# The Persistence of Subjectivity
## *On the Kantian Aftermath*

*The Persistence of Subjectivity* examines several approaches to and criticisms of the idea at the heart of the self-understanding of the modern Western, or "bourgeois," form of historical life: the free, reflective, self-determining subject. Since it is a relatively recent historical development that human beings have come to think of themselves as individual centers of agency and to believe that entitlement to such a self-determining life is absolutely valuable, raising such a question also raises the question of the historical location of philosophical reflection itself. What might it mean, that is, to take seriously Hegel's claim that philosophical reflection must always be reflection on the historical actuality of its own age? In discussions of Kant, Hegel, Heidegger, Gadamer, Adorno, Leo Strauss, Arendt, Manfred Frank, and John McDowell and in examinations of modern institutional practices and modernist art and literature, Robert Pippin challenges a number of prevalent views about both the nature and the value of "leading one's own life."

Robert B. Pippin is the Raymond W. and Martha Hilpert Gruner Distinguished Service Professor in the Committee on Social Thought, the Department of Philosophy, and the College at the University of Chicago. He is the author of several books on German idealism, including *Kant's Theory of Form, Hegel's Idealism: The Satisfactions of Self-Consciousness, Modernism as a Philosophical Problem,* and, most recently, *Henry James and Modern Moral Life.* He is winner of the Mellon Distinguished Achievement Award in the Humanities and was a Fellow at the Wissenschaftskolleg in Berlin.

T0381629

# The Persistence of Subjectivity

## *On the Kantian Aftermath*

ROBERT B. PIPPIN

*University of Chicago*

CAMBRIDGE
UNIVERSITY PRESS

CAMBRIDGE UNIVERSITY PRESS
Cambridge, New York, Melbourne, Madrid, Cape Town, Singapore,
São Paulo, Delhi, Dubai, Tokyo, Mexico City

Cambridge University Press
The Edinburgh Building, Cambridge CB2 8RU, UK

Published in the United States of America by Cambridge University Press, New York

www.cambridge.org
Information on this title: www.cambridge.org/9780521613040

First published 2005

*A catalogue record for this publication is available from the British Library*

*Library of Congress Cataloging in Publication Data*

Pippin, Robert B., 1948–
The persistence of subjectivity : on the Kantian aftermath / by Robert Pippin.
p.   cm.
Includes bibliographical references and index.
isbn 0-521-84858-x – isbn 0-521-61304-3 (pbk.)
1. Self (Philosophy). 2. Subjectivity. 3. History – Philosophy.
4. Philosophy, Modern. I. Title.
bd438.5.p57   2005
126 – dc22   2004062838

isbn 978-0-521-84858-9 Hardback
isbn 978-0-521-61304-0 Paperback

# Contents

# Acknowledgments

Earlier versions of these chapters have appeared in the following publications and I am grateful for permission to reprint. In most cases the revisions for this volume have involved brief expansions or qualifications, or most often additions to the footnotes. The postscript to chapter 9 appears here for the first time.

Two are reprinted with permission of Cambridge University Press: "The Kantian Aftermath: Reaction and Revolution in Modern German Philosophy" will appear soon in *The Cambridge History of Nineteenth Century Philosophy*, edited by Allen Wood, and "Gadamer's Hegel: Subjectivity and Reflection" appeared in *The Cambridge Companion to Gadamer*, edited by Robert J. Dostal (2002). "Negative Ethics: Adorno on the Falseness of Bourgeois Life" will appear in German in early 2005 in a collection of conference papers edited by Axel Honneth and published by Suhrkamp. "The Unavailability of the Ordinary: Strauss on the Philosophical Fate of Modernity" appeared in *Political Theory* 31, no. 3 (June 2003), published by Sage Publishing. "Hannah Arendt and the Bourgeois Origins of Totalitarian Evil" will appear in a collection of essays, *Modernity and the Problem of Evil*, edited by Alan Schrift for Indiana University Press. "On Not Being a Neo-Structuralist: Remarks on Manfred Frank and Romantic Subjectivity" appeared in *Common Knowledge* 6, no. 2 (Fall 1996). "Leaving Nature Behind: Or Two Cheers for Subjectivism: On John McDowell" appeared in *Reading McDowell: Essays on Mind and World*, ed. Nick Smith, with responses by McDowell (New York and London: Routledge, 2002). "The Ethical Status of Civility" appeared in *Civility*, ed. Leroy S. Rouner (Notre Dame: University of Notre Dame Press, 2000). "Medical Practice and Social Authority in Modernity" appeared in the *Journal of Medicine and Philosophy* 21 (1996). "'The Felt Necessities of the Time': Literature, Ethical Knowledge, and Law" first appeared in Italian as "'Percepire le necessità del tempo': Letteratura, conoscenza morale e diritto," *Ars Interpretandi* 7 (2002). "What Was Abstract Art? (From the Point of View of Hegel)" appeared in *Critical Inquiry* 29, no. 1 (Fall 2002). "On Becoming Who One Is: Proust's Problematic Selves" will appear in *Philosophical Romanticism*, ed. Nikolas Kompridis, to be published by Routledge Press.

I am especially grateful to two institutions: the *Wissenschaftskolleg zu Berlin*, where I was in residence in 2003–4 and so could complete work on the introduction, the postscript to chapter 9, and the revisions to various chapters; and the Andrew M. Mellon Foundation, whose Distinguished Achievement Award in 2001 supported much of the final editorial work on this volume. Special thanks to Thomas Bartscherer, Bo Earle, Hugh Liebert, and Jonny Thakkar for their assistance in preparing the manuscript and index.

The Persistence of Subjectivity

*On the Kantian Aftermath*

# 1

## Introduction

### *"Bourgeois Philosophy" and the Problem of the Subject*

I

Nowadays the term "bourgeois philosophy" no doubt sounds an immediate ironic note. It invokes a still polemical, if also a stale and overused characterization of a distinct historical condition, our historical condition, the "modern West." The phrase suggests that there is a sort of philosophy appropriate to a historical epoch and a kind of society, that pursuing some questions makes sense only under certain historical conditions: a certain level of cultural development or prosperity, a certain sort of economic organization, a certain distribution of social power, a certain relation to religion, and so forth. "Bourgeois" is an adjective that is supposed to help direct us to the specific conditions among the possibilities most relevant for understanding why our philosophy looks the way it does, so different from past versions of our own, and perhaps from anyone else's. Since the term has become a kind of epithet, it also suggests a high-minded defense of a commitment to a value, when that commitment is actually motivated by low-minded interests.

If we were to characterize epochs and societies by reference to "highest values," then the heart of such a bourgeois philosophy would have to be a philosophy of freedom. This would be a philosophy that explains how it is possible (whether it is possible) that individual subjects could uniquely, qua individuals, direct the course of their own lives, why it has become so important that we seek to achieve this state maximally, consistent with a like liberty for all, what that means, why it is just to call on the coercive force of law to ensure such a possibility (the protection of liberty, the "one natural right"), and so forth. The basic philosophical claim underwriting such an enterprise is the notion of the independent, rational, reflective individual, one who can act in the light of such reflective results. This is the ontological and the value claim that underwrites rights protection, claims of entitlement, and just deserts, and that begins to make pressing new sorts of philosophical problems: the distinct nature of self-knowledge, the problem of personal identity, skepticism about the external world and other minds, and so forth.

In the European philosophical tradition, "the question of the subject" became quite a speculative one. The most important issue derived from the famous Kantian and post-Kantian denial of any immediate presence to the mind of, or possible direct reliance on, the world (even "the world" of one's own impulses and inclinations), the denial of the "myth" of the given. A human subject is, rather, a meaning-*making* subject (minimally always "making up her mind" in experiencing and so likewise responsible for what she claims to know), a self-conscious subject, in this active, self-determining relation to itself in all experience as well as in all action.[1] This "inseparability of mind and world" claim raised the issue of how rightly to acknowledge the "subjective" character of such experience and the many unique, elusive characteristics of self-knowledge. So the "bourgeois" claim is that there are such entities and that they in fact actually *do* these things in acting and thinking.

The "problem" suggested in my title is that a great many very persuasive writers think that such an ontological claim, in both its socio-political and more speculative formulations, and such a normative ideal, freedom, understood in "the bourgeois sense," are not only fantasies but destructive, dangerous, and self-deceived fantasies. Insofar as one can agree with such a vaguely summarized objection, I agree with this charge but not with the implications most often drawn from it, and I want to explain that agreement and that demurral in the work that follows. (The demurral defines the nature and the limit of the agreement: The basic "bourgeois" picture is not false, a mistake, or "ideological"; in Hegel's terms, it is simply "incomplete." Such an ideal of freedom should be not rejected but properly "realized.")[2]

---

[1] All this under the assumption that any such "self-determination" must be rule bound to really be a determination, that it cannot be an arbitrary positing, either in judging or in acting.

[2] In historical terms, no Western philosopher better represents bourgeois philosophy in this sense than Kant, and the story of an astonishing amount of post-Kantian European philosophy can be understood as a reaction against, a great qualification of, such a conception of a moral and social ideal, such a conception of philosophy's task.

## II

By now that bourgeois label suggests a variety of cultural sins: conformism, consumerist materialism, pompous self-satisfaction, self-deceit, and hypocrisy as a whole way of life. This cultural characterization – self-deceived satisfaction – is often explained as the only effective strategy for dealing with the deep, permanent conflict in bourgeois culture between the inheritance of a largely Christian, altruistic humanism, on the one hand, and a ruthless, remorseless secular capitalism, on the other hand; all ending up in what Nietzsche famously called a "wretched contentment." (There are plenty of other stories about the presumed "cultural contradictions of capitalism" – such as the view that liberal-democratic capitalism requires a kind of morality of prudence and responsibility that it also must undermine by promoting ever more creatively self-indulgence and hedonism, all in order to create the conditions of the expanding consumption on which capitalism depends.) In lieu of any full treatment of the theme, let us say then that in general the epithet is meant to convey the charge of a self-deceived or hypocritical, disguised egoism and selfishness (often parading as entitlement claims), a complacent satisfaction with low-minded, uninspiring, vulgar ends or goals, or, usually, both. In historical actuality, the great ideal of "a free life" is just well-organized selfishness, producing a lowest-common-denominator level of cultural crudity.

There is an aristocratic flavor to this use of the term as an epithet, and that is important to note because it marks a kind of anxiety deeply connected with an important dimension of the problem of the bourgeois subject, and hence important for its ideal (perhaps its compensatory fantasy of) freedom. The bourgeois is originally held in contempt because he cannot act as the nobleman paradigmatically acts – *independently*, in majestic indifference to what unworthy others think of what he does.[3]

---

[3] A brief history of the term: Its original meaning derives from feudalism. Certainly by the eleventh century and long thereafter the term simply designated an inhabitant of the *bourg*, a *lieu fortifé* surrounding a princely household. They were the people who lived inside the fortified walls, and while they were not noble (and so did not have the privilege of carrying arms in service to the king) they were entitled to privileges as *bourgeois du roi* and so, as tradesmen, artisans, and basically what we would call bureaucrats, were distinguished from the group who lived in open houses outside the walls, in the villa or country houses (a *villanus* or villain, a word with its own remarkable history), and certainly from the paysans, the serfs who lived farther out.

By the seventeenth century in France, though, much of the modern meaning of the term as an epithet, or insult, was well established. In French literary works by Corneille,

(In principle, anyway; there is a lot of self-deceit and fantasy on the "aristocratic" side as well.) The world of the bourgeois – indeed for Rousseau the world of modern society itself – is a world of such complex, pervasive and fragile dependencies that for the bourgeois attempting such independence would be economic and social suicide. His range of independent action is limited not merely by his bad, craven character but by the form of society that requires and rewards such cautious, reputation-protecting conduct. This question of the right way to understand the relation between independence and dependence will emerge as one of the most significant complexities in the modern aspiration to a free life.

III

But these problems of dependence, conformism, inauthenticity, and so forth – the cultural dissatisfactions – are only a part of a still larger, quite paradoxical situation. At just the moment in the nineteenth century when Western European societies seemed to start paying off the Enlightenment's promissory notes – reducing human misery by the application of its science and technology, increasing the authority of reason in public life, constraining the divisive public role of religion, extending the revolutionary claim of individual natural right to a wider class of subjects, accelerating the extension of natural scientific explanation – it also seemed that many of the best, most creative minds produced within and as products of such societies rose up in distaste, protest, even despair at

Boileau, Poisson, and most famously Molière, a bourgeois was already a person without dignity or merit, a social climber, vulgar and craven, a philistine, possessed of the means to enjoy the finer of things in life but with no clue how to do so (and terrified that such ignorance would be discovered, such as the man snoring through Wagner or asking how much that Vermeer would cost) and bizarrely obsessed with respectability and the appearances of conventional morality (only the appearances because the bourgeois was also false, a hypocrite, a poseur; the local anti-pornography bourgeois is the one sure to have a huge stash of the stuff in his basement). Now what is interesting about this history is that such expressions of distaste with the bourgeois and the whole way of life that emerges when they become the "ruling class" is that it is almost always tied to aristocratic nostalgia and a kind of aristocratic self-congratulation. To "épater" the bourgeoisie is to demonstrate that one is not a member, and if that cannot any longer place one in the nobility, it can help to inch one closer to the hierarchy of cultural rank established by romanticism and still so influential: the ranks of the creative, authentic, artistically sensitive appreciators of the finer things. This style of critique, in other words, is not political (unequal wealth and unfair advantage are not usually intended in the epithet) but cultural. I am much indebted here to Paul E. Corcoran's informative 1977 article and to Zhiyuan Cui for this reference. For even more detail, see Pernoud 1960 and Pirenne 1939.

the form of life that also made all of this possible. In painting, literature, music, as well as in a kind of avant-garde philosophy in Kierkegaard, Nietzsche, and others, just being "modern," as that was understood in bourgeois terms, became a source of some distinct anxiety, a distasteful fate. A large dimension of the problem had to do with issues not traditionally aesthetic, issues such as how to understand historical time at all, the temporality of one's art, how to locate oneself in a moment that seemed unlocatable given the radicality of the rupture represented by modernity. One can "hear" this accelerating radicality and rupture most dramatically in music from Wagner to Schoenberg and Webern, but roughly the same trajectory (the thematization of art itself, the concentration on form, the assumption of the historical exhaustion of prior forms, a liberationist sensibility demanding "freedom," a growing anxiety about art's reception in a mass democratic culture) occurred in drama, painting, poetry, and novels.

More substantively, the best brief characterization of much of the tone of post-Hegelian European thought and culture is that it is comprised of a profound suspicion about that basic philosophical claim of "bourgeois" philosophy noted above, the notion central to the self-understanding and legitimation of the bourgeois form of life: the free, rational, independent, reflective, self-determining subject. Nowadays, one has to get in the back of a rather long queue of European complainants to register an objection about any faith in such a conception or ideal. Moreover, although much of European modernism was inspired by a revolutionary consciousness and a hope for a rapid acceleration of the modern trajectory itself, such aspirations were often overshadowed by something darker, not just a critical reaction to the aspirations of modern subjectivity but something like a growing high culture "bourgeois self-hatred." Indeed, it has been suggested that the two most successful and catastrophic mass movements of the twentieth century, fascism and communism, seem largely well nourished by this, the former rejecting the ends of peace, security, and individual well-being for the sake of a return to blood and soil, collectivist, archaic primitivism, the latter for the sake of a recklessly rapid acceleration forward, beyond the basic oppositions of "individualist" bourgeois society for the sake of a classless future.[4] This must have something to do with the appeal of such a backward-glancing, even occasionally fascist sensibility to so many modernist artists and philosophers (such as Eliot, Lawrence, Pound, and Heidegger) and the revolutionary leap forward

[4] For example by Furet 1999.

attempted by so many artists and intellectuals (especially after the international crisis of the capitalist system in 1929).[5]

## IV

To return to the question raised by the phrase itself: Is any of this cultural and social history important for philosophy? Is even the original,
sweeping notion of "modern philosophy" of more than bureaucratic use;
is it a *philosophical* term of art? Can such a characterization be taken in
a much more radical way than as the mere date that a standard, historically organized textbook would invoke, an embodiment of the view that
there is simply a subset of the very many, perhaps perennial philosophical problems that as a matter of contingent historical fact happened to
engage the imagination of philosophers in the West from roughly the
seventeenth century to the present? These might be historically novel
problems, it might be conceded, but all of them would be *in principle*
accessible anywhere anytime. Is there instead some common, historically
specific prereflective orientation by virtue of which individual problems
came to make whatever sense they did in *and only in* just this sort of society
in historical time, a society moving toward or having arrived at capitalist
economies, romantic marriages, nation states, liberal-democratic institutions, and by and large an ever greater commitment to natural science as
the highest cognitive authority? Indeed, could there even be such a thing
as "*modernist* philosophy" in the sense in which there is modernist painting
or architecture or poetry? Might a similar self-consciousness about such
a locatability, and an anxiety about how to deal with it, be said to have
produced such a modernist moment in philosophy, first of all in Hegel,
but then more dramatically in the Kantian and Hegelian aftermath of
the European tradition, in many of the figures dealt with in this book?

The premise of such a moment would be a controversial one, but by
no means necessarily a reductionist one: that certain problems rise to
salience because of social and historical characteristics would not make

---

[5] A caveat here or a concession. A contemporary single mother working two jobs, trying to
arrange day care for her children, and taking them to the doctor when they are sick is not
going to be much bothered by how unhappy Franz Kafka was and would understandably
be thrilled to become beset with the spiritual crises of the bourgeoisie. But we should
not also concede too much to such a class-oriented or so-called materialist counter. That
an ideal could be said to be failing need not mean much about the individual beliefs of
particular agents and can be apparent in various social and individual pathologies, and
such shared symptoms can also have a lot to do with the products of high culture. It all
depends on one's diagnosis, the content of the claims.

much sense without some pre-philosophical commonality in underlying, largely practical, and prereflective commitments and in a historically specific way of experiencing the world, the way one had come to experience claims to authority, religious practices, the organization of labor, and so forth.[6] If there is such a prereflective commonality to the topics of bourgeois philosophy, one could perhaps see connections between typically modern problems in philosophy and the various but still quite distinct styles and subjects that characterize the art, literature, and music produced in and for such societies, especially as they became more and more sensitive to their own historicity.[7] Or one could ask: Why should there be such a connection, if there is; and does it mean anything philosophically that there is? For one thing, perhaps there is simply philosophical progress, and the bourgeois world, with its disenchanted nature, atomistic self-understanding, and skepticism, suggests to philosophers a distinct set of problems because those are the (finally) genuine problems, appropriate to this latest, most advanced stage in human progress. Perhaps that is all the modernist, historical consciousness we need.

Even though the question of what sort of ideal this is and why it has become so historically important to us are obviously pretty sweeping topics, it already does not look like a strictly philosophical answer will get us very far, at least it doesn't seem likely to me. It is after all only relatively recently in Western history that we began to think of human beings as something like individual, pretty much self-contained and self-determining centers of a causal agency, only relatively recently that one's entitlement to such a self-determining life seemed not just valuable but absolutely valuable, for the most part more important even than any consideration of security, well-being, and peace that would make the attainment of such an ideal more difficult, that it was even worth the risk of life in its defense. It seems unlikely in the extreme that the so-called bourgeois notion of freedom and that most important implication – the idea of a human or natural right, the capacity just by being a human being (just by "showing up" as

---

[6] Obviously, the question here of what it is for some phenomenon or practice to "make sense" or to fail to is a very large topic (cf. chapter 3). I mean here only to refer to the way a practice might be said to have come to "get a grip" within some form of life, to fit in and thereby have a salient profile, has come to matter; that it has come to seem that something important would be neglected if such a question or practice or possibility were neglected.

[7] I mean here something more than the obvious point that such texts and practices can be said to "express" the "*Weltanschauung* of an age." The idea is that there are dimensions to the problem of this historical self-consciousness that need to be explored and worked out, in various ways that cannot be understood as merely illustrative of philosophy.

it is sometimes put) to place all others under an obligation to act in no way inconsistent with like availability of action for all – should have been waiting around in history unnoticed, waiting for Locke and Rousseau to discover it. That would be as unlikely as an attempt to explain (and to account for the authority of) what may be the greatest social transformation in human history – one we are actually living through – the greater and greater unacceptability of gender-based division of labor and unequal social statuses for men and women – by appeal to some philosophical discovery or new insight.

We can try to quarantine, as it were, the philosophical issues – arguing that the way in which such an ideal got on our agenda is of no importance to philosophy, and we just investigate its rational credentials once history hands it to us. But, on the one hand, that seems quite disingenuous since the notion has a kind of historical and social authority and priority in normative discussions and a dense, complex "lived" meaning to those committed to it that philosophy also needs to understand if it is to understand what the ideal entails and what actual authority is merited. (For example, how could one possibly begin to discuss something like what sort of importance ought to be attributed to modernist art, and why, without being everywhere oriented from an appreciation of what sort of status it has come to have in bourgeois societies and just those, even if one ultimately wants to say that status is too various and disunified for any answer, even if one wants to say that we have lost our way somewhere?)

On the other hand, if it is plausible to consider the origin and even the authority of such normative commitments as unintelligible apart from the place of such commitments in a changing, historical social organization, it is also highly plausible that any particular mode of "investigating the rational credentials" of such commitments is itself necessarily attached to the same historical story. Argument forms determining what counts as a legitimating case also come attached to complex and developing histories and need the same sort of proper location in order to be understood. For example, the idea of appealing to which form of authority "pre-social rational individuals would choose to submit to" is not something that would have made such sense, say, to Aristotle, just as refraining from appealing to the proper natural role of men and women, to natural law, would have greatly puzzled Aquinas.

Now such historicizing tendencies always provoke spirited counterintuitions. For one thing, if all of this is plausible, it also means that the original core notions of seventeenth- and eighteenth-century bourgeois liberalism – right, individual, property, contract, fairness – are also not frozen in some kind of time capsule, to be opened whenever philosophers need something from their tool kit. It is quite likely that our collective experience over time of the hold such notions have on us has changed a great deal, changed us and our sense of the ideal, and this would mean that any such notion must be taken up with a great deal of informed historical sensitivity if we are serious about any contemporary project of normative self-assessment. To be sure, one often hears people insist that, say, the ownership of human beings as chattel is evil, has always been evil, and that it must have always been possible for anyone anywhere to know directly and unhistorically that it was evil. This kind of issue would obviously require several more discussions even to begin properly, but as throughout I am only trying to suggest here that such a rigoristic, essentially moral condemnation is not only implausible (it too quickly lumps together all slaveholders of all times, with no appreciation of the great differences between the ancient Greek understanding of slavery and that of the American South and no way to appreciate the quality of mind of Jefferson, for example, or Lincoln's compromises in the prewar and early war years). It is also *itself* a particular sort of judgment of absolute ahistorical responsibility typical of a historically particular (sometimes called "peculiar") normative institution, morality, a kind of stance toward the world that requires *its own* historical genealogy in all the senses noted above.

To say everything at once: I think that there is (has to be) such a thing as philosophical modernism in the sense suggested above, that the historical location of philosophical activity has become a – perhaps the – central question for philosophy (and where it hasn't, it ought to be), that there is no easy progressivist narrative to explain the contemporary shape of philosophy, and that such issues cannot be properly understood unless the intimate reflection of such concerns in modernist literature and art is acknowledged (or said another way, unless the divisions between philosophy and literature and the arts are treated as the highly problematic, poorly understood, and crudely administered divisions that they are). My suggestion in the following chapters is that this is particularly important in any attempt to understand the fate of the ideal noted above, the free and rational individual subject, the heart of bourgeois philosophy, the philosophy of our time.

The underlying claim that I want to make in these essays about this situation is a difficult one to express economically. It is to try to suggest that the reflection of this tension and complexity in the main documents and work of modern European high culture can sometimes just as much be read as elements of panic, pathological melancholy, and a distorted, hasty appreciation of its own ideals, or as exploratory and unresolved, as it can be read as some sort of accurate record of "what we have become," as a demonstration that fundamental sense-making practices have broken down. Or we should be suspicious about phrases such as "breakdown" and might view the modernist response to some sort of putative collapse of authoritative norms and ideals in bourgeois culture as only partial, hesitant, and, in such partiality, often partly distorted. This could all also be true about suspicions of bourgeois individuality and freedom. It is possible that that suspicion can go too deep or, to say it metaphorically, that reactions to the limitations of such subjectivity can move forward and away, can recoil, too quickly, too hastily.

I have discussed similar issues in several earlier books, especially *Modernism as a Philosophical Problem: On the Dissatisfactions of European High Culture* and *Idealism as Modernism: Hegelian Variations.* Those books were concerned with the general theoretical position at stake in a Kantian version of the project of German Idealism and of Hegel in particular, and the legacy of that tradition in later figures who took it up and in others who explicitly rejected it, and those books dealt with those writers who proposed alternative "modernity theories." And in the latter book, there were also two essays on Hegel's political philosophy itself, framing the collection, offering an alternative view. Here I am concerned with a more focused topic, and besides setting out its dimensions in this chapter, I am also eager to point out the limitations that such a narrower focus brings with it. I have called that problem the persistence of the problem of subjectivity, but in modern philosophy that topic has ranged from questions of self-knowledge, epistemological incorrigibility, first-person authority, and action theory to the nature of autonomy, the scope and basis of rights claims to phenomenological issues (what it is "like" to be the subject of one's experiences and deeds, if it is anything at all). But I am concentrating in what follows on what could be considered a crucial subset of those issues; in more obvious terms it could simply be described as the conditions under which one could be said "to actually *lead* a life," wherein one's deeds and practices are and are experienced as one's own, due to one, not fated, determined by exogenous requirements, under the sway of the will of others, of *das Man*, subject to "the administered life," the imperatives of the work world, and so on, or where such a subjectivity would not be closed off to one because of the grip of some distorting picture, scientism, "reflective" philosophy, the forgetting of "the ordinary," and so forth.

Genuinely leading a life is rightly taken to involve the problem of freedom, and in the Kantian/Hegelian tradition I am interested in, freedom means being able somehow to own up to, justify, and stand behind one's deeds (*reclaim* them as my own), and that involves (so it is argued) understanding what it is to be responsive to norms, reasons. Any traces of genuine subjectivity detectable in a modern form of life often condemned for obliterating it or revealing its fraudulent promises will thus be traces of the presence of practical reason in human practices, a presence beyond instrumental or coordinating strategies. Sometimes this presence can be best detected by the pain and pathologies occasioned by the absence of reason in such practices; that is, if Kant is right that the claims of reason, the insistent call of the demand for normative justification among subjects, is in some practical sense unavoidable and Hegel is right that it is inattention to such a call, or misunderstanding it in terms that have grown historically inappropriate, then that misunderstanding might provide the best explanation for the experiences of certain sorts of determinate failures in a form of life. That phenomenological claim remains among his most interesting, that the breakdown in a practice of demanding from and providing to each other reasons we can share[8] occasions its own distinct sort of suffering, a suffering intense enough to provoke revolutionary transformations in the normative structure of a society.[9] The idea that there can be such traces or determinate absences in works of art and literature has lost much of its appeal, but the viability of such ideas depends, as always, on how it is interpreted, as I hope we shall see.[10]

Stated in the most comprehensive way possible, the counterclaim I am interested in and that circulates so freely throughout European letters and art from the latter half of the nineteenth century onward is that *any* such notion of subjectivity, however far from the Cartesian and Kantian paradigms, if still indebted to them (to the "modern"), must itself be considered a failure, either philosophically incoherent in the traditional sense (or a historically "created" fantasy that can do no real work other than fraudulently securing a new regime of administered power) or a real social "failure," reliance on which has produced nothing but social

---

[8] This is Korsgaard's apt phrase (1993). Hegel also claims that such a breakdown can be uniquely and philosophically explicable, that the course of such failures and resolutions can be shown to have its distinct "logic."

[9] Cf. Honneth 2000.

[10] I have tried to make a beginning of such an attempt in a book on the novels of Henry James (Pippin 2000c).

pathology and massive delusion, not the promised result of individual autonomy.

All of which again depends on just *what* has failed, just what is being relied on, appealed to. Besides extending a radical Kantian claim that these norms are "self-legislated," but collectively and over historical time (a topic worthy of its own book-length treatment), Hegel insisted on two aspects of any such position that set him apart from figures in the Cartesian and liberal traditions and that emerges frequently in the exchanges I set up in the following chapters. He insists on recognizing that such norms *change*, even while not conceding any relativist or pragmatist conclusions (conceding such change, that is, while still maintaining a distinction between norms with genuine authority and those mistakenly taken by a community to be authoritative at a time) and that deliberation about and judgmental application of such norms requires participation in a complex social world, depends on a historically achieved, common like-mindedness. This amounts to treating "bourgeois subjectivity" as a normative status achieved historically and as always inseparable from complex (ultimately recognitive) relations of social dependence.[11] These emphases on the sociality and historicity of subjectivity are the sources of most of the later criticism of Hegel (against his supposed anti-individualism), and while I do not here advance direct defenses of such controversial claims,[12] I am trying to suggest the appeal and coherence of a position on such a historical and socially mediated subjectivity indirectly, by reflecting on the limitations of other figures in the post-Hegelian European and Anglophone traditions, by trying to understand such claims as extensions and "completions" of liberal claims about the subject and by examining various phenomenological manifestations of the problem of subjectivity and sociality in modern literature and modern art and in discussions ("criticism") of both.

## V

A distinction and a brief digression are necessary here. Often when the question is posed this way, it is the prelude to a much more deflationary approach: the question of whether some philosophical outlook, in this case, "the bourgeois outlook," should be called "ideology." This usually

---

[11] That is, one is such a subject by being taken to be one, recognized as one, not as a matter of sociological fact, but normative propriety. Some aspects of such a claim are treated below in chapter 10; others in Pippin 2000e and 2004.

[12] I present such a defense in Pippin forthcoming a.

amounts to a charge that the best specific account of the growing hold such problems began to exercise on such imaginations would be not only a nonphilosophical account but one particular to the material interests of those whose fate was most linked to the success of the new bourgeois world order and its "representative" ideas and norms. The idea is that a particular organization of social power tends to promote a kind of resistance to evidence and argument against such a distribution, so much so that it might create a so-called false consciousness, where such possible tensions and counters are literally not even noticed, or "seen." So when you hurl the epithet "bourgeois ideology" at someone, you mean to indict her with the charge of advancing nonphilosophic and ultimately unacceptable ends with her theses and claims, as when Marx famously called religion the opiate of the masses.

This sort of claim about ideology is not heard much anymore, at least not in that form, and not just because the entire communist ideal seems to have died out. For one thing, it became increasingly hard for proponents to explain how to get *from* some organization of economic power in a society *to* the creation and sustenance of, allegiance to, ideas. There seemed to be no "operative mechanism" by virtue of which some social organization could create so powerfully and uniformly the sorts of incentives and disincentives necessary to make all this a credible explanation. No one has yet been able to explain *how* such interests are supposed actually to operate, to shape or somehow to explain the content of philosophical theories, or to account for the success of some research program or style "gaining hold" or acquiring social legitimacy and authority, selecting some as possible (possibly socially authoritative), rejecting others, all "below" and "prior to" the level of reflection and deliberative resolution.

Understanding how a particular issue becomes a pressing problem, rises to a salience at a time, by understanding how to "fit" the issue into some whole of sense-making practices, and within some narrative of the fate of such practices, is thus not a version of a causal account of the origin and authority of ideas nor a functional analysis of their role in the society. So I am not proposing an ideology critique. But any attempt at something like this "historicalization" as essential to a philosophical account still provokes the same sort of vigorous rejection as ideology critique. This is so because of an intention to keep the concerns of philosophy autonomous, of value in themselves, comprehensible as valuable "strictly philosophically." People who work on reference or reliabilism or the autonomy of psychology or the individuation of mental content can see no need to consider either the historical novelty of their questions or the periodic odd exhaustion that can suddenly befall such "research programs."

(Why is it that philosophy departments with some range of ages among the faculty can look like a historical zoo of some sort, with "species" from various periods locked into programs that have long since ceased to generate articles, books, dissertations? The ordinary language species here, the Rawls-Nozick person there, the deontic logic type here, the Kuhnean there, the intentional inexistence specialist laboring away in this corner, the transcendental arguments skepticism-refuter over there?) There is also very great discomfort with those *particular* socio-historical labels, especially "bourgeois," since they suggest something especially narrowing, regressive, perhaps even philistine.

That is, for the most part traditional philosophy aspires not to have a history like that of literature or art (where times and places seem profoundly relevant) but a history like chemistry (where they do not; no serious working chemist worries about the history of chemistry). But the historical (and the even stranger, much more common geographical – French, German, American, British) labels stick nonetheless and have become part of the daily discourse of philosophy. It seems obvious in *some* sense that the standard list of topics in the modern European/North American tradition could fairly be called pressing or important only within a certain form of life, not some other, and it is understandable that some would say: Granted, we seem to be historically stuck with these problems, but so what? They are interesting and difficult in themselves, and there is not much to be gained by wondering endlessly why we are so stuck. (I mean distinctly modern problems clearly linked to the historical status of the bourgeoisie, problems such as individual natural right, secular foundations for morality, scientific naturalism, the implications of a materialist metaphysics, political legitimacy, the nature of political and social equality, the autonomous value of beauty and art, skepticism about the external world and other minds, self-deception, authenticity, and so forth.)

But the "bourgeois" and "modern" labels are worth pulling into the foreground because so many people have wanted to use them as a kind of weapon. The label can help call to mind how contentious and confusing such a self-identification has become for so many intellectuals, writers, artists (especially writers and artists), and philosophers over the last two hundred years or so.

Moreover, since much European philosophy after Hegel assigned itself a diagnostic, critical, and not merely systematic or analytical role (attentive to the social and historical dimensions discussed above, perhaps even searching for the "social" origins of philosophical problems, sometimes as the best explanation for the recalcitrance of such problems), high on the agenda of anyone working in such a tradition should be some diagnosis of such virulent self-criticism and its historical as well as philosophical implications. And the major players in such a tradition do have their own versions of the historical origin, meaning, and sometimes possible resolution of such negative self-representations, and in the second part below ("Theorists") I discuss elements of both the diagnostic and analytic approach. Alienation, "reflection," inauthenticity, "the forgetting of Being," "the loss of the world," "identity thinking" – some sort of separation from, ignoring of, the roots of all philosophy in ordinary experience – are all offered as diagnostic and analytic tools and are discussed as such below.

## VI

At a strictly philosophical level, things can be narrowed down a bit. In the most obvious sense, in the center of the dispute is the question of whether the assumption of such a free, rational, reflective, responsible individual subject is warranted. Such a subject, that is, must actually possess the several characteristics required for the bourgeois self-understanding and legitimation to make sense and to be defended against objections, and in much post-Hegelian European thought such a claim is vigorously denied. These disputed characteristics especially include the assumption of some sort of self-sufficiency. The core of the notion requires a point in the development and maturation of an individual when it becomes reasonable to attribute responsibility for the future course of that development primarily to the individual herself. This is presumed reasonable because of such a subject's capacity for "reflection," the capacity unique as far as we know to humans, for every single individual to detach herself (at least in principle) from her ongoing commitments and desires and to be able to "reattach" her ordinary commitments (or not) on the basis of some deliberation about whether she ought to do so. The efficaciousness of such a reflectively endorsed will is often thought also to presume a unique causal capacity, a "spontaneity" or an uncaused causal power exempt from the deterministic laws of nature. Even where this is denied, as in various forms of modern compatibilism, the right explicans for an agent's actions is still considered to be what goes on "inside" a distinct individual, usually understood as some interwoven set of her desires and beliefs. (Whatever the subject is made of, or however its results are produced, it, that "subject," is the primary unit of explanation. We punish or praise *that* person, not her family or tribe; that person is the presumed beneficiary of just deserts, etc.)

The constellation of such issues that revolve around the modern subject is not limited to practical philosophy. As I try to show in the next chapter, Kant linked the possible survival of philosophy itself (as nonempirical enterprise, after his own critical attack on the possibility of metaphysics) to the possibility of nonpsychological *subjective* but "*necessary* conditions for the possibility of experience," a strategy that would be repeated and expanded by the "linguistic turn" in philosophy and by Husserlean phenomenology. But this act of salvation came at a steep price. In Kant's view, the only way to make sense of such a subjective contribution was to accept that their status as subjective was also a *restriction* and that therefore we were restricted to possible objects of "our" finite experience ("phenomena," objects qua-so-subject, not "in themselves"). This, in turn, then raised the issue of what sort of subjective restrictions these could be if not psychological and how, if at all, Kant had managed to redeem what has always seemed to be the mark of distinctly philosophical claims: necessity; either that something must be some way, if it is to be at all, or that we must think according to such and such a rule in order to be thinking (or speaking or referring) at all. It is easy enough to be immediately suspicious that Kant's insistence on the restrictive results of subjective conditions is not easily compatible with his attempt to invent new sorts of philosophical necessity ("transcendental" necessity or "practical" necessity in moral theory). And disputes about such issues – what is the right philosophic status to ascribe to subjects presumed to be directing a unique life, resolving deliberatively what to believe, when such are also objects, for others and in nature – made up a great deal of the discussion in post-Kantian German philosophy.

The question has even become part of a dispute about what can only be described as the modern mythology invoked since Rousseau to account for such subjectivity. In contexts that range from Rousseau and Nietzsche to Freud and Lacan to Heidegger and Derrida, such subjectivity is treated as a kind of artifact based originally on some sort of traumatic, perhaps hubristic separation from a previous harmonious or more authentic presubjective mode of being.[13] This "rip in the fabric of being" is then invoked as an explanation of the melancholic realization that such characteristically Western, perhaps violent, attempts at self-assertion and self-sufficiency come at far too high a psychic and social price, require

---

[13] Apparent paradoxes about who or what effects such a split to one side for the moment. The problem is certainly well acknowledged in such treatments.

some tranquilizing forgetfulness or self-deceit, and lead inevitably to various social and intellectual pathologies.

## VII

So for many philosophers, being able to think our way out of a commitment to the bourgeois subject or its ideals (a free life) or to properly defend it is at least the beginning of a philosophical response to the historical situation that seems to raise such a question and demand such a solution. But the critical side has often meant a "throw the baby out with the bathwater" solution, as reflective, rational self-consciousness of any kind, and so the aspiration to a free, self-determining life is jettisoned along with the (admittedly) frequently fantastic notion of all-determining, individual causal agency or wholly self-reliant author of his or her world or a rights-bearing distinct individual. However, the problem of bourgeois subjectivity also includes, as perhaps the major issue, just what a commitment to that sort of reflective subjectivity, which as a norm of sorts underlies various distinctly modern institutions and practices, actually involves or not. Very often such an issue is worked out in an interpretation of some putative modern philosophical defender of some form of such subjectivity, and so a great deal can be at stake in what might seem an academic question of hermeneutics. If philosophical texts can be read as the deepest and most comprehensive attempts at an illumination of and often defense of the basic presuppositions of some form of life, then our ultimate assessments of the worth of such practices might have a great deal to do with what we take a putative defender to be committed to.

Granted, characteristically modern claims about freedom and idealist normativity were certainly not what was most explicitly at stake in the great wave of European skepticism and growing disgust in the world of arts and letters that was to be directed at the culture of the bourgeois world. But at least provisionally, one might take seriously the claims of critics, such as Adorno and Lukàcs and in a very different way Nietzsche and Heidegger, that the self-understanding of the modern world embodied in the work of Kant and Hegel, especially, the high points of the German Idealist movement, best reflected the most sophisticated self-understanding and legitimation of the highest or most important normative aspirations of such a form of life (especially with regard to the meaning and status of a free life). This is, of course, already very controversial and quite reasonably disputed by those who claim that the phenomena at stake are far too various to be addressed by any term such as "bourgeois" or "modernity." But at least if we restrict ourselves to that side of the dispute – the

"Continental" side, as Mill might put it – most linked intellectually to early modern German philosophy (the thinkers, practices, and aesthetic expressions best illuminated by that language), then, with that much at stake and the problem focused in this way, one might be well positioned to ask a broad question about such central ideas.

We might be able to begin to differentiate the object of the philosophical critique, and the philosophical issues presupposed at stake in the cultural and political critique from the actual but not well noticed dimensions of the original idealist positions either directly criticized or at stake, even if abstractly so, in the cultural and political criticisms. (The distorting picture of things, in the grip of which we labor, might better be described as the picture we get from *readings* of philosophy, not as the result of what we have inherited from "the tradition.") Such a process of correcting key elements in the official narrative often taken for granted by proponents or by the cultural critics of the bourgeois notions of subject and freedom might sound at first quite academic and marginal. What is the point after all of, in effect, "grading" Heidegger's or Gadamer's or Adorno's or Arendt's or Frank's readings of individual authors or their presumed narrative of intellectual history and the social history tied to some such narrative? But as indicated above, the point would be more than keeping score; it would be to suggest that the critical potential of the idealist, especially the Hegelian, presentation and defense of a notion of subjectivity and freedom and that account of historical and cultural change by virtue of which such notions came about might have hitherto been undervalued and/or misunderstood and that a rediscovery, reanimation, and perhaps even renarration of the normative elements of this history might still be of considerable value, might clarify better than the standard narrative what it means to have come to live the way we do and what remains to be done and why.[14]

## VIII

Not all the chapters included below directly address as such the issues of what it is to be a subject or what it would be to live a free life. Many do,

---

[14] Disputes about such narratives (many of which have their source in Nietzsche's genealogy or Heidegger's "destructive" attack on the tradition) have become part of the philosophical landscape in the last thirty years or so and have opened up all sorts of possible renarrations. Different ways of stating how we got here often reveal that we are not in fact "where" we thought we were. I am thinking especially of examples such as Brandom 1994; Cavell 1979; Habermas 1987; McDowell, MW; MacIntyre 1981; Rorty 1979; and Rosen 1980.

but I have also chosen recent essays that depend essentially on important aspects and implications of such themes, either explicitly in the work of philosophers or in issues related to such notions: such as the links in Heidegger's work among subjectivity, being-in-the-world, and the failure of such a world of meaning; discussions about social values, such as civility (where the right way to think about individual subjectivity and social dependence is critical); and social disputations, such as the nature of nonpolitical and largely noncontractarian (in this case, medical) authority. Putative normative claims to authority are "at work" in a certain way in modern societies, are best understood as provisional resolutions of a social negotiation that has come to have its own non-negotiable dimensions. (Habermas, on the one hand, and in very different ways, pragmatists such as Rorty and Brandom have their eyes rightly on this aspect of the problem. But we also need a more substantive diagnostic account of the status of such negotiations and the development of what eventually comes to be taken for granted and non-negotiable in them before we can address the assumptions about freedom and therewith rationality at stake in any such conceptions.)

This historical negotiation and normative work also goes on (if Hegel is even roughly right) in literature and the arts as well, so I have also included chapters about what happens when we see modern subjects reflected back to us in literature, how we assess their moral worth and their actions (and so ourselves), and what this tells us about our expectations of art in modernity. (It's all very well, in other words, to insist on, say, the ethical priority of "treating someone as an autonomous person," but I do not think philosophy as traditionally understood can deductively or a priori fix the *content* of such a concept (what it has meant, means now, or could come to mean with respect, say, to women or the role of property, or the relation between religion and the public world). Or, it's one thing to wonder about the conceptual possibility of self-deception, another and more central problem to determine when and why it came to seem important to describe the soul as divided against itself in just that way. That will tell us as much if not more about the content of the notion and its possibility, sending us to Pascal and Diderot, and not just Sartre or David Pears.)[15] So these sorts of diagnostic and historical reflections are as crucial to philosophy as is the continuing attempt to understand the normative force of such evolving considerations (or their lack of such

---

[15] And they cannot be written out of philosophy as just "problems of judgment," requiring a nonthematizable *esprit de finesse.* Such judgmental activity presupposes some sort of resolution of the content issue and does not constitute such a resolution.

force). Hence the inclusion of chapters about the self-consciousness and subjectivity themes in two of the greatest exemplars of aesthetic exploration of that issue: modernist self-consciousness in abstract painting and in Proust's great novel about the modern subject.

In all cases I hope to suggest at least indirectly that the ways in which the question of the modern subject have been posed, whether in terms of a putative conflict between the possibility of genuine subjectivity and the modern notion of nature, or as leading to an alienating and deracinating reflection, or as imposing artificial and alien demands on what had always been recognized and accepted as the touchstone of philosophical reflection, ordinary human experience, or as inherently and deeply committed to a form of "administrative rationality" ("identity thinking") that suppresses and ignores living individuals in their uniqueness, or as supposedly fractured and wholly self-defining as in the practices of modernist art or as solipsistic as the world of Proust's narrator, all have not yet identified anything like the unavoidable and necessary commitments of *the* "bourgeois form of life," and this mainly because we have not yet understood all that well what it means to have started to live so differently in such a short period of time.

However, trying to extend in a different way the claims of modern subjectivity, to raise neglected alternatives, to expose straw men, or to insist that questions cannot be rightly posed philosophically without some appropriate narrative and diagnostic work all have an obvious limit, can be extended only so far. I take issue in what follows with what some thinkers believe has gone wrong in the development of modernity. Although it must seem like mere dogmatism to assert it here, there is no question that *something* has indeed gone very wrong and that all those gathered in this *salon des refusées* have not simply made some correctable philosophical mistake. One might put the point with Adorno by saying that what makes for the success of modernist art and literature (and "modernist philosophy" up to a point) is what it in its own way is getting right about what's going wrong: that is, the implicit (often explicit) attack in such art on the delusions of assumptions about easy historical continuity (or easy historical liberation), the uncertainty and instability of point of view, the insistence on the difficulty of the accessibility of the art work itself, as if deeply suspicious about *any*, even well-meaning, sympathetic audience. Modernist art might even be defined by a loss of audience or loss of trust between audience and artist (as Cavell has famously suggested),[16] making

---

[16] Cavell 1969, "Music Discomposed," 212.

the question of trust, fraud, authenticity, reliability, and philosophical self-consciousness about art itself all wholly new sorts of aesthetic values, and ones that do not seem arbitrarily invented or at all reversible.[17] (In most contexts the name for such attempts at reversibility is kitsch.)

We cannot make any sense of this phenomenon by restricting the account to the history of art or novels or drama or poetry alone, but only by trying to understand what has turned out to be the so unexpectedly poisonous, deracinating, the simultaneously oversocializing and desocializing effects of social and cultural "modernization." One kind of sensemaking or explanation is seeing one phenomenon in the context of something wider and more comprehensive, so that a phenomenon such as Cavell's distrust or loss of audience can begin to look like what we would expect in the aesthetic domain, given some fate for normative expectations generally. I have suggested that this larger context has to do with being called on by a historical situation "to be a subject," lead a life, take up the reins, as it were, and that this is something at which, "modernism" discovers, *we can fail* (oddly, especially when we try very hard to do it). So I think that Cavell is onto something of decisive importance when he says, in a passage that destroys the pretensions of the music critic Ernst Kreneck, "[W]hat in fact the composer has come to distrust is the composer's capacity to feel any idea as his own"[18] and "The entire enterprise of communication and action has become problematic. The problem is no longer how to do what you want, but to know what would satisfy you.... Convention as a whole is now looked upon not as a firm inheritance from the past but a continuing improvisation in the face of problems we no longer understand."[19] But I would start one step earlier here than Cavell starts, with some appropriate astonishment and puzzlement that it could have come to this: *Why* should a civilization in so many ways so successful have produced artists who felt *this* way? *Whose* ideas could "yours" be but "your own"? Who else would know what you want but *you?* How *could* they not be yours, how *could* you not know or claim to know in a way you come to distrust? This all requires a still larger context for us to make sense of why it has happened, and that context, in my view, includes not just the legacy of Kant's revolution and Hegel's reaction, but perhaps even more so the legacies of various readings at

---

[17] Cavell 1969, 184. See also the same theme, varied in many different ways, in the very rich project of Michael Fried.

[18] Cavell 1969, 196.

[19] Ibid., 201.

various times, where such readings and such times, such historical social possibilities and constraints, become so interwoven as almost to allow one to make the relevant point by appealing to either.

It is at least helpful in all of this, I hope, to be able to show that despite whatever else is going on, the culprit is not a distorted, ideological, or predatory "subjectivity" essentially and unavoidably presupposed in the normative claims at the heart of the modern aspiration to a free life. Understanding the core notions of Kant and Hegel, the "normative idealism" at the heart of their account of leading a free life, as "still trapped within the philosophy of consciousness" or within the "philosophy of identity" or "philosophy of reflection" or as the apotheosis of "the forgetting of Being" or as complicit in the loss of the "love of the world" or as having helped "screen" the ordinary human experience of the human, takes far too much far too quickly for granted about those positions and far too radically restricts the materials that we need in order to be able to think ourselves free of these modern anxieties (insofar as thinking can contribute to freeing anything).

But such a recovery gets one only so far, and there is at that point much more work to be done. Hegel, for example, could be taken to have believed that, in his own terms, the "actuality" of modern ethical life, the rule of law, the realization of basic (especially property) rights, a moral notion of individual (rather than tribal or group) responsibility, and the rational answerability of the modern bourgeois family, market society, and representative state were, said all at once, "enough," the satisfactions of a free, self-conscious life. They amounted to ways of institutionally realizing modern freedom without what he saw as the twin dangers of an atomizing individualism or a romantic collectivism. In some fairly obvious sense and in the historical terms he would have to accept as relevant to his own philosophy, he was wrong. None of these institutional realizations now looks as stable, as rational, or even as responsive to the claims of free subjects as Hegel had claimed, even though such criticisms are often themselves made in the name of such freedom. But the nature of that wrong is, I am arguing, also Hegelian, a matter of being incomplete, not wholly wrong-headed. That is, from the earliest stages of his philosophical career in Jena, Hegel's central diagnosis of modern life was to point to its "*Zerissenheit,*" its "torn apartness," stark dualisms and incompatible but unavoidable commitments, producing a kind of suffering and struggle for relief and resolution that he felt he could see in everything from *Rameau's Nephew* to Jacobi's romantic novels and lyric poetry, from the French Revolution to the English Reform Bill. Thus, it is hard not to see his project in terms of a search for a new basis for "reconciliation" (*Versöhnung*) with the world, even a new form of "identification" and satisfaction with one's own practices and institutions. However dialectical and mediated such a reconciliation would be (and most of Hegel's critics on this score set him up as a straw man, ignoring his own insistence on the necessary tensions and strains of modern social existence), it is hard also not to see such a goal as unbalanced in *some* way, not wrong but one-sided, insensitive to an at least equally powerful modern pathology of the sort diagnosed and stressed by the Frankfurt school, especially by Adorno and Marcuse: a "one-dimensionality" and overidentification of modern subjects with their social roles and with a whole social form of life, one that not only tears the souls of its participants apart but also all too easily blunts any effective reflective distance and integrates them all too well into a great anonymous productive machine.[20] "Nonidentity," "the onto-logical difference," "*das Nichts*," "*le néant*," "the other," "*la différence*" are all signs of resistance to this integration, and that moment of the Western experience of modernization deserves in effect its own chapter in an extended *Phenomenology of Spirit*.[21] What more might be said about such a completion I can only begin to suggest in the chapters that follow and in the general reconstructive extensions necessary to allow Hegel's thought to address its sharpest modern critics.

[20] The standard historical narrative of the phases of critical theory, organized by attention to the end ideal, suggests a shift from such a reconciliationist and identity-oriented Hegelianism to the Adornoean and Marcusean insistence on the unintegratable status of the "nonidentical," or a philosophy of resistance, negativity, Marcuse's Great Refusal, and so forth, to, finally, Habermas's communicative turn, where the end goal is *Verständigung*, successful communication. (See the lucid account in Buck-Morss 1977 and Thyen 1989, 64ff, 185ff, on how Adorno thought he could maintain both a logics of disintegration and a pathologically affirmative culture.) This narrative, though, is skewed against Hegel's full position on the end, the source of current dissatisfaction, which is better described as the "realization" of freedom, understood as a collective and institutional achievement. Reconciliation plays only a partial and not a comprehensive role in the details of such a desideratum.

[21] Critics of Hegel never seem to notice that Hegel himself openly welcomed, even required, such an extension. His most famous image of the historical position of philosophy insists that philosophy always comes on the scene too late to play an active role in a particular shape of spirit, that it is possible to understand such a social form only when it has grown old, near its end, that the owl of Minerva takes flight only at dusk, swooping over a gray, desiccated landscape. What must such an image mean for the shape of spirit that Hegel himself brought to rational comprehension, if not that it too is about to die, requiring a different historical-philosophical position? See Pippin 1979b.

# PART I

# SETTING

## 2

# The Kantian Aftermath

## *Reaction and Revolution in Modern German Philosophy*

### I. Kantianism

In 1781, Kant, in his *Critique of Pure Reason*, delivered the bad news that the human mind can (even worse, must) pose important, unavoidable philosophical questions that it cannot possibly answer. These were distinct, perennial philosophical questions answerable, if at all, by pure reason alone, independent of any appeal to experience. (Kant thought the most important ones concerned freedom, the existence of God, and the immortality of the soul, but the scope of his critique also extended to issues such as the nature of the mind, the human good, the purpose of nature, or any attempt to know "things in themselves.") While, according to Kant, we could at least settle once and for all just what those limits to knowledge were and why we were not able to cross such a boundary, that seemed small consolation. Metaphysics, the "queen of the sciences," had understood itself as capable of knowing how things must be or could not be, and so had prided itself on the certainty of its claims and on a rigor in its method rivaled only by mathematics. So it was not for nothing that Kant became known as the "all-destroying."

The skeptical sentiment expressed in Kant's critical work was not, of course, isolated in Königsberg. The latter half of the eighteenth century can be viewed as a collective debate about the nature and even future of rationalist philosophy, or philosophy as it had come to be understood since Plato (especially as the impact and advances of Newtonian physics were more and more felt) and about the right way to state the principles

underlying an ever more popular empiricism.[1] This latter had become
a problem, since to many such empiricism seemed dangerously close to
a radical or all-consuming skepticism, confining our experiential knowledge to subjective states, rendering dubious even the existence of the
external world and other minds, not to mention the truths of religion
and morality. If modern philosophy in some way culminated in Humean
skepticism and Berkleyean idealism (as Thomas Reid, for one, thought),[2]
then not only was metaphysics in trouble, but, many began to fear, so
were any claims to our allegiance made by any normative principle. The
demand for a radical enlightenment threatened to culminate in a par-
alyzing stasis. (This situation was all the more urgent since philosophy
had assumed an ever more public face in Europe. Fewer works were published in Latin, and the political role of philosophy "officials" came to
be a lively, complicated topic.) Just as the Scottish common sense philosophy of Reid, Oswald, and Beattie can be seen as a response to such
skepticism and idealism, there were many in Germany who also began
to seek a balanced position, making room for the legitimacy of general
principles that might not be justifiable empirically but could nonetheless
be shown to have some sort of "indubitable" or otherwise necessary status.
To some extent, although Kant rejected (with stinging contempt in his
*Prolegomena*)[3] the Scottish "descriptive" account of such unjustifiable but
undeniable beliefs, his enterprise can also be seen as the most famous
and successful attempt of this moderating, synthesizing response to what
has been called the "cognitive crisis of the Enlightenment."[4]

Kant did not proceed, though, simply by trying very hard to answer
such metaphysical questions and, in failing often and significantly enough
(or in pointing to the seemingly endless failures of others), by concluding
that it was reasonable simply to give up. (A conclusion such as this would
not be unusual. Often a very good reason to withhold assent to a thesis is
that no convincing argument or evidence has yet been provided to support it, and so a skepticism about philosophy need not involve a general
proof that theoretical knowledge a priori is impossible. One could just
note that for all the argument and evidence advanced, no determinate

---

[1]  The popularity of empiricism, both in itself and as a challenge to philosophy, was growing
in France as well as Great Britain and Germany. See Cassirer 1951, 3–36.

[2]  Actually, Reid believed this about the entire history of philosophy, beginning with Plato.

[3]  Kant, P, 6–8. Kuehn 1987 is an indispensable book on the level of knowledge about, and
degree of engagement with, the Scots on the part of German philosophers in the latter
half of the eighteenth century. Also extremely helpful is Beck 1969.

[4]  Kuehn 1987, 36ff.

conclusion could be drawn.) But Kant thought that he had devised a way of asking first about the very "possibility" of any philosophical or a priori knowledge, or even of any experiential knowledge, a way of determining the conditions necessary to be able to say at all how things are, whether a posteriori or a priori. (By understanding this, we could thereby know why answers to some questions would be impossible.) He invented, in other words, something he called "transcendental" philosophy, and that positive project became in many ways just as influential as his critical results. (He thereby claimed to give "metaphysics" a "secure" foundation for the first time (Bxviii),[5] although he was well aware that this involved a new version of a priori knowledge, not a solution to the traditional problems.)[6] He gave a relatively clear account of this new methodology and quickly sketched and asserted its central presuppositions, some of them tossed off without acknowledgment of their profoundly controversial nature, in the opening passages of the first *Critique*. In the second edition "Preface," he notes:

Up to now it has been assumed that all our cognition must conform to the objects; but all attempts to find out something about them a priori through concepts that would extend our cognition have, on this presupposition, come to nothing. Hence let us once try whether we do not get farther with the problems of metaphysics by assuming that the objects must conform to our cognition, which would agree better with the requested possibility of an a priori cognition of them, which is to establish something about objects before they are given to us. (Bxvi)

And in the "Introduction," he baptizes this procedure:

I call all cognition transcendental that is occupied not so much with objects but rather with our mode of cognition of objects in so far as this is to be possible a priori. (A11/B25)

---

[5] Cf. also Axiii: "I make bold to say that there cannot be a single metaphysical problem that has not been solved here, or at least to the solution of which the key has not been provided."

[6] This would amount to what Paton called a "metaphysics of experience" and in Kant's own terms would prepare the way for what he called a "metaphysics of morals" and a "metaphysics of nature." The possibility that Kant may have been committed to more modest metaphysical claims than in dogmatic rationalism, but still identifiably, traditionally metaphysical, has been advanced for several years by Karl Ameriks. (His claim is that Kant's target is much more specific rationalist arguments – how they tried to get there, rather than the destination.) See Ameriks 2000d, and his views on this and what he also considered a moderate, limited version of transcendental philosophy in Part I of Ameriks 2000c. For a good summary of his position, see his forthcoming exchange with Daniel Breazeale and Charles Larmore in Ameriks forthcoming.

A good deal of both the post-Kantian enthusiasm and the dissatisfaction with Kant's critical project are on view in these unusual formulations. The prospect of establishing something about objects "before they are given to us" is strikingly odd and must have so struck Kant's original readers, used as they were to claims for some special way that objects could be said to be given to, graspable by, "the mind's eye," or the light of reason. Kant was clearly counting on the resonances that such a claim would have had with readers now already used to advances in modern mathematics and the mathematical sciences. This is clear when he cites the examples of Galileo, Torricelli, and Stahl, and notes, "They comprehended that reason has insight only into what it itself produces according to its own design." (Bxiii)

But there is still an air of paradox that arises when that model of anticipatory knowledge of the natural world is imported to philosophy, and Kant is not shy about reminding us of the radical assumptions behind this proposal:

> *Nothing* here can escape us, because *what reason brings forth entirely out of itself cannot be hidden*, but is brought to light by reason itself as soon as reason's common principle has been discovered. The *perfect* unity of this kind of cognition . . . makes this unconditioned completeness not only possible but necessary. *Tecum habita, et noris quam sit tibi curta supellex* (Dwell in your own house, and you will know how simple your possessions are). (Persius (Axx, my emphasis))

As we see below, it is this project – reason's examination of its own possibility and the attendant controversies over the nature of the object of such a study and the right implications to draw from it – that sets the agenda for an extraordinary flurry of philosophical activity in a brief fifty-year period, much of which also set the agenda for a good deal of nineteenth- and twentieth-century philosophy.[7] Whereas some thought of philosophy

---

[7] Kant wavers a bit in sketching the relation between transcendental philosophy proper and "critique." He appears to separate the two, to consider the latter a mere preparation for the former, not part of it, perhaps a "canon." The former would involve a complete, systematic enumeration of all a priori knowledge, including all analytic knowledge necessary to "provide insight into the principles of apriori synthesis." And such substantive transcendental philosophy would presumably still in some sense take as its object our *Erkenntnisart*, not objects. But critique is said to involve no "doctrine" and aims only to supply something like the criterion ("the touchstone") for the actual system of transcendental philosophy or, alternatively, should be understood as an "architectonic" outline of all transcendental philosophy. Yet, on the other hand, "To the critique of pure reason there accordingly belongs *everything that constitutes transcendental philosophy*" (A13/B26–A15/B28, my emphasis). This ambiguity about whether critique is part of transcendental philosophy – or indeed all of it – or whether a mere preparation is a preview of the famous

itself as uncontrollably corrosive, morally and religiously subversive (such as Johann Georg Hamann, Johann Gottfried Herder, and especially Friedrich Heinrich Jacobi, who thought of himself as a kind of Humean)[8]; others thought that the metaphysics in the Leibnizean-Wolffean tradition could meet the empirical-skeptical attacks and survive (Moses Mendelssohn and Johann August Eberhard); and others were more or less adherents of the Scottish common sense philosophy (the Göttingen School), Kant was unique in that he invented in effect a new task for philosophy and so a new way to justify claims about the world (synthetic judgments) that were not grounded in experience, were a priori.

Kant's impact was the most important by far, and by 1830 German philosophy had experienced a number of great Kantian aftershocks. Remarkably, almost everyone of importance in the debates, apart from the parties of metaphysics, faith, and common sense, seemed to profess to be philosophizing "in the Kantian spirit," but their variations of Kantian themes were so radical that they amounted to some jujitsu attempt to use Kant against himself.[9] They seemed out to prove that far from humbling philosophical pretensions, Kant had prepared the way for the ultimate completion of philosophy, or the transformation of the love of wisdom into wisdom, mere philosophy into "science," indeed, a knowledge of "the Absolute." Within this latter group (which we might call, subject to explanation below, the anti-Kantian Kantians), there was, among the many claims, one conclusion that was to prove the guiding inspiration for an upheaval in philosophy's self-understanding at least as great as Kant's revolution, although now mostly in what became known as the "Continental" philosophical tradition. The famous catch-phrase was Hegel's in the "Preface" to his *Philosophy of Right*: "Philosophy is its own time comprehended in thought." Hegel claimed to show that every philosopher is essentially a "child of his time,"[10] even while he insisted that genuinely

---

interpretive problems surrounding the *Phenomenology of Spirit* (whether the *PhS* is the first part of the "system" or its "introduction"). And it is not of course an issue unique to Hegel. Cf. F. Schlegel's remarks, in his Jena lectures on *Transzendentalphilosophie* (1800–1), about the error of attempting to establish the power (*Kraft*) of reason "before" using it (Schlegel 1962, 96).

[8] See the account of Jacobi in Beiser 1993, and for a discussion of the relation between all such schools and the Scottish common sense philosophers, see Kuehn 1987, chaps. 4 and 6.

[9] For Kant's famous defense of the letter of his work, at the same time as he professes his doctrine to consist wholly of the standpoint of common sense, see his 1799 letter to Fichte, PC, 254.

[10] Hegel, PhR, 21; PR, 26.

"comprehending" a time "in thought" was also in some way to transcend it, to understand and to incorporate that time within a developmental process that was in itself, as a whole, rational. Reason can still be said to "have insight only into what it itself produces according to its own design," but reflective attention to what it so "produces," what reason requires of nature and spirit, reveals (1) an essentially temporal or developmental structure to such requirements and (2) that such "producings" were not to be thought of as "imposed" on some exogenous material of experience and so were not subject to Kant's critical restrictions about the unknowability of things in themselves.

These were the twin transformations in philosophical methodology or self-understanding that did so much to influence so much later philosophy. Kant's revolution amounted to his insistence that the proper object of reason's attention was not the noetic or substantial structure of reality, but itself. ("[O]ur object is *not the nature of things*, which is inexhaustible, but *the understanding*, which judges about the nature of things" (A12–13, my emphasis).) This prospect of philosophy as a formal enterprise, not a direct attempt to know something about the world but an account of the way we talk and think about the world, about the normative constraints that govern such claim making, would resonate through later nineteenth-century neo-Kantianism and set the stage for logical positivism and the "linguistic turn."[11] Hegel's claim to link philosophy to its time, to consider it in some sense an expression of an age in the way in which an artistic movement might be understood, would reverberate through the German historical school and romantic hermeneutics and would come to influence the likes of Marx, Weber, Dilthey, the Frankfurt School, and, finally, in a kind of apotheosis of historicism, Heidegger.

There is a narrative link connecting these epochal moments (a link between Kant's invention of transcendental philosophy and Hegel's historical and diagnostic conception of philosophy), one that is of some philosophical not merely historical interest. But to understand this link, we need some sense of that great explosion of system building, theology, and aesthetics set off by Kant's spark.

## II. Dissatisfactions

A great many of Kant's successors were sympathetic to Jacobi's famous complaint that one could not enter the Kantian system without his

---

[11] See Pippin 1982 for an assessment of Kant's attempt at such a formal analysis.

doctrine of things in themselves and their unknowability, but one could not remain in the system and still accept such claims.[12] On the one hand, Kant appeared bothered by no criticism as much as the reaction that greeted the first edition: that his was a version of Berkleyean idealism that reduced the empirical world to mind-dependent states of consciousness, mere representations (the claim that *this* is what objects "conforming" to subjective conditions amounted to). He insisted that he had distinguished clearly between the objects of inner and outer sense, relegated such mental states to inner sense, and had defended a robust "empirical realism," the claim that we certainly did have knowledge of external objects "outside us" in space, even if only as subject to our epistemic conditions. Yet, on the other hand, he equivocated on what "outside us" amounted to, did seem to speak the language of phenomenalism in discussing such external objects, and despite the addition of a *Refutation of Idealism* in the second edition, persisted in claiming that we were forever "cut off" from the true "ground" of appearances, prohibited from knowing things in themselves and are confined instead to our representations.[13] To some (such as Jacobi), he even seemed to apply with gross inconsistency the category he had legitimated only for appearances, causality, to such noumena, ascribing to them the status of the causal origin of the determinacy of appearances.[14] In this context, Kant's claim to have defended synthetic a priori knowledge seemed purchased at a very high price; he had left us unsure as to whether we could count this knowledge of objects-qua-subject-to-our-requirements as real knowledge or as only some sort of second-rate knowledge.

This noumenal skepticism seemed unacceptable, and many set off in search of a way of avoiding such results while still keeping faith with Kant's original transcendental revolution, his break with what many continued to call the "dogmatism" of standard metaphysical realism and its uncritical assumption that what was unthinkable was impossible, what was rationally required was metaphysically necessary.[15] For others, the problem with Kant was not that he had been too skeptical about such knowledge but that he had not been skeptical enough, that he ought to have been skeptical about his own claims to be able to determine the necessary conditions

---

[12] Jacobi 1968, 291–310.

[13] Especially in the Elucidation and General remarks to the Transcendental Aesthetic, A36/B53–A49/B73, and the Fourth Paralogism, A367–380.

[14] Cf. P, 314; 62. See also in the first *Critique* Bxxvi ff. and A251 ff.

[15] By "dogmatism," people meant "without a critique of reason," without an attempt to establish that the kind of knowledge attempted was possible, and if so how it was possible.

of experience. There was no good reason to believe, as some, such as Schulze (or "Aenesidemus"), argued,[16] that reason was at all capable of determining the conditions without which any knowledge would be impossible, and better reason to believe that Kant had merely catalogued the psychological workings of the mind in a way itself open to much doubt and certainly in no necessary connection with what objects, even objects of experience, must be or could not fail to be.

So Kant's project was accused of being "subjectivistic" (his transcendental conditions were ascribed wholly to the subjective side of experience, what we brought to it independent of the content of experience) and therewith of being hopelessly inadequate. Some, such as Salomon Maimon, realized that the heart of the matter on this issue was the strict (and so, many claimed, untenable) separation between the active understanding and the passive faculty of sensibility. It was this strict distinction between the form and content of experience that both made possible philosophy's capacity to issue necessary and universal claims about all possible experience (with such claims based on an analysis of such universally necessary subjective forms, pure concepts and intuitions, analyzable in isolation) and yet that also ensured that the resulting en-formed content would be so "subjectively" conditioned that it could not serve well in any argument about the possibility of genuine empirical knowledge.[17] Kant had wanted to establish the necessary conditions of experience, thereby ensuring that there could be no conceivable contrast between such conditioned results and "what the object might really be." He had even issued such speculative "identifications" as "the object *is* that in the concept of which the manifold is united" (B137, my emphasis)[18] (i.e., that is all that "being an object" could amount to) and "the conditions of the possibility of experience are at the same time the conditions of the possibility of objects of experience" (A158/B197). But he always had to add in some way "necessary for us," and so "only phenomenal objects," and so forth.

---

[16] Schulze 1969.

[17] Maimon even argued that on the Kantian assumptions the very cooperation between such separate faculties was incoherent and that what Kant had established in the Second Analogy was so formal (given any event, there must be *some* cause) as to render it useless in any answer to Hume (Maimon 1965). See also Paul Franks's helpful discussion (2000).

[18] Cf. also, "the unity that the object makes necessary can be nothing other than the formal unity of the consciousness in the synthesis of the manifold of the representations" (A105).

Of course, from the Kantian point of view, the implication of such dis-satisfactions would have to be a retreat to the alternatives he was proud of having undermined and left behind. These were attempts to "sensitize" the concepts of the understanding, as in Lockean empiricism,[19] or to "in-tellectualize" appearances, as in Leibnizean rationalism (A271/B327).[20] Or it would involve a speculative excess he himself seemed to toy with in his *Opus postumum* – a "deduction" in some way of content, of the matter of experience.[21] However it was repackaged, such an attempted a priori determination of the content of experience would have to be regressive, as in, say, Schelling's attempted philosophical determination of what na-ture itself must be. By Kant's lights, by contrast, the separability of intellect from sensibility was merely another way of pointing out the obvious: that we were finite, discursive knowers. Our minds could on their own supply us with no content, must be provided with such data, could know only by judging, actively classifying and synthesizing content provided to it; in a word, that we were possessed of no "intellectual intuition." The *only* win-dow on reality for human knowers was sensory. And if we could not meet the ultimate gold standard of absolute knowledge – God's creating the object he thinks as he thinks it – what we had left was certainly not thereby second-rate. And consistently enough, this – intellectual intuition – is just what Fichte, Schelling, and in some ways Novalis, in some different way Hegel, insisted we *did* indeed have. One strain in such an emerging school of thought (tied especially to Fichte) had it that Kant himself had to be availing himself of some such potency, given that his own determination of the forms of experience amounted to an a priori determination of content (we just needed to extend consistently what Kant had started in this determination of content), and even that the apperceptive character of experience, the way we must be said to be in some self-relation in all relation to objects, was already a manifestation of such an unusual faculty. (By Kant's own theory, such apperceptive activity was neither a judgment nor a manifestation of inner sense, so it seemed already close to a form of "intellectual intuition.")[22]

As in both issues, the phenomena-noumena split and the understand-ing-sensibility split, the great problem, reappearing everywhere in Kant's

---

[19] I.e., to understand concepts as faint copies of, reflected remainders derived from vivid, content-rich sensations.

[20] I.e., to portray the senses as only dimly and unclearly grasping what the intellect could clarify and grasp more clearly.

[21] The best discussion of these late developments in Kant's thinking is Förster 2000.

[22] Cf. Pippin 1989, chap. 3.

project, was the dualisms so prominent and frequent that they were taken as indication of some fatal absence or incompleteness in Kant's formulations. And very often that weakness was understood to be due to a lack of clarity about transcendental or critical philosophy itself.[23] Such dualisms were manifest in the split between practical reason and sensual desire, between understanding ("what we can know") and reason ("what we can think"), between subject and object in general, between theoretical and practical philosophy, and by far the most important and crucially unresolved dualism, between freedom and necessity, the gap between the conditions of morally responsible agency and the conditions of the possibility of experience, between the Rousseauean and the Newtonian origins of the idealist legacy.[24] This was taken to be problematic not only because Kant's dualism seemed so strict or heterogeneous that it made difficult to understand any relation between such poles, but because it seemed that Kant merely began by assuming such dualisms, did not ground them, and confessed to being unable to deduce them from a common source, and this left many with the impression of a residual empiricism, even dogmatism, in Kant's own enterprise. (Indeed, the first, loudest, and clearest voice demanding a more rigorous and systematic beginning and end to the critical system was from Karl Reinhold, the Kantian epigone and popularizer, who did more than anyone to spread the Kantian word.)[25] And again, much more importantly, it just seemed completely unacceptable to claim that the most important condition of the unique dignity of and respect for human being, freedom, should be ruled theoretically unknowable, merely a practically necessary postulate.

Accordingly, anyone sympathetic to such criticisms would also be imposing on himself requirements far stricter than Kant thought could be met. These would especially involve complete systematicity (the required response to the above charge of ungrounded presuppositions). Kant had certainly recognized the inevitable attempt by human reason to "ascend"

---

[23] In his so-called *Differenzschrift*, or his early work *The Difference between Fichte's and Schelling's System of Philosophy*, Hegel was already pointing to the way that philosophical claims should be understood within a larger social and historical context. He treated the presence of these dualisms in Kantian philosophy as an expression of the very general "dividedness," even the "torn apartness" (*Zerissenheit*) of the modern form of life itself, suggesting that these aporias were not philosophical mistakes in Kant but a manifestation of a deeper incoherence, necessary commitments to incompatible options in such a form of life or "shape of spirit." Cf. D, 83, 85; GWe, Bd. IV, 8, 9.

[24] Cf. the summary by Ameriks 2000b.

[25] For a very good summary of Reinhold's *Elementarphilosophie*, see the discussion in Beiser 1993, chap. 8, 226–65, and see also Ameriks 2000c, part 2.

from "conditioned" knowledge to the "unconditioned" but had insisted that we could take on such attempts only as a regulative ideal, could never claim to complete any such series or to work out fully and for all time the determinate relations between the parts and such a whole. Kant freely admitted that the delimited situation of human reason, as his analysis had left it, was an affront to reason and unacceptable, so much so that he even conceded, remarkably, that dialectical illusion, or attempted reasoning about the unconditioned, was a perennial feature of human thought, even after the exposure of such illusion by critique.[26] And indeed, even those who attempted with the greatest ambition to fulfill such a systematic requirement, Fichte and Schelling, recognized themselves that their attempts at a *Wissenschaftslehre* (the attempt to transform mere *Kritik* into a *Lehre* or positive doctrine of science) and a "*System* of Transcendental idealism" were failures, and they both moved later to positions that bore little connection to their Kantian beginnings.

Other attempts to make good on what their criticisms of Kant required did not fare much better. Claims that the problem of knowledge could be solved only by defending a "subject-object *identity*" sounded like bizarre claims that in some way ontologically identified human judgments with objects in the world (or, worse, that such judging activity and the natural world were both aspectual or modal manifestations of an underlying substance and so originally, substantively, identical). And claims that we should not be said to be making judgments about the Absolute, but that the Absolute (the unconditioned, infinite totality) was expressing *its* self-knowledge "through us," made it very hard to understand how *we* could be said to know this was so, given that *that* claim, too, would just be the expression of the Absolute's self-knowledge. Or Schelling's question might be an interesting one – is the subject-object difference a subjective difference or an objective difference? – and it might be reasonable for him to wonder about an original source or substance itself neither subject nor object (but "indifferent" between them), but how or why such a substance would or must differentiate itself so into such subjects and objects, not to mention into cabbages and kings, into thinkings and doings, remained quite dark. And it might be true that, as a historical matter, the rediscovery of Spinoza that resulted from Jacobi's attack on Lessing's Spinozism was an indispensable additional motive in such speculative adventures

---

[26] This intriguing problem – *why* must illusion persist even after it has been exposed? – has not received an extensive discussion in the literature. A very helpful new book about that and related topics is Grier 2001.

(as was the excited importation of so many Platonic themes.)[27] Given the disappointments with what were perceived to be the limitations of Kant's subjectivism, his inevitable skepticism, or his various dualisms, it would indeed be understandable that the most sophisticated and scientifically informed modern form of monism, in which substance could be understood as neither mind nor matter, would be quite attractive. (It also did not hurt that the philosopher proposing the thesis had inaugurated biblical criticism, was a fierce antidogmatist, and a persecuted Enlightenment hero.)

But because so many were in fact motivated by such a desire to "animate" this Spinozistic substance (to see it as alive, a purposefully self-moving life force), to make use of it to articulate the "*hen kai pan*" totality they deemed necessary, or even, like Schlegel, Novalis, and Schelling, to attempt to "synthesize Fichte and Spinoza," all of that is nowhere near even the beginning of a philosophically adequate account of what this could mean, and no one has ever provided one. Not to mention that it is just not very likely that being should be understood as an infinite, self-differentiating, living totality; it is mind-boggling to imagine what a "synthesis of monism, vitalism, and rationalism"[28] could mean; and it seems quite a stretch, when pressed about the epistemic possibility of such claims, to wave over them the magic wand of "transcendental argument," to plead that such monism claims should be counted as necessary conditions for the possibility of determinate experience.[29]

To be sure, the difficulty of demonstrating any of this philosophically was itself a major theme in these discussions, especially in the work of Hölderlin, Schelling, Novalis, and Schlegel. The problem for these artists/philosophers/critics was precisely the discursive nature of

---

[27] On the Spinoza controversy, see Baum 2000, 199–215; Beiser 1993, 44–108; and Henrich 1991, 101–34.

[28] Beiser 2002, 352.

[29] This is what Beiser claims (2002, 589). In general, this is quite a helpful book, but Beiser is quite often given to pronouncing on the "philosophical importance" or "sophistication" of these "vitalist Spinozists" in ways that are not justified by any philosophical demonstration. This late attempt to enlist "transcendental argument" is the strangest, since that strategy is precisely what began all the worries about subjectivism in the first place (that "*we* can't understand the possibility of X without Y" need have little to do with the truth about Y, as Aenesidemus, among many others, was eager to point out). At any rate, nothing Beiser says gives one reason to think that we are in for a new wave of "vitalist, rationalist, Plato-inspired, drunk-with-God" monism anytime soon. For a contrasting narrative of nineteenth-century German philosophy, one that makes much more of the normativity/naturalism and anti-empiricist elements in the Kantian aftermath, see Pinkard forthcoming.

judgment insisted on by Kant. Judgment was an *Ur-teilen*, an original separating of what was not in fact separate (Socrates' being a man, say, or his being white, from his being Socrates), just in order to manifest such unity to finite intellects. But judgment itself thus intimated an original unity, prior to any judgmental articulation, not capturable in limited discursive judgment but nonetheless "present" in some way. Such an original unity, lost in all our conscious judgings and doings, could however be made present in some indirect way by art, especially by lyric poetry. And the problem with this program is one familiar to all such accounts. It is very hard to tell the good intimations from the bad ones, especially since we are not talking about aesthetic qualities alone but a philosophical profundity so profound as to be indemonstrable and of course therewith incomparable with any other.[30]

## III. The Hegelian Spirit

The account above is a bit skewed, of course. Not everything in the Kantian aftermath is best seen as a reaction to Kant's noumenal skepticism, dualism, and incomplete systematicity.[31] Moreover, the general problematic at issue in Kant's philosophy and in much German philosophy of the period, described here as a triple problematic – to concede that not all human knowledge could be empirical, while admitting the critical objections to rationalist metaphysics, and avoiding the appeal to merely practically indubitable elements of common sense – occasioned complex and fruitful controversies outside Germany. William Whewell's claims about the cooperative roles of, yet differences between, what he called "Fundamental Ideas" and sensations, and aspects of his moral intuitionism sound Kantian themes and would be relevant as well. (Although Whewell's concession that there could be moral progress and his claim that there could be empirical discoveries of necessary truths also highlight

---

[30] For philosophically ambitious treatments of the early romantics, see Bowie 1997, 1990; Frank 1997.

[31] For some indication of the magnitude of the problems involved in understanding properly the post-Kantian aftermath, see the extensive work done on the subject by Dieter Henrich and his partners in the "*Konstellationsforschung*" project. Henrich has claimed in this project that we need to be able to separate from the self-understanding of individual thinkers the "inner dynamic" of the positions at issue, always available to such thinkers but often not properly understood and accessible "through" those self-interpretations. Only a proper setting of the actual "constellation" of issues in a nuanced historical context can form the basis of such a narrative. For examples, see Henrich 1982, 1991, 1997.

similarities with Hegel.) But the post-Kantian framework gives us one way of understanding an underlying Kantian aporia that will play its way through Fichte and Hegel and will return us to the alpha and omega suggested at the beginning and so to the lasting influence of this period of philosophy. That concerns the invention of transcendental philosophy itself, or what Hegel called the problem of "reflection," of reason's absolute reflection on itself, eventually the self-authorization of reason's claim to authority.

That is, a good candidate for the deepest, most intractable, and potentially paradoxical of the problems in Kant's legacy would be the status of transcendental philosophy. If the possibility of the synthetic a priori judgments at the heart of modern science (and for Kant, in mathematics as well) needed to be established, required a prior critique, what should be said about the possibility of transcendental reflection itself? By what right do we assume that we have some access to the necessary conditions for the possibility of experience, and if so, how? Unless we can somehow establish what we are up to in such an enterprise, the status of the results will remain as controversial and divided as they have always been. The enterprise will tend to look like a form of psychology or even psychologism (how the mind works, how we have to think about the world, regardless of how it really is) or, on the other extreme, an attempted account of the "logically" indispensable components of the very *concept of experience* (the conditions necessary for "any possible representation of an object" making sense). The former has little to do with Kant's intentions, since he clearly and insistently distinguished between *quid facti* and *quid iuris* questions (A84/B116), and the latter (often associated with Strawson's austerity in *The Bounds of Sense*)[32] will have to depend on some claim about meaning that will again leave unclear the relation between "how we have to think about experience," "the sense we could make of it," and "the nature of the objects of experience."[33]

The issue – what exactly is Kant referring to in referring to "the subject" of experience? – is also at stake in the controversies and the vagaries that attend any discussion of what the idealism in "German Idealism" consists in. Since Kant seemed to be talking about elements in any experience that could not be said to be derived from experience, he fell naturally into the habit of designating *these* elements (pure concepts and the forms of intuition) "contributions by the subject." "Ideal," "formal,"

---

[32] Strawson 1966.
[33] Cf. Rorty 1970, 1971; Stroud 1969.

"underived from experience," "subjective," and "knowable a priori" would all be synonyms in this account. Since, as we have seen, much later dissatisfaction originated in (1) this equation of "subjective" with "formal" (the claim that thinking was judging, was discursive, and could supply itself with no content) and (2) his conclusion that therefore any object of experience could be only phenomenal, knowable only subject to our formal, intuitive, conceptual, and especially finite conditions (only as so en-formed), one might assume that Kant's later critics would want to eliminate this restriction. Since there is certainly no evidence that they wanted to do so in favor of any empirical derivation, it would be natural to assume that they believed that they could avoid Kant's subjective-objective, formal-given dualities and somehow make "the subject" in its a priori self-determination responsible for (constitutive of) far more of experience than Kant had, perhaps even for a substantial portion of the very *content* of experience (at the very least, perhaps for some general but determinate principles of nature, and determinate principles involved in any explanation and evaluation of human conduct). Fichte's doctrine in his 1794 *Doctrine of Knowledge* (*Wissenschaftslehre*) that, in experience, the *Ich* or ego posits not only itself, but also the *nicht-Ich*, or the non-ego, looks like such an attempt to eliminate Kant's dualism between formal and material, spontaneity and the given. But even Fichte had to conclude that such a fully autonomous, self-determining subject of experience was a "*Sollen*," an ideal or "ought," and could be posited only as a goal of an infinite "striving." This did not seem to leave us substantially better off than we were with Kant's noumenal skepticism.

But "ideal" also need not be limited to this subjective meaning. Its original, much more Platonic meaning seems to be playing a role in the post-Kantian reaction as well, and that meaning is, by Kantian lights, a robust realism, the alternative to a subjective idealism. In both Schelling and Hegel, and in the more poetical expressions of the *Frühromantik*, the early romantic idealists, the "ideal" seems to refer to what they designate as "the Absolute," the "unconditioned" manifested in the conditioned world of nature and spirit, such that the latter are intelligible only as such dependent manifestations.[34] The status of finite, individual objects, any subject's particular activity, even historical events were taken to be elements of an "idealism" by being understood as manifestations or expressions of this ideal Absolute. And there is no question that Schelling was

---

[34] This side of the story is told in detail by Beiser 2002. For such a Platonic reading of Hegelian logic, see also Henrich 1982.

greatly influenced by his reading of Plato's *Philebus* and *Timaeus* during
the early years of his idealist period, and that when he refers to an *Ideen-
lehre*, a doctrine of ideas, he means to give a far more substantial status to
Kantian categories and that he and Hegel are given to summarizing their
"idealism" by claiming that finite things, considered in their particularity,
are not fully "real," that only the Absolute is truly real and that delimited,
finite objects, events, and activities are fully comprehensible only from
the viewpoint, as limited manifestations, of this Absolute.[35] It began to
seem, that is, that a reflective knowledge of "subjective conditions" apart
from the material content of knowledge was impossible but that Kantian
reflection had turned us in the right direction (away from the empirical
world as sole authority in knowledge claims). Such subjective conditions
also had to be "objects" of a special sort; "moments" of the unfolding self-
consciousness of absolute mind, knowable in an absolute philosophical
reflection not even bound (which could not be bound) by the normal
laws of logic (the logic of "the understanding").

The details of such putative radicalizations of subjective idealism, on
the one hand, or this inversion of Kantian into so-called objective idealism, on the other, are obviously book-length subjects. But there are three
reasons to suspect, even conceding the inadequacies of such brief sum-
maries, that the directions suggested by these summary formulations are
too narrow and so are potentially quite misleading. These were heady
times in Germany, and a great many different possibilities and developments were in the air, being tried out and quickly discarded, rapidly
reformulated, and so forth. It is probably impossible to give one general narrative that is adequate to all the movements and countermovements. But the major players in the narrative – the early Fichte, the early
Schelling, and Hegel – often gave notice that they appreciated something
of the originality of Kant's formulations and were aware that these merely
"subjective" and "objective" responses were inadequate.

For one thing, one would certainly expect that any such metaphysical
expansion or reversal of Kant's project would have to take quite seriously

---

[35] See Hegel's contrast between subjective and absolute idealism in the Addition to §45 of
the *Enyclopedia Logic*, where he claims that "finite things" are "mere phenomena . . . in
their nature" because "they have their existence founded not in themselves but in the
universal divine Idea," EL, 73; EnL, 122. Hegel either means here that all finite things
causally depend for their existence on a single creative or emanating force or that no
finite thing is intelligible individually, by itself, but fully intelligible only in the light
of intelligibility as such (where intelligibility does not simply mean "thinkability" but is
understood in a post-Kantian way). I have argued for the latter view in Pippin 1989.

the power and scope of his arguments against all traditional rationalism as "dogmatism," would not merely bypass those objections on the way to new system building. (As noted before, there *were* defenders of traditional metaphysics around, such as Eberhard, but the major players were everywhere eager to ally themselves against "dogmatism" of all forms.) It will not do to say that Schelling and the romantics accepted Kant's critique of the traditional claims for reason's power to know a priori, but that they appealed to a different kind of "reason," a synthetic, integrating attention to the "*hen kai pan*" totality within which parts could be understood in their true partiality and finitude. Such a supposedly intuitive appeal to wholeness has even less chance against Kant's critique because there is much less clarity about the source of determinate results, by what right individual claims within any such system can be made and, especially, defended against objections.

And, as if a sign that something closer to Kant's intentions is going on, the constant appeal to "intellectual intuition" as the answer to the epistemological challenge (about how this speculative knowledge is possible) keeps faith with Kant's rejection of the classical notion of a passive intuitive faculty. Any nonsensible intuitive power must, everyone seemed to agree, be an *active*, producing, spontaneous faculty in order not to be limited by, affected by, its object, and there is considerable enthusiasm for the famous sections 76 and 77 in the *Critique of Judgment* for Kant's presentation of the idea of an intuitive intellect. There is also evidence that both Fichte and Schelling were not claiming somehow to know that this self-producing intuitive power was something like the life-force of the universe, as if some neo-Platonic One. (The problem we started with was how any such knowledge of the Absolute might be possible. It is hardly an answer to, in effect, *add* to the difficulty by making what seem like more, increasingly arbitrary claims about what reason knows a priori about the cosmos.) In an 1801 letter to Fichte, Schelling claims that his own idea of "the Absolute" is derived from the *Kantian* suggestion about the "identity of thinking and intuiting" altogether (not just as a feature of God's activity but as a feature of ours).[36] And Hegel is even clearer in his early work *Belief and Knowledge*:

The idea of this archetypal intellect is at bottom nothing else but the same idea of the transcendental imagination that we considered above.... Thus transcendental imagination is itself intuitive intellect.[37]

---

[36] Quoted in a very helpful book on this topic by Horstmann 1991, 214–15.
[37] Hegel, BK, 89; GW, 341.

This is not the end of the story (how this faculty, now considered constitutive of our experience, overcomes the distinction between possibility and actuality, without producing the objects it intuits (the key characteristic, according to Kant, of an intuitive intellect), is a longer story), but the direction suggested does not appear neo-Platonic or Christian/creationist.[38]

Further, there are indications that later idealists were keeping faith with what they recognized to be one of the most radical and far-reaching of the first *Critique*'s innovations. When Kant made such claims as "the object is that in the concept of which the manifold is united" or when he insisted that no unity of experience would be possible (self-ascribable to a single subject over time) were we not able to distinguish a mere subjective succession of representations from a representation of objective succession, he did not intend to be providing something like a description of the operations of our mental faculties. When he claimed that all representation of a genuine object could amount to was a certain sort of rule-governed unification, he was not trying to replace spatio-temporal objects with mental states or mind-dependent products and activities. He meant to point out that any "representation of an object" is a normative (*rule*-governed) claim, a holding to be so and so, subject to the required implications of normative commitments. It is about what in our experience *ought* to be thought together with what, and his idealism consists in accepting the Humean point that such normative unity is not something we can be said to perceive directly in experience. He went on, though, to point out that without any distinction between "this ought to be thought together with that" and "this merely happens to be followed by that," a unified experience would not be possible, and he concluded that it must therefore be the case that some such normative requirements, especially requirements that experience must be able to exhibit very general kinds of unity (categories) for any representation of content to be possible at all, cannot in any sense be understood as "derived" (that normative authority cannot be understood as based on any claim about what we have so far observed) and must therefore be understood as "subjectively" necessary. What is "subjectively" grounded is such a claim to normative *authority*, not mental functioning, ideal archetypes, psychological processes, or episodes of thinking. So all judgment is said to rest on predicative, excluding, and inferring relations that *constrain* what we

---

[38] I have attempted to present a fuller defense of this sort of reading of the no. 76 and no. 77 issue in Pippin 1997a.

can intelligibly think and articulate by normatively constraining "what we ought to think," not by *being* psychological or metaphysical limits. (In this light the objection that Kant's position is a "subjective idealism" is not an opening to a contrasting romantic realism but a complaint that Kant's results should not be characterized as "merely" subjective. They are subjective, but Kant has gone some way to removing such "merely" qualifiers by the claim for these sorts of "identities" ("the object is that in the concept of which . . . ") that later idealists wanted to emphasize.) Thus the true contrasting term to idealism is not rationalist realism, on the one hand, or partial, finite, incompletely real particulars, on the other. The contrast is between what Sellars called the "space of reasons" versus "the space of causes," between an ideal (i.e., not naturally determined) normative domain and a comprehensive or totalistic "naturalism."[39] This is why Kant's book is full of such language as "reason has insight only into what it itself produces according to its own design" (Bxiii), "what reason brings forth entirely out of itself cannot be hidden, but is brought to light by reason itself as soon as reason's common principle has been discovered" (Axx), and even that "reason *does not follow the order of things* as they present themselves in appearances, but frames for itself *with perfect spontaneity* an order of its own according to ideas . . . " (A548/B576, my emphasis). He is pointing to the problem of the source of any such normative order (the "ideal" source of such authority "in us") and raising the great problem correctly detected as such by his successors: *How* could human reason in effect authorize its own claim, and *what*, on such an assumption, could it be said to authorize? What could such a self-authorization look like? (Jacobi's worry that such a project as a whole is a nonstarter (threatens "nihilism," rests on "nothing"), not just in moral theory, is thus not irrelevant.) In this context, then, "absolute" knowledge, pure ideality, would amount to the achievement of such a wholly autonomous self-authorizing.[40]

---

[39] I should stress that this and the following characterizations are preliminary. It would, for example, be a natural (or at least a Kantian) response to such a characterization to ask whether we have any reason to believe that such a rational subscription to principle is at all *possible*, whether freedom, especially as autonomy, is possible. Must we not, as Kant tried to do, carve out some theoretical space for such a possibility? (This is the kind of challenge Karl Ameriks has made, especially with regard to Fichte and my interpretation of Fichte. See Pippin 2000c, 211–16. A full answer to such a question requires a detailed treatment of the "priority of the practical" thesis in Fichte and others, a thesis that ultimately circumvents rather than answers such a challenge, and how that claim is connected with Fichte's insistence on the role of faith, or an original practical commitment in even theoretical philosophy.

[40] See also Pippin 2000b.

The continuation of this problem is clearest in Fichte and his other-wise mysterious references to "self-positing" as ground or origin. He notes in the *Wissenschaftslehre* (*nova methodo*), translated as *Foundations of Transcendental Philosophy*, "The idealist observes that experience in its entirety is nothing but an acting on the part of a rational being." He then notes in more detail what he means by such idealism:

> The idealist observes how there must come to be things for the individual. Thus the situation is different for the individual than it is for the philosopher. The individual is confronted with things, men, etc. that are independent of him. But the idealist says, "There are no things outside me and present independently of me." Though the two say opposite things, they do not contradict each other. For the idealist, from his own viewpoint, displays the necessity of the individual's view. When the idealist says "outside of me," he means "outside of reason": when the individual says the same thing, he means "outside of my person."[41]

Fichte even remarks in a note for his Aenesidemus review, "The I is reason."[42]

Third, it is nicely consistent with this direction that Kant does not discuss concepts as abstract objects or archetypes, and his major successors for the most part were aware of the importance of such a shift. Kant had claimed that concepts should be understood as rules, normative constraints on synthetic and inferential activities:[43]

> All cognition requires a concept, however imperfect or obscure it may be; but as far as its form is concerned the latter is something general, and something that serves as a rule. Thus the concept of body serves as the rule for our cognition of outer appearances by means of the unity of the manifold that is thought through it. However it can be a rule of intuitions only if it represents the necessary reproduction of the manifold of given intuitions that is thought through it. (A106)

The "necessity" referred to here is certainly not a claim that empirical knowledge amounts to necessary truths. Kant is referring to the claim of normative necessity, something that experience can never directly exhibit but cannot violate and without which claims about bodies would not be possible. (In his practical philosophy, where his claims about

---

[41] Fichte, F, 105–6; WL, 25.

[42] GA, II, 1, 287.

[43] The pioneering effort to highlight the importance of Kant's understanding of concepts as rules was Wolff 1963. Jonathan Bennett also appreciated the importance of Kant's characterization: "Kant's actual working use of 'concept' is . . . rather thoroughly Wittgensteinian. For him as for Wittgenstein, the interest of concepts lies in the abilities with which they are somehow associated" (1966, 54).

normative authority are very similar (as "self-legislated"), he refers to this necessitation as a practical necessitation or (normative self-) constraint, a "*Nötigung.*")

"All intuitions, as sensible, rest on affections, concepts therefore on functions. By function, however, I understand the unity of the action of ordering different representations under a common one" (A68/B93). Such a notion would, of course, require also a different theory of what it is to understand concepts, and Kant indeed consistently argues that a concept is a "predicate of possible judgments" and thus that to understand a concept is not to grasp a mental or abstract object or archetype but to understand such a concept "functionally," or how to use the concept in different contexts, as a predicate of possible judgments.[44]

## IV. Hegel and History

As noted, there are so many topics being discussed at once in the post-Kantian world that it would be a major undertaking to trace out such a theory of "normativity and its origins" in the late eighteenth- and first third of the nineteenth century. And while such an approach might suggest a general direction different from the "absolutizing of subjectivity" versus "realist monism" options, numerous very difficult problems remain. How we account for the determinacy of such normative principles or rules, especially if we have decided that there is nothing "in the world" that certifies any determinate candidate, nothing we can "read off" from the architectonic structure of reason, obviously looms very large as a difficulty. And everyone seems to want to avoid the kind of "imposition" metaphor that would require again something like Kant's noumenal skepticism, but how *else* we are to think of such a mind-world relation so as to avoid this is not immediately apparent. The problems are linked, and there is space here only to point to the Hegelian responses.

First, there are several indications in his *Science of Logic* that Hegel appreciates the properly Kantian origins of his project and that he is clear

---

[44] According to Hegel, too, concepts are determinate not by reference to abstract content or real universals but as predicates of possible judgments (understanding the content just *is* understanding such possible and disallowed roles). But for him the question of possible determinacy is difficult to constrain to concepts alone, since the unit of intelligibility for Hegel is not the concept or even judgments and judgmental forms, since judgments are determinate as something like arguments in an inferential system, or as places in what Hegel calls "syllogism." Ultimately, this all means that for Hegel, in his famous claim, the unit of intelligibility is simply the whole, "*das Ganze.*"

about how he understands himself to be altering it. He quotes approvingly the important passage cited earlier here. "An object, says Kant, is that in the concept of which the manifold of a given intuition is unified" (SL, 584; WL, 18).[45]

This is a claim Hegel then quickly translates into his speculative language:

When it is comprehended, the being-in-and-for-itself which it possesses in intuition and pictorial thought is transformed into a positedness; the I in thinking pervades it. (SL, 585; WL, 18)[46]

With these passages in mind, it seems that Kant and Hegel are making a point similar to one made by Sellars in a linguistic context, that the objective grasp of a concept is nothing other than mastery of the *correct* use of a word and, hence, in Robert Brandom's extension of this Sellarsean claim, that the sense of any possible *nicht-Ich*, let us say, any *objective content*, is inseparably linked to the structure of our *asserting and inferring and justifying practices* (the *norms* governing our "*Setzen,*" let us say). (And this would mean that our understanding the possibility of an individual object is linked inseparably with, is a function of, our understanding the use of singular terms, that our understanding a possible *fact* is a function of our understanding what can be asserted by a proposition, and our sense of a natural law is a function of our understanding of counterfactual inferring.)[47]

Admittedly, this can seem like pretty thin gruel when we consider the many passages where Hegel insists that "reason" *is* reality, that all that there is is an expression or manifestation of the truly real, Logos, Reason, the Absolute. But here we have to remind ourselves of the extent to which various assumptions in classical, especially Aristotelian, philosophy stand behind Hegel's commitment to this holism. So, while some

---

[45] *SL* is the translation cited, except for the substitution of "concept" for *Begriff* everywhere Miller has "Notion."

[46] Miller's translation is a little free. The original reads: "Durch das Begreiffen wird, das An-und-Fürsichsein, das er im Anschauen und Vorstellen hat, in ein Gesetztsein verwandelt; Ich durchdringt ihn denkend."

[47] See Brandom 2002. The assertion of *this* identity, I maintain, is the core of what Hegel transforms from Schelling's version into Hegel's own version of "identity theory." See Pippin 1989, 79–88. Hegel's somewhat more speculative formulation of what is the same point is: "The object therefore has its objectivity in the concept and this is the unity of self-consciousness into which it has been received; consequently, its objectivity or the concept, is itself none other than the nature of self-consciousness, has no other moments or determinations than the I itself" (SL, 585; WL, 18–19).

formulations of this holism seem to refer to the emanation of some divine mind into its logically necessary moments until the achievement of its full self-consciousness, it is much closer to the spirit of Hegel's enterprise, I am suggesting, to see the claim about "the rationality of the real" to be an echo of this Greek rationalism with its claim that "to be *is* to be intelligible," that there is no ineffable, nothing in principle unknowable. (There cannot be miracles, or omnipotent, impassible gods who could cause without being caused. "Nature" is the *only explicans*.)[48] This is extended in Hegel to cover not only the domains of nature and human nature but the record of human deeds, too. That is, while Hegel accepts the Greek principle of the absolute universality of reason – that to be is to be intelligible – he also distinguishes in a modern or Kantian way between the intelligibility of nature – its conformity to reason – and the meaningfulness of human practices and institutions – activities undertaken for reasons and intelligible only in the light of such reasons. (The grand division in the *Encyclopedia* is between Nature and Spirit.) That is, Hegel accepts the different meanings of "subjection to reason" when this point is recognized, and a storm, the death of a child, a plague, etc. do not *mean* anything.)[49] We could say that in the human world, we make meaning, are responsible for the subjection to reasons we ascribe to ourselves and impute to others, but that would be only a half truth. "Making" is far too simple a term to capture the claim that the way things mean what they mean – how, in what sense, reasons for their being so can be demanded – are results and that we are in some way (a collective, greatly mediated, deeply historical (temporally extended) way) responsible for such results.[50]

---

[48] There is a great deal of truth in Heidegger's remark that Hegel was the most radical of the Greeks. See the discussion by Gadamer, HD, 107.

[49] Cf. Sellars 1963. The core idea here – the irreducibility, priority, and autonomy of normative commitment in any account of the possibility of cognitive and practical claims – is not a uniform one. There are very different senses of legislation and commitment at issue, even though, I have tried to argue, there is at bottom a common sort of claim for such a priority. See Pippin 1997f, 2000b and the discussion in Ameriks 2001a, b.

[50] While it would yet again be far too involved a topic in this context, we should at least keep in mind that Hegel distinguishes between a genuinely philosophical treatment of such questions of intelligibility and an ordinary pursuit of truth. Different normative issues are at stake, he stresses. Correctness (or *Richtigkeit*), the correspondence notion of truth, is, for example, not something Hegel wants to challenge. For ordinary purposes, that question (Does our "conception" "coincide" with its "content"?) is what we mean when we ask whether a proposition is true. However, truth (*Wahrheit*), as Hegel considers it, is a different issue and, again, concerns "the coincidence of the object with itself, that is, with its concept" (EL, 237; EnL, 323). Moreover, Hegel, in a way that sounds somewhat

Then again we come to all of Hegel's objections to the finitude of transcendental philosophy. Kant introduces the possibility, against rationalism, that the forms of thought (understood as in the above formulations) might *not* be the forms of objects, and thinks he needs to close that gap. He does so with some version of an imposition claim that creates the untenable phenomena-noumena distinction. Hegel makes very clear several times that he thinks this imposition idea is fatal to the Kantian philosophy and its descendants, that it is *the* "principal misunderstanding" (*"hauptsächlicher Mißverstand"*; 21). It leaves us with a kind of second-class and so unsatisfying "truth." The misunderstanding, for Hegel, is the assumption that there is any gap to be closed.

That is, Hegel's response to this is to insist on a Kantian insight that Hegel thinks Kant does not remain fully faithful to. Probably the most well known formula quoted from Kant's first *Critique* occurs at A51/B75. It is the claim also quoted by Hegel at a crucial point in his own exposition of Kant in this section of the *SL*. After Kant had distinguished the faculties of the understanding and intuition, he asserted, "Neither of these properties is to be preferred to the other" and "Without sensibility no object would be given to us, and without understanding none would be thought." He then asserted his famous epigram: "Thoughts without content are

strange to us, also distinguishes, as the bearer of philosophical claims, propositions from judgments. In part, he means to distinguish questions about the structure and truth conditions of logical content alone from the rules and conditions for subjective acts of asserting and inferring (i.e., those dimensions of judgmental logic that would generate later worries about psychologism in neo-Kantianism). But this distinction quickly leads to those speculative dimensions of a judgmental logic that interest him. In the *Encyclopedia Logic*, he distinguishes mere propositional assertions, such as "I slept well last night" and "A carriage is passing by," from genuine *judgments*. These are properly asserted when they are asserted *against* some possible objection or doubt and truly embody our judgmental ability (in the sense recognizable in Kant, and also Aristotle, as the expression of sound judgment or mother wit or *l'esprit de finesse*) all in a way dependent on what Hegel calls the "logical value [*Wert*] of judgments," a dimension he connects with "the logical significance of the predicate." Judgment in this latter sense is not required to determine that "the wall is green" or that "water freezes at 0° centigrade," in the way it is when someone judges that a work of art is beautiful, that some human quality is good, or that some political decision was just. This same judgment is also not required to understand the relation between essence and appearance, or the unconditioned and the conditioned, or force and its expression, or among universality, particularity, and individuality. (EL, §171 *Anm.*) It is also important to remember that at the beginning of the "Logic of the Concept," when Hegel wants to point to the importance of the question "What is truth?" he does not cite as his example Socrates, Spinoza, or Kant. He cites Pontius Pilate's question.

empty, intuitions without concepts are blind." Concept and intuition, even mind and world, must be understood as *inseparable*, but precisely not as *indistinguishable*, as if collapsed into one another (as in many charges of "pan-logicism" against Hegel).

The phrase has become as familiar as the well known implication that foundationalist empiricisms of all sorts, whether early British or later positivist versions, are impossible. The idea of a "given" has been exposed as a "myth." The mere deliverances of sensibility cannot found anything. They are blind. Yet the epigram itself, while so familiar, is also paradoxical, even dialectical. By parity of reasoning, if the understanding and intuition really are inseparably linked (neither contribution to experience can be understood except as already in relation to the other), then not only would a foundationalist empiricism be impossible, but the standard picture of a priori knowledge, or a philosophical "logic," even a Kantian a priorism and a transcendental logic, will have to be revised. That is, thoughts, concepts considered apart from intuitions, are *empty*. Or at least they are *cognitively* empty, without cognitive significance. There is something like a "logical content" in any pure thought (although it is not entirely clear what that is), and this will be appealed to when Kant claims that empirically independent reason can legislate a unity regulatively, if not constitutively, apart from reliance on intuitional content. But Kant still insists that, strictly speaking, the content of the forms of thought considered cognitively, as having objective purport, must count as "empty" except insofar as that content is supplied by intuition. (That is, given Kant's doctrine, there must *still* be a sense in which such merely logical content must also be "empty." That is simply a corollary of the fundamental critical principle about thinking: that it can supply itself with no "content.") But intuitions are supplied empirically, and this seems to make such content always empirically dependent in some way.[51] Kant thought he could provide that content by availing himself of what he actually called at one point, mysteriously, "transcendental content" (A79/B105). He could do justice to the inseparable intuitive content of concepts and preserve a notion of a priori knowledge by appeal to the claim that there were *pure* forms of intuition, and so there could be a way, independent of actual experience, to specify sufficiently something of the experiential nonconceptual content of any pure concept, and could do so a priori.

---

[51] This position might amount to something similar in Whewell and, as we see below, certainly in Hegel, but it is not orthodox Kantianism.

But taking this "inseparability" thesis quite seriously also points to Hegel's response to the second problem about philosophical methodology and determinacy of results. There is a passage from the *Encyclopedia* that already gestures in such a direction:

*Philosophy, then, owes its development to the empirical sciences.* In return it gives their contents what is so vital to them, the freedom of thought – gives them in short an a priori character. These contents are now warranted necessary, and no longer depend on the evidence of the facts merely, that they were so found and so experienced. The fact as experienced thus becomes an illustration and a copy of the original and completely self-supporting activity of thought.[52]

This passage indicates that articulating and justifying the normative authority of the claim, without appeal to a given, a pure form of intuition, or by reversion to an imposition claim *is* what "giving content" the "shape of the freedom of thought" amounts to. And the passage also reveals what Hegel regards as the consequences of Kant's inseparability thesis: the reliance of philosophy on what Hegel took to be *the historical development of spirit*, both in its attempts at knowledge and self-knowledge and in its institution of social and practical norms. The Introduction and the Preface to the *Phenomenology* raise the issue of philosophical methodology exactly that way.

Hegel's claim to be able to replace a "critique," with its conflicting assumptions about both the separability of the form of knowledge from its material and its insistence on their deep inseparability, with a "phenomenology" that rejects any such formal methodology and remains truer to the inseparability claim is the initial manifestation in his project of a way of treating claims to know and to act well that is both much more historicized and more integrative, more concerned with the relation between such norms and a form of life or shape of spirit as a whole. He insists:

Consciousness, however, is explicitly the concept of itself. Hence it is something that goes beyond limits, and since these limits are its own, it is something that goes beyond itself.... Thus consciousness suffers this violence at its own hands; it spoils its own limited satisfaction. (PhS, 51; PhG, 57)[53]

---

[52] EL, 18; EnL, 58. ("Indem die Philosophie so ihre Entwicklung den empirischen Wissenschaften verdankt, gibt sie deren Inhalte die wesentlichste Gestalt der Freiheit (des Apriorischen) des Denkens und die Bewährung der Notwendigkeit, statt der Beglaubigung des Vorfindens und der erfahrenen Tatsache, daß die Tatsache zur Darstellung und Nachbildung der ursprünglichen und vollkommenen selbtständigen Tätigkeit des Denkens werde.")

[53] Hegel, PhS, PhG.

Because of this, Hegel believes he can claim that

> we do not need to import criteria, or to make use of our own bright ideas and thoughts during the course of the inquiry; it is precisely when we leave these aside that we succeed in contemplating the matter in hand as it is in and for itself. (PhS, 54; PhG, 59)

If we simply look on, then the source of the determinate norms accepted and modified or discarded can be said to be experience itself, in the self-examining, ultimately self-authorizing sense Hegel wants to give such a notion.

Claims such as these raise their own questions, of course. They assume a great existential power to the force of reason in human life, all such that

> [w]hen consciousness feels this [its own] violence, its anxiety may well make it retreat from the truth and strive to hold on to what it is in danger of losing. But it can find no peace. If it wishes to remain in a state of unthinking inertia, then thought troubles its thoughtlessness, and its own unrest disturbs its inertia. (PhS, 51; PhG, 57)

And they assume, then, that Hegel can maintain some appropriate balance between what we have been calling the inseparability thesis about concept and intuition, mind and world even, and the distinguishability thesis, the avoidance of either an implausible pan-logicism or some appeal to a divinely creative intellect. He may not have succeeded in either task, but I have tried to argue here only that these are the issues he must deal with and that they represent an important extension of a thesis about the normative dimensions of thought and action initiated by Kant's Copernican revolution.[54]

---

[54] A fuller account of all of this would involve a comprehensive interpretation of his *Phenomenology of Spirit* and the precise relevance of a "historical dimension" to that work. In lieu of that, I would suggest the following. The relevance of history should not lead one to expect the relatively absurd claim that there are actual historical positions corresponding to the basic Consciousness/Self-Consciousness/Reason (or essentially Kantian, *Anschauung/Verstand/Vernunft*) structure of that work. Rather, these putatively ahistorical positions are something like "self-consuming artifacts," putative ahistorical possibilities the failure of which makes clearer their impossibility and the practical unavoidability of a historically inflected "epistemology." These putative thought-experiments are meant to undermine any confidence in the usefulness of such philosophy, not establish it. This issue is quite relevant to chapter 9 and its postscript. See also Pippin 1993.

# PART II

# THEORISTS

# 3

## Necessary Conditions for the Possibility of What Isn't

### *Heidegger on Failed Meaning*

### I

In his famous interviews with François Truffaut, Alfred Hitchcock insisted that while many of his thrillers concerned some piece of information or object, around which all the intrigue and energy of the film swirled, it didn't matter if that object was never identified, that it could even turn out to be nothing at all, of no serious importance in itself.[1] Borrowing from some Kipling stories, he called such an elusive object of attention a "MacGuffin" and went on to say,

My best MacGuffin, and by that I mean the emptiest, the most nonexistent, and the most absurd, is the one we used in *North by Northwest*... Here, you see, the MacGuffin has been boiled down to its purest expression: nothing at all.[2]

In 1987, the great twentieth-century intellectual historian Hans Blumenberg, in a supremely backhanded compliment, noted the effectiveness of Heidegger's "question about the meaning of Being" in functioning in just this Hitchcockean way. In a clever rejoinder to Heidegger, Blumenberg titled his article, "Das Sein – Ein MacGuffin," thereby deliberately invoking Hitchcock's own description of the MacGuffin, "boiled down to its purest expression: nothing at all."[3]

The cleverness of this invocation of the nothingness of the Heideggerean MacGuffin, *Sein*, derives from the enormous if infamous

---

[1] In fact, Hitchcock came to realize that the mystery, intensity, and tension of a narrative is greatly increased if such a presence could also remain an absence.

[2] Truffaut 1985, 139.

[3] *Frankfurter Allgemeine Zeitung*, May 27, 1987, p. 35.

and elusive importance that Heidegger himself ascribes to "the nothing," *das Nichts*. The appeals to *das Nichts* and *die Nichtigkeit* occur just when *Being and Time* begins to indicate how we should understand the meaning of Dasein's very Being, *as*, in a way, "nothing at all." Here is Heidegger from Division Two of *Being and Time*:

> Care itself, in its very essence, is permeated [*durchsetzt*] with nullity [*Nichtigkeit*] through and through. Thus "care" – Dasein's Being – means, as thrown projection, Being-the-basis-of-a-nullity (and this being-the-basis is itself null). [*Das nichtige Grundsein einer Nichtigkeit.*] This means that Dasein as such is guilty, if our formally existential definition of "guilt" as "Being-the-basis-of-a-nullity" is indeed correct. (BT 331/SZ 285)

Blumenberg is suggesting, in effect with King Lear, that "nothing comes from nothing" and that Heidegger's picture of Dasein's angst-ridden realization of its own nullity should be taken as a revelation about the emptiness and misleading quality of the question (or worse, of Heidegger's fanciful analysis), not as the manifestation of the existential abyss. The idea is clearly that while the creation of the expectation of a "comprehensive meaning" (an unnecessary and artificial requirement, in Blumenberg's view) is vital to the possibility of the Heideggerean narration of a person's life (or in Heidegger's terms, vital to being able to "temporalize" (*zeitigen*) temporality, the supreme "condition" of meaningfulness), and while the intimation of a profoundly elusive, almost necessarily *absent* meaning may best of all fulfill a dramatic need (something that preserves what Heidegger calls a complete *Unabgeschlossenheit*, un-closedness, incompleteness, in Dasein's existence), at some point such an expectation is more a dramatic trick than anything else. The "meaning of Being expectation" is already such a trick, Blumenberg suggests, and is *in reality* nothing at all, in the ordinary not Heideggerean sense of: "there's nothing to it."

   This is a bit of a cheap shot, not as cheap as Carnap's famous swipes in "The Elimination of Metaphysics through Logical Analysis of Language,"[4] but unfair nonetheless. However, understanding just why it is unfair, how the appeal to *das Nichts* functions in Heidegger's early philosophy, and especially why the question opens up for Heidegger distinctly philosophical issues (not issues of psychological health, historical diagnosis, social theory, or literary mood) will require several steps.

---

4 Carnap 1959, 60–81.

## II

First, it is important to stress that Heidegger's understanding of the *Seinsfrage* is that it is directed toward what he very frequently calls the "meaning of Being" (*Sinn des Seins*).[5] This is a typical programmatic statement in SZ:

> Basically, all ontology... remains blind and perverted from its ownmost aim, if it has not already first clarified the meaning of Being, and conceived this clarification as its fundamental task. (31; 11)

In his 1936–7 Nietzsche lectures Heidegger characterizes the "decisive question" at the end of Western philosophy as "the question about the meaning of Being, not only about the Being of beings"; and, he goes on,

> ..."meaning" [*Sinn*] is thereby delimited in its concept as that whence and on the basis of which Being in general as such can be revealed and come into truth [*in die Wahrheit kommen*].[6]

This seems pretty clearly to say that the "clarification" spoken of in SZ was of the "possibility" of the meaning of Being at all, rather than any direct answer to the question.[7] It is hard to exaggerate the scope of this question as Heidegger understands it, since it seems to cover the intelligibility, deep existential familiarity, of someone uttering noises at me, of ink marks on a page, of having to make breakfast, seeing that someone is angry with me, or facing a decision about whether to volunteer for a mission. The issue, he keeps stressing, is not what there is, what the basic kinds are, or even (as in the *Introduction to Metaphysics*) why there is something and not nothing.[8] The question concerns the very possibility of intelligibility at all, how it is that sense can ever be made of anything, that there could be

---

[5] I realize that I am here taking a side in a dispute with many facets. But Heidegger seems to me pretty consistent about this, and critics such as Tugendhat are off base when they charge Heidegger with equivocating between asking about the meaning of Being and asking about the meaning of the word "Being." However, I need to charge ahead if I am to get to the issue of interest. See Tugendhat 1986, 147–8. The most comprehensive and convincing refutation of Tugendhat's overall interpretation is Dahlstrom 2001. See also Rosen 1993, chap. 5, 176–211.

[6] Heidegger, N, Bd. I, 26.

[7] That any such meaning must be a "temporal" meaning is an answer to such a possibility question, not to a question about Being itself. Indeed, as we see below, Heidegger's main thesis is that there cannot be such a latter answer, and that that is why the answer to the first question is as it is.

[8] Heidegger, IM, 19.

a *Lichtung*, a clearing or lighting or *Unverborgenheit* that "happens," such that a "sense" of Being is possible.[9] (When pursued in terms of the issues discussed in this book, one could say that Heidegger has formulated in a new and unusual way something like a condition for the possibility of being a subject of a life – making a certain kind of sense to oneself. One's engagements with the world and with others are said to occur within a kind of "horizon" of significance determined or oriented from some abiding, largely unreflective sense of oneself, the meaning of one's being. This is largely a teleological hierarchy of "for-the-sake-of-which" relations that amount to what and why things "matter" as they do for Dasein, a structured network of significances that can, Heidegger would want to say, break down or fail.)[10]

Now a formulation such as "whence and on the basis of which Being in general as such *can* be revealed and come into truth," since it looks very much like a question about the "conditions necessary" for the possibility of any "meaning of Being," seems a project in the tradition of transcendental philosophy, or part of a post-Kantian heritage. Despite his protestations in *Grundprobleme* that his own concept of transcendental truth "does not coincide without further ado with the Kantian,"[11] and his criticism of SZ in the Nietzsche lectures as too transcendental in the Kantian sense,[12] Heidegger certainly takes up what seems the language of transcendental philosophy: "By 'existentiality' we understand the state of Being that is *constitutive* for those entities that exist" (33; 13). The hermeneutic of Dasein becomes a hermeneutic "in the sense of working

[9] Now immediately we have to state such claims carefully. Heidegger is clear that he considers the great initiating moment of post-Platonic Greek metaphysics – the resolution that "to be" was "to be intelligible," to be determinate (delimited by determinate form) – to be in fact a hybristic "resolve," the beginning of Western metaphysics as the imposition of subjective requirements for intelligibility, and so an orientation that obscured to the point of forgetting the "being process" itself, the "happening" or eventually historical character of the meaning of being, and so the intertwined relation between Being and Nothing, between meaning and darkness, nonmeaning. But it is clear that it is meaningfulness itself that is at issue in Heidegger's project, what could be object of any understanding, what could somehow mark the basic difference between "meaningfully being" at all and absent, or what I want to discuss later as failed, meaning.

[10] This is no doubt a way of putting the matter that Heidegger would be uncomfortable with, that it was a merely ontic, perhaps even psychological, formulation, but it seems to me only to restate what Heidegger himself says about *Bedeutsamkeit* and *Sorge* in the quotations below.

[11] Heidegger, *Grundprobleme der Phänomenologie*, in GA, Bd. 25, 460.

[12] Nietzsche, op. cit., vol. II, 415.

out the *conditions* on which the *possibility* of any ontological investigation depends" (62; 37). And most directly,

But in significance [*Bedeutsamkeit*] itself, with which Dasein is always familiar, there lurks the ontological condition which makes it possible for Dasein, as something which understands and interprets, to disclose such things as "significances" [*Bedeutungen*]; upon these in turn is founded the Being of words and language. (121; 87)

There is even what has sounded to some like transcendental idealist language. "Dasein only has meaning.... Hence only Dasein can be meaningful [*sinnvoll*] or meaningless [*sinnlos*]" (193; 151), "only as long as Dasein is (that is only as long as an understanding of Being is ontically possible), 'is there' Being" (255; 212). And even "all truth is relative to Dasein's being" (270; 227). Heidegger is certainly clear that in such passages he is not talking about phenomenalism or subjective idealism. Even though "reality is referred back to the phenomenon of care," this does *not* mean that "only when Dasein exists and as long as Dasein exists, can the Real be as that which in itself it is" (255; 212). Or "Being (not entities) is dependent upon the understanding of Being; that is to say, Reality (not the Real) is dependent upon care" (*ibid.*). And all commentators on Heidegger can cite his famous realism in §44:

What is to be demonstrated is not an agreement of knowing with its object, still less of the psychical with the physical; but neither is it an agreement between "contents of consciousness" among themselves. What is to be demonstrated is solely the being-uncovered [*Entdeckt-sein*] of the entity itself – that entity in the *how* of its uncoveredness. (261; 218)[13]

It is clear from the literature on this issue in Heidegger that passages with such realist and such idealist implications, such transcendental and more traditionally ontological implications, could be produced at great length. The talk of "dependence" still, though, at least suggests some sort of a "dependence of sense," if not existence dependence, in the roughly transcendental, or "condition for the possibility," meaning.[14] Such "uncovering" or disclosedness as discussed above obviously cannot happen without us

---

[13] The same point is made if, following Dahlstrom and in a different way, Haugeland (see below, note 16), we note the limited, ontic frame for "uncoveredness" in the above passage and note that by the time of SZ, the fundamental happening of truth occurs as "disclosedness" (*Erschlossenheit*). Dahlstrom 2001, 389–90.

[14] This is the sense in which Robert Brandom argues that, say, the only grip that the notion of a particular might have for us consists in our understanding the role of singular terms in language. Cf. Brandom 2002, 194ff.

(although that does not mean that it happens to or for us in any straight-forward sense, and since the phenomena Heidegger is interested in are "hidden," his version of phenomenology is also a hermeneutics),[15] and nothing Heidegger says in §44 undermines or contradicts the dependence claim in general. (The entity *in* its uncoveredness, or being *in* its disclosedness, is not the entity "itself," or Being, directly apprehended; there is a "how" of uncoveredness; a distinct event of disclosedness. Or it seems natural to frame the issue as John Haugeland has: that ontological disclosedness is a condition for the possibility of comportment toward entities as entities, of ontical truth.)[16]

In terms of Heidegger's project, though, we can see straightaway both what the first question would be if his enterprise were to be considered transcendental and that the absence of any concern for such a question already reveals that he conceives of his project somewhat differently. The question would be: Why should Dasein's requirements for intelligibility – what Being could come to mean for Dasein – have anything to do with "the intelligibles" as such, with what Being *could* possibly mean? There is no immediately obvious reason not to believe, with Nietzsche, that what we count as intelligibility is the perspectival expression of the will to power or, with Foucault, that there are no power-neutral accounts of such sense making.[17] (Indeed, in his famous *Abbau*, Heidegger himself makes similar claims about the "hybris" and subjectivism of all metaphysics.) Or suppose that "*as far as we can make it out*," Dasein must be understood as "ontologically unique." Is this because we lack the intellectual resources to understand Dasein as, say, a sophisticated machine, or despite appearances ontologically continuous with other mammals, or because Dasein in itself cannot *be* such an object or such a kind, and this is a way not dependent on what we could make sense of?

---

[15] I think Taylor Carmen is right about this in his 2003 book.

[16] Haugeland 2000, 57. For reasons that are apparent below, I don't agree with Haugeland that something like the basic laws of physics, constituting what is to count as a physical object, could be an example of Heideggerean disclosedness. For an influential treatment of Heidegger as "still transcendental," in a way continuous with Husserl, see Tugendhat 1967.

[17] This is the sort of question that emerges for any transcendental account that tries to isolate "that without which" some undeniable feature of our experience or language, such as the difference between the succession of representations and the representation of succession, or the possible reidentifiability of particulars, would be impossible. Even in Strawson's "austere" version of the Kantian project, as delimiting the bounds of sense, the question of the status of his results and so the problem of "verficationism" was raised immediately, especially by Rorty 1970 and Stroud 1969.

The direct answer to such questions would be what Kant called a transcendental deduction, and so a demonstration that the "conditions for the possibility of experience" are, *must* be, "at the same time the conditions for the possibility of objects of experience" (that what "we" require for Being to have meaning is what is required for Being itself to have any possible meaning). But such a deduction, in anything like its Kantian form, would require an appeal to pure forms of intuition or something analogous (something outside "the space of the conceptual," or outside the requirements of the subject, yet accessible to philosophy), and (to make a very long story very, very short) by the middle of the nineteenth century, such an appeal had become largely moot, and there is no indication of such a strategy in SZ.[18]

The absence of that or any analogous argument form in *Being and Time* suggests something like the approach already manifest in Hegel, but which in Heidegger results from his famous break with Husserlean phenomenology. That is, we begin from an original denial of any possible separability of conceptual and material, intuitional elements in any philosophical account of experience in the first place and so an insistence that we did not *need* to cross any divide between "*our* conditions for intelligibility" and "*the* intelligible" and do not need to deduce how our requirements for intelligibility might be said to "fit" what we are independently given. The question itself should be rejected, not answered.[19] In fact, in his Davos encounter with Cassirer and in his *Kant and the Problem of Metaphysics* shortly thereafter, Heidegger presses his account of the finitude of Dasein – the absence of a formal point of view from which to secure any sort of philosophical necessity, even transcendental necessity – to the point of transforming Kant's *Critique* into his own existential analytic. (Heidegger's name, of course, for his version of the inseparability thesis is "*in-der-Welt-sein*" or, eventually, "*Geschichtlichkeit.*")

There is, for example, no argument by Heidegger that purports to investigate what a meaningful engagement with entities and others would be like, were there *not* some comprehensive "horizon" of significance, or some orientation from the meaning of Dasein's Being, and thereby to try to show that such a putative situation is not really possible. He does not

---

[18] See the very helpful account in Friedman 2000. See also Crowell 1991; Dahlstrom 1991; and Kisiel 1995, chap. 1.

[19] Cf. in SZ: "But subject and object do not coincide with Dasein and the world" (87; 60). Without Dasein, there can be entities but no "meaning of Being" question. Speculating about the meaning of being "in itself" is like speculating about what objects could be said to be like, were we to abstract from *any* way in which we could know such objects.

do so because he does not consider the relation between such a comprehensive horizon and determinate intelligibility as that between necessary condition and conditioned, a fact that is dramatically manifest in the possibility that the existential function of such a comprehensive horizon can pass into "forgetfulness" (without any ontic "senselessness").[20]

And we should keep in mind our main topic: In Heidegger's account we are headed toward some sort of claim that whichever conditions we might establish, they can fail, in some way collapse. "Care" is the meaning of the Being of Dasein and the interrelational structure of the world of Care can fail in such a catastrophic way that Dasein will appear not as the world-embedded, open-to-meaning, engaged agent in a shared world that it is, but, all at once as it were, the null basis of a nullity. (Or to anticipate an even more radical challenge: Dasein is at the same time both.) Wherever Heidegger's Kantian talk might lead us, we have to keep in mind how bizarre it would sound to refer to some sort of "breakdown" in the constitutive-conditioning function of the experience-enabling categories of causality or substance.

But where does this leave us with respect to our question: What *sort* of question is the *Seinsfrage*, and how might one go about answering it? It is not, we should now conclude, a transcendental question in Kant's sense (of the sort that might require a deduction), and Heidegger seems to adopt the "inseparability" thesis about subject and object, concept and intuition, Dasein and world, but (to make another very long story very short) without the phenomenological reduction, bracketing, and abstracting that might lead us back to a claim of Husserlean philosophical

---

[20] This issue leads into complicated territory. Heidegger insists that, just as a mode of presence for some meaning can *be* its hiddenness, living in the forgetfulness of the meaning of Being is still *ontologically distinctive*; the question is still present by virtue of its absence. Much more would have to be said about this to counter the impression that Heidegger is stacking the deck against objections to his claim that Dasein "is" ontological. But it remains a problem for any "transcendental account." See Haugeland 2000, 47, where one must cite Heidegger's claim both that the question of being has been forgotten (no disclosure goes on) and that such disclosure is a "condition of the possibility of *any* comportment toward entities as entities" (my emphasis). There are similar paradoxes elsewhere. Haugeland wants to treat Heideggerean fallenness as analogous to what Kuhn calls normality in science. But for Kuhn, this tenacious hold of normality is, as Haugeland notes, *a good thing*. It requires a persistent attempt to solve problems, not to give up on them. But we are "*lost*" in the they, not merely going on as they do. Haugeland himself notes on the next page that, as publicness functions in Heidegger, it has a "tendency to disguise and forget anxiety," the disclosive state that can call us back to ourselves. All such paradoxes stem from the unusual sort of "failure" Heidegger wants to account for.

necessity.[21] So we seem left simply without any distinctly philosophical claim, except negative ones. We might be tempted to conclude that, if Dasein *is*, in some radical sense, thrown projection, always already embedded in its world, if any possible meaning of Being is existential in just this sense, then there is nothing to say about *what it is to be so thrown* except insofar as any such answer is "attested" in the experience of such subjects, in a historical world, at a time.

There is a sense in which, properly understood, making such a claim *is* what fundamental ontology consists in. But everything comes down to "properly understood," and we are therewith in the vicinity of one of Heidegger's deepest anxieties: that this radical doctrine of finitude, a finitude that makes the adoption of a transcendental interpretation of Heidegger quite misleading – will be misinterpreted as the invitation to a historicist philosophical anthropology, a *mere* hermeneutics of what being *has come to mean*; radical only in that considerations of how anything *could* come to mean are included *within* the hermeneutic, not treated independently or *prior* (i.e., transcendentally). Another of his anxieties also lurks in this area: that he is an "existentialist," for whom the horrible truth about the "meaninglessness" or "absurdity" of Dasein's existence is *too* horrible to face, provokes despair, and so on. I think Heidegger is right that both characterizations are inaccurate.

That is, both transcendentalist and existentialist interpretations are hard to make consistent with the fact that Heidegger is manifestly not talking about the finitude and mortality and self-obscuring characteristics of Dasein, on the one hand, and, on the other hand, some considerably more than finite capacity on the part of philosophy to set out the necessary conditions always required for anything to make sense for such a finite being or to state the "real" truth about Dasein's "absurd" existence. Finitude, the consequences of Heidegger's criticism of standard logic, of Husserlean phenomenology and Kantian transcendentalism, and eventually of all metaphysics, is primarily a critique, one might even say an

---

[21] If there really is such an inseparability, then we can only quite artificially isolate condition and conditioned. Each "side" is so determined in respect to the other ("meaning" and "that without which meaning is impossible") that we are smack in the middle of Heidegger's circle, not the realm of transcendental necessity. Thus, when Heidegger invokes transcendental terminology, there is usually some qualification. At SZ 65; 41, "a priori" gets scare quotes; when, at 78; 53, he says freely that being-in-the-world is a "necessary a priori constituent [*Verfassung*] of Dasein," he tosses it off as if a mere preliminary observation and "not by a large measure sufficient" to fully determine the Being of Dasein.

attack, *on philosophy itself*, not a reminder that we all die and are afraid of that, or cannot face the absurdity of our lives.[22] (As early as 1920 Heidegger was writing, "We philosophize, not in order to show that we need a philosophy, but instead precisely to show that we do not need one.")[23] Avoiding though the transcendental or historicist anthropology or existentialist interpretations has everything to do with the radicality of Heidegger's account of *das Nichts*, to which I now turn.

## III

Heidegger presents an existential analytic that is proposed as preliminary, a stalking horse such that progress in understanding the meaning of Dasein's Being could be *the* decisive step in understanding any *Sinn des Seins* (for Dasein). Again, this approach creates a transcendental temptation, as if we are looking for Dasein's conditions of sense, conditions that will set the horizon for the possibility of all sense (even though still "for Dasein"). But I want to suggest that the Dasein analytic is privileged because it is *exemplary* (exemplary of how the meaning of Being "happens"), *not transcendental* in this sense (not constitutive of any possible meaning, as if "necessary conditions" have been found). To see how this works, we need to remind ourselves briefly of the drama that makes SZ so riveting.

The catch phrase associated with Heidegger and Sartre that "existence precedes essence" amounts, minimally, to a denial that any distinctively human "way of life"[24] could be said to simply have an anthropologically fixed, essential, or socially "assigned" nature. Rather, one's existence is always in a kind of suspended state, everywhere oriented and "lived forward" by some prediscursive understanding of and commitment to a

---

[22] Cf. this telling remark from the 1929–30 *Fundamental Concepts of Metaphysics*:

> What if it were a prejudice that metaphysics is a fixed and secure discipline, and an illusion that philosophy is a science that can be taught and learned? ... is all this talk of philosophy being the absolute science a delusion? Not just because the individual or some school never achieves this end, but because positing the end is itself fundamentally an error and a misunderstanding of the innermost essence of philosophy. Philosophy as absolute science – a lofty, unsurpassable ideal. So it seems. And yet perhaps even judging philosophy according to the idea of science is the most disastrous debasement of its innermost essence. (GA 29, 2)

[23] *Phänomenologie der Anschauung und des Ausdrucks*, ed. C. A. Strube, GA 59 (1993), 91. Quoted in Dahlstrom 2001, 385. Note his qualification in the footnote.

[24] To invoke Haugeland's comprehensive term of art for Dasein (Haugeland 1992, 35).

"meaning of one's being" that cannot have something like a resolution or totality or a fixed "grounding" in the usual sense.[25]

And, Heidegger notes, Dasein can "decide its existence by taking hold *or* neglecting" (33; 12). In the historical world that Heidegger interprets (i.e., our world), it is the latter that mostly manifests how Dasein is at issue for itself, by neglecting in some way the call of conscience, calling one back to oneself as a concernful being-in-the-world, living a life only by "taking up the reins," only by *leading* one's life, but constantly "falling," lost in the concerns of *das Man*, attempting to avoid the claims of such a requirement. Dasein's Being is said to "lie hidden," but in a way such that that "hiddenness also belongs to what thus shows itself" (59; 35). And in the most dialectical expression, the *Ich* or I can exist as "not-I," in the mode of having lost "*Ichheit*," or *is* only by having lost itself (*Selbstverlorenheit*; 152; 116). (And it is already important to note, contra the "existentialist" reading, that this does not mean a simple falling away from an authentic selfhood, to which we may resolutely return. The point is the more radical claim that the "*Ich*'s" capacity to exist as "*Selbstverlorenheit*" "is" what it is to be an "I" at all. Achieving some sort of stable "*Ichheit*" would be to cease to be an "*Ich*.")

This account sets the stage for the sort of philosophical question about meaning that Heidegger wants to pose. For the question he wants to ask is not a skeptical one (about other minds, the external world, or the very possibility of a distinction between knowing and not-knowing at all), not an idealist worry (What is the relation between the conditions for our understanding the meaning of our being? and What could being be?), and not an ethical one (How can Dasein remain "true" to itself?), but one oriented from a different question: What could meaning – "fundamentally," preeminently the meaning of Being – *be, such that it could fail, utterly and in a way absolutely fail*? This sort of orientation (examining the nature of significance, meaningfulness in our engagements with others and the world, by taking our bearings from a breakdown in meaningful practices) had

---

[25] In this, Heidegger is closer than he knows to the Kantian and post-Kantian tradition, once one breaks free from Heidegger's Cartesian interpretation. Beginning especially with Kant's moral philosophy, "person," despite the surface grammar, is in no sense a substantive or metaphysical category, but in some way or other a practical achievement, and the attribution of the notion to an other is an ascription not a description. As Fichte would say, the I posits itself; as Hegel would say, *Geist* is a "result of itself." The somewhat confusing but very important point here is that being a subject means being able to fail to be one, something that already tells us a lot about the uniquely practical, not metaphysical status of subjectivity in the post-Kantian tradition. See Pippin 1999b, 2000a.

been methodologically prominent from the very first accounts of being-in-the-world. The "worldly" character of the world itself (*Weltlichkeit*), not just aspects of the world or items in the world, is announced by, perhaps even consists in, such breakdowns as "conspicuousness" (*Auffallen*), "obtrusiveness" (*Aufdringlichkeit*), and "obstinacy" (*Aufsässigkeit*), each a kind of "break" (*Bruch*) in the referential contexts within which *Zuhandenheit* makes the kinds of sense it does. No regressive transcendental argument to necessary conditions of sense is involved in such a making-manifest; Heidegger is appealing instead to the phenomenological evidence of "attestation" (*Bezeugung*), what "shows itself" *in* such experiences of breakdown *as having been at work.*

Moreover, the sort of significance Heidegger is interested in as a matter of fundamental ontology is hardly limited to the dealings and engagements involved in the equipmental world of sense. Dasein's Being is, "fundamentally ontologically," care, its "circumspection" always "concernful." The meaningfulness of its engagements with objects and others involves a layered relation of ends, "for the sakes of which" (*Worumwillen*)[26] in Heidegger's nominalization. Even if the directedness and normative commitments that, as Dreyfuss notes,[27] sustain our comportment in the world "nonrobotically" are not self-referential mental states, this directedness is *sustained*, something evident when that sustaining fails, when, in the simplest sense, care fails, when we cannot care. That is, the accounts of everyday significance and of the meaningfulness of Being are treated as matters of mattering. The prethematic ontological horizon of sense "held open" by Dasein is a horizon of mattering, with saliences of significance and ordered relations of importance always at issue if not directly "*pointed at*" or aimed at or consciously attended to in such engagements. It can be best seen as that sort of sense or mattering when we experience the distinctiveness of its failure, something Heidegger first begins to describe in his account of anxiety.

There he begins to explore this unusual "logos of mattering" with a remark that is not given the usual headline treatment but is astonishing nonetheless. For Heidegger notes an experience rarely treated at all before Kierkegaard on despair, and rarely treated anywhere as of such consequence:

[T]he totality of involvements [*Bewandtnisganzheit*] of the ready-to-hand and the present-at-hand discovered within the world is, as such, of no consequence

---

[26] SZ 97; 68; 109; 78; 117-20; 85-7.
[27] Dreyfuss 1992, 68.

[*ohne Belang*]; it collapses into itself; the world has the character of completely lacking significance. [*Die Welt hat den Charakter völliger Unbedeutsamkeit.*] (231; 186)

Is such a thought even thinkable? *Complete* insignificance? The *totality* of involvements of the *Zuhanden* and *Vorhanden* "collapses into itself"? For one thing, it does not seem likely that this "collapse" could be *so* total that the entire meaning-structure of our everyday engagements could also collapse, such that stop signs, hammers, weather vanes, cooking implements, and the like would intrude into Dasein's existence as senseless objects, the way the discovery of implements from another culture or planet would. It is possible to imagine such a breakdown, but for Heidegger's point about the possibility of failure to be cogent, he need only be talking about the "failure of sense" of the "ultimate for-the-sake-of-which" in this network of relations, the meaning of Dasein's being, the failure of which can in some way throw into relief all other pragmata without introducing some sort of apocalyptic senselessness.[28]

It is not until Heidegger revisits in Division Two the issues here introduced that both the existential dimensions of such an experience, the determinate importance of "the failure of the meaning of Dasein's being," and its importance for fundamental ontology emerge. Having noted that any full account of the meaning of Dasein's Being must take account of Dasein as possibly a totality or whole, Heidegger argues that Dasein can never be such a whole, but its own total significance can come into view by being toward its end, indeed, an ending that constantly threatens Dasein's very Being. He asks,

How is it existentially possible for this constant threat to be genuinely disclosed? All understanding is accompanied by state-of-mind. Dasein's mood brings it face-to-face with the thrownness of its "that it is there." But the state of mind which can hold open the utter and constant threat to itself arising from Dasein's ownmost individualized being is anxiety. (310; 265–6)

This is the preparation for Heidegger's extraordinary account of "freedom toward death" and his summary account of care as "shot through" with *Nichtigkeit,* and Dasein being the null basis of a nothingness.

Heidegger at this point allows himself a no doubt deliberately comic understatement when he then notes, "the ontological meaning of the notness [*Nichtheit*] of this existential nothingness is still obscure" (331; 285). But what he tries to stress throughout his extended account of conscience, care, guilt, and authenticity is the radicality of the failure of meaning

---

[28] I am indebted to Michael Williams and Eckart Förster for discussions about this point.

provoked by the conflict between any sense making, care-ful engagement, and defeat of such attempts in the face of the absoluteness of one's
death. What he describes is a collapse of significance that allows us to
see that what had "kept up" such a structure of significance was "nothing" but our caring to keep it in place, a care originating and failing in
utter contingency. The unincorporability of one's death into this structure of significance, or of mattering, the impossibility that death could
mean anything, brings into experiential prominence the contingency of
care itself, the escape or flight from such a nullity without which leading an existence, temporalizing a time, would not be possible. His claim
seems to be that the experience of the constant impendingness of one's
death can "block" in some way the practical projection into the future
that amounts to the work of sustaining meaning for Dasein. Such an experience does not cause such a breakdown, nor is it merely the occasion
for such a reaction. Heidegger must mean that the sustaining of such
meaning requires the fulfilling of an existential condition, a sense of fu-
turity, a being-toward-an-end, that the absoluteness and arbitrariness of
death calls into question ("calls" as the call of conscience). The idea is not
that death itself is unintelligible or absurd, but what being-toward-death
calls into question reveals that what it means to be Dasein is to be able to
fail to be a "concernful," circumspective "site" of meaning and that the
succeeding and failing cannot be a part of Dasein's project, cannot be
assigned to it as a task, a work. (This begins the difference with Hegel,
whose position I want to bring in below as a contrast.)

A short time later, in his lecture course of 1929/30, Heidegger focuses on a *Stimmung* that reveals a failure or collapse of meaning that
is intuitively clearer but less intuitively connected with responsive action
or redemption. He notes as an ontological phenomenon the possibility
of "deep boredom" (*tiefe Langweile*). The "emptiness" evinced in such a
profound or deep boredom (*die langweilende Leere*) is not the sort one
can will or argue oneself out of, not the sort of orientation one can control.[29] (It should be stressed here that Heidegger's variations in appeals
to various "*Stimmungen*," or moods, attunements, means that his analysis
is not restricted to any particular experience of *death*. He is looking for

---

[29] *Die Grundbegriffe der Metaphysik. Welt – Endlichkeit – Einsamkeit*, GA Bd. 29/30, op. cit.,
244, 248. These lectures are filled with references to the economic and social global
crisis of 1929 and make clearer how Heidegger understood the political implications
of his account of the meaning of Being. They thus give a chilling sense of the kind of
desperation that can be produced if one believes oneself to be in such a situation. See
Gregory Fried's interesting 2000 study.

paradigmatic cases where the whole interrelated practical structure of care can, "on its own" as it were, fail, and then asking what such meaning must be that it could fail.)

And of course Heidegger is not trying to say that the fact of one's inevitable death gives one a *reason* to lose faith in the worth or point of one's projects and goals. In the first place, the character of the significance or meaning he takes to be threatened is, in his terms, "prior" to any belief or project. What fails is care, and this precisely not for any reason. (One must already care about reasons for that to be a possibility, and in that case the mattering of reasons would not fail.) It fails because nothing matters in isolation from whatever else matters, and Heidegger thinks there must be some primordial horizon of significance for such care to be sustained (the kind of primordial horizon that comes into view when the problem of Dasein's totality is in question). What is important in this context is that the practical implication of this failure is what Heidegger calls "guilt," an owning up both to the radical contingency of one's thrownness and to the inescapability of an ever-threatening death, as well as to the practical necessity, in acting at all, of fleeing in some way from such nullity, of "erring" in the ontological sense in order to be, in order to "stretch one's existence along in time." This incompatibility is not a rational inconsistency or a failure to be rational enough. We are simply not "in charge" of whether care fails or not or how to think our way into or out of such an experience. ("This 'Being-a-basis' means never to have power over one's ownmost Being from the ground up. This 'not' belongs to the existential meaning of thrownness" (330; 284). "Being-guilty is more primordial than any knowledge of it" (332; 286).)[30]

---

[30] The radicality and extreme difficulty of the claim that the primordial meaning of Dasein's Being is disclosed in the collapse of meaning, in such a primordial meaning just *being* the possibility of collapse or failure of meaning, are related to what Heidegger says about the nature of our not-being and both the necessity and impossibility of its incorporability into the structure of care. In effect, Heidegger is trying to resurrect an Eleatic, or radical sense of not-being, *to mēdemos on*, not just *to mē on*. That is, he is trying to recover what he considers obscured by the "solution" to the problem proposed in Plato's *Sophist*. Since the sophist says what is not, it might look to an Eleatic as if he violates the proscription on nonbeing, and so there cannot really be a sophist, or a distinction between sophist and philosopher, because nonbeing cannot be. But Plato's Eleatic stranger tries to show that *to mē on* cannot be some sort of radically empty being, just a *Not* Being, but is instead "otherness," a kind of otherness "woven through" all the beings. To say what is not the case is not then to say what is not, but to say what is other than the truth at the time; that is, always to say *something else*, to say of something other than what is the case that it is the case. (In Heidegger's 1924–5 Marburg course on Plato's *Sophist* this issue is brought to a head in §§78 and 79. See PS, 386–401. But Heidegger is so self-restricted there in

This is the predecessor account for all attempts – eventually Carnap's, too – to tame or moderate the existential and ontological challenge of not-being.[31] But our own not-being is not *another way for us to be*; we *are* not something other than alive when we are dead. Death is also not a natural completion, or ripeness, or the lack or privation of life in a material body; it is not – existentially, with respect to Dasein's experience of the meaning of its Being – even a factual "event" to be expected and has its role in such a meaning question only by our "being-toward" it. And, as Heidegger never tires of saying, the ontological problem of not-being cannot be reduced to the problem of a logical operator, the paradigmatic form of treating not-being as otherness; not this being, but *thereby some other being* or some other possible point in logical space. This is the sense of the famous passage from *What Is Metaphysics?* that so enraged Carnap:

> Does the nothing exist only because the not, i.e. negation exists? Or is it the other way around? Do negation and the not exist only because the nothing exists?... We assert: the nothing is prior to the not and the negation.... Where do we seek the nothing? How do we find the nothing?... Anxiety reveals the nothing. That for which and because of which we were anxious was "really" nothing. Indeed: the nothing itself – as such – was present.... What about this nothing? – The nothing itself nothings.[32]

(Even here, it is important to stress, Heidegger is tying this so-called reference to the Nothing to anxiety, or the failure of possible "projection." He is always referring, I think, to the unique Dasein-possibility – failed "lived meaning" – not to any metaphysical nonmeaning.) Death, Heidegger is suggesting, is not simply the negation of life, other than life (but some other state of being). For Dasein qua Dasein (not qua biological organism) is always "dying" (251; 245), always in a way "at" its end, and for it ceasing to be is an absolute nothingness, the meaning of which cannot be captured by the negation operation applied to "life." He goes to an extreme formulation to try to suggest that such radical not-being cannot be domesticated by us, is not the result of what we do to ourselves, bring

---

his role as a commentator that the issue is much easier to see elsewhere in his lectures, when he speaks more in his own voice.

[31] Cf. also another such attempt – Hegel's – especially, in his Introduction to the *Phenomenology of Spirit*, his remark that

in every case the result of an untrue mode of knowledge must not be allowed to run away into an empty nothing, but must necessarily be grasped as the nothing of that from which it results [*Nichts, desjenigen, dessen Resultat es ist*]. (PhS, 56; PhG, 61)

[32] Carnap 1959, 69. This, with the ellipses, is how Carnap quotes the passage from *What Is Metaphysics?*

about in some psychological sense – his infamous phrase is "the nothing itself nothings" – but his contrast is clear enough.[33]

From a Heideggerean point of view, in other words, when Creon and Antigone in Sophocles' play are arguing over what is to be done with Polyneices' body, when the audience is made aware of the utter difference between Polyneices and the thing now rotting outside the city walls, they are enacting what they must enact in order to live, even though both "mediations," both appeals to the Penates, on the one hand, and the city's requirements, on the other, are attempts to reclaim, within a logic of mattering, what cannot make sense in this way; both represent in ways typical of such human flight a refusal to allow Polyneices to die. There is no way to continue to stretch along into the future the world that had Polyneices in it. He is not in it at all; he is nothing; and when in some contingent way the structure of care fails to be able to continue such redemption, the character of such an attempt, its ultimate "*Nichtigkeit,*" becomes unavoidable.

Such a failure of meaning is radical in ways now more familiar from modern literature.[34] When Bartleby the Scrivener stops working, and "prefers not to," what is "uncanny" (in exactly the Heideggerean sense) about his story is that the failure of meaning he suffers is not in the name of what his form of life lacks, what it should have; not in the name of any absence or privation, any "other than what now is." The failure of meaning appears to be complete, not a response to the failure of humanism, of justice, not a response to the brutality of wage labor and so forth. Bartleby has in effect no "everyday" psychology (none we are given by Melville as relevant), no beliefs or aspirations, no reasons. Mattering just "fails" in the way it can (the way it can fundamentally in anxious being-toward-death), *in the way that reveals the utter contingency and fragility of it succeeding when it does.* It happening or not happening *is* the event of truth (the occasion for living "in truth"). The "disturbance" Bartleby provokes in his colleagues is very much as if he is the presence of death among them, the "uncanniest" of guests. In the same way that the nihilistic culmination of metaphysics reveals something about the nature of metaphysics as such

---

[33] He wants to make the same point about the implications of the primordial situation of thrownness, about what happens to us, by coining such neologisms as "Die Angst ängstet sich um das Seinkönnen des so bestimmten Seienden . . ." (310; 266).

[34] Heidegger's example in *Introduction to Metaphysics* is from Knut Hamsun's *The Road Leads On*, where a poet sitting alone by the ocean muses, "Here – nothing meets nothing and is not there, there is not even a hole. One can only shake one's head in resignation" (IM, 29).

and is not a contingent event – philosophers losing faith in metaphysics – so, too, in the existential situation it is the radicality of this failure of meaning that reveals what is most essential about such meaning (that it can so fail). Any partial or determinate failure (of the kind central to Hegel's account of conceptual and social change, for example) amounts merely to an extension of sense-making practices and so blocks any radical reflection on their possibility. ("Only by the anticipation of death is every accidental and 'provisional' possibility driven out" (435; 384).)[35]

But there are no determinate conditions *necessary* for care to succeed, to be sustained, for anything to matter, such that to call the call of conscience, anxiety, and being-toward-death a threat to the existential satisfaction of transcendental conditions is to obscure the point Heidegger is trying to make.[36] There is no way that being-in-the-world can be isolated from its historical incarnations so that we might isolate "conditions" necessary for the pragmata of the world to make the sort of determinate practical sense they occasionally do. Heidegger's accounts of involvement, comportment, falling, and so forth are both (1) primordial elements of how things have come to make sense in a historical world (such that the gradual transformation of such a world into one wherein a predatory technological subject confronts material stuff for its mundane purposes is not a failure or breakdown of sense, but the contingent transformation of the horizon of ontological meaning) and (2) preparatory

---

[35] Cf. the remark in *Introduction to Metaphysics*, "the human being has no way out, in the face of death, not only when it is time to die, but constantly and essentially. Insofar as humans are, they stand in the no-exit of death. Thus being-there is the happening of the uncanniness itself" (IM, 169). It would take several more chapters to try to show that this sort of account of meaning-failure is paradigmatic for what Heidegger wants to say in all contexts about the meaning of Being. But I would want to argue that there are always parallels to this sort of account in those other contexts. Forms of life can also "fail" to mean, and there can be analogous anticipations of death in phenomena such as "nihilism." The language of SZ is reconfigured as a kind of struggle between "Earth" (thrownness) and "World" (projection) in *On the Origin of the Work of Art* and so forth.

[36] It is certainly possible to characterize Heidegger's account as "transcendental" in a rather benign sense. One could say that Heidegger has shown that a necessary condition of Dasein's Being making sense is the possibility of its not making sense; only such a condition can disclose this unavoidable "condition": the utter contingency of such care or mattering or significance when it happens. Or one could say, with Føllesdall, that Heidegger has shown that purposive action is a "necessary constituent" of the possibility of intentionality. But this is too benign to be very informative and can be misleading. Heidegger's procedure is rather to establish a question, demonstrate both its supremely distinct and practically unavoidable character, and then to argue that various possible candidate accounts (such as Cartesian mentalism) fail to answer it. He does not, cannot, argue, say, that nonpractical intentionality is "impossible." See Føllesdall 1979.

to the account of the *failure* of such a way of things mattering when the call of conscience and its attendant anxiety bring the practical structure of care crashing down. Again, Kantian or transcendental conditions cannot "fail." That is the whole point of the case for their necessity. The Heideggerean elements of practical sense making can ultimately fail or even be permanently forgotten. That is the whole point of saying that care is shot through with *Nichtigkeit* and is the null basis of a nullity. This failure, occasioned by the "threat" to meaning posed by one's ever impending death, is not a failure "as yet" to make the proper sense of what seems without sense.[37] There is no horrible fate that we are too fearful or too finite to make sense of. The failure that Heidegger is trying to account for is not a failure to "make sense" of death but an occasion in which the failure to make sense of, be able to sustain reflectively, sense making itself "happens."

This situation, I have claimed, is an exemplary, not a transcendental account. Of what is it exemplary? In existential terms (in Heidegger's sense of existential) it exemplifies the occasion requiring either an "authentic" or "inauthentic" response, an issue that would require several volumes to discuss appropriately. But the basic direction of the book's analysis suggests the obvious answer: What is exemplified is the temporal character of Being, that Being is time, the truth of the meaning of being historical, a matter of *Geschichtlichkeit*. I close with some brief remarks about that sort of claim and temporality itself.

## IV

I have said that for Heidegger mattering can just "fail" and in a way that reveals the utter contingency and fragility of it succeeding when it does; and so that meaning happening or not happening *is* the event of truth (the occasion for living "in truth," in the acknowledgment of this finitude or in flight from it). There is another way to put this point, once we take in Heidegger's most comprehensive account of care, his way of making

---

[37] Or: When Kafka's K cannot find the court that has accused him nor even the charge against him, we are not to assume that if he tried harder or got lucky, he *might have*. In a paradoxical way that exactly mirrors Heidegger's claim, this failure in no way lessens the bewildering guilt K begins to feel, the anxious sense that being alive itself is the situation of being guilty. In the parable of the law and the man from the country that closes the novel, there are three things true of the elements of the fable. The doorway to the Law *is* for the man from the country; he may *not*, though, enter; and these two facts do not amount to a contradiction, but instead "a necessity."

the point cited earlier: that care must be sustained to function as care, stretched along into the future. Heidegger's formulation is that "temporality [*Zeitlichkeit*] reveals itself as the meaning of authentic care" (374; 326) and that the "primordial unity of the structure of care lies in temporality." This is the opening to what he calls "a more primordial insight into the temporalization structure of temporality, which reveals itself as the historicality [*Geschichtlichkeit*] of Dasein" (381; 332). This distinctive historicality (or historicity, as it is now more frequently translated) is stressed by Heidegger in a way not entirely clear in the Macquarrie-Robinson translation:

> The movement [actually this is another neologism, more like "moved-ness" or "motility," *Bewegtheit*] of existence is not the motion [*Bewegung*] of something present-at-hand. It is definable in terms of the way Dasein stretches along [*aus der Ersteckung des Daseins*]. The specific movement [*Bewegtheit*] in which Dasein is stretched along and stretches itself along, we call its happening [*Geschehen,* "historizing" by Macquarrie and Robinson]. (427; 375)

However valuable it is to draw attention to the etymological connections between *Geschehen* and *Geschichte*, it is crucial that the translation capture the sense of contingency connoted by *Geschehen*, and especially regrettable that the translators often make *Geschehen* a verb when Heidegger uses it as a noun, suggesting just the opposite of what Heidegger wants to suggest – the mere "happenstance," let us say, of meaning as a temporalizing, care-ful engagement, and the happenstance of its failure.[38] So the summary claim that he makes should be:

> This is how we designate Dasein's primordial happening [*ursprüngliche Geschehen*], lying in its authentic resoluteness, and in which Dasein hands itself down to itself, free for death, in a possibility which it has inherited and yet has chosen. (435; 384)

There is a lot packed into such claims, but the basic dimensions of the case attributed to Heidegger are visible. What is meaning such that it can fail? Finite, contingent; a *Geschehen*, distinctively temporal, in a way a kind

---

[38] Preserving that connection also makes the relation between the so-called early and later Heidegger considerably easier to see for English readers, the Heidegger who says very shortly after BT (in a 1931–2 lecture course), "Being happens as a history of human beings, as the history of a *Volk*" (*Vom Wesen der Wahrheit*, GA, Bd. 34, 145). Stambough's word for *Geschehen* in her later translation of SZ, "occurrence," is better, but it now conflicts with what has emerged as the preferred translations of *Vorhanden* and *Zuhanden*, John Haugeland's "occurent" and "available" (Stambough 1997).

of event, "*Er-eignis*" (or "e-vent" as it is sometimes translated to capture Heidegger's hyphen), that can happen *to* us, or not, cannot be redeemed or reflectively grounded by philosophy.

This *Geschehen* quality also differentiates Heidegger's position from that other southwest German philosopher, and that can be a final way to make the Heideggerean point. I quote from the "Preface" to Hegel's *Phenomenology*:

> But the life of Spirit is not the life that shrinks from death and keeps itself untouched by devastation, but rather the life that endures it and maintains itself in it. It wins its truth only when, in utter dismemberment [*Zerissenheit*], it finds itself. . . . Spirit is this power only by looking the negative in the face, and tarrying with it. This tarrying [*Verweilen*] with the negative is the magical power [*Zauberkraft*] that converts it into being.[39]

This claim is possible in Hegel's account because such instances of failure, breakdowns in a form of life as a whole, "utter dismemberment," are precisely *not* mere "happenings," events, and so not instances of radical nonbeing. As he notes in the "Introduction,"

> Thus consciousness suffers this violence at its own hands: it spoils its own limited satisfaction. When consciousness feels this violence, its anxiety may well make it retreat from the truth and strive to hold on to what it is in danger of losing. But it can find no peace. If it wishes to remain in a state of unthinking inertia, then thought troubles its thoughtlessness, and its own unrest disturbs its inertia.[40]

There is, of course, no such "magical power" for Heidegger, and this is because spirit does not suffer the violence of death "at its own hands," such that some way can be found to reconstruct the subjective purposiveness inherent in so suffering, in bringing about such suffering (the purposiveness necessarily assumed if this self-inflicted suffering is to count as a deed). From Hegel's (or perhaps from Adorno's) point of view, the Heideggerean experience of death *as* (now, for us) radical not-being, *as* unintegratable in any way with Dasein's projected meaning, *is* "something we have done to ourselves," can be itself made sense of, given the historical situation of late modernity, or late industrial capitalism, and so forth. From Heidegger's point of view, on the other hand, Hegelian death remains Christian; the tarrying of which Hegel spoke is possible because of a faith in "resurrection," and the ultimacy of death in our experience is not being authentically faced but clearly avoided. It is as if Hegel cannot

---

[39] PhS, 19; PhG, 27.
[40] PhS, 51; PhG, 57.

help giving away his dodge and his own uncertainty with that revealing (most un-Hegelian) word or Freudian slip, *Zauberkraft*, "magical power."

But contrary to many interpretations of Hegel, these remarks by him show that Hegel does not treat the failure of some community to sustain a practical "directedness" as a mark of some *ultimately* in-principle *overcomeable* finitude. For, only as long as there is such "violence suffered at its own hands" *is* there *Geist*. According to Hegel, there is a narrative ("rational") structure to our coming to this realization, but *this* is the realization we are coming to (i.e., just the opposite of the jejeune invocations of Hegel as announcing the end of history or a complete "closed" systematicity).[41] But, as I have been suggesting, this realization (a.k.a. "Absolute Knowledge") cannot itself be a Heideggerean "happening" since the realization that only in such "failure" is there success (success at being *Geist*) is an achievement like no other in such historical attempts, is what makes what Heidegger calls the "revealing and concealing" process *itself* manifest. This is why Hegel treats the final problem of reconciliation in the *Phenomenology* (*Versöhnung*) as "forgiveness" (*Verzeihung*), forgiveness not at being "merely" human but grounded in the realization of being "absolutely" human.

Stated this way, matters between the Baden and the Schwabian are left pretty much at a standoff. But Heidegger reminds us that philosophy is "the opposite of all comfort and assurance," "the highest uncertainty," and maintains itself "in authentic questionableness." So perhaps an unresolved standoff, an ending that is not an end, is a good place to close.

[41] Pippin 1999a, chap. 7, "Unending Modernity," 160ff.

# 4

## Gadamer's Hegel

### *Subjectivity and Reflection*

So mußte vor allem Hegels Denkweg erneut befragt werden. ("Above all else, the path of Hegel's thought must be interrogated anew.")

(GW, Bd. 2, 505)

### I

Gadamer's philosophical hermeneutics is as much a reaction as an initiation: a reaction against a relativistic historicism that "locked" speakers and actors "inside" world views, a reaction against the overwhelming prestige of the natural sciences and the insistence on methodology inspired by that success, and a reaction against the "bloodless academic philosophizing"[1] of neo-Kantian philosophy and its perennialist "great problems" approach to the history of philosophy. But in several of his autobiographical remarks, Gadamer singles out an opponent that seems to loom oddly large in his reminiscences about provocations. "Using Heidegger's analysis, my starting point was a critique of German Idealism and its Romantic traditions" (PG, 27), he writes in one such recollection. And in the same essay, he writes of trying to avoid or to "forfeit" (*einbüßen*) "the *fundamentum inconcussum* of philosophy on the basis of which Hegel had written his story of philosophy and the neo-Kantians their history of problems – namely, self-consciousness" (PG, 7). And later, "So I sought in my hermeneutics to overcome the primacy of self-consciousness, and especially the prejudices of an idealism rooted in consciousness" (PG, 27).

---

[1] Gadamer, "Reflections on my Philosophical Journey," in PG, 9.

I want to explore in the following what Gadamer might mean by giving to hermeneutics the task of "overcoming the primacy of self-consciousness" and to ask whether it is really Hegel in his sights as he attempts to do so.


## II

We need first to attend to the conflicting strands of deep solidarity with Hegel, coupled with just as deep a rejection. With respect to the former strand, there is much to cite. Indeed, the selection of Hegel as such a principal opponent is somewhat odd because there are so many passages throughout Gadamer's writings that warmly embrace Hegel as a comrade-in-arms. While the major influences on Gadamer's development of a philosophical hermeneutics are unquestionably Plato, Aristotle, and Heidegger, Hegel is not far behind, as the epigram above already indicates. This is so for a number of obvious and not so obvious reasons.

In the first place, one would expect from Gadamer a sympathetic embrace of Hegel's own reaction against Kantian formalism, an embrace of Hegel's denial of transcendental subjectivity and pure practical reason, an embrace of Hegel's attack on philosophies of transcendence or "the beyond" (*Jenseitsphilosophie*) and so Hegel's attempt to situate or embed the human subject in time, and an embrace of Hegel's attack on all attempts to understand concepts, or language as means employed by a subject or as rules applied by a subject. The Heideggerean and Gadamerean "dialectic" between "being in a world" (and being always already subject to a particular life-world) and "having a world" (being a potentially critical, reflective subject of such a world) was already clearly announced by and explored by Hegel (PG, 36). And Gadamer sees that thereby Hegel had already anticipated a great deal of the dialectic of later European philosophy. Hegel had understood that we would need a way of achieving this rejection of formalism and this socio-historical "embedding" without ending up with a kind of sociological, empirical, descriptive, nonphilosophical enterprise and with a diverse plurality of incommensurable language games (an option already on the horizon in Herder). And all this must be accomplished without, by rejecting this empiricism and relativism, reanimating a new hope for some decisive meta-language or transcendental philosophy of necessary conditions for the possibility of sense making, experience, practical life, and so on, a hope for temporally and methodologically stable conditions, "scientifically" arrived at by a proper "control" or methodology (what turned out to be the neo-Kantian temptation).

It is thus no surprise that, in the exciting calls for a new "life" philosophy swirling throughout Germany in Gadamer's early adulthood, he would recall and astutely take his bearings from such a passage as the following from the Preface to Hegel's *Phenomenology of Spirit*:

> The form of study in ancient times differs from that of the modern period in that study then was a thorough process of education appropriate for a natural consciousness. In specific probing of each aspect of its existence and in philosophizing about all that occurs, it generated for itself a universality actively engaged in the whole of its life. In the modern period on the other hand, the individual finds that the universal [*die abstrakte Form*] is already prepared for him. It would therefore be better to say that in his effort to grasp it and to make it his own he directly forces the inner essence into the open without the mediatory experience of the natural consciousness. Thus the generation of the universal here is cut off from the manifold of existence – the universal does not emerge out of that manifold. The task now is not so much to purify the individual of his immediate dependency on his senses and to raise him to the substance which thinks and is thought, as it is the reverse, namely, to actualize the universal and to infuse it with spirit by dissolving the fixed determinations of thought.[2]

Hegel's attempt to "infuse" the traditional categories of the understanding "with spirit" (*sich begeistern*; HD, 16), and so, in his *Phenomenology*, his attempt to understand the determinacy and authority of such discriminations by understanding the actual roles they play in a social community and their systematic interrelatedness across many different activities of such a community looks like an attempt to construe norms and principles as having a "life" of their own that in principle is quite close in spirit to Gadamer's two-pronged hermeneutical attack on transcendentalism and relativism.

Moreover, any claim that we have lost something "vital" that was a taken-for-granted aspect of ancient Greek life would obviously be welcome to Gadamer (whose great disagreement with Heidegger stems from Gadamer's resolute refusal to see his beloved Plato as "the origin of Western nihilism"), and Gadamer indeed sometimes writes in almost a tone

---

[2] This is a very tough sentence to translate. "[D]ie Anstrengung, sie zu ergreifen und sich zu eigen zu machen, ist mehr das unvermittelte Hervortreiben des Innern und abgeschnittene Erzeugen des Allgemeinen als ein Hervorgehen desselben aus dem Konkreten und der Mannigfaltigkeit des Daseins." G. W. F. Hegel, *Die Phänomenologie des Geistes* (Felix Meiner: Hamburg, 1952), 30. Gadamer quotes it in "Hegel and the Dialectic of the Ancient Philosophers," in HD, 8.

of gratitude for Hegel's philosophical rehabilitation of Greek thinkers as philosophers. He even goes so far as to refer to the Greeks "and their latest and greatest follower, Hegel" (PG, 15).[3] As we see below, Gadamer will disagree with Hegel's appropriation of the ancient art of dialectic, with Hegel's account of the deficiencies in the Greek theory of subjectivity, and with Hegel's readings of key passages, but he still credits Hegel, alone among the Titans of modern philosophy – Descartes, Spinoza, Leibniz, Locke, Hume, and Kant – with an appreciation of the "speculative" moment in Greek thought, an appreciation that remained unique in the history of modern philosophy until Heidegger.[4]

Indeed, only Hegel and Heidegger (and, one should now of course also say, Gadamer) have shown how philosophy itself should be understood not merely to have a history but to be its history, that the work of philosophy itself is a speculative recollection of its history, and since it is so speculative and philosophical, it so "reconceptualizes" (*aufhebt*, cancels, preserves, and raises up) historical "thinking and knowing" that the objects of study should no longer count as merely historical texts. ("The first person who wrote a history of philosophy, that was really such, was also the last to do so – Hegel" (PG, 35).)[5] As we also see below, there are various ways of comprehending philosophical recollection as a living conversation, ranging from Heidegger's "destruction" of the still living, still ontologically pernicious Western metaphysical tradition to Hegel's developmental account of how "they" were trying, incompletely, to accomplish what "we" are still trying, more completely, to accomplish to Gadamer's own account of the eternally inexhaustible residue of meaning in past texts and events, but the denial of any separation between philosophy and its history and so the refusal to see past philosophers and writers as failed versions of us certainly unites them. At the end of the First Part of *Truth and Method* Gadamer writes,

Hegel states a definite truth, inasmuch as the essential nature of the historical spirit consists not in the restoration of the past but in thoughtful mediation with contemporary life.[6]

---

[3] Gadamer means to echo here Heidegger's early remark, that Hegel is the most radical of the Greeks. See "Hegel and Heidegger," in HD, 107.

[4] A well-informed study of the Hegel/Heidegger/Gadamer theme, with a focus especially on the common theme of Greek philosophy, is Dottori 1984. See especially chap. 4, "Hegel und Gadamer," 240–99.

[5] Cf. also HD, 104.

[6] *Truth and Method* (New York: Seabury, 1975), hereafter TM, cited in the text, 150.

Finally, Gadamer makes clear that he understands the radicality of Hegel's enterprise, especially understands how decisively Hegel broke with "the metaphysical tradition" so constantly under attack by Heidegger and his followers. Whatever Hegel is up to in his account of "spirit's experience of itself" in his *Phenomenology* and in his treatment of "thought's self-determinations" in his *Science of Logic*, it cannot be understood as a continuation of the "substance metaphysics of the Western tradition" (PG, 34). Gadamer realizes that Hegelian spirit, *Geist*, refers just as little to an immaterial substance as Dasein refers to human nature.[7] He notes that in pursuing his own life-long goal of attacking traditional, substance metaphysics, "I do not stand alone in all this; Hegel also held such a view" (PG, 34).[8] He even goes so far as to write some things that stand in some considerable tension with what he also says about the need to overcome Hegel's absolutization of the principle of self-consciousness:

In particular, Hegel's powerful speculative leap beyond the subjectivity of the subjective Spririt established this possibility and offered a way of shattering the predominance of subjectivism.... Was it not Hegel's intention, also, [i.e., together with Heidegger after the latter's "turn" – RP] to surpass the orientation to self-consciousness and the subject-object schema of a philosophy of consciousness? (PG, 37)[9]

## III

That question is somewhat rhetorical, of course, and Gadamer's final answer is that whatever Hegel may have intended, his philosophy did *not* completely break free of "subjectivism," and for all his sympathy with the speculative, historical, "Greek," antimetaphysical, and antisubjectivist

---

7 One might say, going beyond Gadamer and anticipating what is discussed below, that *Geist* refers instead to the collective achievement, in various "developing" ways, of a human community, communities more and more successfully self-authorizing and self-regulating over time. This would obviously require a book-length treatment for it to become clear. For some indications, see Pippin 1997b, 1999b, and 2000e.

8 These claims are also somewhat confusing, because Gadamer also attributes to Hegel the intention of reviving "the logos-nous metaphysics of the Platonic-Aristotelian" tradition, but in a way "founded upon Descartes' idea of method" and undertaken "within the framework of transcendental philosophy" (HD, 78–9). This seems to me an impossible, internally inconsistent characterization.

9 Cf. also, in "Hegel and Heidegger," "For it is Hegel who explicitly carried the dialectic of mind or spirit beyond the forms of subjective spirit, beyond consciousness and self-consciousness" (HD, 104).

elements in Hegel, he cannot finally travel all that far down Hegel's
*Denkweg*, the path of his thought.

For one thing, Gadamer is clearly a post-Heideggerean philosopher
of finitude, in several different respects. He judges

> Kant's critique of the antinomies of pure reason to be correct and not superceded
> by Hegel. Totality is never an object, but rather a world-horizon which encloses
> us and within which we live our lives. (HD, 104) [10]

He might have also added his frequent objections to the idea of such
a totality as a *completion*, since any claim for an inner teleology and the
completion of a development would have to be made from some position external to historical forms of life, arrived at by some reflective
methodology, and it would have to suggest that understanding the past
is less a matter of an unformalizable "conversation" and an eventual "fusion" of opposed horizons of meaning (*Horizontverschmelzung*) than it is
a result of the application of some independent theory, with epochs as
instances of moments in that theory. [11] Gadamer is forever returning to
examples from art as paradigmatic problems of understanding, insisting in such passages that it would be ridiculous for someone to claim
that Shakespeare could be considered "superior" to Sophocles because
farther along in such a putative development. [12] Even more important,
such an ideal of a final, absolute self-consciousness, even as a regulative
ideal, runs counter to what Gadamer regards as Heidegger's successful

---

[10]  Cf. the discussion of Aeschylus on "learning by suffering" in TM, Gadamer's claim that
"real experience is that in which man becomes aware of his finiteness" (320), and the
explicit contrast there with Hegel. Cf. the helpful discussion by Redding 1996, chap. 2,
35–49.

[11]  The status of Gadamer's own proposals for a nonmethodological hermeneutics, and so
his somewhat transcendental "theory of the possibility of meaning" and the examples
cited to confirm it (not to mention the status of his model, Heidegger's *Daseinanalytik*),
in the light of this critique of totality and theory, is another, complicated matter. Cf. his
discussion in TM, 306ff, and his discussion in SHR. Gadamer himself has had to face
charges of defending some form of linguistic idealism (from Habermas) and an implicit
teleology in his concept of a fusion of horizons (by Wolfhart Pannenberg), and he denies
both ascriptions in this essay.

[12]  I note that the issue depends on what one means by "superior." With respect to the
realization of art as such, Hegel goes so far as to defend the superiority of Greek art *as
art* over modern art. There is, though, another sense in which he claims that the ethical
life behind Shakespeare's presentation and the kind of self-awareness visible in Hamlet,
say, does represent an advance or moment of progress.

demonstration of the unending, unresolvable interplay of "revealing" and "concealing" in claims for truth:

> Truth is not the total unconcealment whose ideal fulfillment would in the end remain the presence of absolute Spirit to itself. Rather Heidegger taught us to think truth as an unconcealing and a concealing at the same time. (PG, 35)[13]

By contrast, Gadamer somewhat ironically embraces what Hegel called the "*bad* infinite" when he claims that the "soul's dialogue with itself" has no teleological endpoint and no inner direction and so is inexhaustible. As Gadamer is wont to put it, the "otherness" of "the other" in, say, a conversation or an attempt at a textual or historico-cultural meaning, the opacity that originally called for interpretation, is never overcome, can be only partially "revealed" by another sort of "concealing," contrary to Hegel's claim that in modernity, especially (in *some* sense brought to its full realization by Hegel), human beings finally recognize themselves, make their own, what had originally seemed, and is now no longer, other.[14]

Gadamer thus takes sides with the enormously influential (for all later modern "Continental" philosophy) Schellingean and Kierkegaardean insistence on finitude against Hegel and, on this score, is particularly critical of an aspect of Hegel's project that he otherwise praises – Hegel's attempted revivification of ancient dialectic. On the one hand, in Gadamer's view Hegel appreciated that the kind of Eleatic dialectic on view in the *Parmenides* and in Zeno helps one to understand the "interweaving" of and "fluidity" among ideas and especially the way in which statements about certain categorical distinctions undermine the very distinctions themselves (the same must be the same as itself, but also other than "other," and so forth) and so seem to prompt a way of thinking about determinate meaning very different from that possible in standard assertoric judgments. And of course what Gadamer calls the "hermeneutic priority of the question" would lead him to be quite sympathetic to the dialogic, statement and counterstatement, question and answer model

[13] Cf. also TM: "To exist historically means that knowledge of oneself can never be completed" (269).

[14] As is often, indeed endlessly, repeated, this hope for a kind of superceded difference and totality, especially when it reappears in Marx's theory of labor, is held to be responsible for "totalitarian thinking" of all sorts (cf. Gadamer, HD, 98, on Hegel as forerunner of Marx and positivism!), notwithstanding Hegel's repeated insistence that the state of freedom in question, "being one's self in another," still requires the self-other relation be preserved. Cf. Habermas 1987, 36, 42, 84; Adorno, ND, 22–3, and Pippin 1997c.

as the origin for the Hegelian dialectic.[15] On the other hand, Hegel, for Gadamer, greatly exaggerated the possibility that some positive doctrine could actually result (for Plato, especially) from such contradictions and so misinterpreted crucial passages, such as Plato's *Sophist*, 259b (HD, 22). (According to Gadamer, Plato is there, in his famous parricide of Parmenides, attempting to *dissolve* the appearance of unavoidable contradiction with his distinction between "otherness" and "not being," not at all to embrace the results as the beginning of a new speculative doctrine.)[16] Gadamer agrees that the undecidability, aporias, and confusion that result from the Socratic elenchus in the dialogues point to a positive result but not a positive doctrine or anything that can be stated as such. The real speculative moment in the dialogues is the dialogue drama itself, which, for Gadamer, captures the unsayability but yet the presence of what cannot be said. Hegel, on the other hand, according to Gadamer, in passages that represent the extreme end of his criticism of Hegel, tried to present dialectic as a philosophical method and in so doing fundamentally compromised his own insights about the limitations of language, the limitations arising from the historical embeddedness of Dasein and the inherent limitations of natural consciousness itself. Hegel's dialectic is really a "splendid monologue" and "relies far more upon the principles of Cartesian method, on the learning of the Catechism, and on the Bible" (HD, 7). Or: "In his [Hegel's] dialectical method I see a dubious compromise with the scientific thinking of modernity" (PG, 45).[17]

Finally, the most comprehensive criticism of Hegel is intimated by Gadamer's report that one of the earliest influences on his work in ancient philosophy was Julius Stenzel, who observed in Greek philosophy what Stenzel had called "the restraining of subjectivity," what Gadamer refers to as the Greek "superiority . . . in which out of self-forgetful surrender they abandoned themselves in boundless innocence to the passion of thinking" (PG, 9). It is hard to imagine phrases more un-Hegelian than "self-forgetful surrender" and "boundless innocence," unless it is

---

[15] Cf. TM, 325–41.

[16] On this score, about this particular passage, I think Gadamer is quite right. See Pippin 1979a.

[17] See also HD, 79, and TM: "Hegel's dialectic is a monologue of thinking that seeks to carry out in advance what matures little by little in every genuine conversation" (332–3). From Hegel's point of view, in the terms he used early on to discuss such issues of finitude, what Gadamer is defending is a form of "faith" (*Glauben*), not philosophy or knowledge (*Wissen*).

"the passion of thinking." What Gadamer is referring to here goes by the general term "the problem of reflection" (or, said from the Hegelian side, the "impossibility of innocence"), and for Gadamer and Heidegger, Hegel's account of the priority and status of reflection drastically qualifies his achievement in otherwise opening up ways of considering the actual "life" of human spirit without rendering that life an "object" of methodological study.

## IV

And the problem is not an easy one to summarize, especially since Hegel considered himself a fierce critic of what he termed "finite" versions of "reflective" philosophies. We need first to note that the question opened up by Gadamer's restrictions on methodological access to the lived meanings of texts and utterances concerns the possibility of the intelligibility of experience itself. The issue is not a formal account of the interpretive human sciences; the issue is "ontological," or concerns human being itself. Our very mode of being is interpretive; we exist "understandingly," in an always already "understood" world. There is no way of conceiving a subject "before" any act of interpretation and so no way of understanding the interpretations as accomplished by such a subject. The question Gadamer is posing about the role of reflection in this large context concerns, then, the right way to understand the "understandingly mediated," or, said in the German Idealist language, the self-conscious character of all experience, an issue given great weight by Kant but already a key element in modern philosophy as such.

Locke had called reflection "that notice which the mind takes of its own operations,"[18] a view that typified the "theater of the mind" approach of early modern philosophy, wherein what we were conscious of in ordinary consciousness could not be said to be spatio-temporal external objects in any immediate sense but sensory effects, "ideas," "impressions," "representations," and so forth, such that the work of the understanding left us either, for the empiricists, "fainter" and, because more generalized, vaguer "ideas" or, for the rationalists, "clearer and distincter" versions of what was only imperfectly and deceptively apprehended immediately. But for both camps, *consciousness itself was reflective.* (There wasn't first consciousness of objects in the sense of some direct "awakeness" as in the premodern tradition and then, as a subsequent act, reflective attention

[18] Locke, 1967, I, 44.

to our own modes of apprehending. Being aware was being aware already of one's own mental items, *re*-presentings, which then had somehow to be reconnected to their real source or origin.)

This situation (and its resulting skepticism) was unbearable for Kant, and in the course of rethinking it, he came to deny a touchstone for both earlier modern traditions: the possibility of some immediacy and givenness in experience at all, whether of the world or of the self. The mind was, Kant argued instead, active in *any* determinate experience and could not be said ever to apprehend directly a given content, even an idea or impression. This meant that the reflective nature of consciousness had to be put another way. In being aware of objects, say, external objects, of "outer sense," the mind could still be said to be also "aware of itself," but not because of awareness of inner content or of "a self." We are manifestly not aware of ideas or impressions of chairs when we are aware of chairs. We are aware of chairs, but we are also *taking* ourselves to be perceiving chairs, not imagining or remembering them, not perceiving stools or tables, and we are ourselves "holding" the elements of such thinkings together in time, all according to various rules that could not be otherwise if such contents are to be held together in one time (or so Kant argued). We are conscious, in a way, self-consciously, are adverbially self-conscious. In any act of intending, I am taking myself to be just thus and so intending, and there are elements of that "apperception" that cannot ever be said to be due to our contact with the world but must be subjectively contributed.[19] This meant that there was an element of self-determination (a required active element that could not be attributed to the deliverances of the senses) in how I took myself to be engaging the world, and through Fichte and then Hegel, this acquired an almost mythic status as a "divine" sort of freedom. And this element, to come to the decisive point for hermeneutical theory, means that one cannot ever be said simply to be "in" a state of consciousness without also at the same time *not* being wholly "in" such a state, not being wholly absorbed in the intended object, except as an occasionally contingent and always recoverable self-forgetting. As Gadamer puts it in *Truth and Method*, speaking of a subject, understood as in Idealism as a reflective consciousness, "it is of its essence to be able to *rise above* that of which it is conscious" (TM, 306, my emphasis). One cannot likewise just be "carrying on," at some level unavailable to reflective consciousness, the practices

---

[19] I introduce and defend this "taking" and "adverbial" language in Pippin 1982 and 1989, chap. 2.

and rules of a community life. In Hegel's account, *there is no such level unavailable to reflective life, or the activity could not count as an activity belonging to us,* and therein lies the deepest disagreement between Gadamer and Hegel.

This approach ultimately meant that for the post-Kantians, especially Fichte and Hegel, the central act of consciousness was not a representing, picturing, grasping, or simply being in a state but an activity, a construing thus and such, a judging, in *some* sense a making. (Hegel, for all the speculative qualifications, does not abandon this revolutionary Kantian insight, and that is partly what Gadamer means by saying that Hegel remains a philosopher of subjectivity.) [20] The position also required that the mind's relation to itself in such consciousness could not be accounted for in any standard bipolar (subject-object) model of intending. In judging, even in judging about ourselves, we are always judging self-consciously, and so reflectively, even while not judging *that* we are judging. (The judgment does not occur unless we judge and still hold open the possibility of judging rightly or not, and we cannot *do* that without taking ourselves to be doing *that*.) At some appropriately defined level, the proper explanation of why we organize our experience the way we do, and hold each other to account the way we do, is that we, the subjects of experience, and not the contents resulting from our contact with the world, are "responsible" for such elements. When one begins (with Fichte) to insist that we cannot discover such rules "lying ready made in the mind,"[21] but must be understood to have instituted or founded or "posited" such rules, we have begun to move away from any finite reflective model and have begun to attempt an absolute reflection, an understanding of the process itself of such self-regulation and its necessary moments. The ineliminability of the reflexive character of experience is supposed to provide us with the supreme condition by appeal to which our own determinate requirements for experience can be nonempirically developed. And we have thus arrived at the beginning of Hegel's historical and "logical" account of how and why we hold each other to the norms we do.

This is the background behind many of the things Gadamer says about Hegel, reflection, self-consciousness, and about this attempt, as he puts

---

[20] It is also why Hegel's phenomenology is ultimately so different from Husserl's attempt to return to a kind of realism in his phenomenology. For a defense of this claim about the continuities in the Kant-Hegel relationship, see Pippin 1989.

[21] Contra Heidegger, for the same sorts of reasons, we cannot be said to "find" such formal constraints in the world into which we have been "thrown."

it, to develop "the entire content of knowledge as the complete whole of self-consciousness" (HD, 77). For example:

> That, according to Hegel, is the essence of dialectical speculation – thinking nothing other than this selfhood, thinking the being of self itself, in which the ego of self-consciousness has always already recognized itself.... It (pure, speculative reflection) thus discovers in itself the origin of all further determination. (HD, 19)

And, of course, however the particular transitions in Hegel's *Logic* are argued for and however much Hegel attempts to avoid the traditional paradoxes in the subject's attempt to know itself absolutely, the whole idea of being able to make anything like the logical structure of intelligibility "for itself," or explicit, is a nonstarter for Gadamer. There is, in the first place, no way, he claims, to extract such normative dimensions from the "lived" language spoken in a community at a time (HD, 95). If that is conceded, we can then appreciate the full force of Gadamer's Heideggerean objections. We are now (with any concession about the unformalizability or rendering explicit of the logical forms of language) prepared to say something like: "We do not speak such a language. It speaks us."[22] "Language completely surrounds us like the voice of home which prior to our every thought of it breathes a familiarity from time out of mind" (HD, 97).

Demonstrating this point about the limits of reflection, with all its presuppositions, is what Gadamer meant by claiming that his task was the "overcoming of the primacy of self-consciousness." Such a result would involve acknowledging that the expression "the subject of thought and language" involves both a subjective and an objective genitive. The much cited summation of his position is from *Truth and Method*:

> Understanding is not to be thought of so much as an action of subjectivity, but as the placing of oneself within a process of tradition [*Einrücken in ein Überlieferungsgeschehen*], in which past and present are constantly fused. This is what must be expressed in hermeneutical theory.... (TM, 258)[23]

Gadamer, in other words, would have us reverse the canonical relation between Hegel's *Phenomenology* and *Science of Logic*. It is in experiencing the insufficiencies of a disembodied account of our categorial requirements that we would *then* learn the necessity of returning to the lived experience of the "house of being," language. Were a more linguistically oriented *Phenomenology* to be the culmination of this antisystem, one small step

---

[22] Cf. "To What Extent Does Language Perform Thought," Supplement II to TM, 491–8.
[23] The passage is italicized in the original, WM, 274–5.

would have been taken toward Gadamer's ultimate suggestion: "Dialectic must retrieve itself [*sich zurücknehmen*] in hermeneutics" (HD, 99).

## V

Before venturing a brief reaction to Gadamer's invocation of and separation from Hegel, I want to endorse enthusiastically the basic principle of his approach to all hermeneutics. There is no essential historical Hegel whose personal intentions we can retrieve or whose historical world we can objectively reconstruct as the central necessary condition in understanding what his texts meant or mean, and there is no essential or core meaning-in-itself in Hegel's texts, eternally waiting to be unearthed. Gadamer is right: We can only look back at Hegel from where we are now, from within our own "horizon." As Gadamer has shown in a wealth of valuable detail, that does not mean that we cannot be confronted by an "alien" strange Hegel from whom we might learn something or that the necessity of this "prejudiced" understanding prohibits a challenge to and development of our "fore-understandings." But, in my view, this means we ought, at the very least, to be much less confident that we simply long ago correctly boxed up and shelved "the Hegelian option" and can periodically drag it out and invoke his claims about "thought's self-determination," "development," "progress," "totality," or "Absolute Knowledge," as straightforward candidates to be accepted, rejected, or modified. We ought, at any rate, to be less confident about these matters than, it seems to me, Gadamer is.

Consider Gadamer's laudatory characterization of Hegel as hermeneut, cited earlier:

Hegel states a definite truth, inasmuch as the essential nature of the historical spirit consists not in the restoration of the past but in thoughtful mediation with contemporary life [ . . . *in der denkenden Vermittlung mit dem gegenwärtigen Leben*]. (TM, 150; WM, 161)

The question of the modesty just mentioned is obviously most at issue in what one might mean by "thoughtful" (here the objections to Hegel's "dialectical methodology," his developmental, progressive understanding of spirit, and his notion of "totality" are relevant), "mediation" (the issue of *reflective* mediation and so the status of the *Logic*), and especially "contemporary life." There are several aspects of the last issue that raise the first questions for Gadamer's approach.

The "horizon" within which Hegel's philosophy reemerged as of possible philosophical relevance for Gadamer and his contemporaries was first of all the systematic question of the human sciences, the *Geisteswissenschaften*. And so Hegel's sensitivity to all the unique, nonreducible elements in such an understanding and to a "conversational logic" in interrogating the past, his insistence on a self-correcting process of historical change, his stress on everywhere taking account of what Gadamer calls "effective history" (*Wirkungsgeschichte*) in understanding our own situation, and his entire systematic attempt to show that understanding other human beings and their cultural and political achievements could never happen were they to be understood as "objects" attracted a great deal of attention, if also qualification.[24]

But we might look at this as in a way only a first step in clearing a space for understanding the human qua human in the modern world. It is understandable that such an initial strategy would so heavily stress what cannot be comprehended by an objective methodology and that we would be occasionally tempted to argue for such a claim by arguing for a *fundamental* inaccessibility. But we stand now in some sense on the other side of the early debates with relativists and positivists and neo-Kantian, "scientistic" naturalists about the very legitimacy of the category of meaning and the relation between understanding (*Verstehen*) and explanation (*Erklären*). Our own "contemporary life situation" thus helps us to see possibilities in Hegel other than those of importance in Gadamer's appropriation and transformation of Hegel. The debate about what we now call "folk psychology" still goes on, of course, and the notions of "person" or "Geist" or "Dasein," not to mention belief, desire, intention, and so on, must, apparently, still contend with their naturalist opponents. But the original debate that so decisively influenced Heidegger's early work in phenomenology and therewith Gadamer's project was the psychologism controversy and Husserl's response in his *Logical Investigations*. That debate made it appear that the alternatives were either a psychologistic naturalism or some sort of realism about meaning, often a quasi-Platonic realism about meanings, commitment to intentional inexistence, ideal entities such as "values," and so forth. Much of Heidegger's animus against idealism and philosophies of subjectivity and his own insistence on the question of being draw their inspiration from such realist reactions. The effects of that early controversy can certainly be seen in Gadamer and in the various claims about

---

[24] A locus classicus: the discussion of "observing reason" in Hegel, PhS, 139–210.

what must be independent of the constructions of subjectivity.[25] But the situation looks different now. For one thing, there are not many such Husserlean or Fregean realists around anymore. For another, the epistemological problems and the dogmatic implications of such a realism now appear impossible to overcome. For yet another, the linguistic turn, the success of various attacks on the dogmas of conventional empiricism and analytic philosophy, and a great revival of philosophical Kant scholarship have all created a different way of understanding Kantian idealism and so a different way of understanding the post-Kantian idealist tradition. So what has drawn attention to Hegel in the last twenty-five years or so are two issues somewhat different from those that connect Gadamer to Hegel.

In the first place, Gadamer was so concerned to limit the pretensions of a "reflective philosophy" and so to insist on a kind of embeddedness and inheritance not redeemable "reflectively," in either Hegelian or left-Hegelian (practical) or Habermasean terms, that the curious, uniquely modern phenomenon first noticed with such brilliance by Rousseau is difficult to discuss in his terms. One can, to speak somewhat simplistically, come to understand and especially to experience virtually all of one's inheritance, tradition, life-world, and so forth as coherent and intelligible but *not* "one's own" and so as, root and branch, *alien.* I can even, in some sense that requires much more qualification, become alienated "from myself," from my own life; indeed, paradoxically, I can be the agent of such alienation. Or, said another way, all the formal conditions insisted on by modern democratic life as necessary for institutions to count as just (i.e., as somehow products of my will) can *all* be satisfied without any "identification" with such products; as if I made them, but do not see or experience that making as mine.[26] If there is such a phenomenon

[25] In Pippin 1997h, I argue that this sort of Heideggerean critique of subjectivity confuses a compelling anti-Cartesianism with a much less persuasive antisubjectivism.

[26] Gadamer has his own notion of a kind of emancipatory effect of hermeneutical reflection, the results of which assure that "I am no longer unfree over against myself but rather can deem freely what in my preunderstanding (prejudice, *Vorurteil*) may be justified and what unjustified" (SHR, 38). From a Hegelian (or critical theory) perspective, the question of justification raised here, and its historical as well as logical presuppositions, look like a welcome return to traditional notions of reflection, but in the next paragraph, Gadamer makes clear that he considers this reflective justification to be only a "transformation" of some preunderstanding into another, or the "forming of a new preunderstanding." This seems to me to take back with one hand what was given by another, and is responsible for such Gadamerean claims as that every historian "is one of the nation's' historians; he belongs to the nation," and so, whether he acknowledges

and if the language of identity and alienation is as indispensable as the language of rights or the language of finitude in understanding the modern social and political world, then the Hegelian language of subjectivity, reflection, and Geist's "reconciliation with *itself*" will also be ultimately indispensable.[27] And in the last twenty-five years or so, Hegel's approach has come to be more and more in evidence, especially in so-called identity or recognition politics.[28]

The second point can be made by reference to one of Gadamer's favorite images. When he wants to stress the unformalizable and largely unreflective character of everyday human experience of meaning, our mode of understanding, responding to, correcting, ignoring, and so on meaningful utterances and deeds, Gadamer invokes the image of a game and the activity of play. And it is true that in "understanding" how to play the game and in actually playing it, I cannot rightly be said to be consulting the rules of play and/or reflectively "applying" them in practice. The founding argument of Heidegger in *Being and Time* about "being in the world" remains for much of the post-Heideggerean Continental tradition decisive on those points.[29] But this also means that such games (to be games) are normatively structured; there is a right and a wrong way to "go on," and the *active adherence* to such rules on the part of (what can only be described as) subjects doing the adhering makes the appeal to some sort of "entering a transmission event," rather than my sustaining a commitment, hard to understand. Such "game playing" may not be rightly described as "guided" by individual subjects who make episodic,

---

it or not, is "engaged in contributing to the growth and development of the national state" (ibid., 28). Cf. Dottori 1984, 289–99.

[27] I do not here mean the kind of experience Heidegger discusses in *Being and Time*, when "anxiety" detaches me in some way from my involvement in a world and I experience the ground of my being as a "nullity." The phenomenon of alienation in modernity is, for want of a better word, considerably more dialectical. It is also not captured by Gadamer's invocation of Schiller's notion of disharmony and aesthetic harmony, cited as an isse of alienation in Gadamer's "Hegel and Heidegger" essay in HD, 106. Schiller, in the seventeenth letter of *On the Aesthetic Education of Man*, locates the origin of our unfreedom in "external circumstances" and "a fortuitous exercise of his freedom" (85). The puzzling issue in Hegel involves self-alienation and is not fortuitous.

[28] An important event in this development was, of course, the publication of Charles Taylor's influential book *Hegel* (1975).

[29] In SHR, he makes two other important points about this game analogy. No one is "it" or has a privileged position (32); and someone who keeps trying to question or undermine the motives of another player himself falls out of the game, becomes a "spoil sport" (41). (Both claims lead to Gadamer's objections to Habermas's use of the psychoanalytic model of liberation.) One easy summation of Gadamer's Hegel criticism is that Gadamer is accusing Hegel in effect of being such a "spoil sport."

mental decisions, but game playing is nevertheless certainly "minded" and normatively *guided* in some sense, and one of the topics of recent interest in discussions of Hegel has been attention to how he raises and discusses such questions, especially at the institutional level. (I don't mean to suggest that Gadamer denies this aspect of the problem, but I am not sure that his dialogic model of interrogation and "agreement" is adequate to account for it.)

Subjectivity in Hegel, even the collective kind that he is interested in, can then, on such a view of mindedness, be understood itself as a kind of collective human achievement (in no sense, as Gadamer would agree, a traditional substance), that achievement being the establishment of normatively successful, mutually bound communities. As Nietzsche also noted, we have *made* ourselves into creatures with the right to make promises (we are not "by nature" such creatures) and thus, by holding ourselves and each other to normative constraints, have made ourselves subjects and remain subjects only by finding ways to sustain such results.[30] *Geist*, Hegel regularly says in one of his most puzzling and paradoxical formulations, "is a result of itself,"[31] or nothing but the achievement of such rule-following, reflectively rule-assessing communities, and that process must somehow be understood (at its most basic level) as a kind of continual negotiation about normative authority.[32]

Gadamer would be fine with the self-correcting, negotiating, aiming-at-agreement parts of all this, but without Hegel's argument for the relevance of criteria of genuine *success* in such attempts (ultimately, the so-called Absolute viewpoint), we will end up with simply a narrative of what had been taken, as a matter of historical fact, to be failure, success, reformulation, and so forth (insofar as we, by our lights, could understand them now). And there is no reason in principle why such a narrative must be so radically distinct as a mode of knowledge; it seems compatible with a certain kind of cognitive, hermeneutically reflective, historical anthropology (which is what philosophical hermeneutics, without this normative animus, becomes).[33]

The idea of meaning or intelligibility in general as a *result* of normatively constrained or rule-bound human practices, or the legacy of Kant's

---

[30] Nietzsche 1969, Second Essay, 57ff.

[31] Hegel, SS, 7.

[32] For more discussion and defense of such an interpretation, see Pippin 1999b.

[33] The direction suggested by this claim no doubt brings to mind Habermas's exchanges with Gadamer. See Habermas 1971, and SHR, 26–43. For the differences between the position that I am attributing to Hegel and Habermas's position, see Pippin 1997c.

theory of judgment in Hegel (and paradigmatically in Fichte),[34] is, I am claiming, the source of the deepest disagreement between the Idealist and the Heidegger-influenced hermeneutical project, inspired as the latter is by a very different notion of the understanding of meaning and ultimately of truth as "disclosedness" or "unconcealment," and so understanding as "itself a kind of happening" (SHR, 29). On this Hegelian view, understanding cannot just happen (*geschehen*); it does not "occur" as we try to "occupy" or seize (*einrücken*) a place in a "transmission-event."

For reasons again having to do essentially with Kant (this time his theory of the unity of reason and the tasks of reflective judgment), this project assumes also a semantic holism, or understands any instance of a meaningful assertion to involve a variety of other implications and commitments without which such an assertion could not be properly made. And this raises the question of how to present an account of the form any such relation of implication, presupposition, inappropriateness, and so on would have to take were such interconceptual relations really to make possible meaningful assertions. Without attention to this sort of normative dimension and this sort of holism, the project of Hegel's *Logic* would have to look, as it so often has, like a kind of neo-Platonic theory of "concept emanation."

Gadamer's disagreement with this view is why he argues in *Truth and Method*, in a remarkable section on "the limitations of reflective philosophy," against all claims that nothing "prereflective" can determine or condition actions or utterances without our really having reflectively incorporated such a prereflective level, arguments based on the claim that otherwise such instances could not count as actions or utterances. He insists that these always rest on a kind of rhetorical trick of sorts, that though the argument is successful after its fashion, we know the claim is not true (TM, 305–10).[35] It is clearer, I think, with respect to the way the "ineliminability of reflection" thesis descends from Kant through Fichte to Hegel, and with respect to these issues of normative reflection, why one would want to say that the game we are playing with norms always

---

[34] Cf. Pippin 1989, chap. 3; Pippin 2000a; and "Fichte's Contribution," in *The Reception of Kant's Critical Philosophy: Fichte, Schelling, and Hegel*, ed. Sally Sedgwick (Cambridge: Cambridge University Press, 2000).

[35] Cf. Gadamer's formulation of Heidegger's (and his) position in his "Hegel and Heidegger" essay. In discussing "fate" (*Geschick*) and "our being fated" (*Geschicklichkeit*), he writes that "it is a matter of what is allotted [*zugeschickt*] to man and by which he is so very much determined [*bestimmt*] that all self-determination and self-consciousness remains subordinate" (HD, 109).

involves a possible interrogation about reasons for holding such norms and that *only* such reasons can "determine" our *commitment* to norms (or only beliefs can determine other beliefs).

From "where we stand now," the distinctiveness of the "human sciences," following this Hegelian lead, stems from the distinctiveness of human experience in being "fraught with ought," in Sellars's phrase, from the distinctive human capacity we might call our responsiveness to reasons, "oughts." Viewed this way, we can understand why "this is traditional," "this is the way we go on," and so on could never ultimately count as such reasons, however much time it takes us to learn that.[36]

---

[36] This, of course, still leaves a good deal unresolved about how any sort of "universal history" could be possible on such an interpretation, what the Hegelian account of totality would look like, how to understand the relation between thought and language in Hegel, and so forth. All that can be said here is that the direction sketched above does not, I think, lead to what Gadamer calls "the total unconcealment whose ideal fulfillment would in the end remain the presence of absolute spirit to itself" (PG, 35). There is no metaphysics of presence in one of Hegel's most sweeping and helpful characterizations of the task of SL, that this "truth of actuality" must never be represented as a "dead repose" and that

by virtue of the freedom which the Concept attains in the Idea, the idea possesses within itself also the most stubborn opposition; its repose consists in the security and certainty with which it eternally creates and eternally overcomes that opposition, in it meeting with itself. (759)

# 5

## Negative Ethics

### Adorno on the Falseness of Bourgeois Life

I

"Wrong life cannot be lived rightly" ("Es gibt kein richtiges Leben im falschen," MM, §18, 43; 39),[1] wrote Adorno in a famous passage at the beginning of *Minima moralia*. It is surprising enough to hear that what is wrong with modern life is that it is "false." But Adorno is willing to go even further: "Our perspective of life has passed into an ideology which conceals the fact that there is life *no longer*" (MM, 13; 15; my emphasis). This air of paradox is only intensified by the epigram for the book, taken from the Austrian writer Ferdinand Kürnberger: "Life does not live" (MM, 20; 19). Such an evaluation is not unprecedented, although one sees it mostly in modernist literary contexts. T. S. Eliot in *The Wasteland* had compared modern officeworkers crossing London Bridge with the dead as described in Dante's *Inferno* ("I had not thought death had undone so many"), and the accusation (that we have become the living dead) is prominent in Orwell, Lawrence, Nietzsche (of course), and many other modernists.[2] It is, though, philosophically surprising.

It contains an echo of the controversial Aristotelian claim that one can be truly virtuous only in a good polis, a claim reanimated in the nineteenth century by Hegel and his theory of *Sittlichkeit*. Such a claim already

---

[1] As the German indicates, this standard translation already defangs a bit what Adorno is trying to say: that a form of life can be "false."

[2] See Carey 2002, 10.

violates modern intuitions about the self-sufficiency of moral individuals and the possibility of moral heroism.[3] And there is in the aphorism an even stranger appeal to what has been called an ontological theory of truth, something also apparently resurrected by Hegel and quite contrary to the modern insistence that life is not something that *can* be true or false (only propositions can be true or false). According to such an ontological account, what is false with an imperfect, malfunctioning state or deficient friend is that each is "not truly what a state or a friend is." This implies some notion of degrees of "true being" and sounds strange because such an account would seem to depend on a theory of natural kinds, teleology, and metaphysical perfectionism that does not seem consistent with the direction of all modern philosophy, not to mention the Weberean *"Entzauberung"* thesis so important to the critical theory account of modernity.[4]

This raises the most obvious question.[5] The particular way of life that Adorno has in mind is notoriously broad: Western, Enlightenment-era, or liberal democratic, capitalist, technologically and scientifically advanced mass-culture, consumer societies. What characteristics of *that* form of life would lead Adorno to call it not unjust, immoral, or inconsistent with the higher potential of human spirit but "false"?

---

3 Since Adorno remains fiercely critical of individuals who lived in the most "untrue" form of life in all history (and is not merely critical of that objective social world) and since he surely knows of examples such as the Danish rescue of most of its Jewish population in 1943, clearly "a right action" and evidence of some survival of "a true or correct life" even in an objectively "false" life, the claim obviously requires more comment. See Jay Bernstein's account in Bernstein 2001, 411ff. Bernstein does not discuss the compatibility between such actions and Adorno's aphorism.

4 This is not to deny that there are elements of a "reenchantment" aspiration in Adorno, as when he contrasts Heidegger's "death metaphysic" with what he approvingly recalls as a person's "feeling of his epic unity with a full life" (ND, 362; 369). Bernstein has fashioned his ambitious interpretation on such a recovery of "auratic particularity." See Bernstein 2001.

5 There are many others, of course. Does he mean that any attempt to lead a "proper life" in a corrupt, "damaged" [*beschädigt*] social world simply has no chance of *success?* Or does he, in a much stronger claim, mean that it is not even *possible* for such an attempt to *arise,* because socialization of individuals into "false" institutions is virtually total? Is this because the motivating force of such a norm, a proper life, stands little chance of getting any grip on persons so socialized? Or does he mean that a "false life" will always produce and demand allegiance to what appear to be norms of "rightness" that will disguise the falseness of the life they serve so well as to foreclose even the conceivability of any alternative norm? Actually, Adorno appears to intend to affirm all of the above, but the questions then only intensify.

## II

We should begin by noting the extremely unusual strategy employed by Adorno in his most ambitious treatment, the discussion of "Freedom" in *Negative Dialectics*. To demonstrate this claim of falseness, Adorno takes on as a target the philosophical tradition that he clearly wants to treat as the most developed expression of the self-understanding and attempted legitimation of bourgeois society: classical German Idealism. The false-ness of bourgeois society is supposed to be paradigmatically on view in the Idealist presentation and defense of its (and that society's) most sa-cred ideal: freedom. So far, so good. This could amount to a familiar enough claim of "falseness" and could avoid any unusual metaphysical commitments: Bourgeois societies understand themselves as defending and promoting an ideal of individual liberty, whereas in reality individ-uals in such societies are systematically unfree. So something like the *self-representation* of such a society is false, either internally false to its own ideals or as aspiring to an ideal that falsely represents what freedom is. If there really is some essential connection between a distinctly human life and free activity, much in Adorno's sweeping condemnation of modern "life" could then be understood in these terms.[6]

But to demonstrate such a claim, Adorno leads us into the stranger territory mentioned earlier. For "bourgeois" philosophies of freedom – paradigmatically, Kant's – are treated as manifestations of the underlying paradigmatic form of the modern understanding of all intelligibility itself: idealist "philosophy of identity." Once we understand the ideological and so distorted character of this profoundly comprehensive manner of thinking, bourgeois self-delusions about freedom can, as instances of identity thinking, then be subject to the appropriate ideology critique. (Obviously, this attention to identity theory is a close successor to the earlier interest of Horkheimer and Adorno in explaining late capitalism and fascism as culminations of a process of reification (*Verdinglichung*) that, in consumer societies, had become total.)[7]

---

[6] And this is what Adorno does claim, explaining "horror" with the claim "because there is no freedom yet" (ND, 216; 218) and even equating evil with "the world's own unfreedom" (ND, 218; 219).

[7] To be sure, Adorno's project in *Negative Dialectics* can also be understood in more general terms. In his concluding "*Meditationen zu Metaphysik*," it becomes clear that for him the existence of the Holocaust stands as a permanent indictment of the sufficiency of the sense-making practices authoritative in Western modernity. Indeed, Adorno's view seems to be that any attempt to "make sense" of such an event is an obscenity, perhaps a secular form of blasphemy. And he even tries to demonstrate (or at least to suggest) that the

My claim is that Adorno's account is held captive by a distorted (if conventional) picture of this tradition, especially of the moral and ethical project tied to such idealism, so distorted that there is no good reason to accept Adorno's attack or his more general claim about what the tradition stands for (Western modernity, essentially).[8] But I want also to express solidarity with Adorno's deeper insight into the essentially social and historical character of "the problem of freedom" and to offer some further reasons, in the spirit of Adorno's critique, in support of the suggestion that the internal paradoxes of the Kantian moral theory are manifestations of the internal tensions or "antagonisms" of bourgeois society itself, that a philosophical attempt to "resolve" such tensions cannot be separated from a reflection on the sort of social world wherein the "problem" could get a grip, rise to any salience. There is, in other words, an antinomy in the notion of freedom characteristic of bourgeois society, but Adorno has misidentified it.

### III

His style of critique, operating at such a level of abstraction, makes Adorno's claims in the freedom chapter of *Negative Dialectics* very hard to summarize. It might be that in many modern contexts, some sort of over-hasty "identification" occurs, occurs typically, and should be counted an ethical wrong. Perhaps all value is unjustifiably identified with exchange value, all authoritative rationality with instrumental rationality;[9] individuals might be overly identified with their social, that is, market

blindness within such practices to this insufficiency is partly responsible for the possibility of totalitarian mass murder. Hence, *Negative Dialectic*: a kind of defense on behalf of "the nonidentifiable" and a kind of ethics based on such an acknowledgment. And so, for all the fireworks about Heidegger, Adorno's concentration on the subject-world relation (not subject-subject relations) as the original source of the blindness and "coldness" of the modern world, his portrayal of a predatory, hubristic subjectivity, and his characterization of the roots of that attitude in Western metaphysics are all themes that place him far closer to Heidegger than he would be comfortable with. See also note 12 below.

[8] I am interested in a restricted but still very wide swath through the issues linking Kant, Fichte, and Hegel. One could call it their common theory of normativity, and the common problem that arises when appeals to nature or a metaphysics of value is replaced by (by and large) a Kantian kind of idealism about both theoretical and practical constraints. See Pippin 1989. The practical side of the Hegelian case is addressed in Pippin forthcoming a.

[9] See Thyen's (1989) discussion of the similarities between these sorts of claims and Weber 1968, 109.

role;[10] all that there is might be too hastily identified in one genus as mere raw material for technological use. But in these cases the falseness (or "wrongness") at issue is clearly a function of the *content* of the claim, not with the attempted identification itself, with the form of thinking per se. And in more general terms it is not a new insight that forms of thought typical of modern administrative organization, such as quantitative analysis, or strategic rationality, could become so prevalent and could so "identify" in its narrow terms "what there is, that it is, and what is not, that it is not"[11] as to render finally inaccessible to thought and finally perhaps to experience something like "living particularity."

But again these are all *symptoms* of a deeper problem for Adorno, and that problem is supposed to concern "identity thinking" itself, almost as if commitment to such identitarian idealism had its own Hegelian dynamic or logic.[12] Quite surprisingly, according to Adorno what is basically going wrong (at the symptomatic level) amounts to a kind of logical confusion between the status of concepts, or universals, and their relation to instances, or particulars. This, in its simplest sense, is what he means by identity thinking: a regimentation of our experience of particulars such that they are identified by attending only to their conceptually salient aspects, whether these be common markers or common similarities to

---

[10] This is certainly the way Adorno sometimes (but hardly always) talks about the problem. See ND, 149; 146.

[11] To invoke Wilfrid Sellars's famous characterization of modern science (or scientism, depending on your point of view) in Sellars 1963, 173, quoted to good effect by Wellmer 1985, 143.

[12] This is a counterpart claim to the main thesis of *Dialectic of Enlightenment*. There the problem was a kind of "excess" Enlightenment. Having set out to attack superstition and unreason, Enlightenment rationality, blind to its own origins and nature, ended up also delegitimating any appeal to tradition, value, ideals, and so forth, thus consigning us to a natural (unfree) fate, rather than finally liberating humankind. Or, at the moment of the beginning of the greatest human triumph over nature, the bourgeoisie needed more and more to legitimate capitalist competition and resultant hierarchy by appeals to nature and a kind of inescapable natural fate. Here, this "drive," let us say, to identification (or to reject as irrelevant or unimportant everything that could not be "conceptually identified") ends up with a mastery that is also a submission. In very general terms this latter narrative is considerably "worse," more pessimistic than the former. The best account known to me of the differences between DE and ND, one that also shows very well how the latter can be understood as an attempt to resolve the inherent aporiai of the former (the "overdetermined solution" problem, that DE makes its own stance look impossible), is Thyen 1989, 109ff. Her suggestion that ND be read mainly as a historically inflected theory of experience seems to me a valuable one, but it does not resolve the general orientation issue taken up here.

a paradigmatic instance. Elements of experience that do not "fit" what we might conceptually require of them are systematically ignored, even "suppressed," in a way Adorno often links not with a mistake or simple confusion but with "domination" (*Herrschaft*) or compulsion, force (*Zwang*), as if simply thinking in a distorted or simplifying way like this amounts to an exercise of power, even an ethically wrong exercise of power. This very unusual critique underlying what can be more traditionally characterized as Adorno's ethical charges against both bourgeois society and the picture of moral psychology it generates is the most distinctive in *Negative Dialectics* and the one most in need of interpretation.

One step further in the analysis, these axiomatic assumptions about the logic of discursive activity are also invoked (following Lukács to some degree) to explain the most consistent and paradigmatic notion of freedom in modernity: autonomy, radical self-legislation, and its particular moral psychology. That is, the psycho-dynamic criticized as excessively "identitarian" echoes a familiar romantic reaction to Kant. The criticism is that concrete and particular sensuous impulses are not allowed any standing in anyone's motivational economy except *as* permitted, "incorporated into a maxim" by a self-authorizing practical reason. What amounts to an insistence on an individual's total "identification" with what a universal moral law requires, absolutely and unconditionally, is not a development in the history of moral theory that we will be able to understand well, Adorno suggests, unless we understand the more sweeping logic of the "identity thinking" underlying it *and* the "ideological" or social and historical roots of such a logic. While Adorno also wants to maintain his materialist and historicist credentials, and so to claim that this confusion is not simply a logical mistake or is not merely contingently linked to a particular organization of production, distribution, and consumption, the details of that sort of link are not much discussed. Adorno is much more interested in the broader dimensions of a certain way of *thinking* about freedom as a first step in unmasking the ubiquity and "ideological" character of such a way of thinking in general.

Hence the theme of the following remarks: *idealist moral theory* as paradigmatic of the modern *logic of "identity thinking,"* as itself the prime example of the *paradigmatically ideological character* of such a regulation of experience and evaluation. (Foregoing the necessary book-length treatment, I shall take this last claim about ideology to amount to something very general: Certain axiomatic (largely unquestioned) norms governing discursive and practical activity, axioms deeply taken for granted in modern scientific, philosophical, and ethical theory and regulative in modern practices, can be shown to be so philosophically inadequate (even self-contradictory) that we are entitled to suggest that their appeal and authority must reside in their role in the pursuit of nonphilosophical ends.)

IV

This is, I believe, a roughly accurate if very brief sketch of the position defended throughout *Negative Dialectics*.[13] Philosophically, though, this is already not a promising beginning. It seems most unlikely that the right *explicans* for everything from bourgeois hypocrisy to maldistribution of resources to the "coldness" of "the administered world," even perhaps to the slide of some bourgeois societies into fascism and terror politics, has much to do with discursive practices and normatively constrained conduct best codified and defended in German Idealism. (For one thing, such a discursive practice, a drive toward reification or in this version toward identification, functions as pretty much an unexplained explainer.) Second, the book appears to be constructed with such quick, even careless brushstrokes that Adorno can give the impression that he thinks of all predication as a form of identification, as if he has simply confused the "is of predication" with the "is of identity," "Socrates is white" with "Socrates is the teacher of Plato."[14] As has been often pointed out by critics, Adorno should have distinguished between "identifying" and "identity" thinking; successfully being able to determine one object as not

---

[13] Cf. the accurate summary given by Wellmer 1985, 148–9, and his very effective critique based on an analysis of Adorno's philosophy of language, 156ff.

[14] I doubt that Adorno can really mean to conflate these two types of assertion, and he seems to understand and to want to distance himself from the impressions he gives. See his own qualification on his remarks about logical thinking, that he does not mean to criticize but to criticize only its "running amok" (PT, 108ff). But there are passages such as: "Irrationality is the scar which the irremovable nonidentity of subject and object leaves on cognition – *whose mere form of predicative judgment postulates identity*" (ND, 92; 85). The same suggestion is made at ND, 152; 149. The best way to formulate the problem that Adorno is circling around is to see it as the problem of conceptual content, especially the determinacy of content and so the right formulation of the inevitable indeterminacy of such content and what consequences to draw from such indeterminacy. Adorno seems to work within the assumption of an exclusive dichotomy between nominalism and concept realism of some sort, and this misses the revolutionary beginning made by Kant and Hegel in arguing for a functionalist account (concepts as rules, with determinacy ultimately a function of "use").

another is in that sense to have identified it, but that need not mean that the object itself need be *exclusively* "identified" with such determining predicates and certainly need not mean that the object be identified with its conceptually determining markers, whatever that could mean. Likewise with distinctions between "identifying as" and "identifying with," and so on.[15] Moreover, left at this level of analysis, the ethical gesture of the book as a whole, for all the fury directed at Heidegger, the Nürnberg trials, or conventional morality, looks very weak. That gesture would amount simply to a reminder of sorts "to remember the forgotten nonidentical," a plea for finitude, humility, to acknowledge in some way what is lost in conceptual codification, to own up to nonconceptualizable sensuous particularity and something like its ethical claim on us.

Consider the canonical definition of Adorno's whole enterprise: "To change this direction of conceptuality, to give it a turn toward nonidentity, is the hinge of negative dialectics" (ND, 24; 12). The same gesture is made when he writes that philosophy must now amount to "striving, by way of the concept, to transcend the concept" (27; 15). And so on, with resistance to the drive to absolute identity and other "saving urges"[16] on behalf of "the impulse before the ego" (221; 221) or what had otherwise been treated as a mere "addendum" (*Hinzutretende*; 226; 226) and deliberately self-canceling expressions, such as "not to be at home in one's own home" and "Only thoughts which cannot understand themselves are true" (58; 48).

In practice, this seems little more than applying concepts in such a way that an asterisk is always somehow present or implied, as if to add to the invoking of a term such as "factory" or "welfare" or "husband" or "statue": *Caution: Concepts just used not adequate to the sensuous particulars that might fall under them.* If we go further than such platitudes, we end up with interpretations of Adorno that defend some view of a "re-enchanted" sensuous world of particulars, as if we could discover again "auratic particulars" the mere perception of which would count immediately as reason for action (as when perceiving that someone, some singular human being, is in

---

[15] See Thyen 1989, 115ff., and her helpful distinctions between formal, logical, and psychological identity issues. (But her attempt to save Adorno from some of these embarrassments does not seem to me effective. E.g., "Dem 'Wozu,' nicht dem 'Wie' identifizierenden Denkens gilt Adornos Interesse" (118). I do not see how the questions can be separated.) See also Braun 1983, 263ff.; Schnädelbach 1983, 70ff.; Theunissen 1983, 62.

[16] ND, 250; 253; a phrase Adorno borrows from Goethe's *Die Wahlverwandtschaften*.

pain thereby counts *eo ipso* as a claim on the perceiver to do what she can to relieve the pain). But apart from his remarks on the "negativity" inherent in modern art, Adorno, in my view, showed no inclination for both "aestheticizing" and "ethicizing" *all* of human experiences in such a re-enchantment project.[17]


## V

But stopping here would be unfair to Adorno, for a number of reasons. In the first place, for all his charges about the philosophical limitations and the ideological distortion of modern sense-making practices, he makes very clear that he *also* never intended to return to a form of nominalism, even a romanticized form. And he does not at all mystify "the other" as some singular, ineffable "Beyond," or *Jenseits*, before which we must all pay the appropriate mute, respectful homage, à la Levinas:

This much should be granted to Hegel: not only particularity but the particular itself is unthinkable without the moment of the universal which differentiates the particular, puts its imprint on it, and in a sense is needed to make a particular of it.(ND, 322; 328)[18]

And so it can often appear that these dual commitments, anticoncept and antinominalist, can easily land Adorno into a dead end or at least into the kind of deep dialectical dilemma he often tried to cultivate:

All post-Auschwitz culture, including its urgent critique, is garbage.... Whoever pleads for the maintenance of this radically culpable and shabby culture becomes its accomplice, while the man who says no to culture is directly furthering the barbarism which our culture showed itself to be. (ND, 359f; 367)

[17] I agree with Axel Honneth when he claims, "The critical theory that emerges in Adorno's postwar writings thus vacillates helplessly between philosophical reflection and aesthetic experience, not wanting to be one, not able to be the other" (1991, 69). And so I disagree with Bernstein's attempt to propose on Adorno's behalf a nondominating theory of "the complex concept" that would do justice to Adorno's critique of all philosophical reflection but would emerge on the other side as something other than art. That seems to me to leave us with the "asterisk" qualification just discussed.

[18] This Hegelian, even idealist moment in Adorno also helps to explain why, apart from a few references to "common sense" philosophy, Adorno's insistence on the limitations of practical reason and his emphasis on the inextricable role of sensuous impulses and a particular point of view in all action does not return him thereby to British moral sense theory, or the reliance on the sympathetic aversion to suffering so common in Smith, Rousseau, and Hume. The Kantian and Hegelian critique of immediacy has, apparently, barred the door to such "critically naïve" positions.

With such expressions we seem to have passed beyond gestures of acknowledgment, remembrance, and guilt and passed into an impossible world more at home in Kafka's *Der Prozess* or more typically in Adorno, the world of Beckett, the "no-man's land between the border posts of being and nothingness" (ND 374; 381) than in philosophy. To get beyond such occasional expressions of despair as "Thought honors itself by defending what is damned as nihilism" (ibid.), we need to consider in more detail the heart of the issue: what he is really after in his critique of identity thinking: the "bourgeois" notion of freedom and Adorno's treatment of it as ideology.

## VI

Ever since the seventeenth century, freedom had been defined as all great philosophy's own most [*eigentümlichstes*] interest. Philosophy had an unexpressed mandate from the bourgeoisie to find transparent grounds for freedom. But that concern is antagonistic in itself. (ND, 213; 214)

This "antagonism" will play the central role in the story Adorno wants to tell, essentially how the bourgeoisie changed from a revolutionary to a conservative class, how it was "that freedom grows obsolete without having been realized" (ND, 215; 215). To understand this, we must understand how the problem of freedom was posed in its bourgeois form, a form supposedly representative of the requirements of an identitarian logic, and then why the "antagonistic" and unsolvable *form* of that problem is thereby subject to the general "ideology critique" that Adorno applies to such a discursive practice.

There is one aspect of the Kantian formulation of this problem that Adorno returns to frequently, and it orients much of his discussion.[19] That decisive orientation is the Kantian stress on *freedom as autonomy*, the claim that persons are subject to no claim of obligation except requirements they have themselves legislated and subjected themselves to. One is obligated, in the Kantian picture, because, and only because, one

---

[19] Yet again, it is not entirely clear why the Kantian formulation of the freedom issue, and not Locke's or Rousseau's or Hume's, counts as *the* paradigmatic bourgeois formulation. Given the importance of appeals to happiness and sentiment, or at least to security and peace in bourgeois culture, rather than to unconditioned worth and moral dignity, it is an issue that needs more comment than Adorno devotes to it. Perhaps he simply starts from Nietzsche's famous observation that "human beings do not desire happiness; only the English desire happiness."

has obligated oneself.[20] And this could account for the ethical "lack" or negativity presumed by any critical theory, without reliance on any traditional notion of human nature or historical teleology.[21] In the simplest sense so momentous for Hegel: We lack simply *what we have required of ourselves* or "must so require" of ourselves in order to act at all. Indeed, even "human tutelage" (or "maturity," *Mündigkeit*), an organic metaphor, is described dialectically by Kant himself as "one's *self*-incurred tutelage." (This line of thought would later form the basis of the appeal to "determinate negation" and "immanent critique" in Hegel's pioneering *Phänomenologie des Geistes*.)[22]

Perhaps this aspect of the Kantian position is so important for Adorno because, with its denial of a substantive ethics or value theory, it is most consistent with the bourgeois assumption of the absence of objective value in a disenchanted world.[23] Perhaps, beyond expressing the liberal restriction of worth only to what was "freely" achieved by an individual, the general position best expresses the revolutionary aspirations of the bourgeoisie to secular self-sufficiency altogether, expressed not just by an appeal to the supreme authority of reason but now *even* to the "self-authorizing" character of reason's authority.[24] But in speculating on this issue, one runs out of material pretty quickly, since Adorno does not discuss much his reasons for this virtually exclusive focus on Kant and the Idealist ethic of autonomy. I suspect all of the above play a role in his thinking.

---

[20] Hence the will is not merely subject to the law but subject to it in such a way that it must be viewed as also giving the law to itself and just because of this as first subject to the law (of which it can regard itself as the author). GL, 431; 39.

[21] Cf. the remarks on negativity in Adorno and romantic philosophy and links to other aporetic traditions in philosophy in Bubner 1983. Also very helpful in the same volume, Theunissen 1983.

[22] I have tried to make the case for locating the origins of Fichtean and Hegelian "logic" in the Kantian problem of self-legislated law in Pippin forthcoming c, forthcoming d, 2000a, 2000b. See also the compelling narrative provided by Pinkard 2002. Admittedly, this is a huge topic. From Adorno's point of view, there is no way to regard German fascism as some sort of determinate negation of, internally required by, the Weimar Republic, no way to consider its falseness a matter of partiality, incompleteness. Hegel's view is not, I think, committed to such claims, but that is the longer story that cannot be told here.

[23] This is the aspect of Kant's position particularly stressed in the recent work of Christine Korsgaard. I take issue with it in Pippin forthcoming c.

[24] This latter claim for what Hegel called "absolute reflection" is the source of the dialectical logic required to explain its possibility in later idealism and does seem connected with the systematic aspirations of the identity theory that bothers Adorno.

But the idea that all laws to which we are bound must be self-legislated is a complex, largely metaphorical notion, and Adorno notices several interesting things about it. It is metaphorical because the idea of a pre-obligation position, from which obligation is constituted, is so hard to imagine coherently. It would seem that any putative act of self-obligating self-legislation is either already practically required by some principle – on the basis of which it can be rationally justified – or it is not, in which case it can look arbitrary or like some existential leap.[25] The self-imposition of law must somehow be made consistent with the nonarbitrariness of law itself, the moral law, and the *"praktische Nötigung"* for so legislating. But what Adorno notices is the inner "antagonism" in the concept itself: that self-rule is also, at the same time, an act of self-submission; and the absolute and unconditioned rule of reason is also, at the same time, *an act of self-enslavement.* Here are some of his formulations (the first makes clear the expected link with the critique of identity thinking):

That there must be freedom is the supreme *iniuria* committed by the lawmaking autonomous subject. The substance of its own freedom – of the identity which has annexed all nonidentity – is as one with the "must," with the law, with absolute dominion. (ND, 248; 250)

In his most clearly dialectical formulations:

The absolute volitional autonomy implied therein would be the same as absolute rule of one's inner nature. (ND, 253; 256)

And

As he honors freedom, however, seeking to cleanse it of all impairments, Kant simultaneously condemns the person to unfreedom in principle. A person cannot experience this utterly limited freedom otherwise than as a restriction of its (one's) own impulses. (ND, 253; 256)

But in these and other passages where Adorno tries to portray the bourgeois notion of autonomy as conceptually unstable, a self-undermining complex of freedom and unfreedom, he does not present the issue as only a conceptual puzzle. Both the theoretical aspects of Kantian

---

[25] In itself the notion that reason should submit to no authority other than itself, to reason, is not so revolutionary. The difficulty is more obvious when we take the notion of self-legislation (not discovery) seriously and when we tackle the problem from the subjective side: that one can be said to be bound to such legislative results, and this because one can be said to have bound oneself.

freedom – freedom from natural necessity and so spontaneity – and the practical doctrine – freedom as self-legislation – make sense as philosophical problems, indeed as *the* most important problems, only within a certain social and historical world, in this case the "bourgeois" world. The problem of freedom bequeathed to philosophy at this time is a specific notion – requiring radical individual responsibility, individuality as a self-causing, even self-originating causal agency, all in a way consistent with an exclusively natural-scientific ontology – and the paradoxes and incompatible commitments required by such a notion are not the results of poor reasoning or confused philosophy but accurately express both the requirements of the social world in its current form and the limitations *of that world.* So for Adorno, the "contradiction" in the antinomies is not between "dogmatism" and "skepticism" but between two incompatible ways in which modern subjects must experience themselves, "now free, now unfree" (ND, 294; 299). He presents this historical connection in several ways.

Some are expressed in comments about Kant's psychology – "His timid bourgeois detestation of anarchy matches his proud bourgeois antipathy against immaturity" (ND, 248; 250) – thus implying that such desiderata are incompatible in bourgeois society, much less in Kant personally.

But more often he directs his interest to the deepest manifestation of the problem, that revealed in Kant's Third Antinomy, the antagonism between freedom and scientific determinism, and so to dual, inescapable bourgeois needs: an alliance with modern natural science and the scientific world view, on the one hand, and an allegiance to the individual as a self-causing causality, on the other, the latter necessary to justify bourgeois notions of entitlement and desert as well as a distinct moral worth and dignity ("protection" in a sense from the ruthlessness and materialism of bourgeois culture). The fact that these two commitments cannot be rationally combined, so goes the thesis, is not simply a philosophical problem but reflects the inner antinomy or "*Antagonismus*" of bourgeois society itself, the source of its many pathologies:

The dichotomy also refers to progressive scientification. The bourgeois class is in league with this insofar as it promotes production, but it must fear scientific progress as soon as that progress interferes with the belief that its freedom – already resigned to internality – is existent. This is the real background of the doctrine of antinomies. (ND, 214; 214)

## VII

His remark about this situation seems to me exactly the right proposal for beginning to understand the dilemma.

> Reflections on freedom and determinism sound archaic, as though dating from the early times of the revolutionary bourgeoisie. But that freedom grows obsolete without having been realized – this is not a fatality to be accepted; it is a fatality which resistance must clarify. Not the least of the reasons why the idea of freedom lost its power over people is that from the outset it was conceived so abstractly and subjectively that the objective social trends found it easy to bury. (ND, 215; 215)

And freedom was so conceived not because of bad philosophy but because it was the notion of freedom necessary for a world of property-owning, contracting, rights-bearing individuals, deeply committed to the scientific disenchantment of the natural world. And here again Adorno tries to link this misconception to the spell (*Bann*) of identity thinking, as we return inevitably to our first topic. Yet again this seems too great a stretch. It is somehow supposed to be "the drive to identify" persons with absolute spontaneity or with determined bits of matter that accounts for this dead end (ND, 261, 287; 263f, 291f), a drive Adorno links, usually with little or no justification, to the ideological needs of distinctly bourgeois society.

So for Adorno, "Under the conditions of a bourgeois economy this is an unshakable fact; in such an economy there can be no answer to the question whether freedom or unfreedom of the will exists" (ND, 260; 263). But here it must also be noted that what Adorno is proposing (or gesturing toward) is self-consciously an extension and realization of the bourgeois aspiration for realized freedom, including the freedom of individuals. His is definitely a "not yet completed Enlightenment," not at all an anti- or postmodern recommendation. He calls the Kantian morality of reason "Kant's bourgeois sublimity" (ND, 237; 239), praises Kant's Principle of Justice in extraordinary terms, calling the situation of Kantian right "a reconciled condition that would not only be above the bad universal...but above the obdurate individual" (ND, 279; 283) and this even though Adorno must realize the Hobbesean side of Kant's treatment of the state and the great centrality of bourgeois property rights in the famous *exeundum* argument.

And there are utopian anticipations of what the "state of realized freedom" would be:

If the social process of production and reproduction were transparent for the subjects, if the subjects determined that process, they would no longer be passively buffeted by the ominous storms of life. (ND, 260; 263)

This is a goal for critique that clearly takes as its underlying norm freedom and, just as in Hegel's opening line in his *Philosophy of Right*, insists on the full *Verwirklichung* of the value raised to supreme, even absolute importance by bourgeois society. (He even notes in such societies "a potential that would rid men of coercion," resulting in "the objectivity of a reconciled life of the free" (ND, 271; 275).)

## VIII

There is no extended discussion in *Negative Dialectics* that purports to demonstrate that the best way to understand the irresolvable antagonism of Kant's Third Antinomy is the implication of the problem's very formulation in an identitarian logic, nor that the true realization of freedom somehow depends on a new, negatively dialectical way of framing the issue, nor that the "spell" of such thinking is itself to be explained by some lack of transparency in the material organization of production and power in bourgeois society, nor that a different, more "transparent" organization of power is a necessary condition for the effective or real possibility of such a nonidentitarian way of thinking. All this is still distinct from the question of how to state what identity thinking actually is. It is, of course, always open to Adorno and his followers to insist that such a set of questions rests on precisely the assumptions about philosophical account giving that Adorno wishes to challenge and that his own aphoristic, "mimetic," antisystematic "constellation" of paragraphs and topics is meant to be an example of what philosophy can now "catch sight of," as it were, "only out the corner of one's eye."[26]

---

[26] For example, cf. the epilogue in Buck-Morss 1977, 185ff. On the indirect, elusive, and always somewhat metaphorical nature of what Adorno is after, cf. the remarks in EF on "the idea of a happiness in freedom vis-à-vis the object, a freedom that gives the object more of what belongs to it than if it were mercilessly incorporated in to the order of ideas" (30; 21). See also Albrecht Wellmer's remarks on the issue in Wellmer 1985, 135–8 and 158.

This does not seem to me a very interesting response, and at any rate there is one crucial element in any effective "ideology critique" that Adorno certainly does not neglect.[27] As noted before, one very good reason to begin to search for nonphilosophical, empirical factors that might be relevant to an explanation of the content and social success of some normative claim might be that there is very little reason to think that there could be very persuasive philosophical reasons for holding the view. And this Adorno *does* try to show, concentrating on the Kantian claim for the primacy of practical reasons and therewith the autonomy of the normative realm altogether (both supposedly paradigmatic instances of identity thinking). In this section my claim is that Adorno misunderstands this Kantian thesis and in the following, concluding section, that he thereby misidentifies the truly irreconcilable "antagonism" at the heart of Kant's theory of freedom.

The problem with Adorno's interpretation is already on view when he summarizes and criticizes Kant's "answer to Hume." It is quite apparent there that Adorno is sweeping aside one of the most important distinctions that Kant attempted to draw, as in Kant's famous claim in the *Groundwork* that

[e]verything in nature works in accordance with laws. Only a rational being has the capacity to act *in accordance with the representation* of laws, that is, in accordance with principles, or has a *will*. (GL, 412; 24)

Yet it is precisely this distinction that Adorno claims that Kant collapses in the answer to Hume:

Kant's causality is one without a *causa*. As he cures it of naturalistic prejudice it dissolves in his hands . . . but when Kant maintains that the subject *must* think causally, his analysis of the constituents, according to the literal sense of "must," is following the very causal proposition to which he would be entitled to subject only the *constituta*. (ND, 246; 248)

As others have noted, this is quite a puzzling claim.[28] Given what Kant has said in the *Grundlegung* passage and in many other places, why would Adorno be satisfied with basing his charge on the "literal sense of 'must'"?

---

[27] I have to assume here that by "effective" ideology critique one should understand any critique that does not make the highly implausible reductionist, *causal* claim that any and all norms are the product in some way of empirical social conditions.

[28] See the clear account of Adorno's confusion of "*Objektebene*" and "*Metaebene*" and his collapsing of the distinction between "*Gesetzlichkeit*" and "*Kausalität*," in Braun 1983, 145; basically the same point in Beier 1977, 63; and see Thyen 1989, who offers a very limited defense of Adorno (that his claim remains nonetheless "interesting"), 179ff.

Kant so carefully works to separate empirical or natural-scientific claims about what "could not be otherwise" from transcendental claims about "necessary" conditions of experience (a case modeled after the requirements of logic) and from practical or moral necessity (*Nötigung*) that there is no reason whatsoever to think that Kant was confused about the distinction. Only a very crude appeal to the "literal sense of 'must'" could lead one to think that the "must" involved in claims such as "If you believe 'If A, then B'; and you believe 'A,' then you must believe 'B'" or "If you are to be able to represent an event, you must experience that event as necessarily following another according to a rule" or "If you set out to obtain X and Y is the only means to X, you must either obtain Y or give up the goal X" is *the same* as the must in "If copper is heated, it must expand." This is not even to mention the very different sense of "must" in "You must always act under the idea of freedom."

But even in these practical contexts, Adorno continues this rather clumsy reading of practical necessity, always assuming that when Kant mentions reason "determining" the will with a kind of "necessity," he must mean, in a question-begging way, causal necessity:

> With . . . magnificent innocence, . . . Kant utters this in the line about creatures unable to act otherwise than under the idea of freedom – creatures whose subjective consciousness is tied to that idea. Their freedom rests on their unfreedom, on their inability "to act otherwise." (ND, 230–1; 231–2)

There are passages where Adorno indicates that he understands that the traditional notion of *ratio* can mean either reason or cause, but he charges idealism with a dogmatic attempt to conflate the distinction into a causal one. He even goes so far as to claim that because thoughts "must" conform to "logical stringency," this, too, is evidence of the general "unfreedom" of all thought! (ND, 232; 233)

Now perhaps Kant is not entitled to his distinction between "under laws" and "according to concepts of law," but it will take a good deal more than these pronouncements to demonstrate this. Kant's entire critical philosophy depends on the distinction, often defended at length, between normative and causal necessity, between a normative constraint by principle or rule and physical constraint. His claim in the *Critique of Practical Reason* about what he calls the "*Faktum der Vernunft*" can confuse a first-time reader of Kant (and apparently confused Adorno) because the conclusion of his argument is exactly the opposite of the claim that there is any fact "for" reason to discover. He means, as is often pointed out by Kant scholars, the *practically* inescapable "fact *of* reason" itself. That is, from the point of view of the agent or actor, the only determinant one can bring to bear in consideration of a possible action is the strength and quality of the reason that would justify it. I may also believe that all such considerations are themselves causal results of neuro-chemical processes, but Kant's case for the autonomy of the normative depends only on pointing out that knowledge of such processes cannot be *practically relevant* to a deed unless it can be made to serve as a practical reason, all within a complex of reasons about what might be done. (I, qua agent, cannot simply "wait" to see what my neuro-chemical processes will result in.)

This core Kantian claim – the autonomy of the normative domain, the claim that the only thing that bears on the sufficiency of a reason for action is another reason, never a mere state of affairs or cause on its own – is everywhere based on such a practical argument and never on any direct theoretical claim about our intelligible selves. Since we have no knowledge of such, Kant's entire practical enterprise must begin from that noumenal ignorance and from the strict distinction in kind between "practical necessity" and "causal necessity," precisely the distinction Adorno keeps eliding. As noted several times, it might be quite interesting to wonder why what Kant thought necessary to defend the possibility of individual moral accountability drove him to defenses of such conditions that all seem to be dead ends: noumenal ignorance, intelligible causality, absolute unconditional moral accountability. And it might be fruitful to consider nonphilosophical explanations of why he might have found himself saddled with those conceptions and those defenses, matters tied to incompatible yet unavoidable "bourgeois" commitments. But, again, that turn makes a certain kind of sense only if one has first identified properly the philosophical dead end, the place where appeals to bad arguments, un-thought-through premises, and so forth begin to seem manifestly irrelevant in trying to explain the hold some idea has on our imaginations. *That* Adorno clearly has not done.

## IX

Adorno's version of Kant is no doubt influenced, on the one hand, by German neo-Kantianism and its emphasis on the psychological aspect of Kant's theory of knowledge and, on the other hand, by the standard two-world interpretation of Kant's idealism, with its endless problems about nontemporal noumenal causation. This perspective is what leads him to emphasize the meta-ethical dimensions of freedom or the determinism problem as the core "antagonism" not solvable in bourgeois society (as in the earlier quotations about the role of science in bourgeois modernity). And this also highlights the problem of nature, and the status of rational agents as natural, in a way that connects up with themes of interest to Adorno since *The Dialectic of Enlightenment*, as now (in ND) identity thinking and the idealist "rage" for identity with, control of, the natural world assumes the central role in Adorno's narrative ("The system is the belly turned mind, and rage is the mark of each and every idealism" (ND, 34; 23)). Yet this emphasis not only is based on a misleading interpretation of Kant; it prevents Adorno from seeing much more directly the prephilosophic social and historical dimensions of the "problem of freedom" as Kant presents it.[29]

For, in his practical works, Kant rarely portrays the *practical* problem of freedom as the problem of how to achieve "more" independence from the restrictions imposed on human beings by their status as natural animals. His interests seem to lie elsewhere than just in building up something like the "strength" of will "against" our impulses, despite the common romantic picture. Assume with Kant that not being able to act "except under the idea of freedom" is a *practical* necessity, unavoidable from the agent's perspective, that what it means to act under such an idea is to be able to act on reasons, and even, for the sake of argument, that by acting we commit ourselves to doing nothing that violates this condition, doing nothing not in conformity with the form of rationality itself (the moral law, let us say). It is in this sense that we could be said, just by deciding to act at all, to have "legislated" the rule of reason, in both its moral and instrumental sense, for ourselves and to have subjected ourselves to it. If we then ask Kant *why* we cannot always *do* what practical reason requires, indeed often act against our own best interests knowingly or even violate

---

[29] Somewhat ironically, Adorno remains a Kantian. "Negative Dialectics" is not a dialectics at all but a philosophy of finitude and a call for an acknowledgment of such finitude. The "nonidentical" plays an oddly similar rhetorical role as the Kantian identification of the *Ding an sich* against later idealists. See the interesting remarks on the Kant-Adorno relation in Thyen 1983, 133ff and especially 153 and 171. Attempts such as Guzzoni's to domesticate the notion of nonidentity by such appeals to finitude seem to me pure Kantianism. Cf. Guzzoni 1981, 17ff. Thyen's attempt to differentiate her position from Guzzoni's by understanding Adorno as after the "limit concept of the conceptual" end up sounding like a modest empiricism or a Kantian cautionary doctrine (1983, 204ff). Not to mention that, when one considers "the hard labor of the concept" necessary for Kant to demonstrate his own version of the limits of experience, it becomes more obvious that Adorno has simply helped himself to scores of claims without the relevant philosophical work.

the instrumental law of reason we have legislated for ourselves (do not ask directions when lost, for example), Kant's answer does not often rely on our "natural constitution" as such. Occasionally, he will, like a zealous Puritan, point to some boiling sea of riotous passions demanding satisfaction or to our pitiful weakness in doing what we know we ought to do. But more often he presents an *explanation* for that susceptibility and that weakness, and that explanation is profoundly social.

That is, Kant clearly inherited from Rousseau a sense of the role of comparative worth, or vanity in social life, and was impressed, like Rousseau, with some alternate sense of true worth that does not involve the approval of others. (Although Kant, like Rousseau, also thought that this competition has many indirectly positive results. "[T]hanks be to nature," Kant writes, "for the distasteful, competitive vanity" (I, 21; 32).) And in the *Religion* book, while Kant characterizes human evil as self-love, he makes clear that such a self-love acquires *content* – we come to appreciate what would enhance self-love and what would diminish it – only by comparison with others (R, 27; 51). Accordingly, some contemporary commentators have attributed to Kant the Rousseauean thesis that the origin of *all* human evil is social.[30] A life of truly realized freedom, while it is also a morally righteous life for Kant, is praised as well as being a life of maximum self-sufficiency in the direction of one's life. It is mostly in that sense a life of realized freedom, freedom from the requirement that others think well of one, from the need to measure one's worth in comparison with what others have, and so from the endless vices that originate in such ambition and vanity.

More positively, and already paradoxically, especially in his essays on history and his remarks in the *Religion* book about an ethical commonwealth, Kant frequently stresses what his practical philosophy should consider irrelevant: the social conditions of such an independent life. His remarks on education, character formation, historical development, and family life all make clear that while he thinks it is in some sense strictly true that I can always do what I ought to do, no matter what others are doing, no matter my own past, there are social conditions in which this is much more or less likely, and it would be grossly irrational for me or anyone not to consider the long-term influences of these varying social conditions, however theoretically problematic is the whole notion of "influence." And the more he stresses these conditions, the less clear it

[30] Anderson-Gold 1991, and Wood 1999, esp. chap. 9, 283–320.

becomes in just what sense I *can* always be said to be able to do what I ought to do. Such considerations would seem to introduce considerations of moral luck that undermine the absoluteness of "ought always implies can" and that shift our attention from questions of individual fortitude to questions of institutional rationality.

Even in his political philosophy, Kant concedes that while rational agents in the state of nature are capable of following general moral injunctions to injure no one or to restrict the freedom of others only in ways that are reciprocal, they are not capable, unilaterally, of successfully and securely distinguishing "mine" and "yours," the condition necessary before I can observe any rule about not taking what is "yours." This comes close to saying that a form of legal sociality is a condition of the possibility of the mine/yours distinction itself and so of the possibility of an individual's "actualized" independence as a concrete individual. (The way to Fichte's 1796 *Grundlage* obviously depends on the direction of this argument.) In the *Religion* book, after noting that "[h]uman beings . . . mutually corrupt one another's moral predisposition" (R, 97; 108), Kant goes on to state a principle difficult to reconcile with his paradigmatic picture of bourgeois individuality and self-sufficiency:

[T]his highest moral good will not be brought about solely through the striving of one individual person for his own moral perfection but requires rather a union of such persons into a whole toward that very end, [i.e.] toward a system of well-disposed human beings. (R, 97f; 109)

Put another way, the irresolvable tension in Kant's theory is *much more on the surface* than Adorno acknowledges and is best captured by Kant's doctrine, most clearly articulated in the 1784 *Idee zu einer allgemeinen Geschichte in weltbürgerlicher Ansicht*, of our "unsocial sociability" as dialectically tense or "antagonistic" a notion as one would ever want. ("Antagonism" is the word Kant uses (I, 20; 31)). As in Rousseau, the worst form of evil is subjection to the will of another (i.e., being used as a means), and the greatest moral good is a life consistent with the capacity to direct the course of my affairs as a free rational agent (the bourgeois ideal from Rousseau and Kant to Rawls and many others). *But achieving this good is not something an individual can do alone.*[31] Social institutions both to nourish and to develop such independence are necessary and are consistent with, do not thwart, its realization, but with freedom understood as an

---

[31] See Pippin forthcoming b.

individual's causal agency this will always look like an external necessity that we have good reasons to try to avoid. This creates the problem of a form of dependence that can be considered constitutive of independence and that cannot be understood as a mere compromise with the particular will of another or as a separate, marginal topic of Kant's dotage. *This* is, in effect, the antinomy contained within bourgeois notions of individuality, individual responsibility, individual desert and merit, property rights, and so on: the bourgeois notion of freedom. This dialectical relation between independence and dependence is what is really at stake in the paradox identified by Adorno as self-ruling and self-enslavement.

This different stress is not just a matter of getting the scholarly details right. Adorno's critical account of what he clearly regards as the bourgeois "identification" with the requirements of a natural-scientific (technologically powerful) world view and a contradictory and equally unavoidable "identification" with the normative imperatives of bourgeois freedom set up his problem in a way that will inevitably suggest that the only "critical" way out is to show that the former identification is contingent and so ultimately avoidable. This suggests a "reenchantment" project that is hopeless.[32] The collapse of the teleological, scholastic view of nature is not ultimately explicable by appeal to the requirements of new material social conditions. The collapse was rational, responsive to real discoveries about the really disenchanted character of nature and a great human liberation. Once the problem of nature as a whole is simply left behind, the incompatible normative commitments of bourgeois society with respect to freedom can be seen much more clearly and subject to critique much more effectively.[33]

So, in sum, this notion of freedom paradoxically must appeal to a condition of dependence and mediation that its mythic self-understanding

---

[32] It also leads Adorno to collapse distinctions with wild abandon, as in his attempt to show that the "reality" of the appeal of the Kantian transcendental enterprise is the way it mirrors the demands of a society dominated by exchange value. See ND, 180; 178. There is no argument for this. Adorno simply seems to reason: The former requires a formal abstraction, so does the latter, so they must have something to do with one another. See his chapter "On the Dialectic of Identity," ND, 149ff; 146ff, and Thyen's discussion of the self-referential paradoxes such discussions generate (1989, 189–90).

[33] Otherwise, we are always going to endure such claims as: "If thought really yielded to the object, if its attention were on the object, not on its category, under such a lingering eye the objects themselves would begin to speak" (ND, 38; 28). There is perhaps some broad metaphorical sense intended here, but the content of such a plea just seems like a rather inflated form of realism.

must also ultimately deny. And it is an antinomy with no resolution in Kant beyond a theodocical expression of mere hope, a theology that itself borders on mythology. That reconciliation must await the transformation of our understanding of "actualized" freedom as our unsocial sociability to a fuller actualization of freedom, and so therewith a fuller conception of freedom, not one in humble deference to the nonidentical but in the right relation to others, freedom as "being with self in others" (*bei sich Selbstsein im Anderen*), to quote a familiar source.[34]

[34] I realize that from the perspective of Adorno and Horkheimer, this is a false opposition and that in late capitalism no theory of social relations or intersubjectivity can be held up as an *alternative* to a critical theory everywhere oriented from the "domination of nature" theme. This – distinguishing the social as in some way "its own" normative domain – is of course the basic difference among first- and second- and now third-generation Frankfurt school critical theory: Horkheimer, Marcuse, Adorno, et al. from first Habermas and now Honneth. (The best explanation for the increasing reification of social relations in late modernity, according to the original account, is the inevitable influence of the authority of the positivistic sciences, in the service of capital, in transforming and distorting the understanding of such social relations, once it is more and more accepted that human organisms are not qualitatively different from any other bit of the natural.) There is much more to say about this issue, but I have wanted only to make a beginning here to show that in *Negative Dialectics* there are no good reasons given to support this methodological monism and many reasons to suspect that it is not adequate. Ultimately, of course, the direction I am suggesting is Hegelian, not Habermasean, but that is also another story. On the differences between Adorno and Habermas, see the lucid account in Honneth 1979.

# 6

## The Unavailability of the Ordinary

### *Strauss on the Philosophical Fate of Modernity*

In *Natural Right and History*, Leo Strauss argues for the continuing "relevance" of the classical understanding of natural right.[*] Since this relevance is not a matter of a direct return or a renewed appreciation that a neglected doctrine is simply true, the meaning of this claim is somewhat elusive. But it is clear enough that the core of Strauss's argument for that relevance is a claim about the relation between human experience and philosophy. Strauss argues that the classical understanding articulates and is continuous with the "lived experience" of engaged participants in political life. He appears to mean by this the everyday experience of choices, conflicts, and of other human beings as these appear *from* the participant point of view, "within" some sort of horizon established by their various engagements and practical projects. In the modern world, by contrast, he claims that we have manufactured a kind of artificial experience, have created by education and training over the course of time habits of heart and mind that have obscured and distorted how the human things originally make sense just as matters of praxis. Because of this we have been left disoriented and at a loss with respect to the basic questions about how to live that unavoidably appear within this participant point of view. This is the heart of our "crisis."

[*] A version of this chapter was presented at a conference on "Living Issues in the Thought of Leo Strauss: Fifty Years after *Natural Right and History*," in June 2002 at the Carl Friedrich von Siemens Stiftung in Munich, Germany. I am grateful to Nathan Tarcov and Richard Zinman, the editors of the forthcoming volume of those conference essays (*Natural Right and History: A Reassessment*), for permission to publish my essay as a chapter in this book. I am also grateful to Heinrich Meier, Nathan Tarcov, and the participants in the discussions during that conference for several comments on the thesis of the chapter.

This claim by Strauss raises important philosophical issues about the distinct nature of this "ordinary" human experience, the conditions of the possibility of an undistorted or original or genuinely human ordinary experience, how different interpretations of what it is might be adjudicated, and especially the nature of its *claim* on us in Strauss's narrative. (We need, for example, some answer to the skeptical question: Who cares how the practical world feels to us or looks, what it is like for us to experience it? *That* ordinary world is as full of gods, angels, ghosts, wretched probability expectations, primitive fears, and banality as it is, perhaps, full of human meaning, right and wrong, high and low.) Strauss does not address these issues in a straightforward thematic way, but he does address them indirectly by constantly relying on implied answers to such questions, and his treatment is the theme of these remarks.

It is a somewhat sprawling, complex theme, difficult to address economically. The issue of the relation between philosophy and experience, or how there might be a philosophical appreciation of "life as it is lived," is arguably the central theme of all modern European philosophy since Hegel. And it is especially striking that in that tradition the theme is often raised with the same practical urgency as in Strauss. The attempt is to recover some everyday perspective that is said to have been, oddly, not only lost but missing (hard to find). The attempt often is to invoke a radically new sort of philosophy (or a way to avoid or end philosophy) in order to return to "life as it is really lived"; as if without such a reminder, we might become all too habituated to life lived in some inappropriate register, might live in some way out of scale, measuring and directing our lives disproportionately. We might even permanently "forget" what the human scale and measure is like. And the relevant figure or image is often this "remembering" what has been forgotten, and it shows up everywhere in characterizations of the task of modern philosophy. It resonates in Hegel's claims about philosophy as partly a "phenomenology" of experience, in Kierkegaard's remarks on *The Present Age*, in Nietzsche's insistence that we recover a capacity to look at science "from the point of view of life" rather than vice versa, in the popularity of *Lebensphilosophie* in the twentieth century (Dilthey, Simmel, Plessner, Bergson, Scheler, Hans Jonas), in Wittgenstein's assurance that ordinary language is all right, that the extraordinary character of philosophy is evidence of pathology, and in Heidegger's claims about the forgetting of the meaning of being. As Strauss himself puts it, "the problem of natural right is today a matter of recollection rather than actual knowledge."[1] It is a striking and somewhat

---

[1] NRH, 7.

underreported fact that *this* is the company Strauss keeps ("the friends of the lost, missing, but recoverable ordinary").

Obviously, the central issue in such a contrast will be how to distinguish between a picture in which the everyday has been forgotten but is recoverable, layered over or screened behind artificial constructs and fantasies, and a picture in which there can be no such contrast, in which there are historically multiple (if sometimes continuous) everydays, not primordial and derivative experiences. The deepest and most comprehensive version of the latter picture is Hegel's, and so involves the right way to understand what it means to tie philosophy, when understood as reflection on the meaning of human experience, to history, all as opposed to what I regard as this persistent dream of a lost (but findable) everyday, human experience of the human. But a number of preliminaries are necessary first.

## I. Philosophy as *Zeitdiagnose*

The idea of recovering or remembering presupposes some account of what was forgotten and why, how an ordinary experience came to be so layered over with such a distorting screen, and why that is so important. This means that a narrative and a diagnostic element must be central to a philosophical self-understanding, and it is important first to appreciate what is involved in ascribing such tasks to philosophy, especially since Strauss inherits some of these notions without explicit formulation.

Hegel, of course, was the first to claim that philosophy could take as its proper subject matter *historical* "actuality" ("*Wirklichkeit*"), and he went so far as to deny that philosophy was concerned with what it had traditionally taken itself to be about: the "ideal." That there might be a distinctly *philosophical* comprehension of the great swirl of events in actual human history has always seemed highly implausible to most philosophers.[2] For many, Hegel seems to be giving philosophy the implausible task of illuminating the rational meaning of what he called in the *Phenomenology* the "shapes of spirit" (*Gestalten des Geistes*). It appears that he proposes to show in what sense a concrete, shared, historical form of life could be said to be a *rational outcome* of a prior collective experience, especially of the experience of something like a breakdown in a form of life, and that

---

[2] PPH, 56, for Strauss's formulation. Perhaps the first expression of such skepticism is Aristotle's claim in his *Poetics* that poetry is more philosophical than history, able to present broad human problems and general types since not tied to unrepeatable events and unique particulars.

he intends to give philosophy thereby a kind of "diagnostic" and even narrative function. And all this in a way that particularly targets our *ideals* or *norms*; why some come to have the grip on us they do; why such a norm might lose such a grip. (Hegel treats these "breakdowns" in a form of life as constitutive of *Geist* itself, as in his famous remarks about the "life of *Geist*" not shying away from death and *Geist*'s "tarrying with the negative."[3] They are, rather, anomalies in Strauss, signs that something is going wrong, failing, and that is an important difference in their notions of diagnostic philosophy and reliance on narrative.) Hegel's full claim about rational outcomes appeals to a practical, narrative, and collective or institutional rationality that is difficult to summarize economically. It involves not only the attempt, already extremely controversial, to identify a genuinely *common* form of life, shape of spirit, or *Weltanschauung*[4] but an appeal to some sort of transindividual dimension of practical rationality. And finally, the most contentious dispute here (and the one of most relevance to Strauss) concerns Hegel's assessment of European modernization, his account of what it means that we live now so differently from before, and his telling us just what he thinks it does mean: that the realization of human freedom has entered a decisive (because decisively self-conscious) period.[5]

For many, all of this amounts to superficial, armchair sociology, not philosophy, and those same critics might complain that Hegel has a lot to answer for; a lot of bad, pseudo-philosophic profundity about historical actuality, about jazz, professional wrestling, and Disneyland can be traced back to his extraordinary claim that philosophy is its own time

---

[3] Hegel, PhS, 19.

[4] Montesquieu's term of art was the "spirit of laws." Strauss's word is mostly "regime," which he identifies with "the form of life of a society, its style of life, its moral taste, form of society, form of state, form of government, spirit of laws." WIPP, 34.

[5] This is the greatest dispute about the *content* of Hegel's claims. A sweeping resistance to this whole *style* of thought is understandable. There are as many people who cringe in academic pain when they hear terms such as "the" moderns as there are protestors who howl at mention of "the" ancients. Among academics, a professional nominalism, supplemented in the humanities by suspicion of grand or Eurocentric narratives, has become a powerful orthodoxy. Strauss's argument is that such aggregation is justified because (1) classical political philosophies all share the same "specific assessment," that "the goal of political life is virtue," and (2) all modern political philosophies agree in their "rejection of the classical scheme as unrealistic" (WIPP, 40). How (1) would deal with Thrasymachus, Gorgias, Protagorus, and the like and how (2) would include Hoelderlin, Hegel, or Schiller is not clear to me. Strauss later admits there is a Hegelian attempt at reconciliation with the ancient emphasis on virtue, but he indicates that Hegel's reliance on his philosophy of history vitiates that attempt (WIPP, 52–5).

comprehended in thought. But Hegel's invention of this diagnostic role inaugurated a great deal more than café-society analysis. To come closer to some of Strauss's assumptions, later thinkers such as Nietzsche and Heidegger were certainly resolute anti-Hegelians, but they continued the attempt at a *philosophical Zeitdiagnose*, at reaching the proper diagnosis of what was happening to us in the later modern period. And their appeal, too, was to something like *philosophical* fate, not individual genius, the conditions of bourgeois economic life, or one damn thing after another. In a way that we have to think of as modeled on Hegel's account, their claims had it that the most important thing to understand about the civilization of "the last man" was that it was philosophy itself that had failed ("for life"), had now become a thing of the past, had died, and that with this death, the aspirations of enlightenment since Socrates died as well, ceased to have a grip, to be a genuine, possible aspiration. In fact, they claimed, the "lived-out" consequences of such aspirations could *now* be seen to have amounted to a kind of "nihilism," whether in the sense Nietzsche cared about (no possible distinction between noble and base)[6] or the version that Heidegger cared about: the forgetting of the question of the meaning of being.

Two brief qualifications are now needed on such appeals to the causality of philosophical fate, as introduced thus far, before turning again to Strauss's claims.

First, such appeals to philosophical fate in these latter Nietzschean and Heideggerean cases (and Strauss's too) obviously involve a much more *restricted* sense of institutional rationality than Hegel claims. This is the limited sense in which one could be said to have reasons for what one does, even if the overall goal to be achieved might be in some broader sense irrational. One might, for example, have very good reasons for a revenge murder if one is a member of a Sicilian mafia clan.[7] It would indeed be clearly irrational to be a member of such a clan and not plot such revenge. But, one might argue, there are no good prudential or moral reasons to participate in such an institution, and the objective structure and rules of the institution might also be in themselves irrational. Analogously, Nietzsche and Heidegger obviously do not share Hegel's view that the institutions of bourgeois society are in themselves rational (i.e., can be viewed as rational outcomes in a putative civilizational struggle for

---

[6] Nietzsche even describes the "self-sublation" (*Selbstaufhebung*) of morality (Nietzsche 1988, 1886 Preface, sec. 4, 16).

[7] Cf. the very helpful discussion in Hollis 1998.

self-knowledge). They therefore deny that subjects have, in the broadest sense, good reasons to participate. But Nietzsche does argue that "last man" civilization is a rational or rationally inevitable outcome of the original ideals of Christian morality and Socraticism and that we learn something essential about moral ideals by understanding such a development. And Heidegger attributes an enormous range of later ideas and phenomena to Plato and the development of Platonic metaphysics, everything from Cartesian philosophy to the *Ge-stell* of the technological world view. All these are for them in some sense rational outcomes, and they play a central role in how both philosophers want us to understand "the spiritual situation of the age."

Second, Hegel famously does not believe that such a philosophical comprehension of the significance of ordinary normative life is ever able to play a significant role itself in the debates and interpretations that make up that life. Philosophy "comes on the scene too late"[8] and is more like a "priestly sect" than a partisan participant.[9]

## II. Strauss's *Zeitdiagnose*

We need all these controversial notions of distinct historical epochs, a distinctly philosophical diagnosis of an epoch, of philosophical fate, and this broader and more restricted sense of historical rationality, to understand the famous claims by Leo Strauss in *Natural Right and History* and in other texts (1) that it was *modern* European philosophy that was "in crisis," not philosophy as such (the diagnostic claim), (2) that, given its premises, modern philosophy could not but be in such a crisis eventually (here the clear "causality of fate" claim), and (3) that we could recover to some extent, could "remember," what had been lost (forgotten) in the modern rush to embrace the new ideals of power and security and happiness. (That is, a rational development of modern premises is restricted to the assumption *of those premises*, and these premises can be avoided. What modern philosophers have "good reasons" (qua moderns) to believe and do may not be good reasons, all things considered.)[10] Set in context, that is, Strauss, especially in *Natural Right and History*, is clearly carrying on the kind of diagnostic goal given to philosophy by Hegel.

---

[8] Hegel, PhR, 23.

[9] Philosophy of Religion lectures.

[10] "I began, therefore, to wonder whether the self-destruction of reason was not the inevitable outcome of modern rationalism as distinguished from pre-modern rationalism" (SCR, 31).

Strauss's accounts of modern relativism, nihilism, and historicism are not socio-cultural or historical explanations. His account is also an account of the philosophical fate of ideas, and he assumes that philosophical commitments have historical, social, and not just intellectual implications. He clearly assumes that some of those historical implications are relevant to understanding the meaning of those commitments and are relevant to assessing them. A good deal of the account in NRH is narrative, in other words (in the words of Susan Shell, "Who or what killed natural right and can it be revived?"),[11] and the main structure of such Straussian narratives consists in various "slippery slope" claims. Hobbes or Rousseau or Kant may have understood their positions in a certain way, as defenses of the objectivity of certain important values, say, but they did not appreciate the implications of their positions, many of which were made clearer much later (could have been made much clearer only later?) by the likes of, especially, Nietzsche. In Strauss, Nietzsche is alluded to, together with Heidegger, in the claim that "[m]odern thought reaches its culmination, its highest self-consciousness, in the most radical historicism, i.e., in explicitly condemning to oblivion the notion of eternity."[12]

That thought could reach in historical time a culmination, that that culmination should be a kind of self-consciousness, together with the implication that we needed to experience this culmination before we could understand properly what modern thought involved, all sound unmistakable Hegelian notes.[13] So, even though the following might sound odd to attribute to a man who wrote, "The delusions of communism are already the delusions of Hegel and even of Kant,"[14] it nevertheless seems fair, if

[11] Shell forthcoming. One might note variations on this theme: Nietzsche's: "What did natural right die from?" Answer: "Natural causes." Heidegger's: "What did commitment to natural right and all that came with it kill off?" Answer: "An opening to the meaning of being issue." And Hegel's narrative: "Given classical natural right as origin, what will eventually grow from such beginnings?" Answer: "Spirit's full self-consciousness in modern ethical life."

[12] WIPP, 55.

[13] I admit that it is sometimes not easy to see clearly how Strauss wants us to understand such a claim about culmination and self-consciousness. He can also write, in NRH, "The contemporary rejection of natural right leads to nihilism – nay, it is identical with nihilism" (5). I find this "nay" construction puzzling. Perhaps Strauss means that, since the rejection of natural right *inevitably* leads to nihilism, therefore we can say that it is identical with nihilism. This interpretation would highlight even more Strauss's reliance on a "causality of fate" argument in order to justify that "inevitably."

[14] WIPP, 56. I cannot resist pointing out that what Strauss says is a serious distortion of the claims made about human history by Kant and Hegel. It is true that both admit

we assume that Strauss believes that philosophy can take some philosophical bearing from historical actuality, to claim that he looks sort of like a middle-of-the-road Hegelian. That is, he stands "in between" Hegel's full embrace of post-Kantian philosophy and bourgeois modernity as historically rational and the Nietzschean and Heideggerean claim that such a historical world is in the midst of a nihilism crisis that is the historically rational, if catastrophic, outcome of all post-Socratic philosophy (according to Nietzsche) or all post-Platonic philosophy (according to Heidegger).[15] (If we take our bearings from Hegel's claim that philosophy is "the farthest thing possible" from an attempt to instruct the state about what it ought to be,[16] then we can also note Strauss's Hegelian intuitions by saying of Hegel what Strauss said approvingly of Burke: that what looks like "the discovery of History" is really a "return to the traditional view of the essential limitations of theory.")[17] In final summation, then, according to Strauss: There is a modern crisis (this, the anti-Hegel bit); it is due to philosophical assumptions and their inevitable fate (the Hegelian bit); but it is an avoidable consequence of modern philosophy, not philosophy as such (the anti-Nietzsche/Heidegger bit).

Finally, we should note that Strauss's approach ties philosophy itself to a historical fate even more tightly than Hegel's, for whom philosophy is "its time comprehended in thought" and so in some way an expression of that time, of what has already gone on, not an independent *explicans*. For

---

that the "operative mechanism" of historical change is egoism, violence, immorality, even "the slaughter bench." But it is profoundly misleading to associate that claim with "communism" and, presumably, the arrogation by leaders to themselves of the right to commit violence in order to effect virtuous ends. For both Kant and Hegel, the very first premise in their accounts is that major historical change is not subject to the will of rulers or leaders or anyone but works "behind the back" and *unintentionally*. Strauss must of course realize that Hegel says that the owl of Minerva takes flight only at dusk, when philosophy paints its gray in gray, but he does not mention that here in this swipe at what amounts to the gross misuse of Kant's, Hegel's, indeed Marx's philosophy of history by Russian revolutionaries.

[15] Another point of contact: Hegel is the sort of strong critic of modern natural right and so contractarian doctrines of the state that Strauss affirmed in his remarks on Burke, even while distancing himself from any reliance on providence or even prudent compromise with that doctrine (evident, he thinks, in Burke and Hegel).

[16] Hegel, PhR, 21.

[17] NRH, 304. And: "There came into being a new type of theory, of metaphysics, having as its highest theme human action and its product rather than the whole, which is in no way the product of human action" (320). In Strauss's narrative, once the notion of a completed history began to seem implausible, the reactions of Kierkegaard and Nietzsche, on the one hand, and the historical school and eventual Heideggerean historicism, on the other, were the only possible reactions.

Strauss, on the other hand, a historical time can be viewed as philosophy expressed in action.

## III. The Recovery of the Ordinary

We reach now the main topic I want to concentrate on. Strauss himself has a complex version of his own diagnostic claim. First, he has a distinct way of describing such a crisis and of suggesting an escape: The crisis of natural right provokes an attempt to recover in some way what has been so greatly blurred: "the evidence of those simple experiences of right and wrong which are at the bottom of the philosophical contention that there is natural right."[18] To make this claim, Strauss needs to defend a typical assertion in NRH: "It was taken for granted [in modernity] that it [the experience of history] is a genuine experience and not a questionable interpretation of experience."[19] Strauss obviously thinks it *is* "questionable," but there is an enormous amount involved in the claim that persons in the modern world regularly misunderstand their own experience when they understand it as essentially historical, that, especially, their experience of the historically artificial and so mutable is not really an experience of the historically artificial and so mutable. (This would have to be the case if there is *natural* right and if the best reason for believing this is that it is ineliminable in any genuinely human experience.) But this distinction is very difficult to state properly because Strauss is not engaged in a metaphysics of nature or any account of how there could be historically immutable value properties in reality, and he proposes no epistemology that would demonstrate permanently possible, presumably noetic access to such properties. In effect, natural right *is*, is wholly constituted by, the natural-right experience. But on this model, *experiencing* one's social and political world as historical is also *all there can be* to such a world *being* historical. But Strauss must be claiming that modern experience can present us both with intimations of the naturalness of distinctions of right as well as, somehow, contravening experiences.

The way Strauss formulates his claim about a historical crisis is deceptively simple in itself. Strauss could, after all, simply have written books about the claims of Greek and British, French and German political philosophers, offering interpretations and assessments in the usual way of a professional philosopher in a modern university. (Most of the latter,

[18] NRH, 32.
[19] Ibid.

after all, hardly suffer from a historicism sickness. Most contemporary philosophers tend to treat every text as a journal article written yesterday.) There are contemporary philosophers in ethics who consider themselves Aristotelian but have nothing invested in Aristotle being "ancient"; many in the philosophy of mathematics or set theory or ethics again consider themselves Platonists about abstract objects or Platonic realists about moral properties, for whom, likewise, the ancients-moderns issue is irrelevant.

Moreover, the manifestations of a moral crisis, if there is one, might have little to do with philosophy and philosophical fate. Such a supposed modern unwillingness or inability to make and sustain ethical discriminations[20] might be an event with various social and economic causes or might perhaps be due to human frailty, ignorance, fear, or irrationality. The history of political philosophy might just be irrelevant to all that. Said the other way around, there may be a serious crisis in the philosophical understanding of natural right, but the body politic might go on its merry way, unaffected and uninterested, pretty much secure in a robust (but deluded) realist or religious conviction about ethical life. To *philosophize* in the light of the "crisis of *modern* natural right" is already to have required, for philosophical reflection, an epochal "antiquity," a historical other. It is to have suggested that our understanding of classical natural right is in some philosophical sense (i.e., with respect to its meaning) a function now of its alternative historical status, its premodernity. This is almost, but not quite, a historicist premise in Strauss's account, as Stanley Rosen has pointed out.[21]

Second, Strauss argues that the "twin sisters" of a relativist historicism and a value-free scientism must be understood as themselves modifications of a prescientific, natural, or ordinary "human experience of the human," on which such enterprises still depend for their ultimate sense or point. However, he also suggests in various places that the scientific and historicist world view have become so intertwined with experience in daily life that no phenomenology, method, call to arms, or simple appeal

---

[20] If that is the crisis; the present age can sometimes look like the triumph of a self-righteous, naïve moralism.

[21] Rosen 1999, 121. It "approaches" a historicist claim because Strauss need not have invoked any historical epoch to make his point about such "simple experiences." Such ought to be available everywhere and whenever and need require no "special" help from the Greeks. Strauss himself admits this, so it would require a separate discussion to sort out the historicist dimensions of the "ancient-modern" quarrel (instead of simply a quarrel between *any* proponent of nature as foundations, as against history).

to experience can retrieve such experiences in the modern world. (This is another tremendous concession to the power of "the experience of history.")[22] As he puts in PAW, we are "trapped" in some region of ignorance even deeper and darker than those in which the famous Platonic cave prisoners must sit. Because of what our everyday experience has literally become, we are now trapped "below" the cave.[23]

And this all prompts Strauss's third foundational claim (together with his reliance on some claim about the causality of fate and about the "loss" of the ordinary). *Only*, he often insists, a consideration of classical Greek political thought, which, besides being philosophy, also articulates the ordinary experience accessible *before* the modern distortion, can call such an alternative fully to mind, can call to mind the ordinary way in which things make a human sense, especially the simple experiences of right and wrong.

So the claim is that all of our ordinary experience is so intertwined with and oriented from scientific principles, a disenchanted world view, a robust sense of individualism, an acceptance of rapid and basic historical change, and so forth, that it would be naïve and pointless to tilt at these windmills, to rant that this is all some vast mistake. "Our" world, at its most intimately experienced levels, in its most coherent and typical manifestations, does *not* have in it, is not experienced as having any longer, ghosts, witches, angels, interceding saints, or immaterial souls, but it also, just as honestly experienced, does not "point us" any longer to any realm of being higher than the human or to an ordered cosmos within which man has a place, nor does it make available any longer "the evidence of those simple experiences of right and wrong which are at the bottom of the philosophical contention that there is natural right."[24] (At least, such evidence has become very badly "blurred.") This again is the point of tension between Strauss's claims that the modern experience of history is both a "misunderstanding" and that that misunderstanding *is* genuinely new, a deep feature *of* our experience. (There is also an echo here and

---

[22] Cf. his discussion of the "overwhelming power of the past" in "the attempt to solve the Jewish problem" in RCP, "Progress or Return," 233.

[23] Cf. Meier's (1996) note on this image, 22, n. 2. The basic issue is whether we can presume to start out in the kind of "natural" philosophical ignorance that Socrates described and so come to an awareness of our ignorance. (We cannot, straightaway anyway, according to Strauss.) See especially Meier's discussion and citations from Strauss's correspondence on 25, n. 7, where Strauss notes that another reason we live "under" the Platonic cave has to do with the entanglement of Greek philosophy in the tradition of revealed religion.

[24] NRH, 32.

in many other places in Strauss of Nietzsche's claim that, paradoxically, the most important and disturbing *manifestation* of modern nihilism is the absence of any *experience* of such a crisis.) To his credit, Strauss does not shy away from the magnitude of the problem created by this unusual situation.

On the one hand, as his various "slippery slope" arguments suggest, this situation may be said to have created a context in which human life is not coherently livable. We need to distinguish better from worse in a way that is not a function of our simple preferences; we cannot, in such a world, and so experience a great "need" for a modern doctrine of natural right. On the other hand, "A wish is not a fact." And (my favorite Strauss quotation):

> Even by proving that a certain view is indispensable in living well, one merely proves that the view in question is a salutary myth: one does not prove it to be true. Utility and truth are two entirely different things.[25]

And he goes further. The classical natural right doctrine we "need" so badly seems to many to require a teleological view of nature, a view that has been discredited by modern natural science, the most rigorous and authoritative body of knowledge we have available to us. This would seem to require a dualism, a nonteleological science of the universe and in some way a different, teleological "science of man." Strauss considers this the Thomistic solution but he clearly rejects it, boldly insisting, "An adequate solution to the problem of natural right cannot be found before this basic problem has been solved,"[26] unmistakably implying that it has not yet and appearing to promise that he will solve it in the book to follow. (In these terms, at least, he does not, but he does make clear that the "ordinary" he will appeal to, the human experience of the human, since it is not itself based on a theory, is in fact the original touchstone necessary for theorizing to have any point, avoids reliance on an antiquated cosmology, and does not resurrect teleological science since it is itself not a product or object of any sort of science. Hence again the enormous importance of this sort of appeal to experience.)[27]

---

[25] NRH, 6.

[26] NRH, 8.

[27] I think Richard Velkley is quite right to tie this strategy to the influence of Heidegger. Velkley forthcoming. See Meier 1996, 29, n. 10, where he cites a revealing passage wherein Strauss makes very clear his indebtedness to Heidegger and Heideggerean "*Destruktion*."

The strategy proposed in NRH returns us to the issue touched on before: the appeal to a more original, less distorted experience of the human things as such, as human, not as artificially constructed through the lens of some theory. In a word, that word that has circulated so much in twentieth-century thought, in Husserl on the life-world, in Heidegger on pre-predicative experience, being-in-the-world and the everyday, in the later Wittgenstein, Austin, Cavell (and through Cavell's insistence, found anew in Emerson and Thoreau), and recently in two books by Stanley Rosen: an appeal to "the ordinary" as a way of bypassing, avoiding, not refuting, the supposedly reductionist, skeptical, disenchanting, enervating trajectory of modern naturalism.

## IV. Ancient Texts and Natural Attitudes

There are several passages from any number of books that could be cited where Strauss invokes his own notion of the ordinary or prescientific. Perhaps the clearest and broadest is from *Natural Right and History*, so I quote from it at length. After noting that it was in the nineteenth century when it first became obvious that a "drastic" distinction must now be made between the "scientific" understanding and the "natural" understanding (the different way things make sense *in* "the world in which we live"), Strauss makes a general remark that is positively redolent of Heidegger:

> The natural world, the world in which we live and act, is not the object or the product of a theoretical attitude; it is not a world of mere objects at which we detachedly look, but of "things" or "affairs" which we handle.[28]

He then goes on to make an extraordinarily sweeping claim:

> Yet as long as we identify the natural or prescientific world with the world in which *we* live, we are dealing with an abstraction. The world in which we live is already a product of science, or at any rate it is profoundly affected by the existence of science.... To grasp the natural world as a world that is radically prescientific or prephilosophic, one has to go back behind the first emergence of science or philosophy. It is not necessary for this purpose to engage in extensive and necessarily hypothetical anthropological studies. The information that classical philosophy supplies about its origins suffices, especially if that information is supplemented by consideration of the most elementary premises of the Bible, for reconstructing the essential character of "the natural world." By using that

---

[28] NRH, 79.

information, so supplemented, one would be able to understand the origin of the idea of natural right.[29]

There is a historical claim in this passage, the scope and importance of which is unclear. In the introduction to *The City and Man*, Strauss insists that the "scientific understanding" depends on and is secondary to the "prescientific understanding." It is "dependent" because it assumes for its own meaning (presumably its point, purpose, or importance) what is here called "the common sense view of political things," understood as "the understanding of political things which belongs to political life," or "the citizen's understanding of political things."[30] This is the distinction on which he bases another major claim in "What Is Political Philosophy?":

In all later epochs [later than the classical], the philosopher's study of political things was mediated by a tradition of political philosophy which acted like a screen between the philosopher and political things, regardless of whether the individual philosopher cherished or rejected that tradition. From this it follows that the classical philosophers see the political things with a freshness and directness which have never been equaled. They look at political things in the perspective of the enlightened citizens or statesmen. [Strauss does not say here, as he does in his comments on the *Laws*, that these statesmen are always first Athenian, Cretan, or Spartan statesmen, never "statesmen as such."][31] They see things clearly which the enlightened citizens or statesmen do not see clearly, or do not see at all. But this has no other reason but the fact that they look farther afield in the same direction as the enlightened citizen or statesman. They do not look at political things from the outside, as spectators of political life.[32]

I want eventually to claim that this disjunction – "inside" the natural attitude and so originally undistorted by theory, theoretical skepticism, or distortion or, on the other hand, a perspective "outside" and distorting and artificially "screening" such experiences – is not exhaustive or persuasive. But this "screen" theory already seems far too historicist for Strauss's own purposes. If there is such a screen that decisively prohibits our ability now to appreciate or even to imagine successfully the point of view of the participant-citizen, there is no reason given to believe that the insights of classical texts will not be just as "screened" for us in just the same way as the political things themselves, no reason why we will not be bound to treat them as early versions of us, the spectator social

[29] NRH, 79–80.
[30] WIPP, 24–25. See also CM, 10–12.
[31] PL.
[32] WIPP, 27–8.

scientists. And Strauss nowhere argues that the idiosyncrasies of Greek accounts of political life, the application of unusual terms, such as *kalos*, the *polis*, the gods, and so forth, are not likewise also "screens," mediations like Athenian, Cretan, or Spartan. He nowhere shows that they should rather count as expressive of an original experience. Not to mention that Strauss himself in some contexts seems to suggest that this putative historical distortion is irrelevant in the face of the "simple experiences of right and wrong" captured in the two epigrams that begin NRH. The citations seem to be saying, contrary to what seems to be the thesis of the book, that even without the recovery of ancient texts, it is manifestly obvious that the rich man's deed is an evil one and that Naboth is virtuous in resisting the temptations of self-interest and in keeping faith with the Lord. But if we do not need the classical renaissance that Strauss encourages, what is the point of NRH? (Strauss's acroamatic teaching could be that it is the very appearance of self-sufficiency and obviousness in these passages that evinces the darker side or limitations of the natural attitude, with its corresponding presupposition that philosophy is dangerous and corrupting and perhaps, worst of all, unnecessary. Strauss claims that "striving for knowledge of the eternal truth is the ultimate end of man" and therefore that "justice and moral virtue can be fully legitimated *only* by the fact that they are required for the sake of that ultimate end, or that they are the conditions of the philosophic life."[33] But none of this has anything to do with how we "ordinarily" recoil from the act of the rich man or affirm Naboth's fidelity to the law. Strauss, like Plato, never forgets that it was in the name of *ordinary* piety that Socrates was executed. This means that Strauss is obviously aware that he is playing a dangerous double game, calling for a recollection of a form of life potentially quite hostile to philosophy, *the* human perfection. Or such ordinary experience is both the natural home of natural right and, paradoxically, a cave. And adding to the perplexity, Plato's cave image does not suggest any natural way or internal dialectic from the cave to enlightenment; just the opposite.[34] These would all obviously be topics for several additional papers.)

---

[33] NRH, 151.
[34] This cannot be the complete story, of course. For one thing, there are the other images, especially the Divided Line, which suggests that *eikasia* functions naturally in calling attention to images as such and so prompting a journey toward originals. For another, it is indisputable that for the Straussian Plato, the great deficiency of life in the cave is not intellectual but erotic. Life there does not satisfy the deepest human desires, visible only in a few human exemplars. I am much indebted to Richard Velkley for correspondence and for his suggestions about these issues.

Also, it may be that it is just here that the relevance of Straussian hermeneutics is so crucial, that we must understand the "forgotten" art of writing in order to engage in this recovery properly and avoid the objection just stated. This would also be a large and independent topic, but the central difficulty in such an appeal is obvious. On Strauss's premises, the same problems would arise in our being able to recover such an art, as in recovering what we putatively need the art to recover.

## V. Addressing Decent Men

We are now in a position to contrast the competing diagnostic claims: On the one hand, we have the claim that modern culture, let us say, in its practices, politics, assumptions, natural science, skepticism, and denial of transcendence, is rational, the realization of the philosophical fate of humanity. Since I share Strauss's skepticism that this realization could be a matter simply of the application of a methodology, I have been treating such a claim as paradigmatically presented in Hegel's account of historical rationality, that modern culture should be treated as a rational outcome of the experienced insufficiencies, even tragic failings of premodern forms of life. This means exactly what it seems to mean in Hegel: a great subordination of the roles of art and religion in modern life (they both have become essentially "things of the past") and a defense of what Hegel himself frequently calls the "prosaic" character of modern bourgeois life, the unheroic life of nuclear families, civil society, market economies, and representational democracies. Modernity is our unavoidable philosophical fate, and its fate is, at least in essentials, the rational realization of freedom.

Although this is not the "historicist" experience directly treated by Strauss, even the Hegelian invocation of reason would not allow escape from the accusation that such a putative "rationalization" of social and political life in modernity is another distortion of and distance from the ordinary experiences without which the practically necessary appeal to natural right fails.

On the other hand, there is the "screen" or distortion claim of Strauss (and Heidegger) that paradigmatic modern experiences and assumptions arise from, depend essentially on, artificial human constructs that block any genuinely human, original, natural, participant experience of the human. A typically modern experience (presumably the sort described in modern novels, drama, and poetry, as well as in philosophy) is already the expression of a misunderstanding, a distortion of something more original, fundamental, and genuinely revelatory – the experience of distinctions of value (or of being qua being, in Heidegger's narrative). Over and over again Strauss insists that this latter ordinary experience of value is the true basis of the claim of natural right, an intuitive sense of nobility and baseness, high and low, right and wrong that modern philosophy can claim does not exist because modern philosophy has systematically covered it over.

At this point, however, we are prevented from investigating any further such an appeal to prereflective, ordinary lived experience as a *philosophical claim* by the following qualification that Strauss makes in his essay "On Classical Political Philosophy." After noting that classical political philosophy "started from the moral distinctions as they are made in everyday life,"[35] he then introduces a crucial limitation in any philosophical expectations of classical political philosophy. Such a philosophy, he notes, "limited itself to addressing men who, because of their natural inclinations as well as their upbringing, took those distinctions for granted." Or "The political teaching of the classical philosophers, as distinguished from their theoretical teaching, was primarily addressed not to all intelligent men, but to all decent men."[36]

Now Strauss goes on in this essay to admit that once a genuine philosopher enters the inevitable debate about value to which common opinion gives rise, his response will look finally "absurd" or "ridiculous" because he will come to realize and to claim that "the ultimate aim of political life cannot be reached by political life, but only by a life devoted to contemplation, to philosophy."[37] But these original limitations on any philosophical treatment of value – limitations already visible in Strauss's parsing of "political philosophy" not as philosophy about the political things but as about the political mission of philosophy – in effect slam the door on any further philosophical treatment of the debate posed above: "modernity (i.e., understood as what is reflected in basic, orienting experiences of the human world) as rational" versus such modern experience as "distorting." For Strauss is conceding that these putatively original, fundamental experiences of noble/base distinctions and the like require specific conditions that cannot themselves be the subject of philosophical debate and are certainly not results of philosophically

---

[35] In WIPP, 89: "[A]lthough it knew better than the dogmatic skeptic of our own time the formidable theoretical objections to which they are exposed."

[36] OCP, 89.

[37] OCP, 91.

informed political action. These conditions are natural and social (matters of "upbringing"), and one can authoritatively *claim* that they are the true and proper conditions only if one already takes one's bearings from the "simple" or "natural" experiences that are prior to and so the conditions of any further philosophical reflection on value. Without the natural dispositions and upbringing, one will not be able to appreciate such distinctions, and the whole point of Strauss's treatment of classical natural right has been to show that these distinctions cannot be regarded as conclusions of a systematic philosophical account or deduction or policy. You either see it or you do not, and if you do not, there is no way of "*arguing* you into seeing it," part of the indirect point, presumably, of the so-called Socratic and aporetic dialogues.[38]

This last is in some sense a valuable, true point, and I do not want to dispute it. But we should note first that it was precisely this awareness – that our ethical life is woven deeply and in microscopic detail into the web of our lives as a whole and is not a matter of "isolatable" obligation to law or a coordination problem among egoists nor even responsive directly to philosophical critique – that began the so-called conservative reaction to revolutionary politics that, according to Strauss, terminated catastrophically in Hegelian historicism. All we need add to generate that sort of historicist conclusion is something Strauss obviously also accepts: that such dispositions and social conditions change and that they change radically, on matters as fundamental as what it is to be a man or a woman, what is slavery, child labor, and so forth. That claim, together with the denial earlier that the ancient Greek version of such prereflective conditions has any privileged status, will locate such original and all-important bases for moral life in time, and in time essentially, and that will make Strauss's case for, as opposed to his analysis of, the claims of classical natural right fairly weak.

Moreover, since Strauss is admitting that identifying those who have or can have this natural experience establishes nothing philosophically, merely classifies those who already experience the world in these terms

---

[38] And here again one must note that one could read Strauss's narrative as suggesting indirectly and cautiously that what philosophical attention to such experiences helps to reveal is finally that there is only one "natural right," one human activity good by nature, philosophy, even though *this* would never be conceded by the man of healthy common sense. This suggests that what Strauss wants is some revival of the ordinary, natural sense of hostility to philosophy. And just *how* the original recovery would then also lead to a transcendence of the ordinary view that its moral bearings are in order and unassailable is not clear in Strauss (at least not clear to me).

and distinguishes those who do not (and, given their upbringing, most likely cannot), what sort of answer is being provided to those who might admit the existential need of natural right but who are not aided in realizing such a need by being pointed to a community in which such a need was, luckily for them, satisfied? Most of NRH tries to establish the disorienting, crisis-like, even nihilistic consequences of the modern rejection of natural right. That is supposed to be the philosophical or rational fate of such a rejection. But that just may *be* our fate. For the reasons just discussed, that just establishes such a need, and these invocations of ancient Greek experience cannot serve as the answer to Strauss's wise remark about truth quoted earlier. It is worth recalling:

> Even by proving that a certain view is indispensable in living well, one merely proves that the view in question is a salutary myth: one does not prove it to be true. Utility and truth are two entirely different things.[39]

And we should be clear here about the complexity of Strauss's position, a complexity that his "screen" metaphors can often disguise. He is not saying that Greek political experience was in some way in direct contact with human nature, the ideas of the virtues, and so forth, and so the record of such experience in classical political philosophy can guide us back to those originals. The language of metaphysical originals and less-than-real images is wholly out of place here. (For one thing, there is no idea of the human soul, no idea of eros. There *is* only experience as a touchstone here.)

Let me put it another way. It is clear enough from much of what Strauss writes, especially about the Platonic ideas, that he regards an engagement with certain fundamental problems as unavoidable in any worthy human life, that he regards those problems as permanent and coeval with human thought itself, and that the absence of such engagement in much modern thought and even modern experience is not proof against this claim. This is why the image of forgetting is so important; it allows him to say that such nonpresence requires not recreation (perhaps arbitrarily and just as a response to a need) but remembering. It also explains some of the attraction of at least Heidegger's way of framing the issues, because it is obviously a consequence of Strauss's "coeval" claim that he must say, with Heidegger, that we are not, or not yet again, "thinking."

---

[39] NRH, 6.

## VI. The Natural Attitude as the "Way of Despair"

I have been suggesting that the claim about "original" and "distortion" is very difficult to defend with any consistency. The attempt at such a distinction has raised a number of questions about Strauss's position, which I summarize here in the simplest terms possible.

(1) If natural right is *constituted* by a certain sort of experience and if that experience has been lost or forgotten, what status can the claim of natural right possibly have now?[40]

(2) If the epigrams in NRH call to any reader's mind the "simple experiences" of right and wrong that form the starting point of classical political thought, why do we need such a complex historical recovery?

(3) Why should we be struggling to get from one cave to another; why recover the ordinary if the ordinary looks as it does in Plato's *Republic?* Are there better and worse caves? Isn't one sort of darkness like any other sort?

(4) If we, as moderns, are now "screened" from ordinary experience, why wouldn't we be just as "screened" from any deep understanding of the texts that manifest and analyze such experience?

---

[40] I note here, in response to an interesting suggestion made by Nathan Tarcov, that it is theoretically open to Strauss to make much less of the ancients-moderns contrast, to treat it as a matter of rhetorical and pedagogical usefulness, and to insist that our own experience, however fraught with a kind of forgetfulness and willfulness, still does manifest somehow "the claims of natural right" on any experiencer, that a kind of phenomenology of modern life can lay bare in some way what has not been, perhaps cannot wholly be, forgotten. (Something like this is, in essence, Stanley Rosen's emendation of Strauss. See Rosen 1987, 128). I would note here only (1) that this is quite an extreme correction of Strauss's original position and means we will also have to discount the image he used so frequently to describe modern fate, a cave beneath the Platonic cave. I take it that the whole point of that image is to contest the possibility of any such depth phenomenology, and it is not clear to me what, if anything, is left of Strauss's actual position after such a correction. (See esp. PAW, 155–7; CCM, 106–7, 109, 114; see esp. such typical passages as OT, 177, where Strauss makes clear why we are "forced" to attempt a "restoration of classical social science." Not to mention the passage quoted above at NRH, 79–80, where Strauss clearly says that to recover this ordinary experience, one "has to go back" to the ancients, indeed to the "ancient" ancients. I see no indication that he believes we have a choice: either such a restoration or a recollection called forth out of present-day experience.) (2) It is not immediately clear how much, and what sort of detail, can be defended by appeal to such a historical phenomenology. Perhaps an aspiration to be rescued from a confusing relativism, a yearning for some secure distinction between the noble and the base? At best, these would be aspirations and hopes, not answers. I note again Strauss's powerful rejection of philosophy as wishful thinking, at NRH, 6.

(5) It appears (with Strauss's remarks about "decent men") that the only persons who could appreciate the recovered experience are just those who do not need to. What, then, would be the point of the recovery?

These all amount to internal problems suggested by tensions in Strauss's texts. I turn in conclusion to what I take to be the main substantial, philosophical obstacle to recovering or to being able to trust any such putative original experience. This objection is based on sweeping theoretical claims inaugurated by Kant and Hegel. In Hegel's language, modern life has itself become thoroughly "reflective," the first part of what he means in claiming that it is becoming potentially "rational." We assume the roles we occupy, respond to moral claims as we do, in a way now much more self-consciously aware of it being our way, among other possible ways. Such roles are *assumed*, not just *inhabited*, and since we are aware that they are not roles shared by other times and places, we understand that the authority and legitimacy claims inherent in such roles require some justification beyond their *being* our way. To put the point in another way: An enduring, continuous human life is not an event or occurrence, a happening, like others. Lives do not just happen; they must be actively led, steered, guided, which we now, for the first time, fully appreciate. A subject must not only "take up the reins" of a life in order to do this but must do so continuously and with an eye toward the unity and integration without which lives cannot be coherently led. Where there is such unity and integration, it is a result of our work and not a discovery of an underlying human nature. Moreover, leading a life in this way is reflexive because it always involves actively taking a point of view or stand on some relevant event or person or state in the world, and this in an always challengeable and potentially revisable way. If this were not so, any "ordinary" point of view could not be said to be *ours*, to be something for which we were responsible, which we had to "stand behind." (We would not then merit the respect we are entitled to as responsible subjects.) After the Kantian turn, all human experience had to be understood as essentially a judging, a *result*, a holding to be true, a claim to which I commit myself, to which I am not committed otherwise, for which I implicitly pledge a defense, and so forth. In the much more radical (Kierkegaardean) language developed by Heidegger and Sartre to make this point, one *is* a subject (does not flee such an unavoidable self-responsible stance in bad faith or inauthenticity) only by not simply *being* a subject or *being* an anything, even while one is not some free-floating mere possibility, not nothing at all.

It is this reflective character of experience that made all ordinary experience forever afterward seem extraordinarily suffused with what Hegel called "negativity" (an activity or even one's own self possibly not being what it seemed), a question for further questions, rather than an unexplained explainer. In Hegel's *Phenomenology* language, "Consciousness, however, is explicitly the concept [*Begriff*] of itself"[41] and just therein "the pathway of doubt . . . the way of despair" (49). That is, "consciousness goes beyond limits, and since these limits are its own, it is something that goes beyond itself. . . . Thus consciousness suffers this violence at its own hands; it spoils its own limited satisfaction."[42] The only way such dimensions of experience could possibly be avoided would be by a kind of "active forgetting" (which Nietzsche once recommended as a cure for modern homesickness) and not by a remembering of more innocent (or "natural" or undistorted, unscreened) times. (Or, in a claim Hegel shares with Rousseau and Kant, we must lose this naturalness in order to reclaim a form of the everyday as our own. The fall is the greatest human boon, and while a distinctly human existence is a self-inflicted "wound," it is a wound that we can heal, even "without scars."[43])

In saying this, it must be stressed that Hegel, like Strauss (and, for that matter, like Burke, Oakeshott, Heidegger, Gadamer, Wittgenstein, Cavell, and Bernard Williams), rejects the idea of a philosophical enlightenment of and so intervention in the ordinary way of going on, and none of these "friends of the ordinary" think that the everyday can be appealed to as a ground or truth maker, as a component in an *argument* about anything. That would be to miss the whole point.[44] And indeed on one reading of Strauss, to appreciate the genuinely pretheoretical experience is to be able again to appreciate it as a cave, precisely as unenlightenable, and this renewed appreciation would be wholly philosophic, would not involve any change in our ways of going on.

But Hegel is stressing something that many in this club do not: that the ordinary ordinarily tears itself apart, that whole forms of life come to fail catastrophically, to fail to sustain allegiance, can come to seem

---

[41] Hegel, PhS, 51.
[42] This was a major component of Hegel's thinking from early in his Jena days and is given fine expression in D.
[43] Hegel, A, 98.
[44] This is especially true of the complex position defended by Stanley Cavell. I do not claim that anything said here yet bears on his position, one very different from Strauss's, but I would note that there is something different in simply living out the ordinary and feeling some need to call it to mind. That is already something extraordinary.

alien, to lose meaning, often as a result of the skepticism, alienation, the interweaving of self-consciousness, even "everyday" aspects of reflection, all present in everyday sensibilities, and so forth. Hegel is not willing to write off so much of that "tearing apart" as something like a storm or other disturbance. (As the quotations above indicate, he thinks it is something we do to ourselves, and this purposively, rather than merely suffer.) He wants to know whether such breaking down and rebuilding make any kind of sense not, he admits, in and for a life but, as he often says, "after" it, for the "priestly sect" of philosophers. At the simplest and so most misleading level, we can see a clash of images in these accounts of failure and rebuilding: one, Hegel's, invoking some greater self-consciousness and explicitness about our normative "self-legislation," and another, Strauss's, invoking a transformed Heideggerean figure, forgetting, forgetting especially the genuinely human scale, and thereby subject to various slippery slopes and dangerous blind spots once a skepticism about and dissatisfaction with ordinary, always available, prudential wisdom seizes the imagination of the West. (We "tear ourselves apart" for Strauss, too, in other words, but because we in essence do not know what we are doing, not, as in Hegel, because, more and more gradually, we do.)

This is much too large a topic to allow any persuasive defense, but I am trying to stress that the issue at stake does not turn on something as obvious as the great varieties of very different, incompatible historical experiences, something taken for granted by intelligent commentators at least since Herodotus. The Hegelian claim at issue – that the transition in the Western language (and "experience") of self-understanding from roughly "soul" to the "self," or a distinct subject of experience that *cannot* be understood as an object of any sort – seems to capture a wholly different experience of ourselves, not anticipated in antiquity and one that casts doubt on any general appeal to the ancient ordinary. (Any pretheoretical experience would be prereflexive and, if so, not ours, not attributable in the relevant sense to us.)

This idea that consciousness could be in some sort of constant "negative relation to itself" helps us to conceptualize a wide panoply of phenomenological data characteristic of the distinctness of modernity and visible in much modern philosophy and literature, not to mention media such as film. (The experience in question is also very different from the "Socratic" sense that many of our beliefs might be false. It is closer to the slow realization that there is nothing in the world that makes our beliefs about "oughts" or norms true, that sustaining a commitment does not look like finding such a truth maker, even while we cannot give up such normative bindingness.) The nature of a free life could be reformulated on such an understanding, could be said now not to consist in substantive knowledge of the eternal and the proper human place within it or in a spontaneous causal power, but in the proper, new sort of relation to oneself, something that must be achieved and, according to Hegel, only also in relation to others.

This is, in my view, the real philosophical issue at stake in what Strauss calls the "second wave" or Rousseauean stage of modernity (although it is never discussed in these terms, as the problem of autonomy, by Strauss),[45] and it involves the most ambitious philosophical claim of all modernity: that the source of all normative necessity is self-legislating spontaneity or freedom, a claim that presumes the negative or reflective notion of subjectivity that we discussed above. A treatment of this question would be necessary before we could know an answer to a very important question (an answer to what would be Strauss's obvious skepticism): whether this emphasis on self-legislation could preserve a robust notion of *law*, "real" normative force, or whether we have begun to slide down another slippery slope, from spontaneity to the creative imagination to the will to power to resolute deciding.[46] (And in Platonic terms, the most difficult question would arise: whether, at the most fundamental level, human eros, a yearning for completeness and totality, for some "ultimate" sense, for what Strauss calls "eternity," could be said to be satisfied by such a human, self-legislating whole. And what follows if it is not?)

In these terms, the question of whether some fundamental element of the modern philosophical tradition is fated – philosophically fated – for a nihilistic culmination is directly addressed only if we can formulate a response to this question about the relation between spontaneity and law, rational freedom and normative necessity. This is the doctrine that in post-Kantian Idealism renders unavailable the ordinary as normatively sufficient. The ordinary, like everything else in human experience is, in Sellar's famous phrase, "fraught with ought," and there are no original, natural oughts; they are always, in the language developed here, results,

---

[45] Cf. Pippin 1997g.

[46] In the words of Stanley Rosen, the question is whether "freedom begins its long decay in what one could call historical libertinism. Post-Kantianism is the story of that long decay" (1999, 165). In this case, I think the Kant to Nietzsche to Heidegger progression is adventitious, not logical or internal. What Nietzsche "took" from the Kantian and Hegelian notion of spontaneity and transformed into or revealed as will to power was not what was "there" in Kant and Hegel. In other words, Nietzsche planted the bomb he then exploded.

commitments. In Hegel's language, such experience is always a manifestation of the "labor of the Concept," more an epiphenomenon of such work, than an "original basis for assessing." This is the heart of the claim that there is no *prereflective* or natural human experience of the human; there is rather only the *implicitly reflective*, already "negative," not yet fully explicitly reflective human experience, if it is to count as human.[47] The counter-Straussian claim is that even the most ordinary of lives has to be understood as a complex of commitments, not mere habits of heart and mind, and that on the modern understanding of freedom (or the post-Kantian) these must ultimately be redeemable by reason in some way for them to be ours, for us to be able to stand behind them, even for them to count for us as significant.

If it is true that we cannot be said to inhabit, embody, be wholly absorbed in a natural attitude, but that such an attitude is even "originally" reflexive and thereby self-negating, always potentially destabilized and disorienting, then philosophers do not either "look farther afield in the same direction as the enlightened citizen or statesman" by also inhabiting and extending the participant point of view *or* stand outside the practical world and explain its motions from a third-person point of view. Philosophy should rather be understood as rendering explicit the original *self*-transformation of the natural attitude into what it always is, implicitly: more than natural by being a *second* nature; therefore itself by being "beyond itself." Strauss claimed that classical political philosophers did not "look at political things from the outside, as spectators of political life"[48] in the way that, he charges, all modern political philosophy did. I have been trying to suggest that this is not an exhaustive disjunction when applied to certain strains of modern philosophy, but this for an unusual reason. From the point of view I have been trying to suggest, there is no such "outside versus inside" duality. Or said in Hegel's dialectical way, everything inside always already has *its own* "outside." And, perhaps more important for the spectatorial, theoretical attitude that Strauss is worried about: vice-versa. Every "outside" already has its "inside," is an expression of a form of life, a "shape of spirit." Philosophy is and is nothing but its own time comprehended in thought.

---

[47] The first argument of the *Phenomenology of Spirit* is a denial, a reduction to (determinate) absurdity, of the claim that there can be a prereflective acquaintance with the world.

[48] WIPP, 27–8.

# 7

# Hannah Arendt and the Bourgeois Origins
# of Totalitarian Evil

## I

In modern philosophy, "the problem of evil" has become less and less the theological or theodicy problem, "justifying the ways of God to man." It can appear in that form, of course, in Leibniz, to some extent in Kant, in a revised form in Hegel, and in Marx. And it can assume different but still very similar forms – not as a straightforward question of reconciling God's goodness with the created world in which the innocent suffer but as a problem about the "meaning" of the world as such. The "Grand Inquisitor" passage in Dostoyevsky's *The Brothers Karamazov* has become a *locus classicus* for this version of the problem: Could I ever be "at home" in a world with so much evil? What does it *mean* that there is such evil, or could one ever make sense of the brutal persistence of such events in human history? What sort of burden is it (if it is) to live a life permanently unreconciled to or alienated from such a hostile world, if no such sense can be made? And so forth. But for the most part, the philosophical problem is now more restricted and even prior to such worries. There are two dimensions to "the modern problem of evil," once the question of "natural evil" for the most part gave way to the problem of moral evil, the evil acts human beings commit. (1) Does the concept of evil really pick out anything in the human world? On what authority do we invoke it and condemn by so invoking it? (2) If there is such authority, can we "account" for such evil, understand why someone chooses to commit an evil deed with indifference to the claims of the good and the right or even with complete acceptance of, embrace of, their perfidious nature?

As the traditional story goes, we make sense of someone else's deed by first understanding how it made sense for him or her, and that means understanding which reasons they had for doing what they did, and that means understanding in what sense they thought one course of action was more justifiable than another (justifiable even if in a restricted or relativized sense). And this account is often supplemented by the realization that at this point we might also need to invoke objective historical, sociological, or anthropological factors to account for why some sort of consideration would be experienced as decisive then and there.[1]

This second set of issues has, especially since the end of World War II, come to seem to many mysterious or to raise painfully unresolvable questions, even to lie on the other side of the limits of human sense making in general. This sentiment is perhaps most associated with Adorno, who, in the last section of *Negative Dialectics* ("Meditations on Metaphysics") suggested several times that the very attempt to comprehend the evil of the Holocaust was something like an act of obscenity, a betrayal of the magnitude and horror of the victims' suffering.[2] (Lyotard's comparison of the Holocaust with an earthquake that destroyed not only lives and buildings but also any instruments with which it might be measured is also apposite.)[3]

Hannah Arendt has no common cause with such "mystifiers" and is in some sense famously on the exact opposite extreme. But her notorious claim about the "banality" of evil in *Eichmann in Jerusalem* (and the all-too-human origins of such evil in "thoughtlessness") must be read together with a much fuller, more historically detailed attempt to make sense of such total or totalitarian evil in her earlier book, *The Origins of Totalitarianism*. In that treatment, there is a two-stage "account" of the sense of such barbarity. On the first level there is a recognizable, straightforward

---

[1] This familiar "rationalizing" account is given an exceptionally clear treatment in Williams 2002, chap. 10.

[2] There are, of course, many well-known versions of this reticence: that a respectful, horrified silence is the only civilized response to such deeds, that no poetry could be written after Auschwitz, and so on. While it can fairly be said that Adorno's main theoretical project was to develop an account of intelligibility and its limits that could do justice to this failure to understand (and so to develop a notion of an exclusively negative dialectic), the full implications of regarding any human deed as in principle unintelligible (not subject to our conceptual ordering requirements, however one wants to put it) were not fully addressed by him.

[3] As cited in Neiman 2002, 251.

claim about origins. It relies not on some nomological notion of explanation, but instead on the intentionalist and contextual, common-sense approach we noted above. Once put into the right historical and social context, discussed in terms of the motivations and aversions that would develop in such contexts, the sense of such acts, why they would have occurred there and then, begins to come into focus. Then there is another more ambitious level as she draws some conclusions about what such an explanation says about the human condition. What turned out to be missing in such contexts were, she asserted, aspects of human life essential for any affirmable human existence.

I want, however briefly, to discuss both aspects of her case. Her answer to the first seems to me astonishingly sweeping but expressive of powerful currents in later modern thought that we have not yet come to terms with well. I disagree with her answer to the second set of questions and want to argue that she introduces a somewhat arbitrary theological dimension into what had been an admirably (as far as I am concerned) secular narrative.

## II

Hannah Arendt's *The Origins of Totalitarianism* is one of those books that reads better backward rather than forward. Only when one has come to appreciate her thesis about the nature of totalitarian movements and regimes, advanced in the third part, is one in a position to appreciate what the questions are that the first two parts – on anti-Semitism and imperialism – are trying to answer. It turns out that that question is a very difficult one because her thesis in the third part is so bold and in many ways so unsettling. For she argues, famously and now quite influentially, that twentieth-century totalitarianism is a unique form of political evil, absolutely unprecedented in history and completely unanticipated in any political philosophy. She considers her analysis in this section (rightly, in my view), to be groundbreaking and fundamental at the level of her model, Montesquieu. To his list of republic, monarchy, and despotism, she argued that we must, sadly, add another, new, fundamental type of regime: totalitarianism.

Second, once we appreciate why the categories of single-party rule, dictatorship, fascism, and even the most sweeping and most ancient concept of political evil – tyranny – are inadequate, we also have to face the fact that these unique totalitarian movements grew out of, were responses to, social and political experiences in relatively literate, technologically advanced civilizations and that these regimes were nevertheless capable of things never dreamed of by even the most hard-headed and realistic of modern political prophets, even men such as Machiavelli (famously referred to by one historian of politics as "the teacher of evil") and Hobbes. If this is so, and our traditional descriptive and normative categories are inadequate, then a whole set of issues needs to be reframed and rethought if we are to get close to the question of the "origins" of this new type of regime and evil in these unprecedented experiences. She presents an interesting list in describing the historical situation: the collapse of the nation-state (or the seizure of the state by the nation), the consequent spread of anti-Semitism (the impossibility of either integrating or ignoring culturally and economically important European Jewry into such thoroughly nationalized states), the linking of Europe's economic fate with imperialism – eventually, unavoidably, a race-based imperialism – the creation of large masses of stateless and finally, in her words, "superfluous" peoples as a consequent of ethnic nationalism, and the intra-European imperialism it spawned, the "breakdown of the class system" as a source of social identity in Europe and so the creation of an atomized mass of desocialized individuals, for the first time addressable and manipulable as a single amorphous "mass."

So for Arendt, as noted already, this historical evil is, while unique and unprecedented, certainly not in some fundamental way mysterious, signaling à la Adorno the limits of intelligibility as such. Indeed, the task she clearly sets herself is precisely to render the phenomenon intelligible, to include it in a historical narrative of the genesis of a new human condition, all without such an explanation rendering the phenomenon too familiar or expectable or unavoidable (it is, after all, new, unprecedented) and certainly without rendering it in some way excusable.

Her most evocative and poetic descriptions of this new human condition portray it as burdened with an intolerable loneliness, as having lost something like the "love of the world," the artificial human world of civilization. (She shares here her teacher Heidegger's epochal warning that human beings can lose, perhaps forever, the characteristic that makes them distinctly human, that these characteristics are not natural, species characteristics but fragile achievements that have to be tended and nurtured.) These unprecedented experiences are also what prompt her urgent call in the 1950 Preface for "a new political principle," a "new law on earth" necessary now because "human dignity needs a new guarantee" (OT, ix).

Third, this explanatory task – an explanation that would connect these novel experiences with totalitarian regimes – will be difficult because any sort of historical phenomenology of such "experiences" does not consist of simple (or even complicated) empirical questions, and Arendt's claims to account for "origins" is not causal in the sense we might expect from a sociological or economic analysis. It is, as just noted, contextual, and seems to appeal to something as elusive as it is indispensable – something like the "logic of historical life" – how a certain style of political oratory, a certain appeal to violence, a certain indifference to pragmatic issues, a certain invocation of nature or history or especially race would come to *mean* what it did to audiences in a certain context at a certain time (and ultimately come to provide them with reasons sufficient to account for their actions).

There are thus both methodological and concrete questions that arise immediately in an account such as Arendt's. There is no prolegomena about method or goals in the book. We just plunge in and must figure out on the fly just what a question about "origins" is about, given that it is obviously not a causal or even empirical question. (One of her scattered meta-level formulations in a later discussion is that the study would be "a historical account of elements which crystallized into totalitarianism.")[4] Moreover, Arendt herself seemed to realize that large elements of her analysis fit the case of Nazi Germany much better than the Soviet Union, and there has been voluminous criticism of her on this point. One can almost sense her reminding herself to add a couple of sentences about the Bolsheviks at the end of several paragraphs about the Nazis. To make her thesis work, she has to claim that the Soviet Union was a totalitarian regime only after the early 1930s and until Stalin's death and that Stalin in effect had to create the conditions of his own origin: "Stalin had first to create artificially that atomized society which had been prepared for the Nazis in Germany by history and circumstances" (318). (To be fair, her analysis of the *nature* of the totalitarian state fits Stalinism quite well, but the etiological account seems off-base for, essentially, a coup d'état in a largely preindustrial society. And it is hard to see how Stalinist totalitarianism could be understood as in any way a *product* of mass society.)[5]

---

[4] R, 78. Arendt also uses the "crystallization" image in OT, the "Preface to the First Part of Origins," xv. In the "Reply" (to Voeglin), she admits that the book "does not really deal with the 'origins' of totalitarianism – as its title unfortunately claims," and she stresses that "the elementary structure of totalitarianism is the hidden structure of the book."

[5] Cf. 378. It is not easy to connect pan-Slavism with Leninism, either.

## III

Given the book's structure and the questions that structure generates, I need first to engage in some brief exposition about the part of her thesis that I find the most compelling – the claim about the uniqueness of totalitarianism – then attempt to characterize her basic thesis about "origins," and then finally offer some reflections about it. My main point in doing so is to a large extent simply to register a measure of astonishment at the radicality and sweep of that thesis and then to offer some demurrals. For there is a target coming ever more into view as Arendt wends her way through the Dreyfus affair and the Protocols of the Elders of Zion and the Boers and Cecil Rhodes and "intra-European imperialism" and tries to find the culprit in her dramatic and often depressing narrative. And that target is not found in the specific national histories of Germany or Russia, nor in the well-documented mass German resentment against the terms of the Versailles treaty, nor tied to the evil genius of Hitler or Stalin as individuals nor to their charismatic power, nor found in the massive economic chaos of post-Weimar Germany. It is, astonishingly, *bourgeois modernity* itself that we find holding the smoking gun. Of course, there is a well-known neo-Marxist thesis that connects fascism with the late stages of capitalism and that thus portrays that distinct sort of evil as due to something like the logic of this degenerating or "contradictory" form of life, almost as if a natural pathology. But Arendt shares so few premises with such a mode of analysis that I think we should be astonished that *this* protagonist should shoulder so much of the blame.

Consider first the uniqueness claim, and we can then work our way back to the issue of what can only be called Arendt's virulent contempt for the bourgeoisie.[6]

According to Arendt, totalitarian regimes are not just more extreme, cold-blooded, or technologically more powerful versions of despotisms, dictatorships, one-party rulers, or tyrannies. They differ essentially, in kind. The main qualitative difference, manifested in several different totalitarian phenomena, is a largely negative one: the absence of the usual "utilitarian" logic of strategic action, with its commitment to the most efficient means for the achievement of a definite and desirable end, even if it is an end or goal that we would regard as immoral or heinous, such as the pleasure of the tyrant. For one thing, a totalitarian

---

[6] For a good discussion of the differences between Arendt's account and the "traditional" accounts of twentieth-century totalitarianism, see the helpful essay by Canovan (2000).

regime is not a rule by a clique, out for its own self-interest, the most obvious sort of goal one might want to attribute to a violent, lawless regime. There *are*, of course, such lawless, tyrannical regimes in modernity, and we know of some in recent history (Duvalier in Haiti, Idi Amin in Uganda, Saddam Hussein in Iraq), and there are clearly also hybrid cases, especially in Eastern Europe in the twentieth century (such as Ceausescu in Romania), cases where an individual or gang seizes control of the totalitarian apparatus and continues to direct the secret police and maintains terror, but for the sake of their palaces and dachas and often with contempt for party philosophy, which they invoke only as a means or screen.

These cases complicate matters because for Arendt they no doubt manifest what she would regard as the end of totalitarian rule and the beginning of one-party or ruling-clique dictatorships. An economic logic and so a kind of caution and prudence will have entered the picture, and so a kind of predictability, and with that we lose the radical *totalization* of efforts, come what may, that characterizes the two regimes in question. Some aspects of appearances to foreign observers begin to matter; leaders do not want to go so far as to kill the goose that is laying their golden eggs, and so on. But with Germany after 1938 and in Stalin's Soviet Union from 1930 until his death, since neither profit nor power was the fundamental issue, then, as Arendt writes, "common sense trained in utilitarian thinking is helpless against this ideological supersense, since totalitarian regimes establish a functioning world of no-sense" (OT, 458). (One has to assume that this striking appeal to a "supersense" that is in reality a "no-sense" is an intentional paradox and, as discussed below, is meant to differentiate this species of evil from its most familiar relative in the post-Christian world, egoism. The extremity in question in extreme totalitarian evil cannot be accounted for simply by the ruthless indifference to the fate of others in the pursuit of one's interest. Hence the inapplicability of "tyranny.")

Arendt is definitely onto something here, and some of her words, given recent events, sound a chillingly accurate note, especially when she notes "[t]he inability of the non-totalitarian world to grasp a mentality which functions independently of all calculable action in terms of men and material, and is completely indifferent to national interest and the well-being of its people" (419). But there is already that tension in her account between "senselessness" and some "supersense," as in that very sentence just quoted. She can sometimes write as if totalitarian action is simply purposeless, a senseless hurricane swirl of violence, torture, terror, and destruction for their own sake, "an air of mad unreality" (445). But it is also important to remember that she does not doubt that the Nazis were quite serious about their ultimate purposes – the extermination of the Jews and world rule by the Aryan race – and they could be quite efficient about elements of these when they wanted to be. And "achieving a classless society" is not an empty or meaningless goal; it was certainly a goal taken deadly seriously by Stalin and his henchmen. But according to Arendt, as employed by totalitarians both are not "projects" in the usual sense, with debates possible about efficient means or much concern with what in any detail such end-states would amount to. The language is chiliastic, and the realization of the goal will clearly require several lifetimes. It therefore does not fit into the secular calculation that Hobbes paradigmatically introduced, where the worst calamity for any individual is death, and no good can be a good for me if I am not around to enjoy it. The point of proposing either totalitarian goal is to evoke an ultimate and "total" commitment to whatever the leader says is necessary now, as if the leader were the voice of destiny or fate, not someone proposing a policy, justified with reasons consistent with the secularism of bourgeois modernity. (Therein we already have a clue about the origins of such a totalitarian demand: in its sweeping *rejection* of the limitations of bourgeois modernity and in its assumption that a life without "meaning" might well seem a far worse fate than an early death.)

So, the point of totalitarian revolution itself is not simply to replace the leaders of state and civil society and army institutions with true believers who would then put into practice party ideas. The point was utterly to transform every such institution into an instrument of the party whose ideology had very little to do with policy details and much more to do with world domination, based on some iron law of necessity about either nature (racial struggle) or history (class struggle), all as infallibly interpreted by the leader. The specific details of ideological doctrine were nearly irrelevant, given this commitment to what Arendt called this "supersense." If the "total" transformation of society required, say, the arbitrary synthesis of right-wing blood and race nationalism with some sort of communal and worker solidarity, then "national socialism" was as fine a label as any other. If Russia was ludicrously unsuitable for a Marxist revolution, a vanguard theory could be created and implemented. What mattered was honesty about the ultimately unbreakable laws of nature or history and a willingness to throw oneself into a great cause, the success of which has more to do with the perpetuation of the great cause than some ultimate realization of a goal.

Further, the point of totalitarian regimes is not even the power and wealth of the *nation*. Germany itself was surprisingly insignificant to the Nazis, and the German population was even held in some contempt by its own leaders. The point is a vast, generations-long struggle for Aryan supremacy, and with such a goal strategic planning and careful calculation are irrelevant. Uncompromising commitment and dedication are again what matters, *especially if* some sacrifice is imprudent, unnecessary, or pointless. The more pointless and wasteful a sacrifice for the party, the greater the symbolic glory.

In keeping with this contempt for the give and take of strategic debate, the Nazi and Soviet systems were, Arendt writes, nonsystems, hardly smooth running machines (395). In her famous word, they were simply "shapeless." They did not even feel bound by their own legal precedent, the laws *they* had passed, and had no problem revoking and revising at will, as circumstances and their own interpretations changed rapidly.

Now here again, we seem to stray close to traditional categories. The ancient definition of tyranny was rule without law, for the sake of the benefit of one man or clique. But as we have seen, many Nazi policies were hardly designed for the security and well-being of the leaders, and nothing substantive replaced law as an institutional boundary of sorts in human interactions. In tyranny, what replaced law was to some extent, at least, the predictable benefits of the tyrant. Unless he or she was completely insane, you could figure out where the danger points were and avoid them, could figure out how to advance your own interests while escaping notice, and so on. You knew what mattered to the tyrant and knew he would leave you alone if you stayed well clear of any and all danger points. Not so in totalitarian regimes, where *only terror replaces law*.

This last is in many ways the most important point about this qualitative uniqueness claim. What characterizes totalitarian regimes above all is a kind of ultimate non-sense or abandonment of utilitarian thinking. With respect to the main means of governing, this means that terror was employed against one's own citizens – that is, violence, torture, intimidation, the full invasive array of secret police tactics – well *after* such a citizenry has been cowed into absolute, uncompromising compliance, in the absence of any threat to the regime. For the first time in history, people were characterized as enemies of that state with no regard at all to what they did or might do even with any microscopic possibility (cf. 322). They were tortured and killed simply because of who they were or even who some distant relation might have been. Jews, gypsies, the disabled, the mentally ill, homosexuals, and in Stalin's Soviet Union, intellectuals, teachers, writers, or even loyal party members who had been involved in a policy demanded by Stalin that was now deemed untimely could all, arbitrarily, at any moment, be labeled "objective" enemies of the movement in a way for which there was no defense or recourse, since the charge was not based on any claim of "subjective" guilt. These measures can be understood as serving not the goal of "the security of the regime in power," but rather the goal of "total domination" (422). As she explains, just as totalitarian claims to world rule can look like imperialist expansion but not be so, because the former really recognizes no difference between a home and a foreign country (domination is not desired for the sake of the home country), so the secret police in a despotic and a totalitarian regime can look very similar. But there is a crucial difference. The despot's secret police are searching out the secret thoughts of potential enemies, and they make heavy use of the age-old technique of secret police, provocation. A totalitarian secret police avoids the trouble of trapping someone in a guilty maneuver or presenting evidence of what he said. You are guilty if the state apparatus designates you as objectively guilty. Obviously, the secret police have immensely more power in such a regime.

## IV

Thus, life under such a regime was a life of complete, constant terror, and the result was exactly what the regime wanted: an internalization of the police's gaze and accusation, a constant internal self-monitoring and self-vigilance, a combination of selfless commitment and ever anxious uncertainty about whether such commitment was ever "enough."[7] But even this was of no use if you were Jewish, and it is with respect to the camps that Arendt makes her strongest claim to the uniqueness of totalitarian evil. Here she enters the domain of paradox again, both pointing to the gross disutility of the camps, the wasteful irrationality – especially at the end of the war in spending so many resources and so much rolling stock for the extermination camps – and yet also claiming that that "anti-utility is only apparent" (456). Rather, she claims, the camps "are more essential to the preservation of the regime's power than any of its other institutions" (ibid.).[8] This is not so for strategic reasons, as if they really

---

[7] Her account anticipates Foucault's famous analysis in *Discipline and Punish*. See esp. 325.

[8] Cf. PRD, where she claims that totalitarianism is genocide, but one undertaken systematically, "within the framework of a legal order" (187); quoted by Kateb 1983, 76.

believed that the Jews were potentially enemies in the military sense. (The attempt by the German historian Nolde to claim something like this is what started the bitter *Historikerstreit* in Germany, and one can understand why.) The camps, rather, if one can put it this way, allow the Nazi regime to fully manifest itself, to express almost without qualification "total domination," their vision of what total rule could be like. (The point of the policy and action is not purposive in the usual strategic sense, but expressive.) It is almost as if, Arendt seems to be suggesting, they needed to manifest *to themselves* their own seriousness about this totality. They wanted to create a fact; a fact that would put the lie to the bourgeois claim that rule such as this was "unrealistic," that such a total transformation of oppressor and oppressed was simply impossible, given "human nature." In one of the book's most chilling and compelling conclusions, Arendt argues that in this, at least, they succeeded: "[W]e have learned that the power of man is so great that he can really be what he wishes to be" (456).

These are the elements of her "uniqueness" claim that make the "origins" question so difficult. This abandonment of common sense, the appeal of a risky, dangerous, and especially total commitment, the absence of calculations of self-interest either for oneself or for the nation, the relative indifference to ideological depth or substance or even consistency or plausibility, the appeal instead to an ideology of fatality and necessity, denying not only the usefulness but the possibility of "creative action" by individuals in concert with others, the shapelessness and unsystematic, arbitrary and unpredictable nature of totalitarian rule, the totality and irrationality of terror as a method of administration (replacing law and the appeal to law), the concomitant use of the secret police and the unchallengeable category of "objective enemy," and finally the camps as at once an experiment in total domination and brutal evidence for the seriousness of Nazi faith in its possibility all create a very difficult *explicandum*.

And there are already controversies aplenty. I have already indicated that Arendt seems to waver on the role played by actual ideological content in the realization and self-maintenance of such regimes, as well as on the importance of a serious revolutionary goal. A biological racialism must have played a greater positive role in the appeal of Nazism than she discusses, and not just among the mob but among the masses. One would think that the totality of commitment on the point of a mass society to a single leader, the psychological infatuation with a charismatic personality might merit some more attention in discussions about uniqueness. And there are some things she mentions but does not develop, such as the unusual role played by hatred, resentment, and paranoia in all modern mass politics (including our own) or the role played by an enormous leap in the technology available for despotic rule. (Sometimes a great quantitative leap in despotic power such as this can itself amount to a qualitative difference.)

But many of these issues will lead us quickly into the "origins" side of things, so I turn there now, noting first that there are a number of different emphases and directions in her account, and I am not sure that they can all be made consistent. At points she describes events, such as the "breakdown" of class identity, the "destruction" of the nation-state, and the withering away of institutional boundaries, as if these events create gaps, breaks in the fence through which an ever-lurking animality (itself rendered more appealing by an ever-growing fatigue with the burdens of civilized humanity, responsibility, sociality) is ever ready to leap and is finally unleashed with the gamble of the German bourgeoisie mentioned earlier. (At one point, she speculates darkly on the possible attractions of totalitarianism not just to "mass man" but to "normal people around us," those who, she muses, experience a "growing incapacity to bear the burdens of modern life" and who might be quite attracted to a program that absolves them of individual responsibility (437)). This is all in keeping with the philosophical theme most identified with all of Hannah Arendt's work: her multivalent insistence on the autonomy and centrality of the political, on the priority of *citoyen* over *bourgeois*, her defense of republican virtue and constitutionalism, and her constant warning that this domain, since artificial, fragile, and requiring attentive tending, was at great threat of vanishing under the bourgeois onslaught in modernity. Much of her language in *The Origins of Totalitarianism*, especially her account of the camps, suggests this notion of barriers, fences, limits, and institutional mediations, without which we inevitably become the worst of beasts (without "politics"). This all culminates in one of the best passages in the book, in the "Ideology and Terror" chapter, when she notes that when "all human activities have been transformed into laboring," when any "relationship with the world as a human artifice is broken," *homo faber* becomes the *animal laborans* and anything is possible (475).

On the other hand, she often stresses not the failure of what would otherwise keep such insane attractions of animality at bay but the active, historically specific, and positive embrace of totalitarian ideology as if a consistent outcome or extension of the bourgeois apolitical world, its creation of "superfluous" because economically useless peoples, and of the pettiness, venality, and materialism of the bourgeois form of life, all prompting an eager (and ever smaller) leap into the Nazi abyss. This "consistent outcome view" is suggested by such amazing claims as "the bourgeois's political philosophy was always 'totalitarian'; it always assumed an identity of politics, economics, and society, in which political institutions served only as the façade for private interests" (336). It is hard to know what she could possibly mean here, since "the bourgeoisie" as a form of life also includes the modern romantic family, with partners chosen on the basis of love – a distinct experience of subjectivity or an "intimacy" with oneself unknown as such in prior eras – the family as a "haven in a heartless world," the refusal to treat children as property or as economic assets, and on and on.[9] The "bourgeois" creation of a rich private sphere is hardly exhausted by the desire to accumulate property and capital. The subject of bourgeois literature, more than anything else, by a factor of hundreds, is romantic love, not the totalization of economic life. What can she be talking about? At any rate, this is the repeated claim I want to focus on, but we also need the general context of her various claims about origins.

## V

As we have seen, for the most part, Arendt looks for her origins in the three decades from 1884 to 1914. This period looked like "the golden age of security" but in hindsight we now know that it was then that the

---

[9] Here and throughout Arendt refers to "the bourgeoisie" as if a collective agent in her narrative. This ought to give one pause, and a fuller account of her interpretation would have to take up in some detail what she could have meant by such a reference. In his indispensable 1982 book, Richard Hamilton distinguishes the empirical question of Who voted for Hitler? from the necessarily much more speculative question of Why did people vote for Hitler? Admittedly, Arendt is after some sort of answer to the second question. But it is obvious that we also need a solid answer to the former question first before we can proceed. As Hamilton shows in detail, the conventional view that the attraction of National Socialism (especially in the crucial last relatively free election in July 1932, when they won 37.3 percent, before the Nazis could mobilize their position to influence the vote (the March 1933 election with 43.9 percent)) was due to some sort of middle-class panic, or was a phenomenon largely limited to the petite bourgeoisie, is very misleading at best, simply false at worst. To try to come up with a common description for "the supporters of the NSDAP," when they ranged from Protestant farmers in middle Franconia excited by Nazi promises that they would forgive all debts to Jewish cattle traders to selected elements of the bourgeois elite, is extremely difficult, and generalizations are dangerous. Perhaps one should simply read "the bourgeoisie" in Arendt's accounts and in discussions of her interpretation as always in scare quotes, a placeholder for a further long qualification on the empirically establishable referents of that term.

storms were forming that would finally amount "to an almost complete break in the continuous flow of western history as we had known it for two thousand years" (123). This is the period when the unsteady balance between nation and state came unbalanced and when anti-Semitism grew and deepened its roots; it was the age of European imperialism, necessary and unavoidable for capitalist expansion but justified only by race thinking; and it marked "the political emancipation of the bourgeoisie." And these issues are all linked. While the modern nation-state relied on a common historical experience and tradition of the native speakers of one language, in a common geographical locality with a common sense of place and a linked fate, its claim to rule was based on its claim to be a genuine state, an independent political body, that is, on the universalist aspirations of the French revolution – the protection of the rights of man – and its claim to rule a class-divided society in a way independent of class interest, above and over such class struggles. Here is Arendt's most concise account of what happened next:

Only when the nation-state proved unfit to be the framework for the further growth of capitalist economy did the latent fight between state and society become openly a struggle for power. During the imperialist period neither the state nor the bourgeoisie won a decisive victory. Nationalist institutions resisted throughout the brutality and megalomania of imperialist ambitions, and the bourgeois attempts to use the state and its instruments of violence for its own economic purposes were always only half successful. This changed when the German bourgeoisie staked everything on the Hitler movement and aspired to rule with the help of the mob, but then it turned out to be too late. The bourgeoisie succeeded in destroying the nation-state but won a Pyrrhic victory; the mob proved quite capable of taking care of politics by itself and liquidated the bourgeoisie along with all other classes and institutions. (124)

The link with anti-Semitism is made by reference to the racialism that imperialist expansion required and especially to the changing social role of European Jews throughout the formation and disintegration of the modern nation-state.[10] This story, with its emphasis on the role of Jewish banking families in the early financing of the nation-state, when rulers could be above class struggle only by being beholden to no class, and then on the later redundancy of the Jews and resentment against

[10] I think that Kateb summarizes as well as anyone the relation between the first two parts and the third: "The real continuity between the earlier movements and totalitarianism is found in the readiness of European peoples to think in racist and imperialist categories, to accept the normality of, sympathize with, or embrace ardently such modes of response and half-thought" (Kateb 1983, 56).

them, as the bourgeoisie, which had been content in its indifference to all politics not directly tied to economic policy, came more and more to control (and finance) the modern political elite, is a rich story, but not the issue I would like to focus on here. The deepest issue, which Arendt links with anti-Semitism, imperialism, and nationalism all at once, is already visible in the long quotation just cited, with its emphasis on the eagerness of the bourgeoisie to "use the state and its instruments of violence for its economic purposes," and in her giving the bourgeoisie the central role in "destroying the nation state."

Such claims and several others that we examine below raise the question of the German bourgeoisie's dissatisfaction with the limits of politics as such ("the state") and what accounts for the intensity, almost the insane intensity, of this dissatisfaction, to the point of "staking all" on the Hitler movement. And it is here that Arendt proposes several explanations that recall again a Marxian strain not often prominent in her thinking, as she suggests an inevitable dynamic in any bourgeois society, destructive of an independent political community, godless, secular, materialist, and, especially, insatiable in its desire for wealth at any cost (all of which, of course, Marx cheers on rather than laments). Her account slips regularly from any specific attention to the history of the German bourgeoisie (a focus that would help to explain the specifically German gamble, as distinct from the British, Northern European, and to some extent French and Italian bourgeoisie, where this dynamic did not spin so wildly out of control) to remarks about "the bourgeois world" itself (capitalist, liberal-democratic mass societies) as at bottom the most prominent "origin" of totalitarianism, the context within which the totalistic appeal of Hitler would look like a welcome escape. Consider the most important passages.

For example, Arendt's underlying attitude to bourgeois culture suffuses her whole text, not just in her explicit account of origins. Early on, a claim such as the following about the deep consistency between the bourgeoisie and imperialism makes that attitude transparent:

The very fact that the "original sin" of "original accumulation of capital" would need additional sin to keep the system going was far more effective in persuading the bourgeoisie to shake off the restraints of Western tradition than either its philosopher [she means here Thomas Hobbes] or its underworld. It finally induced the German bourgeoisie to throw off the mask of hypocrisy and openly confess its relationship to the mob, calling on it expressly to champion its property interests. (156)

We have already heard about the totalitarian character of bourgeois polit-ical philosophy; now she anticipates Francis Ford Coppola, among many others: Capitalism is not *like* the mafia; capitalism *is* social rule by the elite of a mob, and vice versa.

Later in the section on totalitarianism, she gradually comes to speak more broadly of bourgeois "culture" or "values," and not of just those who own the means of production. This is because she claims that the class system had "broken down." She seems to mean that there was a wide spread of middle-class values, without any identification with a so-cial position above or below anybody. Shopkeepers, accountants, truck drivers, dental assistants, mechanics, plumbers, secretaries, teachers, and so forth were neither working-class nor bourgeois, even though what the nineteenth century would have identified as bourgeois values were domi-nant everywhere.[11] The primary characteristic of such a value system was indifference to all politics not affecting the middle class directly. "The competitive and acquisitive society of the bourgeoisie had produced ap-athy and even hostility toward public life." (Our contemporary view of politics as "interest group" politics counts, for Arendt, as no politics at all. The issue she is raising can be heard in what we mean when we say, "That remark he made was political." We usually mean, "It was said in a way de-signed to appeal to a certain constituency; it was about keeping or acquir-ing power, it was unprincipled, not about the truth.") And in her narra-tive, what finally got the bourgeoisie politically active were the irresistible imperialist possibilities opened up by African and Asian adventures and the inability of the traditional nation-state to manage such possibilities.

Arendt is not shy in this antibourgeois, antiliberal role:

Simply to brand as outbursts of nihilism this violent dissatisfaction with the prewar age and subsequent attempts at restoring it (from Nietzsche to Sorel to Pareto, from Rimbaud and T. E. Lawrence to Jünger, Brecht and Malraux, from Bakunin

---

[11] Much of the picture that Arendt paints is painted with a broad brush and often very quickly. Here, a fuller account of the adequacy of her claims would have to enter into a complex and interesting debate among historians about, for example, the nature of and relative importance of and political behavior of the petite bourgeoisie, or lower middle class, *Kleinbürgertum*, all as contrasted with the grande bourgeoisie of classical Marxist theory. For an interesting beginning to such an account, see Arno Mayer (1975) and his characterization of that class (not a class "for itself" but still "in itself," Mayer says) in the late nineteenth and twentieth century as always "suspended between hope and fear" (417) (hope of ascent, fear of sinking back into the working class), all such that these anxieties "in the event of sharp economic adversity, may well predispose it to a politics of anger, scapegoating, and atavistic millenarianism" (423).

and Nechayev to Alexander Blok) is to overlook *how justified disgust can be in a society wholly permeated with the ideological outlook and moral standards of the bourgeoisie.* (328, my emphasis)

To some extent, she goes on to identify herself with this "desire to see the ruin of this whole world of fake security, fake culture and fake life" (ibid.). Or,

Since the bourgeoisie claimed to be the guardian of Western traditions and confounded all moral issues by parading publicly virtues which it not only did not possess in private and business life, but actually held in contempt, it seemed revolutionary to admit cruelty, disregard of human values and general amorality, because this at least destroyed the duplicity upon which the existing society seemed to rest. (334)

Her term of art for the bourgeois, with his "single-minded devotion to matters of family and career" and his "belief in the primacy of private interest," is "philistine" (339), and she goes so far as to cite as the typical example of such a small-minded philistine, Himmler.

## VI

But all of this poses an obvious problem for her. Why would a selfish, narcissistic bourgeois philistine become a dedicated fanatic, ready to sacrifice all for the cause? (Arendt makes clear in her Preface to the Third Book that she wants no part of that view of either German or eventually Russian totalitarianism that pictures a cowed and frightened population tyrannized by a ruling clique. She insists that the evidence is unambiguous for massive, enthusiastic support for both Hitler and Stalin.) Isn't the prudent, ever-calculating, timid, sheep-like, conformist, weak, unheroic bourgeois the *last* person you would expect to make up the core of Nazi sympathizers? The "mob," for sure; the down-and-out, maybe; the resentment-filled unemployed, marginalized, and desperate people, perhaps. But the bourgeoisie? (As Adam Smith reminded us, bourgeois culture tends to be pacific; one doesn't kill one's customers.)

She has, as far as I can see, two answers to such questions. The first is more in the way of a suggestion about the possibility of an explanation. In a typical passage, she notes, "Nothing proved easier to destroy than the privacy and private morality of people who thought of nothing but safeguarding their private lives" (338). She means again to highlight the antipolitical attitude and civic vices of the bourgeoisie and to suggest some sort of apt historical irony, that their own obsession with their private well-being is what (by their inattention, willingness to compromise almost anything, and resentment about inequalities among their own class) made possible a regime completely indifferent to the well-being of its citizens. The bourgeoisie were all too willing to look the other way as the storm clouds grew on the horizon and should not have been surprised at the virulence and fanaticism that they ignored until it was too late.

But this obviously does not yet go to the positive affirmation of the Nazi program that, Arendt maintains, was most characteristic of the German bourgeoisie. To explain the transformation of the sheep-like, apolitical bourgeois into the enthusiastic Nazi, she needs to establish in some way that those most concerned with their own well-being above all else would also come to experience that "range of significance" in their life, let us say, that well-being, as the be-all and end-all of human existence, as profoundly unsatisfying, almost desperately unsatisfying. This is indeed what she suggests in a number of ways. We have already heard her account of the difficulty of bearing the weight of the many hypocrisies of, let us say, "Christian-capitalist" culture, and she now highlights the odd expressions of relief and even enthusiasm among many intellectuals for expressions of (at least) "honest" anti-Semitic hatred. Her chief example is Céline's *Bagatelles pour un massacre*, in which Céline proposed massacring all Jews, a book that was greeted by André Gide with the sort of "delight" at its frankness that she is noting. Her summary remark:

How irresistible the desire for the unmasking of hypocrisy was among the elite can be gauged by the fact that such delight could not even be spoiled by Hitler's very real persecution of the Jews, which at the time of Céline's writing was already in full swing. *Yet aversion against the philosemitism of the liberals had much more to do with this reaction than hatred of the Jews.* (335, my emphasis)

These remarks are not developed systematically, but they touch on an important point, one made a great deal of by François Furet's magisterial *The Passing of an Illusion*.[12] It has to do with a very unusual aspect of nineteenth- and twentieth-century bourgeois literature, especially the fact that most of the great literary documents of this civilizational epoch continue to express (from Balzac to Philip Roth, from Romantic poetry to Larkin and Lowell) a *deep bourgeois self-hatred*. There are exceptions (I would count Jane Austen, Henry James, and even Proust, whose tone is comic, not bitterly ironic, as exceptions), but the long melancholic list

[12] Furet 1999.

is well known and might indeed be said to have played a factor in the *bourgeois allegiance to totalitarianism* (which allegiance is, again, the most important aspect of Arendt's account of origins). An "inability to bear the burden of modern life," to use her earlier phrase, might indeed amount to an inability to live such a prosaic, small-scale life, filled with some domestic felicity and more security and a better living standard than ever in human history, but filled also with hypocrisy, brutal competition, and constant anxiety, a disenchanted, crushingly prosaic existence that can manage to express itself poetically only in an apparently endless melancholic lament and in intensely critical self-consciousness.

This side of Arendt is best given voice in Nietzsche's work, and there are versions of Nietzsche's lament over the bourgeoisie (which he called "the last man") and similar Arendtean calls for a more heroic, noble, or beautiful existence throughout her work. But in this book, she focuses on one aspect of bourgeois existence that must count as the chief unbearable burden of the bourgeoisie, the intolerable aspect that makes most plausible for her the bourgeois gamble spoken of before.


## VII

This is the account of loneliness in the book's last chapter. She notes that totalitarian regimes require atomized and disengaged individuals, who cannot act in concert and require this both as a precondition and as the outcome of their policing policies. This sort of disconnect (with respect to action) she calls "isolation," an isolation that she again connects with the totalization of labor, and so an outcome that she attributes to the effect of capitalist or bourgeois culture. ("This can happen in a world whose chief values are dictated by labor, that is, where all human activities have been transformed into labor" (475).) And again she invokes the word that, I have been suggesting, plays the most important role in her account of origins: When one's capacity to "add something of one's own to a common world is destroyed," then "isolation becomes *altogether unbearable.*"

This situation is even worse in the state of "loneliness," which, she says, concerns "human life as a whole" (ibid.), and it is connected with other phenomena that she has laid such stress on: "uprootedness" and the feeling of being "superfluous." Her descriptions again echo her account of the condition created by the bourgeois or broadly modern form of life: "to have no place in the world, recognized and guaranteed by others," "not to belong to the world at all." In such loneliness, "I am deserted by own self" and am closed up in my mere, that is, insignificant, even meaningless brute particularity. This situation, which, she claims, had been a marginal despair suffered in earlier epochs, say, only in old age, "has become an everyday experience of the ever growing masses of our century," and again we hear her basic thesis: that totalitarianism represents "a suicidal escape from this reality" (478).[13]

Is this so, or is Arendt, in a bizarre irony, simply assuming the totalitarian premise: that a life without a transcendent, heroic, or noble purpose would be "unbearably" petty, would be to consign ourselves to being the endless butt of the jokes directed at the bourgeoisie by so many nineteenth-century novelists? Put another way, how can Arendt separate out what she admires in bourgeois culture – its constitutionalism, its assertion of fundamental human rights, its equality before the law, its insistence of a private zone in human life, exempt from the political, its religious tolerance – and condemn what she disagrees with – its secularism, its cynical assumption of the pervasiveness of self-interest, the perverting influence of money on human value, its depoliticizing tendencies, and the menace it poses for tradition and a sense of place? It suffices to mention the one institution essential for *both* positive and negative tendencies – private property – to suggest that such a separation is facile. Or, while from a traditionalist point of view, religious tolerance might just look like a timid unwillingness to assert one's faith against an infidel, from another it might look like the courageously rational refusal to dogmatize in what has become a profoundly uncertain, pluralistic world. (Part of that courage might be the courage to admit that secular modernity comes with frightening risks and that one cannot eliminate the risks, "restore" what was "lost," without abandoning all the aspirations characteristic of modernity itself.)

That is, this sense that the bourgeois world has "lost" something, without which it is so "unbearable" as to make plausible the "suicidal escape" of totalitarian self-assertion (whether what we have lost is an attentiveness to "the meaning of being" as claimed by her teacher, Martin Heidegger, or whether it is the "care for the world" embodied in public life that she espoused), often assumes that such a lost something can be recovered.

---

[13] Perhaps Arendt herself realized some of the difficulties with this appeal to the phenomenon of the masses and its inherent loneliness when she came to write her account of Eichmann a decade later. In that account, published in 1963, the notions of compartmentalization, administrative logic, and the absence of "thinking" play a much more prominent role, and there is little to connect those phenomena to the problem of masses and loneliness. See the excellent discussion in Kateb's chapter on "origins" (1983), esp. 70–4, also his remarks on her change of mind about "radical evil," 79.

Hence the tendentious language of "loss," rather than rejection, almost as if it was hastily misplaced on the way to modernization. But such ambitions might have been set aside for a reason, and the fact that without such a deep or transcendent or political dimension, the human condition would be unbearable might just amount to showing that it is in fact (now) unbearable. Our need for what was lost establishes nothing at all (sadly enough) about what can be coherently affirmed in the context of all else we are bound to affirm in modernity, and critics of Arendt have complained long and loud that aside from remarks about revolutionary councils in the German revolution, and some comments on the American founding, it is not at all clear just what Arendt thinks these common political deliberations will be about, when and if such a common care for the world is restored. She simply concentrates much more on how ignoble life was in Germany and is now, without such a dimension.

## VIII

When Arendt points forward to such a possible restoration in *Origins*, she is not hesitant about adding some conditions to this possibility that are not only, in my view, intrinsically unacceptable but arbitrary invocations in this work of historical analysis. In the context of a discussion of the dubious status of rights without a community to realize them and in the midst of her usual attack on the ignoble bourgeois limitation of politics (and so rights talk) to what is merely beneficial or useful, she makes a revealing claim:

A conception of law which identifies what is right with the notion of what is good – for the individual, or the family, or the people, or the largest number – becomes inevitable once the absolute and transcendent measurements of religion or the law of nature have lost their authority. (299)

The paragraph ends with an appeal to a quotation from Plato: "Not man, but a god must be the measure of all things." (All this from someone who, presumably, knew her Kant very well, to mention only one alternative to the either-or she gives us here.) And this all echoes her apocalyptic warnings, such as that given at the end of Part Two where she reminds us that we will be "punished, so to speak, for having forgotten that man is only the master, not the creator of the world" (302). (All such remarks echo her acknowledgment in one of her letters of her "childish trust in God.")[14]

---

[14] As quoted in Neiman 2002, 314.

As I have tried to indicate, I do not believe that Arendt has made a case that it was something like the unbearableness of the bourgeois world that prompted the totalitarian "suicidal escape." But even if it did, her response is still baffling. If we will be saved only "by the measurements of religion or the law of nature," by a god measuring all things, by recalling that there is a creator of the world and we are not its masters, or, again in the words of her teacher, by the fact that "only a god can save us now," then we are in some serious trouble. Or at least those of us philistines for whom there is no such religion, god, or creator will, it seems, be left out of the moral rearmament Arendt proposes. Either that or we are headed for totalitarian leaps. Surely, those are not the exclusive alternatives.

# 8

## On Not Being a Neostructuralist

### *Remarks on Manfred Frank and Romantic Subjectivity*

My theme in the following is Manfred Frank's interpretation of "postmeta-physical" European philosophy.[1] I want to express some solidarity with his hesitations about the program he calls "neostructuralism" and also to raise several questions about the "counterneostructuralist" program that Frank has been defending in many works since the early 1980s, especially about the nature of his appeal to complexly linked themes in German romantic philosophy, preintentional theories of self-awareness, hermeneutics, and Sartrean existentialism. As my chapter title already implies, for Frank, not to be a neostructuralist is to have taken up some strong stand on the irreducibility and ineliminability of subjectivity, especially on the nature and importance of self-awareness and on the implications of such a possibility for any general theory of the intelligibility of anything. (Although the "problem of subjectivity" is a well-known formulation, I note that, in this context, I understand claims about "the priority and irreducibility of the subject" to be simply the name for the counterposition against "objectivism," the position that holds that the knowing, perceiving, and acting subject must be understood as just another, however unique, object in the world, in the best way objects in the world are understood, by modern natural science. Reference is thereby made to such topics as the reality of consciousness – that awareness or disclosure

---

[1] My principal text for this interrogation is WIN. I am now not sure of the extent to which Frank himself continues to think that any engagement with the neostructuralists (even his own 600-page *Auseinanderstezung*) is a worthy way to interrogate the ideas important to him, given his remark in SVL in 1995, that Jacques Bouveresse's book on Wittgenstein gave him "the incentive to turn from shallow neostructuralist critique to analytic philosophy" (32), but I have pressed ahead anyway.

of the world must be something well beyond a receptor's capacity to re-
ceive and process and respond to sensory data, it must be an awareness;
to that quality of experience that can be described as its being "owned"
individually, that it is mine, my point of view or path through things and
that all the experience I have is accompanied necessarily by this prediscursive sense, for me, of its being mine or my way; to the unique lack of
a being/seeming distinction for mental states and so their ontological
uniqueness;[2] to absent qualia and de re/de se distinctions;[3] to my knowledge of me, in no way capturable by some vast set of propositions about
Robert Pippin; or to the claim that human deeds are intelligible only as
such, as actions, if explained by reference to a subject's reasons, taken by
the subject to be sufficient reasons to act thusly, and so forth. In general,
I have some doubts that the latter (the strong stand on the primordiality
of the individual subject) is necessary for the former (avoiding neostructuralism), although it may, as Frank persuasively argues in many areas, be
sufficient, and along the way in expressing those doubts, I want to suggest
an alternative conception of "not being a neostructuralist."

Put another way: I want to agree that Frank's formulations of the self's
experience of itself do help to show that much of neostructuralism's actual attack on the self-conscious subject mounts a vast army against a great
chorus of straw men, that neostructuralism is not attacking "the subject"
but particular Cartesian and "reflective" accounts (or even rather stale
and potted, formulaic, text-bookish versions of Cartesian and Lockean
positions), and that there is no reason to throw the subjectivity baby
out with the Cartesian bathwater. But I have some doubts that attention to the unique nonpropositional, nonthetic ways in which a subject is aware of itself goes all that far in helping to establish any positive philosophical project. Or at least I have not yet understood how
Frank understands the way in which certain phenomena of subjectivity, such as self-familiarity, bear on a general, ambitious alternative to a
structuralist, neostructuralist, naturalized, or intersubjectivist account. (I
have no doubt that in Frank's version of a self-reflexive hermeneutics,
there is indeed such a connection: "I am convinced that neither structuralism nor neostructuralism nor, for that matter, any other form of
systems theory, has truly succeeded in explaining the processes of signification [*Prozesse des Bedeutens*] and of the alteration of signification
[*des Beudeutungen-Veränderns*] without relying explicitly or implicitly on

---

[2] Searle 1992, 121ff.
[3] Jackson, Shoemaker, and so on, and even Lewis.

the category of individuality" (WIN, 10–11).)[4] The "category" of self-aware individual consciousness and agency, as Frank deploys it, still seems to me more like a very small waystation, however initially reassuring, within which to take refuge against the structuralist, neostructuralist, intersubjectivist, and reductionist waves. Or put another way: I should declare myself here at the outset with Hegel and against Schelling, deeply suspicious of the value of any claims about the ineffable, the irreducible, the simply and eternally unrepresentable, although pursuing that issue that way would also take us deep into Frank's speculations about what Blumenberg has called "the persistence of myth.") More important and more to the eventual point, I am not convinced that individual minds are the primary bearers and sustainers of linguistic and general meaning and want to raise (not in Habermasian or Wittgensteinian ways, I should caution) the issue of the normativity and socially sustained normativity of meaning.

Frank's reconstructed, modernized hermeneutical position, though, and the issues themselves are so complex that I have not been able to do more in the following than to present these doubts and suggestions as just that: mere doubts and suggestions. I do not pretend to have done justice to Frank's full position nor to have adequately defended an alternative. I hope only to provoke discussion.

Again, although the specific topic forms only, officially, one-third of the themes treated by Frank, the basic issue throughout, or at least the one I want to focus most on, concerns the general possibility of meaning and this in the dual sense now familiar in such discussions: the special case of linguistic meaning (what it is for vocalizations and physical marks to possess a determinate sense) and the possibility of mental content *überhaupt*, the directedness or "aboutness" of mind: intentionality. (The problem, I am suggesting, around which the "subject versus structure" contestation will swirl, is then the general problem of semantic and intentional content; how it is that one can mean A and not -A, whether one is uttering A, believing A, or thinking about A; or also, so as not to beg any questions, in an alternative formulation, how some sign could just count successfully as the sign of A and not -A. Focusing, eventually, on such a consideration will have to mean giving shorter shrift to the broader contrast at stake in Frank's work (at least his earlier work), between "German"

---

4  Or, with reference to Kant and Fichte, "it is only on the basis of a priori and 'transcendental' consciousness of self that reference to worldly objects (events, states of affairs, and so on) first becomes possible" (Frank, SVL, 40).

transcendentalism and hermeneutics and "French" positivism, structuralism, and neostructuralism, but obviously space is limited.) As we shall see below, as Frank clearly realizes and as many have discovered, it is not easy to have any position about such issues without also taking stands in the philosophy of mind, epistemology, metaphysics, and even moral theory. But there is a particular trajectory through the many things Frank has written about the relation between the possibility of meaning and the putative primordiality of the subject and the subject's experience of itself that I want to follow here, a specific context of discussion. That context is the analysis of neostructuralism.

So, to some general expressions of solidarity: First, I agree with Frank's obvious hermeneutical premise, that it is important to try to understand the main figures addressed in his book together, within some comprehensive whole of interanimating oppositions and lines of influence. These main figures are Foucault, Lacan, Derrida, Deleuze, and Lyotard, but what Frank has to say obviously has implications for the now crowded field of epigones and spin-offs, from the social (as opposed to subjective) constructivists all the way to "libidinal materialists": the Serres, Latour, Nancy, Lacoue-Labarthe, Baudrillard, Kristeva phenomena. Frank is surely right: These positions are not strings of possible arguments, accessible in some Platonic warehouse. They have somehow grown together and have been nourished out of some common ground, "organically," let us say. What is that ground?

Among the many recent books that attempt such a comprehensive account of "what has happened to modern and thereby French thought (and thereby to us in America via comparative literature and cultural studies) post-1968" – Habermas's *The Philosophical Discourse of Modernity*, Honneth's *Kritik der Macht*, Lyotard's *The Post-Modern Condition*, Rorty's *Philosophy and the Mirror of Nature* and later essays, Charles Taylor's *Sources of the Self*, Alasdair MacIntyre's *After Virtue*, Bruno Latour's *Nous n'avons jamais été modernes*, Frederick Jameson's fulminations against postmodernism, Stanley Rosen's *Hermeneutics as Politics*,[5] or recent works by Gianni Vattimo or Albrecht Wellmer – Frank's treatment of individual authors is distinguished by its close and fair-minded treatment of so many authors and texts, by the facility and economy of his organization of topics (the approach to history, to subjectivity, and to meaning), and especially by the persuasiveness of the case suggested by his controversial title, his answer

---

5 One of the best deflations of structuralist aspiration remains Rosen's short, brilliant 1973 piece.

to that "ground" question: that the best way to understand this complex of antirationalist, antimetaphysical, antihumanist, counter-Enlightenment, postmodern, near anarchic *Gestalt des Bewusstseins* is within, not outside, the original French fascination with structure. This allows him to present an ambitious account of the fragile fate of the "subject" in all post-Kantian European thought and to discuss as a general and as the most fundamental theme the intellectual origins and actual case for the putative "death of the subject." So, while, I think, the term would be fiercely resisted by all of the authors under discussion, "neostructuralism" seems to me the right "whole," not the now familiar "poststructuralism" or the even more uninformative "postmodernism," a much better and a more honest designation than "discourse analysis" and the now meaningless "deconstruction." As he puts it in Lecture no. 2, the key premise shared by the likes of Saussure, Levi-Strauss, Barthes, Althusser, on the one hand, and Derrida, Lacan, or Lyotard, on the other, is that "for structuralism the sensual is not a reflection or expression of something nonsensual in the sensual itself. . . . [B]y no means is there a prior world of nonsensual psychic or cognitive states or processes that then might be represented by a world of symbols. On the contrary, the nonsensual world of thoughts is itself constituted as a result of differentiation and combination in the realm of the sensual-phonic" (24 and 25). The key rejection in later (what might also be called) "anarchostructuralists" turns on the implications of "constituted as a result of" in this quotation and the strong structuralist claim about a closed and necessarily regular system to account for the rules governing such originary "differentiation and combination." Their challenge is not, as Frank points out, a rejection "of Saussure's conception of a differential articulation of the sign," but rather a challenge to "the idea that this articulation takes place in a theoretically comprehensive and enclosed system. . . . The 'structure' of the neostructuralists no longer knows any specifiable confinement; it is open subject to infinite transformations . . ." (25). If structuralism is, in Ricoeur's phrase, a "Kantianism without a transcendental subject," then neostructuralism simply cannot be far behind, turning the structuralist's own arguments against a subjective or intersubjective center into an argument against any argument for a center at all or systematicity in general. Successfully meaning, intending determinate content, would be and could only be differentiability within a regulated, closed, structure agree the structuralists and neostructuralists, against all mentalisms, representation theories, phenomenologies, agent semantics, and speech act theories; and so the central theme of neostructuralism is simply a heretical variation within the same sect: The variation proposes the ultimate unavailability of such determinacy-providing closed structure, and so the availability only of the familiar traces, supplements, fissures, silences, and always endlessly differing and endlessly deferred meaning.

So, what, then, is neostructuralism? Well, the framework of questions about structure and subject summarized above allows Frank to sum up and to connect together economically the many familiar neostructuralist claims, now the bread and butter of many a comparative literature first-year graduate seminar. (In fact, I hope these themes are by now so well known – and at any rate, they are spelled out so clearly by Frank – that I can drag each on stage for only a very quick bow.) We have already briefly touched on the "end of metaphysics" theme and the neostructuralist rad-icalization of structuralist suspicions about the "nonsensible" as source or ground, whether understood as souls, ideas, ideal senses, or mental states such as beliefs or certainly if understood as divine. This radicaliza-tion was largely inspired by Heidegger's interpretation of metaphysics as a limitless, almost predatory subjectivism, culminating in a thoughtless and nihilistic Age of Technology. This is not a theme all that internal to the development that leads from Saussure and Levi-Strauss to Derrida's essay, "Structure, Sign, and Play in the Human Sciences," but it obviously motivates the kinds of dissatisfaction with structuralism there expressed, and indeed the theme plays an obvious role in the post-1968 attack on the sufficiency of all "systems" and "totality" approaches.

Other strands have also already been alluded to. Structuralism itself, despite its emphasis on rules and regularities, is not a particularly "ratio-nalist" approach and so, especially in its neostructuralist variations, can look continuous with the emerging nineteenth-century strands of antira-tionalism. (I mean by "not rationalist" that structuralism does not tie the possibility of meaning or the distinctiveness of agency to the having or promising of reasons by individual participants in a practice. Such ges-tures are like mythic practices; only a different sort of circulation of The Code. As is now a commonplace since all the Wittgenstein controversies: Regularities of "differentiation and articulation" need have nothing to do with the "following" of rules or with the proprieties of use, with the commitments and entitlements and material implications that all that en-tails.) We return below to the issue of the relation between reasons and intentional content; here the point is the sympathy between the formal-ism and the materialism of structuralism and a kind of antirationalism that begins to emerge in the European tradition against Hegel, first in the form of a defense of the priority of "life" and the individual in Schelling and Kierkegaard, later in doubts about the possibility of a "pure" or universal reason (and thus reason itself) in the name of language and history, in Herder, say, and then in a full-blown countertheory of intelligibility and agency replete with talk of codes and signs, not reasons and motives.

As Frank shows, the kinds of doubts about the sufficiency of structuralism typical of the neostructuralist project also play a role, either as paradigmatic of a general approach or as actually intellectually motivating, very sweeping claims in Foucault and Lyotard against the possibility of historical teleology or any sort of "grand narratives" and in favor of a much more discontinuous, archaeological, even "geological" approach, as in Sartre's early (and, still, I agree with Frank, absolutely compelling) criticisms of Foucault. This doubt about any sort of universal or continuous, comprehensive human history then shifted attention to a new way of understanding historical change, one much more attentive to massive contingencies in such change and "explained," if it all, by reference to that vague term so useful to the later Foucault: power. Since so much of Enlightenment and post-Enlightenment thought is defensible only by reference to some sort of universal narrative (otherwise "being modern" is just being located at a time, not "having rationally rejected the premodern"), neostructuralism was also postmodern as well as being antirationalist, postmetaphysical, and antihumanist. The notion of that ever-floating signifier can, apparently, do a lot of damage.

As noted already, I understand the fulcrum of Frank's response to all this to rest on a very general interrogation into the possibility of intelligibility and the status of subjectivity in any such appeal. And I want now to return to that argument, this time by way of Frank's own historical genealogy of the roots of the directions taken by neostructuralist thought. Before doing so, though, one brief comment on genealogy.

At one early point in his lectures, Frank invokes that phrase of Jaspers since revived by Habermas's edited reports on the issue, "*die geistige Situation der Zeit*," and so brings up the most ambitious genealogical problem for the modern West: the origins and significance of the fact that, in ways largely linked to the strategies of these French thinkers, so much academic culture in the humanities (outside of Anglophone philosophy departments, anyway) has become so ferociously skeptical, so much about and so hostile to itself; the canon is a colonial canon, centuries of Western attempts to understand the East are mere ideological Orientalisms; literature itself is taught "against itself," when it is not being understood as one among many "case studies" of the apparently endless and (in neostructuralism) mindless attempts at the social control of imagination in the service of the gender or class or nation or race in power. To make a long story short, as I understand him, Frank sees the neostructuralist phenomenon as a reactive phenomenon, to use Nietzsche's famous word; a reaction to what turned out to be the historical impotence of any moral appeal to the traditional humanist subject, whether of classical liberalism, Rousseau, or German Idealism, an impotence over against "a world that is becoming uniform and totalitarian" (9) and an "understandable" reaction against what is finally only the metaphysical and political complicity of the structuralist theoretization of this grim dialectic of Enlightenment. This "understandable" reaction, the attempt to maintain the possibility of negation, noncomplicity, and resistance without what was regarded (falsely according to Frank) as a "naïve" or nostalgic hope for any court of appeal in the claims of moral individualism, would then be the neostructuralist appeal to the self-dissolving, infinitely open, failure of all attempts at closure, resolution, the self-regulation of systems. One author not prominent in this particular version of Frank's analysis,[6] a great diagnostician of the Enlightenment phenomena provoking both the last gasps of Enlightenment subjectivism and the skeptical countermovements of neostructuralism, is Weber, with his original account of Enlightenment rationalization of the life world. Subjectivism (with its earlier manifestions in romanticism, idealism, and hermeneutics and its later irrationalist voluntarism) goes this trichotomy, or a complicit, somewhat cynical theoretization of the phenomena (structuralism),[7] or a "happy positivism" (Foucault's phrase) in which the failure of subjectivity is countered only by a complex "tu quoque" response to structuralism in neostructuralism.

I agree with what I take to be the tenor of Frank's analysis of this state of mind, but the framework suggested by Frank proposes a kind of revisionist or even revivalist mentality, a return to neglected aspects of the romantic, hermeneutical, and existentialist options. Given the "straw men" problem noted above, there is certainly something sensible in this, and I engage in a version of it myself below, with respect to Kant, but we also need to understand post-Hegelian philosophy in a more ambitious Hegelian way, I think. Although no one has yet succeeded in doing so, we need to understand the frustrating historical failure of the original

---

[6] On Weber and Weberianism, see also Frank's TC, 72–73, and KH, 28ff.

[7] When all is said and done. I realize the original political animus behind the anthropological variants of structuralism, especially, was against any appeal to a totalizing system and an insistence on the plurality, incommensurability, and equal legitimacy of different "cultures."

Enlightenment notions of individuality, contract, mentality, and reason, as well as the later modern, romantic, expressivist, and existentialist appeals to individuality, to master decisively the imagination of the West in the last four hundred years. The historical, social hold of such notions, whether linked to ideals of rationality or authenticity, has just proven to be (thus far) unaccountably fragile. It is not likely that this failure stems from a lack of appreciation of Kant, Schelling, Kierkegaard, Schleiermacher, or others, and it is as deeply disturbing a failure as any in human history, easily dwarfing the internal failures that provoked the so-called collapse of Rome, the Reformation, or Copernicus and Galileo.[8] The two chapters that would have to complete Hegel's *Phenomenology*, were he to complete a sequel today, would have to include oddly parallel accounts of both the great expanding confidence and influence of modern science and technology (and so also everything from Comte and the futurists and *Principia mathematica* to logical positivism, naturalized epistemology, neuroethics, and the ever more insipid Mr. Gates) and the coincident ever-growing pessimism that all of that, and much of anything else, matters all that much (and so Schelling, Nietzsche, Dostoyevsky, Dali, Beckett, and so forth). These are trajectories that can join forces in odd moments, as in a "happy positivism" or more darkly as the "reactionary modernism" described so well in Jeffrey Herf's book. But these issues soon grow unmanageable; I take refuge in being a humble commentator, and move on.

The detailed genealogy presented by Frank is, by contrast with the genealogy just expressed, rather bookish and often proceeds internally, by reference to the self-understanding of the individual authors. Much of his account of the romantic precursors of neostructuralist views on subjectivity and history is especially valuable. He shows very well how the "self-critique" of the German Idealist tradition anticipated and helped to provoke the neostructuralist doubts about any progressive self-propulsion of history by subjects and helped to create the radical doubts about subjective self-sufficiency in Nietzsche, Heidegger, and thereby in the neostructuralists. (These moments are tied to such things as the later Fichte's

---

[8] There is some question, of course, as to whether such questions are answerable or interesting philosophical questions, given the manifest folly, vanity, and irrationality of the human species. Whichever explanation of such phenomena there might be might best be cast in the language of pathologies and ideology, rather than by linking such happenings to any putative insufficiency or incompleteness in the civilizational ideal itself. The Hegelian aspiration is the latter and I am just echoing it here. And of course, the options need not be exclusive, either.

image of the "inserted eye," a gaze that cannot fully ever see itself, and so a subject that cannot ground or absolutely understand or justify itself, must even, finally, experience itself in Schleiermacher's sense as "absolute dependence.") But there is one particular point within Frank's account of Foucault's *Order of Things* and *Archeology of Knowledge* and in Frank's treatment of the kind of philosophical alternatives that Foucault saw opening and closing in modernity, that I want to concentrate on. Foucault's own neostructuralist rejection of the subject is clearly motivated by his understanding of such available alternatives. Frank, too, makes use of such a conception of alternatives to motivate his own interest in prethetic and predescriptive modes of self-consciousness that cannot fall under Foucault's suspicions and response, because they are a neglected alternative. I do not so much want to disagree with this claim by Frank as to suggest now that there are other neglected alternatives in this presentation of alternatives.

It does not all come down to

- non-discursive self-awareness, a neglected and largely misunderstood sense of self which can help establish the reality and priority of "the subject"

versus

- the traditional "modern subject," experiencing by being aware of its own states of mind as if aware of entities, full of aporias and blindnesses about its own origins and activities

versus

- the postmodern play of subject-less discourses, fields of power, texts, etc.

These are not the alternatives,[9] I want to suggest, and seeing why they are not goes back, as does virtually everything good in life, to Kant.

The central presuppositions about "the alternatives" are difficult to state economically, especially because Frank's analysis of Foucault's treatment of the origin of modern subjectivism (or, in Foucault's terms, the

---

9 Actually, I have the impression that the basic alternatives are even more stark for Frank. In discussing Derrida's idea of difference and the impossibility of presence, he says that the comprehension of this idea "will essentially decide whether we can join sides with neostructuralism and its critique of systems, or whether we want to remain with metaphysics" (71). My vote is "neither."

rejection of classicism's views on representation and the rise of, eventually, the historical, making, self-propelling subject) is very well and subtly done, full of a great irony in pointing out how nostalgically premodern or classicist Foucault the revolutionary can seem. (Is it really so "advanced" a view to celebrate all those absent subjects in *Las Meninas*?)

The issues I am interested in begin in Lectures no. 7 and no. 8 with Frank's treatment of Foucault's *The Order of Things*, especially Foucault's account of the transition from preclassical notions of the "natural" link between *form signante* and *form du signe* ("to search for meaning is to bring to light a resemblance") to "the classical episteme" and the claim that signifier and signified could now be linked not analogously or by similarity but by representation ("Representation, therefore, does not belong to the natural order, but has its origins in convention: the sign becomes, in short, an instrument of the analytically controlled use of reason, of knowledge") to the new paradigm of historical consciousness. This last transition, replete with the subjective humanism that Foucault is out to undermine, is introduced by noting the many themes in Kantian and post-Kantian epistemology that attack and reformulate "classical" or Enlightenment conceptions of our mental life. Here is how that attack and reformulation is supposed to work:

It [the new humanist-historicist conception of language] states that the rules of reason, on whose timeless validity the Enlightenment uncritically relied, are the precipitates of synthetic activities behind which, in the final analysis, there is a "transcendental," vital, or laboring subject that founds values and meaning and simply institutes the circulating signs or life functions or commodities into their respective order and to this extent is not part of this order itself. (WIN, 130)

The great transition from classical orders of rationality and representation to what remains the main current of our own philosophical world is a shift from "the paradigm of analytic reason to that of synthetic reason" (WIN, 130), and this claim locates all our supposedly false hopes for the subject in Kant and Kant's claim for the priority of the apperceptive, synthetically active, experience-founding, and morally responsible subject. Thus:

From this, there springs an almost infinite series of consequences – of unlimited consequences at least, since our thought today still belongs to the same dynasty. In the first rank, we must undoubtedly place the simultaneous emergence of a transcendental theme and new empirical fields – or, if not new, at least distributed and founded in a new way. (WIN, 243)

Since this Kantian claim to a "new founding" will have a very large role to play in any kind of antiobjectivism that is something more and more positive than a sophisticated gloating about the inevitable "failure" of objectivism, structuralism, and the determinacy of meaning, and so in any case for a true subjectivism, the stakes here are very high.

A conventional view of what is happening with Kant's Copernican turn, a view clearly dominant in Foucault and not directly challenged by Frank, is this: Kant's place in modern thought is believed to lie in his innovations with respect to claims about the necessary role of the subject in knowledge. The basic antiobjectivist (Husserl would say antipsychologistic, we would now say antinaturalist) line in philosophy is the claim that any question about being must be understood to be a question about the possible meaning of being or just is a question about our asserting something or interpreting something. And no mere happening could account for such a disclosure of meaning. Happenings are just happenings; events, motions, states. They do not mean or explain anything (ditto for neural happenings). If the world is understood as disenchanted, then the source of all possible significance must be the intending, disclosing, or synthesizing subject. But then the temptation to an idealism and so a skepticism is deep. Being seems to turn into a subjective datum, an impression or idea, something never just "there," but re-presented in the mental life of a subject, which mental life must be understood in all awareness to be reflecting, turning always to itself and its own states in its rendering intelligible. Either we know only our own ideas or all there really is are ideas.

But such pre-Kantian approaches still seem to animate "ideas" and "impressions" with forces and relations and internal properties, such as clarity and vivacity, that we have no philosophical right to ascribe to them. Kant's turn, by contrast, must be right. We do not just "grasp" these mental or ideational contents; we synthetically determine them to be the contents they are; we engage the materials of our experience under the conditions necessary for us to unify such elements successfully over time within one subject, in order for there to be a transcendental unity of apperception. The "conditions of the possibility of experience are at the same time the conditions of the possibility of objects of experience."

We now have an acting, founding subject (mysteriously not itself an element of the "objects of experience" it makes possible (WIN, 238, 240)) and a source or ground soon to become entangled in the impurities of language, history, the imperatives of life, the will to power, still having to struggle with the "lost world" of premodern harmony and so with an unresolvable skepticism, but such is the price we pay (according to Foucault)[10] for the arrogance of such original subjective self-assertion. Understood this way, as the introduction of some founding act of all-constituting human *Spontaneität*, responsible for but outside the formal coherence of experience and therewith the possibility of semantic and intentional content, the stage is set for revisionism and retrenchment, whether inspired by Schelling's worries about already "grounded," "existing" prediscursive individuality, Heideggerean worries about technology and the technological *Ge-stell*, or motivated perhaps by the French scene in the years following World War II, when the issue of direct individual responsibility, and so individual guilt, all so uncomfortably insisted on by the magisterial Sartre, could have all sorts of uncomfortable personal dimensions. It would indeed be understandable if, struggling out of this blind alley, one conceived the alternatives of either deflating the attempted autonomy and purity of such a subject and revising radically its original relation to itself in all experience (rendering it less bipolar, paradoxically present and absent to itself) – the Schellingean-romantic move I associate with Frank – or of promoting a much more radical paradigm shift: one where "language speaks," not us; one where history does not belong to us, we to history; one where we do not produce commodities, they produce us; and so on.

It is clear that Frank prefers the former option, but as I suggested, evaluating such options depends on the original alternatives. He wants that former option for a clear reason. I quote from a somewhat more informal essay published ten years after *What Is Neostructuralism?*:

In contrast to the particular, the singular or the individual is an element or a part that can never be derived logically from a universal concept in a finite number of parts. Individuals cannot be deduced from a concept (a structure, a code, a system, etc.) because it is in them that the concept of a whole first originates. To put it differently, the meaning of a whole has no existence outside the consciousness of individuals who internalize the universal in their specific and unique ways, and who return it to a state of public accessibility by their actions. (TC, 82)

Frank's agent-centered notion of meaning thus buys into a good deal of the narrative sketched above and robustly endorses that notion of the active subject under attack by Foucault, but he veers off only in denying that the right way to conceive of the subject's self-disclosure is on the "reflective" model alluded to above.

[10] See OT, 299.

What I want to claim is that this approach and the alternatives that seem to motivate it seriously underestimate the radicality, the anti-Cartesian animus, and the implications of Kant's original turn. Once this is appreciated, an alternative to the individual agent–centered view just endorsed by Frank will I hope at least begin to become evident. It might come as no surprise that such a claim will also involve a claim that the first philosopher to appreciate all of these distinctions was Hegel, not Hölderlin, Novalis, or Schelling.

The key Kantian innovation was not any claim about the originary status of the subject's activity. It lies in his understanding of that activity, in the explosive claim that all thinking is judging, or the even more important implication of that claim, that the content of a concept is fixed by the role it can and cannot play as the "predicate of possible judgments." To make use of a concept is thus to subscribe to a norm, not to be subject to a law. It must be the former rather than the latter because the theory has it that the possibility of content involves a capacity of commitments and entitlements and permissions of use, that the use of a concept can be the intending or communicating of content only if one can maneuver about and in some sense be committed to other priorities of use. Thinking can always only be an attempting to get it right, requiring subscription not regularities of performance. Leaving the linguistic dimension to one side for the moment, the denial that thinking a thought (or imagining an episode or believing a claim) can ever be the grasping of a content, whether a mental or metaphysically ideal content, forces on Kant the question of an alternative picture of thinking, and judging is what he comes up with. But that means that his notion of what it is to think turns into the notion of subscribing to norms, as he says, obeying rules. To understand ("to think") a concept such as "table" or "explosion" is to be able to make use of some such set of *Merkmale*, other concepts, in their proper roles within other judgments. Without this propriety, there is no possible content. All of this raises immediately the problem of the ultimate source of this normativity: the rules that originally make possible the complex of judgmental possibilities within which "table," for example, can function properly in judgments about tables and related objects and properties.

The daring of Kant's project grows as he pursues the implications of the claim that all thinking is judging. He is clear in the *Critique* as to how he sees the alternatives at this point. There are only two: either objects directly make possible this complex of inferential possibilities or "thinking" itself must make possible the identification and classification of objects. Kant famously takes the latter path. If the thinking activity that fixes and regulates content cannot be regulated by exogenous content, it must be ultimately self-regulated; an a priori dimension to such subjectivity is clearly unavoidable; and the question of German Idealism is set: How does such self-regulation work, come about? Without this emphasis on the problem of normativity (i.e., judging is always regulation by a norm; thinking is trying to get it right) and without the anti-empirical and antirealist arguments in view, Kant's position will be misunderstood.

Kant is not then working primarily on a theory that describes how an allegedly pure subject outside, not an element of, experience "makes" or constitutes experience. His line of thought tracks the problem of the normativity of thought and experience, the regulation of predicates of possible judgments necessary for there to be any possible content in thought/experience, and he follows up the implications of the requirement that all thinking is judging to its conclusion: that nothing given or exogenous can fix or regulate these contents originally. (This is not to say that there cannot be self-determined rules specifying the ways in which sensory manifolds can be allowed to fix proprieties of use in acquired predicates. Kant of course calls these rules "categories." Synthetic a priori judgments are thus not first-order factual claims; not the use of concepts but the original rules determining the possibility of use and so content.)[11]

Because Kant's interest lies primarily in the normativity of judgment and the source of this normativity and because he realizes the unavailability of realist or empirical answers to this question and presses on toward some theory of self-regulation, it is a serious and almost universal error within the post-Kantian European tradition to understand his theory in terms of mysterious metaphysical or psychological activities going on "behind" or before experience, like some Transcendental Wizard of Oz behind the curtain. Whatever subjects are made of, whoever they are, whatever they are dependent on, or however their brains work, what we are interested in philosophically is what proprieties of use, what norms, what reasons, they must be subscribing to in order to be thinking with content. And whatever we come up with, I submit, will be neither a metaphysical nor a structuralist/antimetaphysical position. Oddly enough, Fichte, who traditionally is seen as not only promoting such a subjectivist reading but as ludicrously exaggerating it, does not, I have argued elsewhere, make this mistake, and neither, I think, did

---

[11] Brandom 1994, 10.

Hegel. (Historically, in my view, the real culprits here are Reinhold and the shadow thrown on these problems by Jacobi and the *Pantheismusstreit*, or the early "attack on humanism" in the counter-Enlightenment.)[12]

There are other implications of stressing this element in Kant, many relevant to the direction taken by Frank's thought and for his alternative to neostructuralism. Of course in one sense, the general line of thought is quite sympathetic to Frank's objections to neostructuralism or to what he later took to calling "linguistic idealism." A structure of possible differentiability or articulability, a language or cultural code, an episteme, a discourse field, the system of forces of production, does not and cannot do anything to make possible intentional or semantic or symbolic content. In this version of Kantianism, thinking or uttering A or in any way being directed toward A by an utterance or sign or image is possible only if intending A has various other material implications, if intending A entails various other commitments and entitlements and exclusions.[13] Elements of a code, material signs in a system, cannot take up and follow through such commitments and proprieties. They do not dwell with the "space of reasons" necessary for thought. What this means in Kant's terms is that, if concepts are to be understood as fixed in their content by being predicates of possible judgments, then the content of judgments is, by parity of reasoning, fixed by the role of any such judgment within possible inferences, and given Kant's understanding of logic, this means within the forms of syllogistic inferences. Hence the *Verstand/Vernunft* relation. Hegel then took the further step of locating such a system of judgmental inferences within a more (most) comprehensive normative structure, *der Begriff*. We allow the inferences we do, and so the judgmental forms we do, and so the conceptual content all this makes possible, as necessary components (we learn over historical time) in order to make possible a common practical goal, the self-realization of *Geist.*

But I return to safer territory. The importance of this account of normativity for the issues Frank has been raising since *What Is Neostructuralism?*

---

[12] As Brandom has pointed out, the post-Kantian philosopher who appreciated this insight most clearly, whether independently or because of Kant, was Frege. "I start out from judgments and their contents, and not from concepts.... [I]nstead of putting a judgment together out of an individual as subject and an already previously formed concept as predicate, we do the opposite and arrive at a concept by splitting up the content of a possible judgment." Frege 1960, as cited in Brandom 1994.

[13] I would not say that the content of A is equivalent to such material and practical implications, as Brandom apparently does. He seems to me not to be explaining intentionality by his theory of doxastic commitments and social score keeping but eliminating the former in favor of the latter.

is, I think, somewhat supplementary, but in a decisive sense. Structuralist and neostructuralist accounts of subjectivity and intentional content do not just make it impossible to understand the distinctly personal, individual character of experience or the unique prelinguistic character of self-familiarity. What is neglected in such accounts, in a way largely connected to a false perception of alternatives and a misreading of Kant, is the ineliminable role of reasoning, inferences, commitments, entitlements, proprieties, and the offering and considering of reasons in the original possibility of mental and semantic content. (Frank is, of course, quite keen to stress the role of argumentation in distinctly philosophical discourse, but I am referring to a deeper connection between reasoning and intending at all.) I would thus even have no objection to those critics of Frank who want to reinscribe linguisticality "everywhere," if they realize, as they often don't, that the possibility of such linguisticality already depends on the normative force of judgment and so requires an account of the space of reasons. (For those who know of Frank's criticisms of Habermas, I concede that, with respect to this point and the one to follow, a discussion of that *Auseinandersetzung* would be relevant here, with more time. I do not finally think Habermas is relevant because his communication theory, while it strongly emphasizes the normative aspirations of any performative dimension, does not, in my view, have a theory of content and is so formal that it can indeed look like what Frank claims: subjects struggling to dissolve their subjectivity in intersubjective consensus.)

Second, the trajectory of this way of looking at the problem of modern philosophy and the significance of Kant will ultimately lead us in a basic direction much different from the trajectory of Frank's work. Consider again the quotation cited earlier: "[T]he meaning of a whole has no existence outside the consciousness of individuals who internalize the universal in their specific and unique ways, and who return it to a state of public accessibility by their actions." This and many other things Frank has written suggest an individualist, agent-centered semantics, one that would return us to some of our most natural intuitions about meaning. These emerge most quickly in accounts of language, where the question of how vocalizations and marks mean what they do seems naturally answerable by appeal to the thoughts, beliefs, or pragmatic intentions of individual minds or speakers, collectively "sustaining" such a support for meaningful discourse and mentality. But this model is obviously unavailable for the explanation of original intentionality or to explain the problem of content we have been tracking through Kant.

(Intentions conferring content already presupposes that intentions have content, and it is very unlikely that the latter can be explained, without a vicious regress, in the same "conferral" sense.) "Thinkings" cannot involve the "internalization" of some "universal" by an individual consciousness, if Kant is right. It must be a subscribing to a norm, not any private internalization, and if a norm is to be a norm, it must be backed by reasons, implications, and commitments. Once we realize that these norms themselves are not conceivable Platonically, but must be understood as the results of social interactions within communities over time, collectively self-constituted norms, we have all the elements in place for the "Hegelianism" I would want to defend. The important point here is that these are engagements with public matters not realizations in private. Whatever sense I can make of anything, even in the most immediate and direct way, my sense of myself, if it is to be a making sense, must involve this aspect of normativity and thus the space of reasons, the public "We" and the deep connection between my sense of others and any possible sense of myself (myself as always and necessarily, first of all, one among others). Agents cannot confer content or determine sense (any "sense," even the most intimate) individually, any more than their utterances, texts, myths, or actions can be mysteriously fixed with content just by some "place" or location (or failure to be located) within some structure. If those are the options, I would rather pass than bet, but for reasons stated, I realize, so crudely above, I do not think they are the alternatives.

# 9

## Leaving Nature Behind, or Two Cheers for "Subjectivism"

### *On John McDowell*

Custom is almost a second nature.
(Plutarch, *Rules for the Preservation of Health,* 18)

### I

It is not difficult to imagine quite a credible narrative of the history of philosophy that concentrated mostly on the concept of nature and the various uses to which appeals to nature have been put.[*] For many scholars, the idea that everything in the cosmos was intelligible in itself, that "what it was to be" anything was accessible to human reason as such, marked the origin of a distinctly philosophical approach, and "What is it?" or "What is its nature?" remained the question constantly close to the heart of the philosophic enterprise. All of this could be imagined while conceding that the variations in such appeals are very wide and the links between such uses sometimes difficult to make out.

Almost always, though, some great *opposition* is at stake and the use of the term is meant to distinguish and contrast. In the everyday sense, the contrast is between the familiar, what happens for the most part, what is expectable and normal, and what is uniquely unexpected, out of the ordinary, strange, "unnatural." In early philosophical uses, the important contrasts are between "by nature" and "by art," between *physis* and *techne,* and between nature and custom, *physis* and *nomos.* It is with Lucretius, and *De rerum natura,* that what would eventually become the great issue in modernity first appeared with clarity, even if in an undeveloped form: the

[*] I am indebted to Charles Larmore, Terry Pinkard, and Nicholas Smith for comments on an earlier draft of this chapter.

186

claim that *everything* is natural, and natural in pretty much the same sense, and so *all* bound by the "bond of nature" (*foedus naturae*), including the unusual, the freakish, and even the instituting of, and changes in, human customs and laws. And it is quite important that this most comprehensive appeal should be so immediately associated with the idea of being bound, since this sets out the contrast with our common-sense experience quite well – that we seem to be not ourselves bound but to be able to evaluate and settle on claims about the empirical world and to initiate action as we deem best, not in the way that bees build hives or bloodhounds sniff out trails or water flows downhill.

I mention the range, complexity, and importance of the theme of nature as a way of appreciating the ambition and impressive scope of John McDowell's *Mind and World*.[1] McDowell believes that a specific understanding of the realm of nature, due largely to modern natural science, has had philosophy in its grip for some time, and this in a way that then creates the appearance of unavoidable and largely unanswerable problems: How could meaning be possible? How could we be responsive to and act on reasons, given that we are the natural beings we are? These become such critical questions and their topics begin to look "spooky," or possible only because of nonnatural capacities, when natural being is understood as it is by modern natural science, where all intelligibility, understanding, and explanation are tied to subsumption under scientific law and so to notions of causal necessity. This take on the problem is, broadly speaking, post-Kantian (in the sense of Kant's Third Antinomy, and his dialectic between mechanism and teleology), but McDowell's response is not. For him, we do not need Kant's noumenalism, however that is interpreted,[2] nor do we have to rest content with an "I don't know how freedom is possible, but as agents we are simply stuck with the assumption" approach, the practical point of view. Likewise, he does not plead for the various antidualist positions popular in recent years: functionalism, anomalous monism, dual aspect and emergent property theories, supervenience logics, and so

---

[1] See McDowell, MW. Page references to *Mind and World* are given in the text.

[2] That is, McDowell's point holds whether the noumena-phenomena distinction is understood as a metaphysical dualism, a veil of perception phenomenalism, or a purely methodological, "dual aspect" theory (i.e., in line with the rejection of the "two-world" interpretation, a rejection and methodological reinterpretation pioneered by Graham Bird in Anglophone criticism and Gerold Prauss in the German literature). All of them make the Kantian assumption that McDowell is out to free us from the assumption about the realm of nature itself, and that is what is important for his claim. For a good discussion of the Kantian counterattack, see Sedgwick 2000a.

forth.[3] (He is not optimistic about "social pragmatist" approaches either, as we see below.) None of these, he claims, addresses the root problem – our starting point, nature as the realm of law, that is, the domain of that explicable by subsumption under causal law – and as long as we do not address our unbalanced and narrow commitment to that starting point (the realm of nature as *exhausted* by that notion of explicability), such answers will always seem the unsatisfying hedges that they are. We do not then need a better solution to the post-Kantian problem – how the organic, evolution-produced, biological entities that we are could mean anything or *really* respond to reasons. What we need, instead, is an "exorcism," a way of freeing ourselves from "the starting point" assumption about nature that makes it seem, *prima facie*, that such capacities are simply impossible (147). We need to understand that the dispositions and potentialities with which we come naturally equipped can be "actualized" in adult human beings by a process of socialization and education that goes far beyond anything that might be explicable by reference to the natural events and properties of the biological world, even while it involves nothing non- or supernatural. It is not our nature simply to come to occupy, in response to biological imperatives, an evolved niche in our environment; it is our nature to orient *ourselves* in a world by exercising, perfecting, and critically revising our unique capacity for reasoning, for justifying claims about the world and for explaining and justifying our actions to each other (115–16). Adopting and maintaining such normative stances is just the opposite of "unnatural." It is how we go on as the kind of beings we are. Everything of importance in McDowell's exorcism and, let us say, his "pacifying" of the mind-world tension thus comes down to his ability to convince us that human nature can be said to be a realization

---

[3] Strictly speaking, the objection (especially to Davidson) is not to the ontology dimension of anomalous monism (see MW, 75ff). McDowell shares the intuition behind attempts to render the space of reasons *sui generis* and autonomous. But to conceive it as simply autonomous, with nature conceived wholly as the realm of law, will lead, he thinks, inevitably to a frictionless coherentism. We thus need in effect some overlap between what is possible naturally and our responsiveness to reasons, and Davidson's position does not allow that. Similar sorts of objections, I assume, would be raised against supervenience theories (where the "base," nature, effectively and exclusively determines the truth conditions for any supervening property talk, and such a nature is, again, conceived entirely as exemplification of scientific law).

In TSN, McDowell is comfortable admitting the possibility of "looking for a scientific explanation of the place of, say, ethical discourse in disenchanted nature" (187). He is there interested only in showing that such a "counterpart" account of the causes of and results of ethical discourse is not a competitor with the actual exercise of ethical logos. This sounds more Davidsonean in spirit than the passages in MW.

of a "second nature," still natural, even if second. (It is second because essentially acquired, not the simple, untended maturation of biological properties. There is something of the sense of this natural-yet-cultivated second nature, or tended growth, in the modern notion of culture, another translation for the word McDowell leans heavily on, *Bildung*.)

I want to raise several questions about that attempt, most of them reactions to the many fascinating things McDowell says about the post-Kantian legacy in modern philosophy in general, more specifically, reactions to the way the terms of his account open onto a set of issues in the modern German philosophical tradition.[4] My main question will be whether we gain that much, free ourselves from that much, if we can come to see our capacity for normative stances as "second-nature natural." I want to offer some suggestions that we are better off leaving nature out of the picture altogether and that doing so begs no questions. This will involve a limited defense of what McDowell, in a sweeping indictment, calls "subjectivism."

Although the historical issues are too unwieldy to be treated here, the theme that I want to pursue amounts to one way of understanding the difference between Hegel, on the one hand, and Schiller, Schelling, and even the Kant of the third *Critique*, on the other, at a crucial period in modern philosophy. The latter three all still felt the force of the question *What must nature be like* in order for meaning in nature – conceptually informed sensibility and practical reasons having a grip, for example, but also purposive life, organic wholes – to be possible? This is the question McDowell wants to avoid, as he sometimes puts it, with a "reminder" about, or a pointing toward, a "partially enchanted nature."[5] But ultimately, Hegel did not feel the force of this question. There is, of course, a *Philosophy of Nature* in his *Encyclopedia*, but as anyone who has slogged through it knows, there is a lot there that seems to turn no other wheel elsewhere in what Hegel says, and very little in the *Philosophy of Spirit* seems to depend on it or refer back to it. Said very crudely, the developmental "direction" of Hegel's system (a systematic account of forms of intelligibility, ever better explanatory adequacy) is "away" from nature

---

[4] Perhaps the most important image in the book is a Hegelian one, the "unboundedness of the conceptual," so relied on in Lecture II. As McDowell also writes in Lecture IV: "the way to correct what is unsatisfactory in Kant's thinking about the supersensible is rather to embrace the Hegelian image in which the conceptual is unbounded on the outside" (MW, 83).

[5] There are several articles that discuss the relation between McDowell's position and the German Idealist and Romantic traditions. See Bird 1996; Bowie 1996; Friedman 2002; Sedgwick 1997, 2000a; and Stern 1999.

and "toward" "spirit," *Geist*; his "logic" concerns more the inadequacy of *appeals* to nature as *explicans*. And so he rejects as misguided such "how possible" questions, questions it seems to me that McDowell, despite the "quietism," is still grappling with (even if not answering) by appealing to the possibility of second nature.[6] It is not that McDowell wants to re-animate a romantic or Schellingean philosophy of nature, but even his "reminder" remains tied to the problem of nature, and I want to propose the nonmetaphysical character of the *Natur-Geist* distinction in Hegel as a better way of leaving first nature behind.[7]

How do philosophical exorcisms work? McDowell is candid at the end of his book in admitting that it is unlikely that the considerations he advances will themselves, alone, free us from the grip of this distorting picture (177; for one thing, it is unlikely in the extreme that the origin of this hold was lack of attention to a neglected alternative). His procedure in working at loosening the grip of modern naturalism has, broadly conceived, two steps, or two kinds of moves. One step is the demonstration that our starting point has created unsolvable and unacceptable aporias, especially in epistemology. We end up, he thinks, oscillating between various versions of the Myth of the Given, on the one hand, wherein our putatively decisive, guiding contact with the physical world cannot, paradoxically, be said to play any real normative role in a knowledge claim (we try to understand how such claims could be constrained from "outside" the conceivings we seem able to control and direct, and we fail), and, on the other hand, we give up the idea of exogenous normative constraints or normative foundations and end up with a coherentism in epistemology that looks like a "frictionless" spinning in the void, normatively unconstrained by the way the world is. Appreciating that these are dead ends should then motivate us to search for the assumptions that are

---

[6] I realize that by McDowell's lights, I seem to be asking for exactly what he wants to foreclose, a "*theory* of second nature," which McDowell writes "would be a refusal to take the reminder [of second nature] as I intend it" (C, 123). But McDowell himself seems to present a good deal of theory in explaining the relevance for perception and action of a second-nature reminder, and I do not understand how the various transcendental questions he raises could be addressed by such a reminder alone. I am indebted to Nick Smith for comments on this issue.

[7] Strictly speaking, nothing is ever "left behind" in Hegel's synthetic account, but "*aufgehoben*," or preserved, even while transcended. In this case, the logic of appropriate explanations of nature is not external to and imposed on the natural world, and Hegel has to show how. Hegel's radical insistence on the inseparability of thought and content is at work here as elsewhere. And the concepts required for an account of *Geist* require nothing "unnatural," even if natural accounts are themselves insufficient.

causing things to go so wrong. McDowell's second step is the crucial one, when he diagnoses the origin of such aporetic symptoms and reaches the fundamental claim of his book: that that origin is an unjustified presumption, a distorting picture of the fundamental situation, basically a restricted conception of nature ("the realm of law"). We can "free" ourselves from this conception or begin to work at freeing ourselves from it by appreciating a naturalism that could encompass both a first- and a second-nature naturalism. Once we accomplish that, the problem and the anxiety dissolve (or begin to dissolve).

Such an exorcism rests on three turning points in McDowell's book. There is first the epistemological dilemma sketched in the first two lectures, oriented from Kantian issues and presented in a way designed to disabuse us eventually of the assumptions about nature that generate the dilemma. Second, there is the presentation and defense of the idea of second nature itself. And third, there are various issues introduced by McDowell's invocation of a Wittgensteinian "quietism," or a case for a diagnostic and nonrevisionary version of philosophy, as against a constructive or positive role. I concentrate here on the first two issues, although the last is probably the most important to him and will turn up periodically.

McDowell's starting point is Kant's famous claim in the *Critique of Pure Reason* that "thoughts without content are empty; intuitions without concepts are blind."[8] Contentful human experience requires the cooperation and relation between both faculties. But the statement of the principle already exhibits its paradoxical quality. If intuitions without concepts are blind, how could the application of concepts ever be said to be guided by the intuitive content of a sensory manifold? There would not be any content unless already conceptualized, and if that is so, what could possibly guide the application of the concept? The other side of the dilemma is harder to state but no less real. To explain how concepts without intuitions are empty, Kant has to distinguish between formal logic – where of course concepts are not meaningless and have a certain sort of determinacy – and transcendental logic, where Kant must defend his principle about emptiness and the need to add or supply conceptual content but still allow for the possibility of synthetic a priori knowledge, independent of experienced content. He argues that concepts do not just "acquire" intuitive content from experience. That is, pure concepts must be able to have content that is intuitive even if not empirically derived.

[8] Kant, A51/B75.

Since he must hold to this distinction, even while he insists that a "pure content" is possible for pure concepts, the doctrine of a "pure formal intuition" must supply such a possibility. McDowell underplays the latter issue, preferring to see much of that a priorist strand in Kant as a kind of bald subjectivism, motivated by a sense of nature's complete disenchantment. That issue reappears in a couple of ways below. But it is the former paradox that McDowell is most eager to avoid.[9]

He does so by means of a partly Sellarsian strategy: denying that the concept-intuition distinction is congruent with the spontaneity-passivity distinction. (It is partial because Sellars himself also defends a theoretical role for something like "sheer receptivity.") Our sensory contact with the world is through and through "already conceptual," even if still basically receptive and even if not a product of a fully spontaneous synthesis or judgment. It can thereby stand as a possible reason for a cognitive judgment about the way things are and so play a justificatory role in the normative claim of empirical knowledge. If we do not get this point right, such sensory contact will be conceived in too immediate a way (the Myth of the Given) and can then play only a causal and "exculpatory" role, not a justifying one; or we will make Davidson's error and read such conceptuality as evidence of no real guidance "from without" and opt for a radical coherentism – the frictionless or empirically unconstrained "spinning" that McDowell charges that Davidson leaves us with.

We are, McDowell suggests, so impressed by the fact that sensory looks and feels and smells and so forth are real natural events, occurring in space and time in the same way that fires start and lives end, that we feel constrained to treat such events as our modern notion of nature teaches us to, and that leaves us only with some causal story about how our conscious states got to be the way they are and with no room to introduce the normative language of knowledge claims. We are also impressed, overly impressed according to McDowell, with the accomplishments of higher-order, perceiving animals and so think that our perceivings must be possible like *that*, apart from any complex conceiving or spontaneous mental activity unique to human animals.

Before we get to the diagnostic issue, McDowell needs to make clear just what it is for. Here a variety of locutions are introduced: conceptual

---

9 McDowell does not deal with Kant's category theory in MW. There is a hint of the interpretation he prefers in HWV. There, the dependence of experience on a prior categorial structure is glossed: "[W]e can make sense of objects coming into view in intuitions only because we can see how objects fit into a view of the world" (465). I find this and the argument behind it in Lecture II persuasive but concentrate here on MW.

capacities to be "operative" not only in judgments but "already in the transactions in nature that are constituted by the world's impacts on the receptive capacities of a suitable subject" (xx). This is to be distinguished from the claim that conceptual capacities are exercised "*on* nonconceptual deliverances of sensibility" (39, my emphasis). For McDowell, by contrast, such deliverances are *always already* conceptual, or "capacities that belong to spontaneity are in play in actualizations of receptivity" (66). "In play" in *what* sense, then, if not in an assertoric judgment?[10]

Consider that Kant, for example, had a devil of a time trying to find the right way to put this point, and it might be useful to remind ourselves of the nature of his difficulty.[11] The first *Critique* spoke of a "synthesis of apprehension *in* intuition" but only, apparently, as a component or moment of a full judgmental synthesis, including reproduction and recognition.[12] There was also an obscure notion of a "figurative" synthesis (*synthesis speciosa*) to be distinguished from an "intellectual" synthesis,[13] and that looks like an attempt to invoke the imagination to make the point McDowell is after. And there is a dense, infamous footnote in the second edition that, whatever else is being claimed, appears to assert that any manifold conforming to the intuitional constraints of sensibility already requires a minimal conceptualization, that *intuitional* unity itself "presupposes a synthesis which does not belong to the senses."[14] But neither passage offers much concrete help with the "in play in *what* sense?" question; they just give rise to the question in different ways.

In the *Prolegomena*,[15] Kant goes much further in insisting on the conceptual character of our first "take" on how things are, and he uses language that seems compatible with some of what McDowell wants. There he claims that there is a difference between "*judgments* of perception," which have only subjective validity (but which clearly do involve the exercise of conceptual capacities, if only problematically) and "judgments of experience," which claim objective validity, and that "all our judgments

---

[10] That is, any interpretation must keep faith with Kant's principle: "[T]he senses do not err – not because they always judge rightly, but because they do not judge at all" (A293/B350).

[11] On the important difference between epistemological issues raised by this issue and "transcendental" ones (i.e., the very possibility of objective purport), see McDowell, C, 121.

[12] *Critique of Pure Reason*, A99.

[13] Ibid., B151.

[14] Ibid., B160 n. See McDowell's gloss in "The Logical Form of an Intuition," 456, n. 6, LFI, and the discussion in Pippin 1989, 24–32.

[15] See Kant, P, sec. 18.

are at first merely judgments of perception" and can on reflection "become" judgments of experience. Judgments of perception might thus, following Gerold Prauss's interpretation, be considered mere "seeming" judgments, first takes on the world, first "looks" prior to cognitive commitment, awaiting some sort of objectifying reassurance. The first take, "it seems to me that the sun warms the stone," could become, on reflection, a cognitive commitment, "the sun warms the stone," or "impressions of the sun are regularly followed in my experience by impressions of the stone's warmth" could become "the sun causes the stone to become warm."[16]

Now McDowell, in his introduction to *Mind and World* (xvii), makes clear that he does not want to rest a theory of empirical knowledge on "appearings" or seemings. His ambition is a more common-sense one; or he wants empirical claims to be answerable to the world, not to appearances or impressions, and he certainly does not want some phenomenalist picture in which experience is constructed from subjective states. But Kant, too, is not treating judgments of perception as subjective states out of which experience is built (they are indeed first takes on the way *the world* seems, as *it* first presents itself to me), and much of the language McDowell later introduces suggests this Kantian direction. An early distinction that McDowell makes sounds like Kant in the *Prolegomena*: "How one's experience represents things to be is not under one's control, but it is up to one whether one accepts the appearance or rejects it" (11). He wants, in his account of sensory contact, an account of "the world, as it appears or makes itself manifest to an experiencing subject, or at least seems to do so" (39). "A judgment of experience does not introduce a new kind of content, but simply endorses the conceptual content, or some of it, that is already possessed by the experience on which it is grounded" (48–9). This first "seeming glimpse of the world" (54) already involves the exercise of conceptual capacities because "having things appear to one a certain way is already itself a mode of actual operation of conceptual faculties" (62).[17]

---

[16] Prauss 1971. Prauss also makes extensive use of a *Prolegomena* metaphor that resonates with many of McDowell's interests: that it is necessary "to spell out appearances" first, in order to be able to "read them as experience" (P, sec. 30). There are a number of similarities between Prauss's view and McDowell's, but Prauss does not attend much to the dimension of "seeming" judgments that (rightly) so interests McDowell – that character of being impressed *on* the perceiver, of being immediately (in some sense) how things just seem ("wrung out of one"), and Prauss is content enough with the problematic, "judgmental" quality of such "*Wahrnehmungsurteile.*"

[17] There is a great deal more detail about what is involved in such conceptual-but-not-fully-judgmental, sensory takes on the world in the Woodbridge Lectures, much of it extremely

Although for McDowell, as we see below, there is a parallel practical issue that forces the question of nature on us (how do any claims of reason
come to have a grip on us, move us, as the natural beings we are, to act),
it is clear in his numerous replies to critics, and in his Woodbridge Lectures, that it is the concern about perception as an originally intentional
natural state and about the role it must be able to play in a knowledge
claim that bears most of the burden in the whole enchantment argument. McDowell's concern is about the *immediate* "world-directedness,"
intentionality, or "objective purport" of perceptual states, something that
requires, he argues, a normative context in a special sense if we are to get
that world-directedness right. It is this requirement that any Fichtian talk
of a merely *self*-constrained spontaneity and Hegelian talk of social bases
of normativity threatens to miss.[18] McDowell is clearly convinced that, for
the individual observer, a kind of object-relatedness *happens* in perception, as part of a "transaction *in* nature," all in a way that requires we most
definitely cannot "leave nature out of it."[19] Any such strategy will not allay

helpful, but beyond the scope of one chapter. See "Lecture II: The Logical Form of
an Intuition," LFI, 440–1. What McDowell is doing is essentially reparsing the Kantian
notion of immediacy, away from "conceptually unmediated" and toward something like
"involuntary" just seeming so, not yet subject to our judgmental affirmation, and so forth.
This allows him to account for how such sensory takes "contain" claims in ways quite
different from the way judgments make claims. See especially ibid., 458–9.

[18] McDowell's claim is that there would be nothing for a "context of justification" to be
*about* if we could not account for this objective purport independently of it. This emerges
frequently in his "exchanges with Brandom" and is no doubt how he would reply to
Michael Williams's suggestions in Williams 1996.

[19] McDowell's condition on what the nature of rational constraint in perception amounts
to is one of the most important elements in his response to Brandom. See Brandom
1996, and McDowell's P, where McDowell writes: "Brandom's less demanding reading
of the constraint does not yield anything genuinely recognizable as the rational vulner-
ability of thinking to the world" (293–4). He means, as the next paragraph makes clear,
recognizable for the subject, even as he also admits that this subject cannot be detached
from the languages and traditions into which he has been initiated. Throughout his
discussion and replies, if what it amounts to for conceptual capacities to be "in play"
in the looks or takes "wrung out" of one by contact with the world are (and are for the
experiencer) what it *would be* for a judgment to have been made, and this capacity is itself
rich with "tradition" and so sociality (what it would be to judge is a matter of what else
I would be committed to backing up, etc.), then I do not see the need to drag nature
into the discussion. I should note again: Sometimes McDowell gives the impression that
*he* means to say: "I don't have any particular stake in a possible appeal to nature, but
anybody who *was* dead set on orienting all possible explanation from what was 'naturally possible' would not find himself fated to be a reductionist if he could appreciate
second-nature. If he doesn't start off with naturalist assumptions in the first place, I've
nothing in particular to say to him." See McDowell, C, 122–3.

our philosophic distress about the possibility of such a prejudgmental but conceptual state.

That "normative context" is conceptual structure and discrimination, or the way in which perceptual takes on the world are conceptually normative, if in a special sense. For the way in which claims are embedded in perception is not the way claims are actually made in judgments. Any immediately experienced, conceptually determinate state is not itself the result of a judgment (that would have to require a nonconceptual manifold, and the merry-go-round would start again) but presents us with a conceptually contentful "item" that is an element in what it would be to have so discriminated judgmentally (as in a "this-cube perception" and not "there is a cube here").

But I do not see that, having traced the issue to this level, we have yet met up necessarily with the problem of nature and second nature. Even if this sort of relatedness claim is normative in a *special* sense, it still of course means at least having already understood, mastered, the proper conceptual role of "cube," all in such a way that having *such* a perception "wrung out of one" is recognizable *to* one and so must be understood as the product in some way of a discriminating activity. But if we are proceeding in a roughly Kantian context, then such concepts are "predicates of possible judgments," and understanding the content of the concept means having mastered its role, understanding how it can and cannot be combined with other possible concepts. And it is not much of a leap from here to claim that the discriminatory capacity essential for and operative in objective purport thus already requires and draws on a general claim-making competency, the *content* of which derives from the proprieties and prohibitions of a predicate's possible use in judgment. This sort of discrimination, even if problematic, cannot be said to have been simply "wrung out of one." It would be a long story, but not an unfamiliar one, then to see such proprieties and so forth (i.e., norms) as essentially social and some of them as not "due to experience" at all but "due to us," if Kant's worry about a priori knowledge has any purchase. The presence of a perceptible cube does not then just "wring out of us" this-sphere perceptions; the possibility of that content requires a receptiveness that is also already actively, even if provisionally, *discriminating.* If normatively constrained, then (the longer story would go), it would be *socially* informed and socially constrained. It is that activity, training, and sociality (a historical and social, not a natural result) that make possible such determinate intentionality, and the more we emphasize this, the more the question of answerability shifts from answerability "to the world" to "to each other." Or at least those two issues begin to seem inseparable, even if distinct.

McDowell is right that in such first takes, I assume no "responsibility" for such content; it just seems that ____. But how is it that such a first take is going to play a role in what we ultimately determine that there is? If such a "look" counts as a reason to say there is such an object *because* it was wrung out of us involuntarily, then its sheer "wrungness" looks like a nonconceptual consideration, close to causal considerations, the "guiding from without" that McDowell wants to avoid, an exculpation.[20] If the determination that there is a cube here is reasonable because such a first take coheres with other takes and perceptions and with what others are willing to say, all "according to a rule," then the question of normative propriety will lead us back to some form of social normativity again, and the "take" (*even with respect to its content*) will be parasitic on that capacity, not on "nature." Or it could so depend on such a capacity, understood as so constituted; that would be one sort of explanation, and that is all I am claiming. No re-enchanted nature need apply.[21] Moreover, without something like a *theory* of second nature, something more than a reminder about such acquisitions, it is not hard to imagine all sorts of bald naturalists nodding in agreement, convinced that the "training up" of "neural nets" can handle second-nature considerations just fine.

Put a different, much more general way, the relevant image for our "always already engaged" conceptual and practical capacities in the German Idealist tradition is *legislative power*, not empirical discrimination and deliberative judgment, and the force of this image of legislative power makes it very difficult to integrate what McDowell says about the overall effect of

---

[20] See Williams 1996, 106.

[21] Or Sellars could be right about the possibility of what he calls "noumenal science." He distinguishes between "the conceptual framework of which nature was the cause" and the "freely elaborated conceptual frameworks with which we now challenge Nature" but notes that the latter is "free" only because the reality about which it ultimately theorizes is in principle unobservable and incapable of effecting within experience a causal alteration in our theories. So the framework is only "free" *relative* to the objects it is about and is in itself a (noumenal) causal system. Where McDowell thinks the paralogisms leave open the possibility that the I is an embodied, natural (second-nature) subject, Sellars thinks they leave open that the I is a "system of scientific objects, the true counterparts of Kant's things-in-themselves." See Sellars 1969, 248–52. McDowell states his criticism of Sellars on this general point at the end of LFI, 467, but his remarks there still seem to me open to the Sellarsian rejoinder that McDowell has not taken full enough account of the fact that Sellars wants the "sheer receptivity" guidance "from below the line" to be an object of such a noumenal science, purely theoretical and postulated and not to be confused with the "guiding" constituents of experience as experienced.

*Bildung* – that it simply "opens our eyes" and allows us to "see the reasons that are always there whether we notice them or not" – with the Kantian and even Hegelian elements he has also imported.[22] And I mean that those elements that McDowell would want to call "subjectivist," given the starting points common to McDowell and the Idealists, cast reasonable doubt, raise appropriate questions, about McDowell's position. The point is not a historical one. One can see this more clearly in considering the manner of his invocation of the notion of second nature.

The transition to that topic might be introduced this way. The most complex and potentially the richest idea in *Mind and World* (and in the later Woodbridge Lectures) is the notion that one can regard sensible in-tuitions as always already conceptually shaped, even though still genuinely receptive. If we can hold onto this somewhat slippery idea, we can reject mythological givens and still find a way of explaining how the world "has its own say" in how we take it up and eventually make judgments about it. But, as noted above, the "conceptually shaped" part of that claim has already altered what it could mean for "the world to exercise constraint." "Conceptually shaped" means shaped in one form rather than another, and if our conceptual array is not *all* as it is because everywhere and in all decisive senses responsive to experiences of the world, then we would seem inevitably pushed away from a comprehensive empirical interpre-tation of "constrained by the world" (although, again, not away from the notion of constraint altogether). What *counts* as constraint and the no-tion of a collective *self*-constraint (what we allow each other to claim as justified) look to loom larger. After all, if the world is said to be *doing* all the constraining, we start sliding back toward foundationalisms and mythic givens. McDowell wants to resist what he regards as quite an under-standable move at this point, were it the case that all meaning had been expelled from nature. Namely, he wants to resist relying heavily on the social dimension of normativity, socially "made" criteria about what is ap-propriate or not, justified or not, within some social practice, all in order to "reintroduce" such meaning. This is a kind of "subjectivism," an inter-subjective kind, which he wants to avoid, together with all other forms of meaning-making subjectivism. Again, we (supposedly) resist *his* option – that our "conceptual capacities" are "operative also in our perception of the world apart from human beings" (72) – because we do not think nature or our nature could embody such meaning. We can avoid *that*

---

[22] We cannot, of course, legislate arbitrarily; the *quid iuris* question must still be addressed.

anxiety – and so the social pragmatist and all subjectivist temptation – if we are just reminded that second natures are possible and that with the right acquisition of such a second nature our normative response to the world will not be a species of the subjectivist or "social pragmatist" genus. We will simply have our "eyes opened" to what is and what ought to be.

## II

How does this occur, so that we end up "resonating" to reason in the space of reasons? Much of McDowell's discussion in *Mind and World* and elsewhere is oriented from a very important and valuable negative answer; that is, an account of what such a resonating *is not*. It involves a compelling interpretation of Aristotle on the acquisition of second natures. The basic point is that we should not understand the proper exercise of practical reason to be in some way based on some known fact about nature, neither a teleological fact about how natures perfect themselves and flourish nor some Hobbesian fact about passions, fears, and interests, which then functions as what we appeal to in order to justify what we decide to do (78–81). As he points out, there will always be some gap between any claim about what members of my species do, how they come to flourish, what they must avoid to stay healthy, and so forth and what reasons bear on what I must face at some moment, as an individual. Such facts do not on their own give *me* a reason to do anything; I can always acknowledge them but count as a more compelling reason for me free riding, deceiving, malingering, taking a risky gamble, or whatever.[23] Likewise, we should not take this to mean that the formative powers of second-nature training only habituate our dispositional and emotional characters to be inclined to obey, to submit to, what *phronesis* or practical wisdom dictates. We will not get Aristotle or the point right, McDowell argues (especially not Aristotle's puzzling indifference to ethical justification or his insistence that he is writing only for people already properly brought up), unless we take full measure of the fact that practical reason itself is formed, shaped, wholly dependent (even in its self-correcting aspects) on a proper formation within an ethical community.[24] *Its* exercise and authority, not just our willingness to submit, can thus be understood only within and

[23] See McDowell, TSN, sec. 3.
[24] See ibid., 184, n. 33.

as a "natural" product of such a community. A practically wise man does not know something about nature that helps him to see what to do or to justify his actions, and he has not merely been made malleable to what practical reason demands. His rational nature itself has come to be formed in a certain way, or it is not what it would have been had he been improperly or otherwise brought up. It is *because* it has thus been shaped that *different aspects of the practical landscape look different to him, have a different salience,* all in such a way that he has, just by virtue of how he understands what is happening, reasons to act that he would not otherwise have.

Taking such a full measure means we will be able to resist what I have already indicated that McDowell's account (enthusiastically) leaves out in his appropriation of the German tradition (and what I want to claim cannot be omitted): what he calls "subjectivism" in ethics. We are tempted, he thinks (especially if we are some species of Kantians), toward a number of bad alternatives by virtue of having come to think that *all* there really is are the objects of the modern sciences. If the exercise of practical reason must always occur in a way naturally explicable, can be conceived as having some grip only in a way continuous with the kind of emotional and responsive being one is by nature, and if we think of that nature as disenchanted, the realm of law, and so on, we will then face the obvious alternatives of pointing to what our natural (first-nature) psychology *can* handle as motivating such a grip: passions, self-interest, contingently acquired desires, and the like. Or we might take the opposite tack and insist on the radically nonnatural status of the faculty of practical reason altogether, insisting that it owes nothing to our empirical natures and instead issues commands based on its own authority alone. Meaning in McDowell's extended sense would then be understood as made by subjects and projected onto a disenchanted nature. For a variety of reasons, McDowell argues that in the latter scenario we could never explain how such a conception of practical reason could ever have a grip on us, that is, ever produce reasons for me to act.

On almost all the major points here, I think McDowell is right, and, along the way, he has also managed to state with great economy the nature of a deep, persistent, fundamental worry in the German tradition after Kant, from Schiller to Hegel to Nietzsche to Heidegger. It was first made noticeable by Schiller's "rigorism" critique of Kant, but Hegel's early critique of the "positivity" of the Christian religion and his use of the same notion to criticize Kant (his insistence that we must find a way to understand how the demands of reason could be said to be "embodied," *verkoerpert*) surfaces with surprising regularity afterward with respect to all sorts of ideals.[25]

But any response to such a worry should, I think, once again leave nature out of it and accept and work within a basic distinction between spirit and nature, *Geist* and *Natur*. These are, in other words, all images and are not meant to invite us to ask how a rational consideration can literally become part of nature, in some way not explicable by subsumption under natural law. The problem concerns a kind of historical achievement – an achievement that has now, in the modern world, become much harder than it ever was, perhaps even impossible. The question is: How does a claim of reason or a commitment to an ideal or goal become part of the fabric of some form of life? How is the achievement of a genuinely common-mindedness (something quite different from a codified, explicit belief system, or subjective commitment to ideals) possible? How could there be a common-mindedness such that our reactions to conduct that is objectionable have become so intimate and such a part of that fabric that the conduct being the sort of conduct it is counts *thereby* as reason enough to condemn it? But to understand this, we do not need to know anything about growth, organic life, cultivated nature, and so forth. We need to understand "the labor of the Concept" in time.[26]

In Hegel's *Encyclopedia* presentation such a line between appeals to nature and appeals to intention, between practical reasons and purposiveness, is not a sharp one. There is a kind of overlap of the sort that interests McDowell, but it has a human meaning for Hegel only as an "expression" of a historical spirit. In his "Anthropology" (the first part of his "Philosophy of Subjective Spirit"), he is concerned to preserve and understand properly (in their relation to other sorts of accounts) certain kinds of explanation that must partially appeal to the natural conditionedness of human life. We know, for example, that a person's outlook, the way she thinks about everything, is some sort of a function of her natural age; we know that diet and climate are not irrelevant to cultural practices; we know that the body, especially the face, can carry and convey a meaning like no linguistic event; and we know that in our erotic

---

[25] See, e.g., Kierkegaard on the difficulty, the impossibility, of truly becoming a Christian; Marx on alienation; Nietzsche's way of raising the problem of whether truth could be "incorporated," *einverleibt*; and Heidegger's accounts of "falling" and inauthenticity.

[26] For more on the subjectivism issues, and an especially clear statement of why his rejection of "projectivist" versions does not commit him to a straightforward realism, see PTE, esp. 159. See also Wiggins 1987, and for a valuable account of the empirical/philosophical distinction at stake in this problem, see Lear 1998.

life, we are hardly projecting a subjective meaning onto a disenchanted machine. And Hegel has his own way of accounting for the "place" of such appeals, but that way does not require any second *nature*. The plot for his narrative concerns attempts by human spirit to free itself from a self-understanding tied to nature, and these anthropological elements are understood as initial, very limited successes.[27]

McDowell's invocation of a kind of natural development and training of our conceptual-discriminatory and judgmental-evaluative capacities, by contrast, soon does invoke the teleological language of "actualizations of our nature" (76). In the same vein, he writes that "our mode of living [with its educated exercise of spontaneity] is our way of actualizing ourselves as animals" (78). Moreover, there is a lot of talk about appropriate upbringing and "proper" training. This latter is either window dressing, that is, philosophically idle ("proper" just *to* any old community, by *its* lights; the Talibans, for example, in which case "proper" doesn't distinguish much). Or it is substantive, in which case, while participants need not base what they do on a knowledge of what is naturally proper, somebody, McDowell, for example, had better be able to defend the idea of "*by nature* proper/improper" for the claim to have any philosophical purchase. If all *that* comes down to is producing something like "critical reasoning skills" and that is "proper" because it "can open a human being's eyes" to "the demands of reason," it would be nice to have some examples of the latter with which to reassure ourselves about the direction this is heading.

The former, developmental, teleological language also seems relatively idle. It is all very well to claim (and it is a fine way to put it) that "certain bodily goings-on *are* our spontaneity in action, not just effects of it," and that this "is central to a proper understanding of the self as a bodily presence in the world" (90, n. 5), but there does not seem to be a lot for "*nature*" to do in any concrete account of the various possible realizations of such spontaneity-in-body. Given the unbelievable variety in human culture, it seems safe to say that first nature radically underdetermines, even while it conditions, any second nature. And while Aristotle's hylomorphism might help us to see here how one might in general avoid dualism (the soul just *is* the being-at-work of the body), there is no reason I can see not just to stop there with the Stagirite and not buy into his or any other account of species-specific and determinate forms of *natural* actualization (small cities, patriarchy, natural slaves, slow gait, deep voice, and so on).

[27] For a fuller discussion of this point, see Pippin 1999b.

If the point is simply that given the various biological and neurological capacities we are endowed with by nature and evolution, human beings have (as a matter of natural fact) the capacity to make, sustain, hold themselves to, and pass on in historical memory various kinds of normative institutions and can form the characters such institutions require and can create practices that allow for developing and revising the various claims for institutional authority inherent in such institutions, what is then gained by declaring so insistently that all of *this* must be understood as a "realization of second nature"?[28] To adopt Rortyean rhetoric, it sounds more like an attempt at an exaggerated compliment than a substantive point. Unless we need to claim, as some objection, something brutally obvious, say that some such possible realizations are in themselves grossly unnatural – that is, unless we are talking about institutional practices that try to educate human beings to perform like ants or beavers, and so on, and I take it that we are not – then "second nature" just means "*deeply* habitual," a historically achieved result (not naturally achieved, in any sense of "due *to* nature"), the observance of which eventually becomes largely unreflective. A culture (*Bildung*) in this sense, while it is something we must have the requisite natural, enabling capacities to build and sustain, *is only* something that we build and sustain. "Subjectivism" then, directing us as it does toward the historical dissatisfactions and tensions responsible for the institutional change we effect, seems unproblematic enough and to be directing us properly, toward history, not nature, as the domain where accounts of human practices are to be based. In Hegel's somewhat puzzling language, while "*Geist*" is not nonnatural or immaterial, it *is* "a product of itself."[29]

The notion of practical reason gaining some purchase in our lives, having its distinctive grip, thus plays a role in McDowell's theory parallel to his claims about a sensibility in which conceptual capacities can be activated. We need both, he thinks, in order to avoid the bad alternatives and aporias that stem from the implications of accepting the modern notion of nature, and, he thinks, only a "partially re-enchanted" nature,

---

[28] Given how little content there is in McDowell's own appeals to second nature, perhaps this all simply *is* his position, and second nature *is* only an image, the point being to disabuse us of the notion of taking up or discarding norms as the result of reflection or choice. Historically acquired forms of life are (but are only) like nature in *that* sense.

[29] Hegel kept flirting, of course, with the idea that one might understand nature as "dormant" or implicit or "sleeping" Geist, as if nature had a *conatus*, striving to be *Geist*, but he also succumbed to his better side, as in the *Lectures on Fine Art*, where *Natur* is called simply "spiritless," *geistlos*. See Hegel, A, 12.

this second nature, will allow us to maintain consistently both such a purchase and such an activation. But defending a "partially enchanted" nature seems quite a high price. A "*gezauberte Natur*," after all, is a "nature made magical," and there seems no good reason to be driven that far. What one wants to object to in bald naturalism is not so much what gets counted as "occurring in nature or not" but what gets counted as a sufficient explanation, and there is no necessary connection between the latter and the former issue. There are some philosophers who obviously think there is and who are convinced that a naturalist ontology has to mean that it will "one day" be possible to explain naturalistically, perhaps through evolutionary neurobiology, why Germans voted for Hitler and why the Yankees won the pennant, but surely the right response to them is "I won't hold my breath" and not a rush to enchant nature.[30]

In sum, if the space of reasons, as a historically constituted human practice, is autonomous, *sui generis*, not explicable in first-nature terms, not supernatural, subject to revision and critical correction, then what is going wrong with what McDowell calls "subjectivism" just seems to be some distorting implications of the "projection" metaphor. This would include, of course, the possible inference that, since such subjectivity is unconstrained by the world or by a direct perception of what ought to be done, it is unconstrained, period. It is thus understandable that that charge was the first blast in German romanticism and in the German counterenlightenment led by Jacobi. However, such implications stem from limited interpretations of such subjectivity and not from the basic point about subjectivity as source.[31]

---

[30] This is in effect what McDowell says in his *Précis* for P, in response to Fodor, 238. But he takes himself to be entitled to it only by having defended an enchanted nature, whereas I think the radical reductionist and eliminativist position begs the question of "explanation" at the start.

[31] Of course, we are also going to need a different sort of argument about the ineliminability of such a domain, something other than an appeal to the proper realization of our nature. That appeal will have to be one to some sort of practical unavoidability and it will not be easy. That is, we cannot content ourselves with just noting the *physis-nomos* distinction in the way Williams does (1996, 104). From even well before Lucretius, it was possible to claim that what *looks* like *nomos* is really *physis* again (the rule of the stronger, and so forth); the nature of its "self-regulating" potential is not easy to make out, and the basis for insisting on the autonomy of a kind of explanation, *without* an enchanted nature ontology, present difficult problems. There is a hint of this sort of strategy in McDowell himself when he distinguishes between the "forms of intelligibility" proper to explanations in nature and forms that belong in the space of reasons. But that seems to him due to the difference between first and second nature. See Rorty's comments in Rorty 1998, 144.

The more direct, obvious, erroneous implication of the projection image is that such normative commitments are viewed as "up to" individuals conceived in isolation from the world or from their tradition and community, as noumenal beings, rational choosers, or projective responders. The error is to think that such commitments can either be adopted and abandoned as the straightforward result of, as objects of, reflection and imposed on a blank content or a formless life or that lacking anything in the metaphysical world to make the projections true, we decided that there is no way to evaluate subjective stances at all.[32] But we can take on all those points – the rejection of dogmatic empiricism as well as a transcendentalism that separates concept and content, the subjective stance from its occasion in the social world, and concepts from their historical and social authority – and still insist on the autonomy and revisability of rationality, without needing to wave that "red flag" of a "partially enchanted" nature.

---

[32] See again the valuable points made by McDowell in PTE, especially on the "earned versus unearned truth" distinction.

# Postscript: On McDowell's Response to "Leaving Nature Behind"

The preceding chapter first appeared in *Reading McDowell: On Mind and World*, edited by Nicholas H. Smith (2002). McDowell responded individually to each of the essays in the collection, and the Cambridge University Press referees for this manuscript all suggested that I make use of this occasion to write a response to that response. I respond at some length (quite a bit more than the three pages of McDowell's rejoinder) because the theme of this book – the persistence of the difficulty in understanding what it is to be the subject of thought and of action and the importance of the post-Kantian struggle to understand that issue – comes up in an important way in McDowell's recent work in general and in these rejoinders, and I hope to make use of this occasion to try to clarify some controversial issues.

I try first to summarize McDowell's counters. There are five points. First, since much of "Leaving Nature Behind" (LNB) argues that one of McDowell's worries, "subjectivism," should, when properly understood, not be seen as a danger and that there is no good reason to drag "nature" into the discussion, McDowell first complains that I am inflating his use of such an appeal in order to complain about it. "Bald naturalists" are the worry. For anyone who thinks that nature, as understood in modern naturalism (or physicalism, or scientism, etc., as the domain explicable by subsumption under law), raises a great puzzle about how natural objects *can* be meaningful, responsive to reasons, act on reasons, and so on, then the discussion of nature in MW can "exorcise," help to rid them of the picture that generates the anxiety. They will complain that, since sensibility "is part of our natural endowment," there is no way to understand our conceptual capacities as "actualized" in such sensibility, and since anything not within the scope of "natural-scientific understanding" is ruled out as queer or spooky, this will appear to create a philosophical difficulty about the objective purport of the deliverances of sensibility (leading, ultimately, to the unacceptable alternatives of only "causal" guidance from experience, or no guidance, frictionless spinning). In sum,

> The transcendental work – the work of making objective purport unmysterious – is done here by the idea that conceptual capacities figure not only in free intellectual activity but also in operations of receptivity outside our control. Nature is relevant only in connection with a possible threat to that idea. (RM, 274)

Second, McDowell accuses me of not appreciating properly that he, too (without hesitation or reluctance), embraces the idea that a "social framework" matters to the very idea of the conceptual, that McDowell's account of objective purport is meant not to be some sort of competitor account of cognitive normativity but to complement our "answerability to each other" with the right sort of account of our "answerability to the world." And he is not out simply to "reverse the order" of these two. "In my picture answerability to the world and answerability to each other have to be understood together" (275). Anyone who (like me) does not properly credit this sort of connectedness and who thus conceives of McDowell as if he is defending an "individualistically conceived taking in of reality" will likely be misled into trying to find a greater role for nature in the overall account than is warranted.

The third point, about ethical contexts, mirrors the first. *If* some bald naturalist, by virtue of being so, thinks that "the capacity to know what there is reason for one to do" cannot find a coherent place in such a nature and so is tempted to reconstrue our ethical lives in a radical way so as to line up such practices properly with the "modern" notion of nature (and so in explanations of the norms persons hold each other to – why these, why so important, etc. – will happily invoke insect behavior, evolutionary struggle, brain chemicals, etc.), we simply need a way to help him to see that he is starting off in the wrong direction *unnecessarily*. "Being initiated into an ethical community" is what helps to form the second-nature responsiveness, sensitivities, discriminatory capacities, and the like that some biological organisms (us) inculcate in their communities over time. And so, "once my reminder of second nature has done its work, nature can drop out of my picture too . . ." (RM, 277).

Then there is the issue of the Germans, Kant and Hegel. The fourth point concerns my worry about just what it could mean, especially in a Kantian context, for capacities that belong to spontaneity to be "in play" in episodes of receptivity. My suggested readings are said either to be unhelpful (drag with them more problems than they solve, e.g., the *Prolegomena* doctrine of "judgments of perception") or to misstate what "in play" amounts to. McDowell cites A79/B104–5 of the first *Critique* to explain his (and Kant's considered) position: "The same function which gives unity to the various representations in a judgment also gives unity to the various representations in an intuition." This is taken to mean that "the logical form of an intuition is none other than the logical form of a possible judgment of experience" (RM, 276). And again, understanding what McDowell is really concerned with (preserving the role of receptivity without a crude empiricism or bald naturalism) will further calm any concerns about nature doing any "heavy transcendental lifting."

The fifth point concerns Hegel and the compatibility (or lack of it) between elements of McDowell's realism (my term here, not his) and what McDowell concedes is the basic "normative model," let us say, in all of Hegel's work: self-legislation. McDowell suggests that my claims about this potential incompatibility derive from far too strong an interpretation of what self-legislated normative authority amounts to. Rather, "our freedom, which figures in the image as our legislative power, must include a moment of receptivity" (RM, 277). If it does, then that is autonomy enough (i.e., that we accept no constraint on our actions other than what it is reasonable to do – in this sense we are subject only to "ourselves," and are so self-legislating). It deserves either three cheers, understood in this way, or none at all. (In a note, McDowell remarks that Brandom is also committed to a position "that brings norms into existence out of a normative void" (ibid.).)

On the first point, I begin with a remark that may seem to have me arguing against myself. I think McDowell has been largely misunderstood by commentators out to get straight above all and before all else "the adequacy" of his appeal to Kant and Hegel in support of his now well-known and often summarized MW strategy: to avoid the Myth of Given and Frictionless Coherentism by diagnosing the assumption that gives rise to the dilemma – disenchanted nature – and then to exorcise the spell, as it were, cast by that notion by means of his second-nature reminder. It is pretty obvious that McDowell's own statement of the problem – the worry that "conceptual phenomena cannot be integrated into the natural as they [the bald naturalists] conceive it" (RM, 303) and the worry that, since sensory interchange with the natural world is obviously such a natural event, such contact can guide either only causally or not at all – is certainly not an explicit worry of Kant's. (Trying to find something close to this in

Kant leads Friedman to think the problem must be like how to connect up mathematical procedures and structures with the empirical world, how mathematics and physics, as synthetic a priori knowledge, are possible. This then leads him into a history of logical positivism and, I think, quickly away from Kant's and McDowell's problem.) [1] McDowell is, rather, looking for "the best approach to Kant for us" (RM, 271), and he sees in Kant, especially Kant's second edition deduction, a way of understanding the actualizations of conceptual capacities in receptive, passive deliverances of sensibility that can serve as a constraint on judgment, even though naturally occurring episodes, and that this notion, when supplemented by a non-Kantian doctrine ("second nature" instead of "transcendental subjectivity" – here the Hegelianism emerges) can pacify the anxieties of the (or of a certain sort of) naturalist.

Fair enough, but that strategy is rather narrowly directed *only* at that naturalist whose main worry about constraints on thought concerns the naturally occurring (caused and causing) status of sensory episodes; Davidson, say. But if we are to look for the "best approach to Kant for us," then, I wanted to suggest, we must do full justice to his worry about naturalism and its general threat to the possibility of a space of reasons, the threat to the possibility of what Kant called "spontaneity." That is, suppose that someone is worried whether natural organisms like us *could* be said to be responsive to reasons in general, rather than causally impelled into a piece of linguistic behavior that a community would be disposed to treat in a certain, common predictable way. We want "answering a demand for a justification by trying to give one," not "provoked into an utterance of a type." (This is the same worry in cognitive as well as practical contexts. We want the episode or statement, "such and such is occurring," to be a normative commitment to a claim, not the causal activation of a trained-up disposition.)

That is, Kant's worry was about a naturalist skepticism directed against the possible *spontaneity* of thought (associationism is one way of giving in to that skepticism), and he was not himself worried about the guiding role of a naturalistically conceived sensibility.[2] (This is particularly clear in the *Groundwork*'s treatment of the "spontaneity of thought.") We need to get that in view, too, in order to see and possibly learn from the full Kantian response. When we do, I doubt that that person is going to be much impressed to hear that a good deal of training and socialization is

---

[1] Michael Friedman, "Exorcising the Philosophical Tradition," in RM, 25–57.
[2] Granted, he should have been more worried. See Pippin 1982, chap. 2, 26–53.

necessary before what some social community will count as a response
behavior will be possible. We can throw in lots of neural-net, training-
up, self-monitoring, self-correcting software jargon into our picture of
how such sociality works and we will do all the justice we need to the
second-nature point. (This same complex of issues and problems will
also arise for the third point McDowell makes.) Put another way, there
is a reason why psychologistic (naturalist psychology) readings of Kant
keep reappearing, whether or not we add into the Kantian picture conceptual capacities operating in the uptake or trained-up second natures.
(All of these are in principle "naturalizable.") The reason is that it is
not clear how to describe the "transcendental" point of view in general
(likewise with a second-nature, but reason-responsive subjectivity), coupled with the conviction that, *whatever* we are up to in getting the world
right, it must be explicable naturalistically because we are, after all, bits
of matter in space and time. There were plenty of naturalized episte-
mologies (of a sort) for Kant to worry about (Hume, especially Tetens),
and worry about them he did, all in a way I think is not yet touched by
the second-nature point. This may not be the point McDowell was trying
to make (he has a certain kind of naturalist in view and is leaving the
very possibility of a space of reasons out of the picture for now), but I
was trying to suggest that it will enter the picture very soon if we want a
full address to the "threat" posed by a disenchanted nature, and when
we do broaden the issues, the second-nature response does not help
much. (We will, I think, have to move directly to the question of what
best explains our subject's conduct, and then straight to what counts
as adequate explanation, something I claim underlies the Encyclopedia
system.)[3]

The second point – McDowell's denial that his picture of objectivity,
the right way to think about what constrains our judgings, our claims
to normative justifiability, overemphasizes individuals' sensible contact
with objects, or receptivity in general, and so neglects the social nature of
such constraints – and the fourth point – how McDowell understands A79,
"The same function which gives unity to the various representations in a
judgment also gives unity to the various representations in an intuition" –
need to be discussed together. The point at dispute concerns both the
right way to understand the Kant-Hegel relation (and so the role of appeals to sociality in philosophical disputes) and the issues themselves.
The former is relevant because one way to understand that Kant-Hegel

[3] Pippin 1999b.

relation is that Hegel's very different approach to the problem of a concept's objectivity involves the role of sociality in his *Phenomenology of Spirit*, an approach that will eventually introduce a whole social and historical conception of subjectivity, rather than a formal-transcendental account.[4] This means that an appeal to "answerability to each other" will play a stronger role in Hegel than, I think, McDowell will want.[5] This is all something best understood by understanding Hegel's notion of the failure (as well as the achievements) of Kant's transcendental deduction, an issue that will take up as critical passages such as the A79 passage above.

That is a lot of balls to heave into the air at one time. It is best to recall first that Kant's Transcendental Deduction involves quite a complex relation to a skeptical challenge. On the surface is the challenge to the possibility of synthetic a priori knowledge, the claim to be able to know something (distinctly philosophical or mathematical or scientific) about any possible object of experience and to know this independently of any actual experience. The Deduction's version of the problem is "the objective validity of the pure concepts of the understanding." (By and large, McDowell follows Strawson in neglecting this goal in favor of a more modest inquiry into the necessary elements of any possible concept of experience.) But responding to this skepticism, for Kant at least, requires responding to a question Kant claims philosophers have not even raised as such: whether we can account for the very possibility of any representation of an object, or the possibility of experience itself, what McDowell calls the possibility of objective purport. In Kant's mind, of course, these are deeply linked: Answering the second will resolve the first. Objective purport, the very possibility of experience, can be shown to require categorical discriminations that cannot be accounted for empirically (they are conditions necessary *for* such a possible experience), and we thereby can demonstrate the objective validity of pure concepts, but only as such necessary "subjective" conditions for experience (something Kant takes as a serious limit on the proof, a claim that Strawson and McDowell dispute).[6]

---

4 Something itself similar to McDowell on "second natures."

5 Although nowhere near as strong as in Richard Rorty's account, where answerability to others replaces answerability to the world in a wholesale way, and the latter is treated as an unacceptable restriction on freedom. See "Solidarity or Objectivity?" in Rorty 1991.

6 There is also, of course, garden-variety modern skepticism about the external world and other minds. Kant is not terribly interested in this form, thinks it a scandal for philosophy that it keeps reappearing, and tries to swat it away forever with his famous "Refutation of Idealism."

Unfortunately, this whole issue now turns on an interpretation of the endlessly complicated second edition Deduction and how to understand what appears there as something like a blurring of the sharp boundaries between the twin conditions of experience set out by Kant, the pure forms of intuition and the pure concepts of the understanding. But I have not been able to think of a way of responding to McDowell's second and fourth points without getting into the issue.

Hegel applauds this blurring, or collapse; so do I; and so does McDowell. Kant is heading away from a claim that our ability to render our experience intelligible, to account for the necessary conditions of this possibility, works only in some limited way, and this because the "aesthetic" conditions of our experience, the forms of intuition, must be understood as restricting the claim for the objective validity of our pure concepts. They restrict that objectivity from "outside" thought, as it were. (We are just stuck with discursive thought (intellectual intuition is a logical possibility, Kant concedes) and just stuck with spatio-temporal forms of intuition.)

McDowell's notion of how to understand the "unboundedness" of the conceptual enters here. He wants to "correct" Kant's tendency, once he gets rolling in this blurring-the-boundary project, to understand even the formal (nonderived) aspects of our immediate contact with the world as *manifestations of apperceptive spontaneity*, a tendency that McDowell thinks would greatly exaggerate the misleading "imposition" image of idealism and would contribute to the general picture of post-Kantian idealism as devoted to self-generated systems of pure thought, as if thought could determine its own content.

A standard way of looking at Kant's own strategy would be the following. We want to know why being-minded as we are is not subject to skeptical doubt (i.e., why it is not the case that our forms of mindedness are mere impositions and, since impositions, cut us off from what the world would look like in itself, from the view from nowhere, etc.).[7] What we want to know is how to deal with the "merely our way of categorizing" suspicions, especially if we are not appealing to any empirical fact of the matter to establish our being so minded. One way (Kant's way, I think) would be to show that the sensible presence of the world in our immediate, receptive contact with it just *could* not violate the requirements of our mindedness. To do *this*, though, we have to be able to formulate a way to describe formally, "all at once," as it were (a priori),

---

[7] B138; A158/B197.

something necessarily characteristic of such a putatively prejudgmental manifold that we can then "use" to make the argument about the impossibility of any "non- or bad fit" with conceptual requirements. We need the mere *forms* of givenness as such, and to do their job, they have to be "outside" thought, independent conditions. This leads to the standard picture of transcendental idealism, because this latter move has to look like a restriction and like a strangely psychological fact about our finitude.

McDowell (in MW and elsewhere) offers a correction. The possibility of (phenomenologically) prejudgmental, perceptual objective purport *only* requires us to be in the possession of certain conceptual capacities. It is not the case that we are actively judging by means of these capacities or that we are spontaneously at work in any way in intuiting the world. We need only argue that the kind of unity possessed by this theoretically isolated element in experience – the passively intuited, outside-our-control, merely-happening-to-us elements – *be the kind that is characteristic of judgment.* This presumably means that a given manifold must just *exemplify* a potential unifiability into subjects and predicates, ultimately (once the argument of the deduction clarifies what is at stake and we understand the schematized categories as modes of time consciousness) underlying substances and properties, antecedents and consequences, ultimately causes and effects, and so forth.[8] (McDowell also says that if we were to understand in the right way the independent world we experience in genuinely receptive, not "up to us" ways, then we would not be tempted to see it, to use Hegel's language, as an infringement from outside on apperceptive spontaneity. It would be understood as the "medium" *in which* such freedom would be exercised.)

Now ultimately, since Kant's strategy in the Deduction is to argue for the inseparability of conceptual and intuitional elements in experience, a great deal of weight will always fall on just what "showing inseparability" actually shows. If it shows that any deliverance of sensibility is to be understood as partly a result of the exercise of some active construal or prejudgmental activity (and not just that these elements must somehow manifest or express the forms of judgmental unity, as if they just "happen" to come that way, fortunately for us, given our own unavoidable requirements), we might seem to be heading toward the world of frictionless

---

[8] There is a remark in a later paper by McDowell, "Self-Determining Subjectivity and External Constraint," that makes me unsure as to what the relation is between the full Kantian claim about what such a conceptual unity in intuition involves and what McDowell thinks (6, draft).

spinning. But McDowell, in his proposed moderation (which, because it preserves receptivity, again seems to give us all the check on that spinning that we need), seems to me just to help himself to what Kant thinks must be established by the hard work of the deduction. When Kant claims *to show* "from the mode in which the empirical intuition is given in sensibility that its unity is no other than that which the category prescribes to the manifold of a given intuition in general" (B145), he is clearly making a promise he needs to redeem. He has to *rule out* the possibility that the intuited manifold's unity is *not* that which the category prescribes. It is possible that it is not; we do not know that it is. (It is possible that the "same form" conceptualizable elements in an intuition are only the elements that can manifest themselves in a way we could take some notice of; those that cannot are not attended to. There would not then be genuine guidance in the way McDowell wants it.[9] Passivity alone will not do it.) And by his lights, he can do that only by appeal to a specific, nonderived, quasifactual aspect of our cognitive apparatus: that we happen to experience the world successively. Thereby, he thinks he can show that *mere* successiveness could never be the experience of a unified apperceptive subject. Since mere successiveness is the only temporal *intuition* we could have, the discrimination that we require (between subjective and objective succession, made possible if there are objectively valid pure concepts) is one that we can claim valid for all possible such experience, given the only form of temporal intuition we have. A putative form of intuitive-mindedness not allowing such a differentiation between a succession of representations and a representation of objective succession is not a possible form of mindedness. This he proceeds to try to show, all the way through the argument of the Analogies. And so on. Kant, to remain Kant (the one who thinks he needs a Deduction), *cannot*, as McDowell suggests, treat what he (Kant) takes to be a limitation as rather what ought to be understood as a "truism."[10]

I agree that this seems to give with one hand (conditions for the possibility of knowledge of objects) what it takes away with the other (knowledge conditions only for discursively minded intuiters like us, so something more like knowledge), but I think Hegel was right to point this out, that Kant is in trouble on this score and that Kant cannot be fixed by McDowell's correction. The worry about frictionless spinning is dealt with

---

[9] This may be what led Sellars (1968) to try to squeeze in a more directly causal element, a second role for sensibility, and see the discussion in Pippin 1982, 46–53.

[10] He would lose his moral theory, for one thing.

by Hegel in another way and avoids what McDowell has simply assumed: that the deliverances of sensibility must exhibit the kind of unity that would allow their thinkability. Hegel agrees with McDowell that there is genuine receptivity in knowledge and that it must be considered a "moment" in a subject's self-understanding. But how we understand just *what* such a deliverance constrains or guides or what role the constraining element will play in further inferences or exclusions or permissions and so forth is not and cannot be a function of the element's having been received. The sort of "authority" or normative force a bit of experience has is parasitic on normative constraints that Hegel does not think can be read off from experience and whose authority is basically "self-legislated," a point we need to return to below.[11] Moreover, since Hegel cannot help himself to McDowell's claims about "the unity" manifested in a received manifold, he has to deal with the general skeptical worry another way. The real worry, as Hegel sees it, is that if our being-minded as we are is at some level relatively independent of the deliverances of sensibility and cannot be "tied" down in some determinate way to the form of such sensibility, then we could be minded other than we are, and the status of our conceptual requirements look more psychological or historically contingent. The simplest way to put Hegel's claim at this point is that we can establish that we could not be other-minded than we are (and so that our form of mindedness counts as the form of objecthood[12]) not deductively but developmentally, by appeal to a retrospective account of attempts at rendering self-conscious the necessary, unavoidable elements of any form of shared mindedness (the so-called relative or historical a priori). (The retrospective perspective is important; that is obviously not how Aristotle or Spinoza thought about what they were doing.) And the crucial addition that Hegel adds to the Kantian picture is an account of how normative constraints on judging and acting come to be understood as having a binding hold on us as social norms, as indispensable elements in our answerability to each other.

As far as I can see, McDowell's appeal to sociality is only a gesture toward the unavoidability of socialization into a community (some community or other), a matter of acquiring a shared form of mindedness. Whether such

---

[11] So for Hegel, one cannot say, as McDowell does often, that "objects" simply "*occupy* a position of authority." They only have the authority bestowed on them, and Hegel is out to show why that granting is necessarily social. See the discussion of point five, below.

[12] If being minded (at some level) other than we are is ruled out, then our being minded about objects in such and such a way, and possible objects, cannot "come apart"; there would be no place for the skeptical possibility to take a stand.

a particular form or other involves genuine answerability to each other (where "genuine" has something to do with real mutuality of recognition among free, rational beings) and how that requirement works as a constraint in determining what answerability to the world amounts to is hard to tell from his account (which is more Gadamerian on this score than Hegelian). The question of the success of such an achievement seems answered in a way similar to his helping himself to the intuitional unity that will get Kant out the difficulty we agree Kant is heading for: Societies are said to be struggling to help each other "see" the reasons there are to act, and that there would be such reasons whether people saw them or not. That leads, though, to point five.

That point consists in McDowell's worry that the self-legislation language I employ is extreme and seems to be committed to normless situations mysteriously becoming norm-governed and the norms being created out of the void. Here are two examples of that putative danger in German Idealism:

The will is thus not merely subject to the law [*dem Gesetze unterworfen*] but is subject to the law in such a way that it must be regarded also as legislating for itself [*selbtsgesetzgebend*] and only on this account as being subject to the law (of which it can regard itself as the author [*Urheber*]). (GL, Ak. 431)[13]

This kind of language, to say the least, caught on. It reaches a kind of crescendo in Fichte's language of the *Ich* positing itself as well as the *nicht-Ich* but clearly influenced Hegel as well, as in the following:

[B]ut if we ask what Spirit is, the immediate answer is that it is this motion, this process of proceeding from, of freeing itself from, nature; this is the being, the substance of Spirit itself.[14]

Hegel later in this passage invokes the paradoxical expression that spirit is a "product of itself" and that "its actuality consists in the fact that it has made itself what it is."[15] (In his speculative logic, Hegel's frequent, similar mode of expression is that the *Begriff* "gives itself" its own "actuality," which I have interpreted to mean that it legislates its own actual authority, to refer to the "self-authorization" of reason by itself, and

---

[13] See Korsgaard 1996b, 100.
[14] Hegel, SS, 6–7.
[15] Ibid.

have argued is the source of a number of the speculative formulations in Hegel.)[16]

He is well aware, of course, that this is quite a different, nonstandard way of putting the issue and the nature-spirit duality:

> Spirit is usually spoken of as subject, as doing something, and apart from what it does, as this motion, this process, as still something particular, its activity being more or less contingent.

And Hegel's contrary view is now clearly stated:

> [I]t is of the very nature of spirit to be this absolute liveliness [*Lebendigkeit*], this process, to proceed forth from naturality [*Natürlichkeit*], immediacy, to sublate, to quit its naturality, and to come to itself, and *to free itself*, it being itself only as it comes to itself as such a product of itself; *its actuality being merely that it has made itself into what it is.*[17]

And again, as above, finally: "[I]t is *only* as a result of itself that it is spirit."[18]

If we begin with Kant, there is a rather sober way of putting his point that might save us from these later, clearly more extreme variations. It seems prudent to say that, despite appearances, there must be no paradox here, no normless situation becoming norm-governed, no pre-obligation state becoming an obligated one through the self-imposition of the law. Kant is just insisting that as rational and free beings, we must determine "for ourselves" what to do in any case (to think for ourselves), not simply to accept, or let ourselves be directed by, guidance from without. This is a condition of living a free life, indeed the most fully realized free life, autonomy. (Something paradoxical already begins here, since Kant does not say something like "we have good reasons to live in this self-directing way," since such an appeal can be addressed only to someone who has already accepted it.) There is, for Kant, only one way of realizing this requirement (whatever it is) of self-direction or self-determination: Following the dictates of practical reason, to do nothing that you cannot rationally justify. To be autonomous is to constrain our action only by rules and principles we can justify with reason, that we can defend to ourselves with reason. (We can thereby "stand behind" our actions, as our own.) Finally, though, there is for Kant only one way to realize *this* condition, since pure practical reason, according to him, *has no insight*

---

[16] Cf. my "The Realization of Freedom: Hegel's Practical Philosophy," in Ameriks 2000a; Pippin 2003a, 2003b.
[17] SS.
[18] SS.

*into which ends are universally worth pursuing.* So whatever the requirement of self-determination amounts to, it can be fulfilled only by ensuring a formal rationality in our maxims: to act on no maxim that cannot be held simultaneously and universally by all.[19]

As noted already, it is difficult to state even the more prudent version without paradoxical elements appearing. Matters get worse when we stress that point made above, that for Kant, practical reason has no insight into any substantive good that can be called authoritative for everyone. We all seek happiness, but there is no common version, no human end or telos. So if we simply say, "All Kant means by autonomy is relying on our own reason to determine what we should do," we have not reached any level of interest to him in his practical philosophy. Yes, in means-end reasoning, we should deliberate about the most efficient means, and perhaps we can say we should have a life plan, a way of ordering and prioritizing our ends. But that has nothing to do with autonomy, since it is not ultimately up to us which overall ends, even very general ones, appeal to us. Likewise, this prudential interpretation is too weak to rope in Kant's unique position. As Kant himself was aware, subjecting ourselves to the rule of reason (and thereby becoming self-determining) is exactly the way his rationalist predecessor, Wolff, described his moral project, and whatever else is true of Kant, he did not see himself as a rationalist perfectionist.

How, then, does Kant describe what reason demands, if being rational is the crucial condition for being the free agents we are? (We should leave out for the moment the very difficult question of the status of the requirement that we act as the free beings that we are.) The passage quoted above seems to make two claims. The first is: We ("the will") are subject to no law that we do not subject ourselves to, "legislate for ourselves." This is very typical of Kant's so-called Copernican revolution in ethics. "Moral insight" is of a peculiar sort in Kant; seeing that anything is the case – say, that this is the principle that a purely rational being

---

[19] That is, this formal constraint on the form of our maxims (universalizability) is the only way, Kant concedes, that our pure reason can be practical, that we can be said to do things just for reasons. That increases the difficulty of answering the question of why must I be said to be subject to *this* constraint? He then tries to say: Because in doing anything at all, you have already *subjected yourself* to that constraint, not an easy thing to show. It would be easier if Kant were not this sort of a deontologist and were more of a substantive value theorist. Everyone could then be said to have reason to realize a value such as freedom, the universal human good. But I do not think that such a position can be defended as Kantian. See Pippin 2000d, 2001a, 2001b.

with a finite will would adopt – in itself in no way constrains our action, does not function just thereby as a norm.[20] He always uses language like "being obligated is placing ourselves under the law," submitting or subjecting ourselves (*unterwerfen*) to it. So if we consider the question of *Why* are we obligated to act on maxims consistent with the demands of pure practical reason? we have to say something like "Because we have obligated ourselves to it." The self-legislation language – I make this a law for myself, submit to its authority – is not expungeable from Kant, and there is thus no "receptivity" in the account of being *obliged*.[21]

And there is more. The law of pure practical reason is not a law like those in the natural law tradition. Laws, to be laws, require legislators, and once a divine legislator is excluded, "we" are the only candidates left. That is, contrary to the wishes of the fans of receptivity,[22] Kant clearly insists that we are the originators or authors *of the law* (*Urheber*). No "result of second-nature socialization allowing us to see a reason to act that would have been there anyway" has a place in this Kantian world. Nature in all relevant senses remains strictly disenchanted in Kant; if it is to be re-enchanted, we are the ones who have "made" it that way. We do not, of course, simply "make up" what the requirement of a pure practical reason determines, what it is for reason, in a nonempirically guided way, to determine what one ought to do. But just *noting what that is* has no practical effect for Kant. We author *the law*, legislate this principle as universally binding, and thereby submit ourselves to its authority (or not, which is also important to remember).[23]

None of this need mean that there is a privileged moment of "election" or ground decision in a life, when I must determine in the existentialist void whether happiness or moral rectitude shall be the hyperordinate principle in my life. But it is easy to see why Kant's language would have led some commentators (Korsgaard, apparently) to move in this direction. And the situation looks at least *less* paradoxical in Hegel's account of

---

[20] See Henrich 1994a, 1994b.

[21] I think Schneewind has established in great historical detail how Kant was led to this unique position on obligation. It is his solution to the problem of the law's authority that plagued the natural law tradition, and it is just as radical as it sounds. There is no prudent version of it. See Schneewind 1998, esp. chaps. 22 and 23.

[22] Or at least friends of a receptivity that can, on its own, do some serious transcendental heavy lifting.

[23] I think that this complex of issues is what is behind what worries Axel Honneth in Honneth 2002, esp. 256–8. That does not come out so clearly in Honneth's presentation or in McDowell's reply, a discussion too centered on Aristotle for the issue I am raising to be apparent.

ethical life (*Sittlichkeit*), since there is never any "ground zero" for such "submission" but an ongoing and collective "legislation" about how one ought to live, and in various individual acts and submissions, frequent requirements for reflection and possible resistance. In that picture, it can be said that some sort of second-nature *Bildung* has made it possible to see a reason "in the world" that exists as such a reason even if unacknowledged by many. Antigone's perception of what has happened to her brother and her awareness that he is her brother just thereby gives her a reason to act. But that it is a reason is because of what has in effect been collectively "legislated" at a time (what would not be there had it not been so legislated), because of the role the family has been determined to play in Greek political life, a role that is cracking in effect under the pressure of the incompatible commitments created by the overall legislated (Hegel's word is often actualized, *verwirklicht*) results within this community.

So here again, as in the cognitive case, we do have a kind of receptivity, but the kind of role it plays is a certain sort of result of free activity.[24] And that will remain so in Hegel's account of the modern world. Someone's being a partner in a contract, a mother, a businessman, or a citizen just thereby gives him or her reasons to do or forebear from doing (if he or she has been properly socialized). But such "reasons" do not and cannot play the particular role they play "on their own," as it were. They are results. Indeed, as Hegel says, a common human-mindedness, *Geist*, is essentially a "result of itself."

---

[24] So when Hegel's full position is at least sketched, it begins to sound like what McDowell approves of in his response to Bubner in RM, that forms of life "are both products of drawn-out historical evolution and dependent for their continuation on continuing whole-hearted participation by mature individuals, those who have acquired the faculty of spontaneity" (297). All I have done here is to put what I regard as the appropriate stress on the words "products," "dependent," and "spontaneity."

# PART III

# MODERN MORES

# 10

# The Ethical Status of Civility

## I

Civility, as its name implies, denotes a quality or social form characteristic of a particular kind of human association: a civil society. In its idealized form, civility can be said to be the distinctive virtue or excellence of the civil association, in the way that courage is for military associations or industriousness for enterprise associations.

This means that the topic of civility can be discussed in any number of ways, depending on what one understands to be taken in by the notion of civil society. Minimally, a civil society can simply designate the rule of law, and civility would then mean law-abidingness or an enduring, stable disposition toward law-abidingness, together with various manifestations of such a disposition. Any fuller understanding of the meaning and various dimensions of civil virtues and their relation to civility (virtues such as public-spiritedness, civic responsibility, and patriotism) will then depend on one's theory of the modern polity itself – the *civitas*, its origins, social purpose, and authority – all in order to define the nature of a *civis* and the various virtues of such a human type. Here the original or fundamental question would be: What makes a human association a civil one (or to use our more familiar but now quite complex and confusing term, a "political" one)? and such a question leads one quickly to the land of philosophical giants, to the likes of Aristotle, Hobbes, and Hegel and to very daunting, intimidating issues.

(Although complicated enough for a whole book, there is also a historical dimension to the question. Virtues *like* civility, such as hospitality, decorum, dignity, and politeness, have often been desiderata of various societies at various times. Civil society is, however, a modern notion, meant to refer to a public sphere, a certain ethical bond among free individuals, distinctly characteristic of modern societies, committed in common to that value as the highest good, to the value of a free life. At least, that is what I assume in the following, conceding that much more discussion would be necessary in any adequate treatment of this historical dimension.)

However, the question of civility can also be detached from the issue of the rules of civil association, and the virtue in question can mean much more than accepting and abiding by those rules as one goes about the pursuit of one's private ends; it can mean much more than law-abidingness. There need be nothing illegal (although there could be, as we see below) about such things as sarcasm and hostility in academic exchanges, rudeness in cab drivers or waiters, insensitivity in the telling of ethnically offensive jokes, screaming fits and "road rage" on the highways, suggestions, just this side of the libel law, that a political opponent is a criminal or a cheat, and so forth, but something is clearly going wrong in such exchanges and that wrong seems natural to characterize as a lack of civility. This seems something more important and far-reaching than issues of politeness but also (and here again the point that has become so arguable in the last fifteen years or so) not a sanctionable violation of rights, not the sort of injury we think is subject to the state's great coercive power. This is the sort of notion of civility, or the virtue of "appropriateness" in public conduct affecting other presumptively free subjects, that is my topic. It is the sort of category that often comes to mind in questions of what is "offensive," and why it is wrong to be offensive, as in the issue of "appropriate" language or content in television shows or advertisements, obscene messages on T-shirts, the display of pictures of dead fetuses in abortion debates, public vulgarity, belligerent administrators, and so on, as well as in more subtle forms of indifference to others that qualify not as moral harm but as an absence of solidarity or acknowledgment of others that we nevertheless consider morally important in some way. As already intimated, this "virtue" sense of the issue of civility is today inseparable from the "legal" sense of civil regulation. But that will introduce a special problem in what follows.

And, as already apparent, civility in this sense can be very hard to identify. The moral phenomenology and category problems introduce phenomena intertwined with issues of decorum, politeness, beneficence, and respect and so make a simple categorization difficult. In a rough and ready sense, we can all recognize incivility as a kind of disrespect, disregard of, or indifference to others (especially a disregard of their status as addressees of reason and therewith as potentially free, self-determining subjects), a disrespect that is serious but does not rise to the level of immoral treatment of others. (Of course, such things as assault or cheating are also "not civil," but what we are trying to understand are forms of incivility that are not illegal or immoral but, in some sense that is to be identified, still wrongs. Imagine, for example, that you are teaching a seminar and imagine the difference among – especially the question of different, appropriate reactions – seeing a student (1) attempt to steal a fellow student's purse, (2) attempt to lean over and copy from another's paper, or (3) express contempt at the contributions of others by rolling eyes, sighing loudly, or muttering obviously sarcastic, giggling side comments to a neighbor. I think it is reasonable to note that (1) is illegal, (2) or cheating, is immoral, and (3) is uncivil, and although a form of impoliteness, not quite like arriving late, leaving early, forgetting classmates' names, or other common forms of impoliteness.)

Conversely, we can initially note a few positive characteristics. As the name implies, we are looking for the distinctive form of association among *cives*, among participants in some sort of ethical community, and, therefore, civility should not be confused with a universal respect for and decorum toward *all* others. *Civil* acknowledgment always rests on an appreciation of some commonality and mutual dependence, or so I try to suggest. Indeed, civility itself could just be said to be some acknowledgment or lived enactment of a dependence on one another in some way, a way of regarding and being regarded that takes this dependence into active account. Aristotle's claim is worth calling to mind: that civility's closest kin is friendship, albeit a "watered down," thinned-out form. Such an acknowledgment of this "watery friendship" avoids the great pretense or fantasy of incivility: the possibility of self-sufficiency or individual autarky (a fantasy often encouraged by anomic modern forms of life, especially urban life, with its corresponding, widespread pathology, narcissism). The thesis here is that incivility can look like the necessary cost of a society of free, competitive agents in honest, aggressive exchanges and relations. Rather, it evinces a false and fantastic sense of independence and self-sufficiency. By examining the nature and importance of civility, we can learn something about the collective nature of a free life and the more mediated, complex relation between social dependence and individual autonomy.

The further assumption in this way of stating the problem is that public life in modern societies cannot be understood as extensions of or even relations among familial or tribal groups nor as managed, directed, or wholly "steered" by coercive state power, or law. As developing societies dominated by familial oligarchies and post-Communist societies emerging from the legacy of state totalitarianism and totalistic legal regulation have discovered, modern societies require a distinct social bond, something other than kin loyalty, submission to legal authority, or even "self-interest rightly understood," a kind of trust and fellow acknowledgment, among, essentially, strangers, even if members of the same community. These fellow *cives* aspire in their trade and professional associations, universities, civic clubs, corporations, and charities to a kind of distinctive ethical relation with one another, civility, a relation we hope will also hold society-wide, not just in such private associations. There are three points that I would like to make about this ethical relation.

## II

First, this relation has a *distinct* ethical status. Modern societies are able to function because of some reliable expectation of civil treatment among their participants, and this expectation is a normative one. It is what ought to happen; a society is better, more like what it ought to be, if there is a high degree of civility, and such civility is a form of trust and mutual respect or recognition. As already noted, it is of course hard to isolate exactly what is expected in the expectation of civility. That is just our problem now; the notion is loose and imprecise enough to look like many similar valuable aspects of human sociality. But being civil, I want to suggest, is more than being polite and different from being morally righteous in general.

Even so, such expectations are clearly normative (or, broadly speaking, still moral) expectations; that is, they would be misunderstood if reduced to social strategies of interest satisfaction. If I offer you the signs of respect and trust only because I want you to offer them to me, and that only because that will simply help me to get what I want, then we are not being civil but are pretending to be civil in order to gain a certain end, and our theme here is being civil, not pretending to be civil.

However, as just suggested, this expectation also cannot be understood as a moral claim or entitlement. Persons *are* entitled to respect as moral "ends in themselves," to use Kant's well-known language. No one is morally permitted to make use of another as a mere means in the pursuit of one's ends, or as an "object," not a fellow "subject," and one is thereby morally obligated to respect another's freedom, the other's entitlement to pursue his or her own ends, all in like acknowledgment of the claims of all others. But this requirement basically expresses a moral duty to do no moral harm, and a society in which persons were morally righteous in this sense, simply refrained from injuring or interfering, in which we all minded our own business, would not necessarily be a society with a high degree of civility. Being civil to one another is much more active and positive a good than mere politeness or courtesy, but like many other important goods, such as generosity, gratitude, or solidarity, it is not the sort of thing that can be "demanded" as a matter of duty, such as a moral entitlement. Being generous only because you have a moral duty to be generous, for example, is not *being* generous. It is simply giving more than strictly required in some context, something that can be done reluctantly or fretfully and *not* "generously." Likewise with gratitude and, I would want to argue, with civility.

(That a morally righteous society need not be a particularly civil one is a point made with great regularity in American literature; the point is almost part of our national mythology. In one familiar representation, persons who are products of New England, puritan societies, ever on the watch for the radical evil or original sin in human nature, harshly judgmental about egoism and the failure of moral intentions, obsessed with guilt and the prevalence of sin, as well as driven by genuine passion for moral rectitude (as in the abolitionist movement), are often portrayed in our literature as cold, unloving, isolated, alienated, spiritually deformed in some way, however righteous and public-spirited. Their social lives are proper and, while not uncivil or hostile, are full of enough suspicion, wariness, and separation to make the point about the possibility of a general lack of civility, even in the presence of politeness and moral rectitude. On the other hand, Southerners are often portrayed as the very embodiment not only of chivalry and courtliness and a warm charm and regard for others but of civility, some form of life that actively embodies the sort of recognition and trust associated with that virtue. This has something to do with the role of British and French aristocratic culture in the South in America, and the contrast with the culture formed by denominational groups fleeing religious persecution in the North, but that is another story. So are similar manifestations of this mythic image, as in the contrast between urban incivility and small town or rural hospitality and civility, and so on. The point now is the simple if still controversial one: that this mythic contrast helps one to see that civility can be an ethical or normative matter without being (without even being able to be) a matter of moral entitlement and that morally righteous societies need not be, and in many interesting ways, just are not, civil societies. Perhaps the best book that one might use to make this point and explore it would be one that focuses on this North-South contrast and the problem of civility and moralism – Henry James's *The Bostonians* – with the contrast there between Olive Chancellor and Basil Ransom, though the point shows up in the treatment of moralism in America in everyone from Hawthorne and Melville to Faulkner.)

Second, there is another point that separates civility from such similar (not "demandable-as-entitlements") social virtues as generosity or gratitude: the degree of its importance. Civility is of fundamental importance in a modern civil society because the end of modern civil societies, our highest good, is a free life, and civility is of vital importance in the collective pursuit of a free life. As a social form, it is not, I want to claim, a marginally good thing but indispensable in the possibility of a worthwhile common life in a modern world so committed to freedom as its supreme value. To understand this, one needs to try to imagine what in fact would go missing, would be so wrong, unacceptable, incomplete, or whatever if a society were either only successfully rationally cooperative (in the Hobbesian, egoistic sense of cooperative rationality) and only apparently, not really, civil or if persons were individually morally righteous but not, in the loose and imprecise sense so far discussed, particularly civil. What would be amiss, in the context of this issue – a modern commitment to a free life – without civility?

Third, there is the question of contemporary U.S. society and the question of the compatibility of a social virtue such as civility within an extremely competitive, relatively anomic, ethnically diverse, rapidly self-transforming, consumer culture. The proper form of an ethical relation of trust and acknowledgment among strangers is one thing; when the strangers are intense competitors or also very different culturally, other and even more difficult questions are raised. (Or to invoke the occasionally more optimistic suggestions of Mr. Smith, when the strangers are all potentially customers, does the situation look better?) The question also looks different if we assume an important emphasis on romantic notions of originality, individualism, and, above all, authenticity (especially in U.S. popular culture since the 1960s), by contrast with which a code of civility can look (at least to many Americans) conformist or repressive or stultifying.

I am particularly interested in this last question about the United States and civility since I have spent a few years living in Germany and, like many Americans who have had this experience, came away mightily impressed with the daily rituals of civility one encounters in German as well as in

Italian and French communities. People, even strangers whose eyes simply meet randomly, greet each other more frequently and warmly than they do in the United States; forms of greeting and departure are elaborate and regular (lots of hand-shaking and *auf Wiedersehens*); conversations on buses and trains are quieter, more respectful of others, bikes are left unlocked outside stores; people not only are willing to give directions to a lost stranger but will often walk out of their way for a while to point someone in the right direction. The honor system on buses and trams functions quite well. (In the years that I have lived in Europe, on almost all the occasions that I have ever been on a bus or Strassenbahn that was controlled, all the passengers had their tickets.) Billing for services is much more relaxed; people trust each other, without much paperwork, to pay with a bank transfer in the next few days, and easily and without anxiety give out their bank account and bank transfer numbers. (We once were a few hundred dollars short at a department store in paying for some bedding. The sales woman, without checking with anyone or asking for identification, took our name and address and asked us to please transfer the rest of the money in the next few days.) You still don't have to pay first at gas stations. Sale and consumption of beer and wine are much more prevalent in public, on the well-founded assumption that everyone will indulge responsibly. There is no need, at movie houses, that some announcement be shown reminding people that they should not chat loudly with each other. And so forth.[1]

Let us designate these problems as: the question of the distinct *normative status* of civility, its degree of *importance*, and the *conditions* under which it flourishes or is threatened.

### III

I have suggested that the distinct feature of such a norm is that it cannot be demanded as a right or entitlement. Even though one "ought to be civil" (or grateful or generous, to cite some companion cases), one need not be immoral in not being civil, and civil treatment is certainly something one cannot claim as a legal right with the coercive force of law as a sanction. Indeed, one way to state the uneasiness many people feel about so-called

---

[1] Of course, one should not go overboard here, and there are serious regional differences. Berlin, for example, resembles New York with respect to daily civility more than it does Munich or Tübingen, and something transformative and a bit bizarre happens to almost all Germans as soon as they hit the Autobahn, as if everyone suddenly has permission to act out aggressive fantasies held in check in all other areas of life.

political correctness legislation is that it makes precisely this mistake, or tries to inspire with sanctions and punishment what simply cannot be secured by sanctions and punishment, even if an ethical loss when not present: that persons be civil to each other. A society so regulated and so coerced is not civil; it merely looks that way.

To understand why this should be so, we need to explore a bit more the elusive question of the nature of civility itself. As already suggested, the social form in question amounts to a very general way of regarding and acting toward others, and that way has something to do with an active acknowledgment, even the affirmation of each other as fellow members of some sort of common, important enterprise (in the broadest, most relevant sense, in "civilization" itself). If this is so, it already means that such an expectation must be conditional on the actual prior existence of this commonality. There must be some basis on which we can recognize each other as a fellow participant or part of some fellowship in general. (Again, there are certainly general forms of civil conduct indistinguishable from hospitality or politeness, but the question is whether there is a unique form of acknowledgment for a fellow *civis*.) This is part of the reason why it is so easy to imagine natural, seamless relations of openness and trust so similar to civility among members of the same tight neighborhood, among members of an ethnic group with a common history and common experiences, or even among alumni of the same military unit or university. "They" are part of what "we" are, almost as if I cannot be "me" (or have become "me") without an equally intimate acknowledgment of "them." Such a commonality is not the sort of thing one can demand as a moral or legal entitlement, as if it could be constituted or created by will or out of duty; it either exists already or it does not; and if it does, then not acknowledging it in one's actions might be dishonest in some existential sense but not in any immoral sense of dishonesty. This, in turn, means that we might say that civility in general involves a kind of enactment of mutuality, or said in the more convoluted way suggested earlier, a way of acknowledging through social forms an open recognition that we are *not* wholly independent, a way of avoiding a dishonest pretense of solitary independence. No one can be said to be *entitled* to such an open acknowledgment of dependence, or to the avoidance of the pretense of independence. Again, a society of suspicious, sarcastic, cynical, judgmental, or self-involved persons – let us say, a world full of *Seinfeld* characters – need not at all be immoral, even unvirtuous (as long as, for example, for Kant, they develop their talents somewhat and are marginally beneficent), and are certainly not criminal. (The *Seinfeld* characters *are*, of course, often immorally indifferent, sometimes criminally negligent, and so forth, but that is not the point here.) In this sense, part of what is wrong in such incivility is not only the dishonesty just mentioned, but that such indifference or disregard corrodes, undermines the dependencies and reliances central to the modern civitas.

Civility, then, involves some sort of appreciation of the dependence of my life on others within some community of dependence and the en-actment of social forms appropriate to that dependence. It is not what we owe others as their right; it manifests an already existing social bond. If there is such dependence, we ought to expect it to be manifest, sus-tained and promoted in the rituals of daily life; we ought to be able to expect that such daily life not involve the pretense of self-sufficiency, indifference, suspicion, and hostility typical of that classic stereotype of American incivility, the average New Yorker.

But what form of dependence, at what level, are we talking about, and to anticipate the second question, why should it be very important (as opposed to it simply being a "nice" feature of daily life in small towns)? Why especially should it be important in our ability to lead free lives? In the context of modern civil society as sketched above, it is easy enough to begin to understand how a collective commitment to a free life entails certain legal and moral constraints. We depend on each other in collec-tive support for a system of law that protects individual rights. We are morally entitled to demand from each other equal treatment as moral subjects, always one among many equally entitled, self-determining sub-jects. What more in the collective, mutually dependent pursuit of freedom is required?

This can turn out to be a very broad question, for what we are asking is something like the following: If, within a democratically elected regime, individual liberties were legally secured and constrained only as little as possible, enough to ensure a reasonable level of common welfare and equal opportunity, what else might be lacking, in order to secure the full realization of a just civil order or even for the empirical stability and reproducibility of that society itself? The Hegelian name for that lack (or Mead's) would be a lack of "recognition," some experience of solidarity, civility, and mutual respect without which (the thesis would be) individual free lives in that society *could not* be effectively or meaningfully led. At least that is the kind of claim that would justify taking civility, understood as such mutual recognition, so seriously.

Then the question is: What argument might show that civility, properly understood in this way, is not merely a matter of politeness and decorum, or important for psychological health and a psychological sense of self-importance, but an essential element of the possibility of any individual's own "free life"? Why should we believe that there is a distinct form of harm, disrespect, say, that must play its own role in the evaluation and assessment of social processes and social change at some foundational level, especially in modern civil societies committed to freedom as an ideal?

## IV

Civility has now become, it would appear, a fairly abstract topic. We are still talking about active forms of respect and affirmation and solidarity, and all of that is still linked with our intuitive understanding of civil conduct, but the direction of these last remarks suggests an importance to the issue that might now appear unmotivated, far out of proportion with a simpler claim of defending civility as one of many sorts of social goods it would be better to have than not to have. The suggestion was that this broader claim to importance has to do with the particular nature of the modern ethical community, *what* modern civil cooperation tries to realize. The link in question is between civility and the supreme good in modern societies, that capacity on which all respect is based, individual freedom, and the conditions under which individuals could lead free lives and sustain such freedom.

Incivility and disrespect (or what such practices are now taken to imply, the presumption of unequal status and privilege) have come to be understood in modern societies as an implicit or often explicit disregard of the other's status as an equally free subject. (I should make clear again that I am not talking about actual abuse or immoral treatment but about a more general incivility. And the direction in which we are going need not imply any problem with the assertion of authority or hierarchical relations of real or socially constituted inequality where they are appropriate, such as that between parent and child, teacher and student, or officer and soldier. The issue is still that these hierarchical relations must also be exercised "civilly," with proper regard for the status of the other as an equally free, end-setting agent. And as a final qualification, there are obviously moral and social limits to any such claim for the importance of civility. The uncivil may certainly merit an uncivil rebuff; the general good of social respect need not imply moral neutrality or the weak, uncertain, timid toleration of anything that, say, Nietzsche worried about as a consequence of liberal societies.) Indifference to the cultural sensitivities of others, their own moral codes, their abilities to converse on the beach next to my loud boom box or to hear the class discussion because of my conversation with a friend, a teacher's willingness to humiliate a student for a laugh or even to stress a pedagogical point, and so forth are now understood as ways of disregarding that other as a subject with his or her own ends, freely set and freely pursued, just like mine. And finally, of the many dimensions of freedom current in the modern self-understanding, what seems particularly relevant here is that the other's status as a free subject is being disregarded because the other's status as a reason-giving and reason-responsive being is disregarded. Rather than simply offer objections to a point made, the uncivil student we mentioned above attempts to manipulate conduct and reaction by expressions of contempt and impatience that cannot be rationally responded to because they have no rational content.

But this interpretive point still just pushes the issue back a step or two. If civility is understood this way, as the enactment in daily rituals of our equal status qua free agents, as some acknowledgment of and respect for such status as rational and thereby free agents, all within a cooperative enterprise or tradition that seeks to realize and protect such individual freedom, then what would be so *wrong* with a city of uncivil individualists? If I *could* moderate my conduct in a civil way, as a way of acknowledging another as an equally free, rational participant in an ethical community but do not (because I want to express myself more vigorously or because of my passion for some issue I care about), what is that "wrong," if anything, if this sort of indifference to the other's status as free-because-rational is not legally wrong or morally injurious?

There are, of course, first of all, various psychological and other empirical ways of stating the "damage" done by widespread, frequent expressions of the disrespect we are discussing. At the social level, one might try to establish that such phenomena not only "manifest" a disintegration of a collective attempt to establish and secure precisely the individual free agency the uncivil agent insists on so stridently, manifesting only narcissism and egoism, not a value freely pursued, and that such conduct also, as an empirical fact, undermines and gradually makes less likely the social will and collective effort necessary to sustain and promote such a social good. One might also try to show, on the psychological level, that the successful formation and sustaining of a stable individual identity is a complex and relatively fragile process. It might very well be that a necessary condition for the possibility of any successful identification with a social or familial or religious role is the existence of some social community willing to recognize and affirm the adoption of such a role. A civil state of tolerance, mutuality, and active recognition and affirmation might not just be in some external way confirmatory of one's individuality but constitutive of its possibility "internally," that one, as a matter of psychological fact, just *isn't* who one takes oneself to be unless "recognized" as such. There is certainly evidence of something like this in studies of child development and in other accounts of socialization as the internalization of the point of view of the other, of the way one is regarded, and it is not stretching too far to make use of the claim in discussing something like social pathologies, and so in making a good deal out of this deep dependence on others and the importance of manifestations and acknowledgments of it in civil conduct.

More philosophically, one might also appeal to arguments, such as those used by Kant about the virtues, or to our broad, imperfect duties toward others. I know, as an empirical, psychological fact, that it is quite possible that the morally significant respect I owe to all others might well be undermined, that I might well become more and more indifferent to the morally salient aspects of such owed respect, were I to live in an uncivil, socially hostile, overly competitive community. I cannot simply count on myself to do the right thing, always, automatically; dispositions must be trained, emotions guided, habits cultivated, sensibilities educated, and so forth, if I am to be better able to appreciate what I must do and to be better able to do what I must do. (This has always seemed to me the Kantian version of the "Mayor Giuliani philosophy" about how large problems can grow out of small ones, and it is not an insignificant argument in favor of civility as an imperfect duty with broad discretionary latitude in judgment, but basically a duty nonetheless.)

Finally, though, the importance of such civil recognition, and so the nature of the wrong in its absence, can also be stated in quite a philosophically ambitious way. This would have to do with the status of freedom itself, the nature of the link between freedom and rationality, and the social character of rationality, and all that again leads us fairly quickly into very deep waters. But the direction can at least be suggested. It has to do with the difference between treating the issue of freedom as a categorial, metaphysical, substantive issue, on the one hand, or as itself a social (or even "socially constituted") norm, on the other hand; not a property we possess, but a norm we train ourselves to abide by. In the former case, the question of freedom, especially in the Christian tradition and its philosophical descendants, was treated as a question about substance, usually immaterial substance (the soul), and about the possibility of a kind of causation exempt from the necessary determinations of nature. Such a voluntarist position usually tries to show that our normal intuitions about agency and especially blame and responsibility require this "uncaused cause" or "always could have done otherwise" notion of agent causality, and the problem is then how to defend such a requirement either with a traditional or "practical" metaphysics.

On the other hand, being a free agent might be understood to be something like a *norm* subjects hold each other to, a constraint and orientation in our actions that is best understood as a result of subjects binding themselves to such constraints, responding to others and initiating actions on appeal to reasons. Being such an agent would not be a natural metaphysical kind, like being a featherless biped or being female (although it is nowadays hard to imagine any category in our historicist age that might not be subject to such constructivist talk), but would be better understood as a social category and norm, such as "being a professor" or a practice "being the collection of rent," not a part of the furniture of the universe but a result, what some parts of that universe have determined to hold themselves to.

The most radical implication of this way of thinking about the issue, and its relevance for our topic, are both immediately clear. The implication is that being a free individual somehow just consists in being regarded as one, being taken by others to be one, and the relevance is simply that, absent the modes of civility that make up such forms of recognition, the decisive aspects of such a self-description can get no purchase. Were we not to treat each other as rational and so self-determining and free beings, we could not be such beings, at least not fully or "really." That is the nature of the dependence mentioned above and already indicates the role that civility must play in such a realization.

All the objections to such a historicist claim about this sort of human dependence are also easy enough to call to mind. It might be that there is nothing more to being a college professor, say, than the social system and rules establishing the practice and the actual practice itself of certification and daily recognition. Absent the satisfaction of such rules and your regarding me as one, I just could not be one, no matter who I thought I really was. But it seems a great and dangerous stretch to make similar claims about an issue that seems more like a matter of scientific or metaphysical fact: whether my deeds happened because of my decision, whether I could have decided otherwise, and what I am entitled to because of who I am.

Although this is not the place to go further into such waters, it is worth keeping it in mind in trying to understand, partly, why and how some of the traditional issues of civility, respect, and recognition have come to occupy such a large place on the post-Marxist political stage, why the "demand for recognition" has become so crucial a theme in so-called identity politics. The strategy crudely sketched above was always central in post-Hegelian accounts of class consciousness and of true human liberation: being a free or nonalienated subject by being in a *condition* where one could be *taken* to be, treated as, such a subject. Many of the underlying premises of that tradition are still at work in such contemporary claims about the centrality of recognition to identity itself, where such recognition is now not only the "watery friendship" of civility but the constitutive condition of freedom itself. What has changed, though, has been the odd coupling of such claims about identity with the language of rights and entitlement and the whole agenda of liberal democratic politics, as if something could be done to "manufacture" such mutuality and civility. Understanding the centrality of civility in the way suggested above may be leading somewhere interesting, but, for reasons that we have seen, it cannot be leading toward a moral or certainly not a legal demand to be recognized or treated civilly. (In the classical left-Hegelian tradition, that would be like trying to "legislate" the conditions of socialism or create them by revolutionary will.)

## V

I have a few last words about the U.S. context and the problem of civility. I have already tried to suggest why a more intuitive American understanding of sociality – a "mind your own business" individualist attitude and a morally proper set of social forms – could not really count as the virtue of civility. The term is, of course, loose enough to define in various ways, and I have no real counterargument to anyone who wants to insist that such a negative state – the avoidance of the improper and the absence of unwelcome intrusions – is "civility" enough. But I have tried to suggest that the virtue in question has traditionally been more affirmative and positive; it involves somehow being able to count on each other, all on the assumption that we depend on each other in both interest-based and even more fundamental ways. But the modern issue of this dependence and trust is obscured somewhat by the admittedly artificial invocation of the Latin roots of the notion: the nature of the *civitas*, the status of the modern *civis*, and so on. We are, of course, really talking about the virtue of the good modern "burgher," the bourgeoisie and its so complicated modern representative, the bourgeois gentleman and lady.

The connotations of that term already suggest an important American resonance: the ambiguous standing of the bourgeois virtues, and so the ambiguous standing of civility itself as a virtue in modernity. If you tell a contemporary U.S. college student that a practice or some aspect of conduct is bourgeois, it is likely that he or she will think you mean: conformist, hypocritically righteous, timid, or perhaps even soulless, materialistic. That same worry about conformism, the same concern with a contrasting, supposedly more desirable individualism, also underlies our experience of the claims of civility, even as so much of our popular culture attacks the incivility of the city. That is, the ideal of a civil society, both law-abiding and actively cooperative, has an uneasy hold on the American imagination. It is sometimes held up as an ideal, often as a small town or rural (perhaps premodern) ideal against an urban (perhaps modern) individualism perceived to be a rootless form of egoism (the Frank Capra version). Just as often, though, especially in modernist and high-culture novels and films, such cooperation is portrayed as regulatory in the extreme, thoughtless, repressive, and secretly obsessed with what it regulates and bans (the Woody Allen version.)

Of course, as Tolstoy long ago pointed out, successful bourgeois life is not a very interesting aesthetic subject, so it might not be a good idea to take one's bearings from the way modern bourgeois societies aesthetically represent themselves to themselves. It would be quite hard, though, to establish empirically whether, in particular, American society, given this ambiguity, was in fact more or less civil than other modern societies in the West, or than any other modern societies, such as Japan, under similar economic and historical conditions. I have already suggested that my own intuition is that it is less civil, and, if we can simply consider that to be a hypothesis for the moment, some of the considerations introduced above might be relevant in understanding why.

If civility can be understood as an enactment in daily life of a mutuality or the actual establishing of the norm of rational agency, as an active attempt to recognize and help to promote each other as free beings, then, as suggested, such a dependence and commonality must already exist and be experienced in daily life as existing. If we return to European examples and more mediated, somewhat more traditional forms of civility, we should not neglect the important role played by long common traditions and even ethnicity in the experience of such a common fate and so in the social bond of civility. Germans are quite civil to each other and to most other Europeans who have become part of their societies (although serious tensions and even hostility among Germans, especially between North and South and now East and West, should not be un-derestimated).[2] But even third-generation Turks or Arabs in Germany report different experiences. The strains on French civility (which until recently seemed much more tied to language than to what the Germans still unblushingly refer to as German "blood") are more and more obvious in provincial and national elections. It seems to me quite an open question whether in the United States, still quite a young country, the idea and experience of being "fellow Americans" can overcome the mis-understandings and often suspicions characteristic of a community with so many different national traditions, experiences, and religions. Civility, I have tried to suggest, cannot be understood as a duty, a responsibility, or an entitlement. It is already a manifestation of something else not subject to moral will or legal coercion. It is an indispensable human good, but no amount of moral lecturing or even moral education, and certainly no amount of legislative constraint (whether mandating a common language or regulating speech or representations of women, etc.) can create it.

Second, as already noted, there is also the question of how much civility we really want, not just how much we can have. And this has to do with the way we understand the great orienting ideal of our polity, leading a free life, and the various, complex dimensions that that can have. I have suggested that at least one way to interpret incivility is that it reflects or betrays a false, self-deceived sense of self-sufficiency and independence. This already presupposes a contrary view, a view of a free life as an un-avoidably collective achievement, or said in its most paradoxical forms, that one cannot be free alone, that being free must involve being recognized as free. A civil order would then be, and be experienced as being, not a restriction on individual entitlements but a way of leading a free life in the only way it can be led, civilly, or in common.

---

[2] There are also, of course, still serious class tensions and the enormous problem of "iden-tity," the complex problem of belonging, affirmatively, to Germany, given what "Germany" has come to mean on the world and local stage. See the discussion in Elias 1996, 405–33.

# 11

# Medical Practice and Social Authority in Modernity

During the same twenty-five-year period in which medical or bioethics established itself as a serious discipline in mainstream philosophy and medical education, an extensive literature on medical institutions and practices, work in the history, sociology, and anthropology of medicine, also appeared.* However, philosophical problems have often been posed in ways that have not allowed such social scientific analyses of medicine to contribute much to what have come to be regarded as the major ethical issues in the field. My attempt in the following is to suggest a way of framing the ethical problems in modern medical practice so that consideration of the historical, social, and cultural dimensions of medicine must play an essential, not merely illustrative or incidental role, in what comes to count as an ethical problem and its possible resolution. This will require some (inadequate) attention to quite a comprehensive claim – the dependence in principle of any philosophical assessment of norms on a comprehensive social theory – but for the most part the defining issue in the following is the problem of the social authority of physicians. I attempt to draw out from a consideration of this issue implications that suggest a possible alternative to liberal, voluntarist (or informed-consent) accounts of "legitimate authority" as well as to familiar attacks on such

* An earlier version of this chapter was delivered to a faculty workshop at the University of Chicago's Center for Clinical Medical Ethics. I am grateful to the director of the center, Mark Siegler, for the invitation to speak and for the workshop itself, to the participants in this group for a spirited discussion that led to a number of revisions in the earlier draft, and to referees at the *Journal of Medicine and Philosophy* for a number of equally spirited and challenging comments. I am also much indebted to Terry Pinkard for a number of invaluable criticisms and suggestions.

liberal notions of authority, attacks that might all be loosely labeled "ideology critique."

(Another large issue surrounding these problems, especially the latter issue, which should be mentioned but cannot be pursued, is the long history of attempts to render problematic or to criticize social modernization itself, attempts to attack the philosophical presuppositions underlying the official self-understanding of Enlightenment culture. In this context, the link between the social authority of modern science and, eventually in the twentieth century, the scientific status of medicine is straightforward. In fact, in many ways, medical practice involves the most direct, everyday example of the social and ethical transformations involved in "Enlightenment culture" and so in the social implications of the growth of the authority of modern natural science.)[1] I do not want to deny that, however described, framed, or posed, individual physicians face very difficult concrete ethical "dilemmas," calling for unusual casuistical and reflective sophistication. But it is reasonable to suggest that a number of aspects of what come to be experienced as dilemmas or problems, at a time, within one sort of social configuration of production, power, and culture and not another, cannot be fully understood without some attention to the function of institutions and institutional roles, the authority of institutional roles, and the historical origins of the sources and even the meaning of such authority. As noted, this is particularly true of the growth of professional authority in the United States and the role of technological and scientific expertise in that story. Within this modern context, if the radical social critic Ivan Illich is even roughly right about the relatively recent transformation of doctors from artisans of a sort exercising a skill on a personally known individual to scientifically trained technicians applying an institutionally sanctioned procedure to a class of patients,[2] then many interesting questions arise about the nature of the social authority exercised by those who possess technical expertise (understood within modern norms of expertise), especially when that exercise is also a market function (and so where we might have reason to suspect the beneficent motives of the entrepreneur-physician) and when it must take place within a modern political culture where notions of liberty and egalitarianism exercise quite a strong social constraint on the conferring of any authority.

---

[1] Cf. Pippin 1999a.
[2] Illich 1976.

I

I suggest the following thesis: that contemporary medical practice raises the problem of medical authority, of what a physician is entitled to do, prohibit, interpret, and so on because he or she is a physician, and that we can understand the legitimating sources of such authority only in terms of the secular resources of public or official Enlightenment culture as a whole, by reference to a theory of such a society, and not primarily in terms of the formal characteristics of the exchange or therapeutic relation between the individuals. This requires discussion of a few points about the notion of authority.

Most obviously: You exercise authority if you can get someone to do or forebear from doing certain things. You tell someone what to do and he does it, because you told him and because you "have authority." Somewhat less obviously, you also exercise authority if you can get others to accept your view of the meaning, significance, or value of some deed or state of affairs. These capacities count as authority if you can compel such compliance without direct reliance on coercive force or persuasion. The former is simply power; the latter suggests equals searching together for the resolution of problems. Obviously, the sources of authority have something to do with legitimacy and some sort of sanction. A professor's authority to credential students who take exams from her stems partly from some trust that her decisions are based on superior knowledge and judgmental fairness; a manager's authority in a business is linked to some acceptance of legitimacy, but usually has more to do with the power to dismiss someone from work.[3]

Authority relations, then, are relations of inequality, involving some sort of suspension of private judgment; in the cases in which we are interested, it is a voluntary suspension, based on some assumption of superior competence and usually some fear of the bad consequences of acting "disobediently." In Mommsen's general description of authority, it represents "more than advice and less than a command, an advice which one may not safely ignore."

Now, to get the discussion started here, we should simply assume that the physician does in fact exercise some such form of social and cultural authority. Physicians, and credentialed physicians alone, are authorized to determine what must be done in various cases or what forbidden, and

---

[3] Starr 1982, who also relies on Lukes 1978; Sennet 1980; and Weber 1968.

are the only ones who may authoritatively state in various circumstances what is happening, what is "serious," or even what is "hopeless." These capacities obviously include access to drugs and treatment; diagnostic authority difficult for the lay patient to comprehend or question; unilateral ability to frame and explain options; and ability to determine with real social effect when a complaint can be labeled a symptom, whether someone can be pronounced sick even if he or she does not complain, and when to deny another the social benefits of being labeled "sick," even if the individual is in great distress.

In one sense, pointing out that physicians exercise authority is just to point out that physicians, like other professionals, fulfill functions determined and limited by law. They are licensed to do some things, such as dispense medications and certify injuries in disability claims, and are proscribed by law from other things (having sex with patients, experimenting on their own with drug therapies, etc.) In Flathman's sense they are "in authority," and we can at least in part explain their authority in the way we explain much political authority, by pointing to the existence of publicly sanctioned rules and procedures and by reference to the legal institutions that originally instituted, and so legitimated, such rules and roles.[4]

However, a physician is also "an authority" in Flathman's sense, entrusted with authority by an ill or injured person not just because that physician is authorized or permitted to intervene, but, much more positively, because of a belief in the physician's superior expertise and (here a much more complicated point) because of some sort of trust that a physician will make use of such expertise beneficently, in consideration only or mostly of the patient's welfare and/or autonomy and not for mere profit, or in consideration only or mostly, of the outcome of some peer panel's evaluation in an HMO review procedure. So, while the issue of the status of the legal, rule-bound authority of a physician might be an independently interesting question, the larger problem at stake here encompasses the role of the physician both in authority and as an authority. This is because the basis of the willingness of societies to create positions of authority, backed by legal sanction, and a willingness in private social exchanges to entrust physicians with authority to act, to recommend, and to interpret, reflect, to speak loosely, the same "societal attitudes," historical conventions, values, and so forth. (At least, this

---

[4] Flathman 1980.

would be so for anyone who is not a strict legal positivist.)[5] In the following, I concentrate mostly on the normative status of the social and not on the legal character of a physician's authority, but the outcomes could apply, mutatis mutandis, to any consideration of the bases of legal authorization.

Several interesting problems arise here, even if one just concedes this much. The most immediate is the empirical and historical question: In what ways and on what basis do societies come to authorize suitable uses of a physician's capacities and the appropriate entitlements deriving from possession of such capacities? This, I take it, is the proper topic of much medical history, medical sociology, and medical anthropology. In the case of the United States, the story of how a profession held in low esteem and mired in a complex and unwieldy competitive system managed to create a degree of professional sovereignty and social authority unprecedented anywhere else in the world is a fascinating one (told with great intelligence in Paul Starr's book).

To understand, though, that this issue (the historical and variable bases of such social authority) raises a variety of normative questions (and it is those questions, rather than the sociological and historical controversies, with which I am concerned), one also has to concede a potentially controversial point: that the putative link between a physician's abilities to predict certain outcomes and intervene successfully and the degree of her social authority is not simply a direct or transparently rational one (as if the entire basis of such social authority is a rational assessment of the benefits to be gained and the harm avoided from trusting the professional judgment of a physician, from submitting to such authority).

In the first place, even if this rationalist account were true, it would still raise as a question how some collectively assigned "value" or meaning to the particular sorts of benefits a physician could provide were originally assigned or authorized, in competition, if you like, with other possible benefits and goods. As is familiar from many well-known discussions of contractual or preference satisfaction models of rational exchanges, we must assume that the partners in such an exchange not only know what they want but have come to want what they want in some sort of undistorted or acceptable way, all in order for the whole account (at least as an account of rationality) to get started. In the case of trusting a physician's competence in exchange for some benefit, the ambiguities inherent in the notion of "benefit" and the way the commercial nature of the

exchange suggests a potential conflict of interest create immediate problems. We return to such issues in the discussion of "ideology critique"
below.

But the basic problem in such a naïve approach is that it ignores that
we also authorize physicians to frame the question for us originally and do
not merely authorize them to perform a specific, mutually agreed-on service. So whatever contractual relation exists is complicated by many more
ambiguous technical and even psychological dependencies, all surrounding matters whose meaning and significance have come to be perceived
as central to all of life. In other words, we authorize physicians to tell
us, in effect, what we are authorizing them to do. When it is a question
of alternative treatments, "quality of life" evaluations, risk assessments,
and so on, physicians do not merely transmit information. We must even
depend on them to help us find ways to be able to disagree with them.

To some extent, this complexity arises in all exchanges that involve
specialized expertise and, as in all such cases, can be addressed by consci-
entious and patient explanations by the more technically competent and
(at least for some middle-class consumers) by soliciting second opinions,
reading physician reference books, and so forth. No one pretends, however, that such measures compensate for years of medical school, training,
experience, and so on or, therefore, that the rational transparency, contractual model tells us all we need to know about the bases and meaning
of physicians' authority.

That model also ignores the fact that physicians are socially authorized to do or recommend in ways that greatly exceed any empirically
strict account of their healing capacities (this is, of course, particularly
true of psychiatrists). And, in general, the difficulty of containing or precisely defining the meaning of the desideratum of a "health benefit" is
becoming widely appreciated.

Moreover, if it were simply rational to suspend private judgment and
cede authority for the sake of a benefit, one could safely ignore the fact
that in consenting to treatment for a disease, one would grant wide authority to affect other aspects of one's life affected by such treatment. This
would imply that all sorts of indenturing and submissive practices would
be acceptable, if benefits could be produced by a competent technician,
in a noncoercive original bargain. And it also ignores the wide cultural
and historical varieties of social authorization.

As conceded, there are certainly inequalities in knowledge in many
other professional transactions, and many of the same questions about
the social function and meaning of various professional roles would have

to be raised about the authority of those occupying such roles. But the very general point at issue now is simply that there is something distinctive about medical authority, a distinctiveness that makes the relation between ethical and social issues quite prominent. We do sometimes suspect that the social authority claimed by other professionals (chiropractors, say, or some psychotherapists or education experts) is more easily challengeable or is based more on chance than defensible criteria (corporation managers, perhaps). And it is certainly true that the relative wealth of physicians, the litigious nature of American society, feminist criticism, and other dissatisfactions have come to complicate the issue of physician prestige and even authority. But the relatively higher and in some sense unique status of physicians with respect to other professions clearly has to do with the "authority" of science itself, something that helps to set the social function of physicians apart from lawyers and accountants. Because of that, we simply do authorize doctors to intervene in and control individual lives to a far greater extent than other professions, and a great deal more (life, death, or the quality of life) is at stake in such authorization.[6]

Once this normative problem about authority is admitted, the more clear-cut question about physicians' authority can be raised: Independent of what a given society might authorize, what is the best, most fitting, just, fair, morally sensitive exercise of such power?

Now, for reasons I do not need to go into, these simple facts alone (the physician's social authorization to act in some respects unilaterally or at least without many of the usual constraints) can, in a modern, democratic ethos, generate ethical worries about injuries to a person's general right of self-determination or to the fundamental natural right in modern societies, freedom. So, at the first level, this concern represents the most obvious problem stemming from the exercise of social authority by physicians. This worry would obviously be increased if one also suspected that persons were being encouraged to be or even manipulated into being excessive or profligate consumers of health care for essentially commercial reasons. If we think that people are being manipulated into thinking that more and more aspects of their daily lives are "medical problems" that they are not competent to manage and so must be turned over to experts, whose advice must be strictly followed on pain of irrationality, our worries about paternalism and manipulation will increase.[7]

---

[6] The unique nature of patient dependence in medical cases, and the corresponding issues of trust and, therewith, authority, are discussed in Zaner 1988.

[7] Illich 1976.

In general, traditional discussions about the compatibility between the exercise of professional expertise and the egalitarian ethos of liberal democratic society often focus on this paternalism problem. The outcome of such worry about paternalism and a potential conflict with the supreme modern normative principle – respect for patient autonomy – is usually an ever greater and sometimes utopian standard of "informed consent" (that is, once the importance of such autonomy is conceded and the centrality of beneficence in physician-patient relations is replaced by the centrality of autonomy). So, one way to allay worries stemming from a rights-based political culture, where human dignity and self-respect are essentially tied to the capacity for self-determination, is simply to integrate such an ethical consideration much more self-consciously and in a much more detailed way into the transactions between patients and doctors. Thereby the fundamental liberal principle – *volenti non fit iniuria* – is preserved. No injury can be done to the willing or, here, the well-informed health care consumer.[8] (One should already note the importance of framing the problem of paternalism and autonomy in a relatively abstract way, as typical uniquely of modern civil societies, dominated by exchange relations among, essentially, strangers, who experience no other ethical relation (family, nation, religion, class) binding them together except a presumed shared commitment to a maximum liberty for each consistent with a like liberty for all. Keeping this larger frame in mind could suggest other aspects of the history and implications of such a social form that might be relevant to the social authority issue. It might also help to raise the question of how much "weight" such a thinly shared ethical principle can and cannot bear.)

This informed consent solution, though, is obviously still a much de-bated question. In the first place, the approach does tend to make some of the "rational transaction" assumptions we were just discussing. These assumptions are clearly reasonable but only up to a point. Part of the issue they raise are the social conditions that define that "point." That is, the underlying assumption is that the authority of physicians basically stems directly from the consent of those affected, on the rational expectation of the benefits that will follow (once various obvious worries about subtle co-ercion, self-knowledge, real consent, and so forth are somehow allayed). Aside, though, from the problem of what could count as autonomously conferred consent in situations of such dependence and ignorance, this

---

[8] See Goldman 1980, and for the definitive treatment of the legal status of the notion, Faden and Beauchamp 1986.

model of authorization frames the ethical issue in a relatively thin or formal way. It must, that is, concentrate attention on procedural issues surrounding conditions of voluntariness, and so is "doubly permissive," as Engelhardt points out: It is a model that permits all interventions to which the participants have consented, and it makes that permission the key element of all bioethics.[9] This would mean that on strict (and thereby fairly radical) libertarian assumptions and without further considerations of greater social harm, we would on such contractarian assumptions permit the sale of spare organs, all sorts of euthanasia, assisted suicide, new industries such as commercialized surrogate parenting, or volunteer experimental subjects, and so on (all as long as the putative great measure of legitimacy, consent, were not feigned, coerced, or in some other sense nonvoluntary).

Moreover, and more famously, some claim that just providing "lots of information" inevitably produces misinformed consent or resistance, that in some contexts some sorts of information are necessarily misunderstood, that most patients are incapable of understanding rudimentary probability figures and become unreasonably terrified of statistically irrelevant side effects, that encouraging patient autonomy in decision making often creates intense, unmanageable anxiety and makes people sicker, that false optimistic prognoses can produce beneficial "placebo effects" otherwise unavailable, that it is possible to determine what a patient "would really want" to know and especially not know, no matter what they say (such that their "real" consent is being protected), that the whole issue is a fixation of the educated upper middle class and irrelevant to the realities and limitations of most medical practice, and that, anyway, modern specialized medicine makes adequate explanations of procedures and implications simply impossible. (I am thinking here of such things as Anna Freud's famous warnings about the inevitable role of "transference" in physician-patient relations and Howard Brody's narrative of the classic clash between more authoritarian and more consensual medicine at the beginning of *The Healer's Power*.)[10]

To such standard doubts about the vagaries and utopian implications of the informed consent justification of the social authority inherent in medical practice, one can (and I think should) add some concerns that begin to raise even larger issues. A hint of such concerns can already be detected in something of a shift in discussions of normative issues in

[9] Engelhardt 1991.
[10] Brody 1992.

medical practice, away from micro-ethical issues toward more macroan-
alytic accounts of institutions, distribution of resources, and what might
be called the "original position" within which any negotiation between
physician and patient already goes on. What, let us say, "The Institution"
itself already makes possible (and impossible) for both physician and patient is now often regarded as as crucial a constraint on self-determination
and autonomy as any action by an individual physician. Most obviously,
this can be an economic constraint, where treatment and long-term care
options are severely restricted by economic class and insurance status. Or
the exercise of medical authority may not only threaten a paternalistic injury to the right of self-determination; it might be, in ways independent
of individual judgment and fault, institutionally unjust, no matter the
good will, conscientiousness, or casuistical sophistication of the individual physician. Extending this point, along with others relevant to section
II below, might already begin to show that such constraints on authority
and judgment, even meaning, do not just raise other, different sorts of
medical ethics problems but that any such problem is misconceived if
framed independently of such a context, as if, in the traditional sense,
a moral problem arising between an individual physician and patient.
(Along these same lines, criticisms that health care makes little or no
difference in general health or may even have a negative effect and that
there was no longer any correlation between greater expenditure and
greater health all began to be voiced in the late 1970s.) [11]

There are various responses to such worries. Perhaps the most intuitively obvious autonomy-based solution would be Kantian or Rawlsian
in spirit. Individuals must not only consent to the authority exercised
over them; it must be possible to assume that they would have consented,
without prejudice or special interest, to the whole system of health care
delivery, and this on considerations of maximum benefits consistent with
equal opportunity of access (i.e., with universal conditions of consent).
However this would work, the problem of legitimating the institutional
authority of health care also raises an even broader class of criticisms.

Here the question is not whether the transactions at issue are consensual, well informed, consistent with moral notions of autonomy, or of real
benefit. The question is what has originally come to count as consent, relevant information, the meaning of free action or what counts as a benefit
or even health. The worry is that such issues are obviously not themselves
objects of free and open negotiation, have always already been decided,

---

[11] See Fuchs 1974; Illich 1976; and Wildavsky 1977.

and, so goes the suspicion, are very likely historically contingent manifestations of the interests of entrenched wealth and power, demonstrably shifting as such interests shift, socially authoritative in ways so deep and unreflective as to avoid critique or open interrogation.

## II

While aspects of such charges can be found in many well-known indictments of the medical profession (such as in the work of Ivan Illich, Barbara Ehrenreich, and Susan Sontag), the best known examples are in the works of "ideology critics" (neo-Marxist, or critical theory writers) and more recently in the institutional histories written by Michel Foucault and those influenced by his genealogies and "discourse analysis." In the former or critical theory case, the general idea is this: Suppose that there is a growing tendency in modern society, shared by both doctors and patients, to think of doctors as highly skilled body plumbers, whose job is to attack a disease and kill it, or mend a body part, such that a greater and greater reliance on technology has changed the very experience of sickness and injury, transforming it into a technical problem and patients into malfunctioning objects or essentially consumers. The central claim of *Ideologiekritik* is simply that this should not be understood as individual moral failure on the part of individual physicians, a kind of secular sin, a dehumanizing indifference to others for the sake of selfish ends, all of which can be rectified by moral enlightenment and the exhortations of professional ethicists. The problem, supposedly, is much deeper and requires another kind of analysis, one sensitive to the issue of a fundamental "false consciousness" and the connection between privileging a wholly "instrumental" reason and the inexorable expansion of capitalism and the culture and social relations unique to capitalism. (Of course, for some second-generation critical theorists, such as Adorno, the fundamental problem is common to both capitalism and instrumental reason and is something like the whole dynamic or "dialectic" of modernization, or "Enlightenment" itself.)

For the technology issue (and, throughout, the same kind of analysis could be given, mutatis mutandis, of the commercialization of health care) the question thus is: Has our "relation to objects" and to others been so influenced by technical instruments, the power of manipulation and production, and so on that our basic sense of the natural and human world has changed and changed so fundamentally that our reflective ability to assess and challenge such a change is threatened? That our very "consciousness" is "false"?

And with this sort of claim we reach another level of abstraction, arguing now that the central modern issue in caring for the sick is not respect for and the realization of autonomy, not the economic constraints on any possible such realization, but the very meaning of autonomy or beneficence or rationality at issue in any such social negotiation. The problem is not the personal moral obligations of physicians nor the problems of distributive justice but the inevitable (because inherited and deeply prereflective) ways in which health care is experienced in a highly technological, modern bureaucracy. In the last case, the assumption is that the influences of entrenched wealth and power and the presumed "reifications" and "fetishizations" of Enlightenment culture have already "distorted" the ways in which such assumptions constrain the very perception of alternatives and courses of action. (The "medicalization" of birth and of death are frequent topics in such discussions.)

Foucault's case is even more radical. His histories of modern psychiatry and modern medicine raise as many questions about methodology as they do about the subjects themselves. Yet it is obvious that books like his 1963 history of the origin of modern medicine (as he puts it, the transition from the question "What is the matter with you?" to the question "Where does it hurt?") are meant to be deflationary and skeptical, even if, on the surface at least, much less so than his account of psychiatry. The final move in the origination of a distinctly modern medical paradigm, Bichat's success in moving pathological anatomy to the center of medicine, is portrayed as a contingent social decision, one made possible and necessary by new bourgeois institutions and one linked to the emerging social values of the French Revolution and not to the ever better march of science.

Accordingly, this enterprise is a familiar example of the cultural politics of, let us say, the postsocialist left. The assumption here is that, now, uniquely, at the center of the nature of the authority of most modern institutions is not primarily representative legitimacy, as in traditional liberalism, or consensual exchange relations, or beneficence, the optimum satisfaction of collectively satisfiable desires, or even traditional class conflict, but a claim to a kind of cognitive authority (or perhaps thereby a new sort of class relation), the possession of the most universally and disinterestedly certifiable method for solving problems. Possessors of such method alone know what sorts of desires can be collectively satisfiable, know who is sick, who healthy; who sane, who not; as if a firm, objectifiable criterion of normalcy, health, and, especially, rational calculations of interest and so on are possible. The major institutions of late modernity are not states and churches; they are hospitals, prisons, universities, bureaucracies, MBA-managed corporations, and so on, and the basis of the willingness of subjects to grant such authority is the founding claim for epistemic privilege. This claim is not simply false, it is claimed, but the extent of the authority claimed on its basis is due to contingent social and class interests (or, more broadly, the "interests of power"), not a necessary or rational implication of the possession of such a competence itself.

Aside from the theoretical complexities of such analyses, the approach immediately raises a number of very good questions, particularly about contemporary approaches to public health issues, and helps to show that any discussion of the problem of medical authority must attend to the issue of who gets to define what is a medical problem and on what basis. That is, for more concrete examples, we know that a very high percentage of people who smoke will get any number of diseases, so we think of smoking as a public health problem. But do we know "what causes smoking"? Is that question a "public health" question? We "know" that people without a high school diploma are much more likely to smoke. Should we define "the problem of education" as a health issue? Is urban violence a health care issue, to be classified and investigated as such by epidemiologists, in the way in which the Centers for Disease Control might take under its wing the problem of homicide against children?

Whatever the questions raised, though, the recurrent problem with such an approach can be stated briefly, if therefore also somewhat unfairly. The notion of some fundamental distortion of consciousness, or the notion that the historical rise to prominence of some scientific authorization in medicine is a prejudiced illusion, presupposes that a nondistorted exchange between physician and patient is possible or that some alternate history could have been written under less biased, more ideal conditions. This, in turn, then raises the question: within the resources available to a modern, secular public culture, and given the unavoidable requirement that some basic social transactions will be authority-based, and so inegalitarian, under what assumptions could we assume that the normative constraints or ethical norms relevant to the trust and dependency necessary in relations to physicians could be anything other than the limited, thin, formal appeal to respect for patient autonomy or the narrow and easily abused appeal to technological competence and scientific authority? Neither source of authority may provide us with very pleasant implications, leading either to a consensual commercialization that is at once both naïve (about consent) and cynical (about what is permitted) or to the authoritarian, paternalistic practices that few defend today.

(It is true that in Foucault's case, it sometimes seems as if for him any discourse of legitimation is itself a contingent exercise of power, rather than a kind of redemption of its use. I do not think that this is true of his position, especially in its later manifestations. But for the moment I simply assume that the rhetoric of his histories, especially in offering to speak for those who have been silenced, promises or hints at an emancipatory moment that would necessarily lead to questions such as the above.)

Another way of putting this would be to concede that ideology and genealogical critics have identified an important problem in any reliance on consent or rational expectation of benefit as the source of medical authority. But the better way to put the point would be to claim not that such consent or expectation is itself distorted or the result of some social manipulation but that such consent and expectation is insufficient to account for the kind of authority a physician must exercise. This would mean that we may not ignore considerations of respect for autonomy and the various thorny problems of impaired consent, surrogate decision making, contractual obligations, and so on that flow from such a concern. But it would be a distortion of the nature of the physician's social authority to rely on such a necessary condition as if it were sufficient. (An even stronger and much more theoretically complicated claim would involve showing how attention to such an ethical requirement – respect for the patient's autonomy – itself requires the physician and many others to do various things and participate in various institutions in norm-bound ways not themselves the results of respect for autonomous subjectivity; that such a norm is itself embedded in some wider ethical practice.)

### III

This brings us to the following results. First, we can safely assume that in patient-physician relations, some sort of uncompromisable respect for the patient as the subject of his or her life, as an autonomous agent, however ignorant, superstitious, or strategically irrational, must be some sort of historical given, an unavoidable starting point. For any number of reasons, we could not be the modern agents we are without such a starting assumption. Let us also assume that, in cases of great and momentous uncertainty in patients' lives, some sort of general trust in the institutionally sanctioned results of modern scientific research procedures is rational or at least more rational than any available alternative.[12]

The problem is that this is all much too minimal a set of assumptions. We still face all the relevant worries. Yes, there ought to be informed consent, but observing that norm only rules out grossly impermissible acts of domination or paternalism and leaves unresolved all the ambiguities:

- What would count as true consent in situations of great pain, confusion, and dependency?
- What would count as informing someone about options within the economic constraints of modern institutional life and the often quite contingent, historically variable assumptions about "relevant" or "significant" information?
- What is the affect of all the libertarian, commercialized nightmare situations already alluded to?

On the other hand, treating a physician as some sort of representative of an institutional power whose history is basically or primarily a story of class interest or the maintenance of power, while it might tell us a great deal about what contributed to the modern administration of medicine, psychiatry, or prisons and the way in which claims to cognitive authority helped (unjustifiably, perhaps) to legitimate quite contingent configurations of power within such administrative structures, does not exhaust the account we would want to give of medical authority in general. Such an approach leaves unclear what sort of alternative history, and so what alternative source of authority, could have occurred, consistent with all the manifold concomitant events of modernization: the collapse of (at least public) religious authority, the intellectual collapse of hierarchical, teleological views of nature, the centralization of authority in the modern nation-state, the proliferation of new markets and the growth of privately controlled capital, and on and on. (At least Marcuse realized that his critique of "one-dimensional man" and technologically dependent societies would simply be Luddite without some account of an effective

---

[12] On the more general issue of trust and the role of dependent, ill patients in creating and sustaining medical authority, see also Zaner 1988 and Pellegrino and Thomasma 1993.

"alternative" technology, a solution that traded utopian romanticism for Luddite opposition.)

This would be a confusing and disheartening result. But it is not at all obvious that these dissatisfying options are the only clear sources of authority consistent with the implications of social and intellectual modernity, to put the problem in its most general terms. If it were, then (1) conscientiousness about patient autonomy, (2) a general, good-faith dedication to fairness and social justice in the institution of health care, and (3) a general watchfulness about various forms of bias and prejudice already built in to the language or discourse of health care negotiations would be all we could expect with respect to the proper exercise of a physician's authority. A certain Weberian resignation about the Faustian costs of modernization would be the appropriate response to worries about the limited, formal, excessively procedural aspects of such norms. However limited and formal, it is the price of modernization.

This would all also mean that anyone who is worried about the limitations of such approaches to the ethical dimensions of medical authority, for reasons such as those cited above, has got a far greater task ahead than might at first appear. Reconceiving some sort of modern social fabric, some inherited ethical and political culture, still consistent with a vast diversity of religious and historical traditions and with, for ever expanding numbers of citizens, the great absence of such traditions, is what is at stake. Among other things, such a reconstruction would involve showing which forms of social cooperation and institutional norms must already be involved just in the pursuit of respect for individuals as autonomous agents, the origins and so the full meaning of such an ideal, and what else must be involved in such practices besides fair contractual relations or procedural neutrality about the good. This seems to demand that, to do full justice to the conditions under which the individualism and autonomy assumptions central to social modernization could be respected, a full theory of the norms of modern society, and so a full theory of society, must be presented. (Writers who object to the role of a principle-based moral theory in modern medical ethics and who defend the idea of a "moral community" and a virtue ethics[13] also seem to me to be committed to the task of this sort of complex, daunting historical reconstruction. It is not enough, in other words, to argue that the moral discourse necessary to articulate a satisfying, rich medical ethics is impoverished without the

---

[13] Like Pellegrino and Thomasma 1993, and in a different way, Zaner 1988, or in May's 1983 account of covenants, cited below.

recognition of the importance of communal roles or the role of virtue in moral judgment. Our moral discourses may simply be unavoidably impoverished, given what else we cannot give up if we are to remain "us.")[14]

In fact, of course, critical theories of society have been concerned to understand such associations and activities for some time, and I have tried to suggest that there is clearly merit in the critical theory suspicion that individual, moral problems of conscience are misunderstood in isolation from the modern ethos in which they are experienced. But many classical critical theories have not sufficiently freed themselves from either a basically materialist methodology, on the one hand, or a satisfaction with a purely "negative" dialectic, on the other, in providing an account of such a presumed and determinative distorting ethos.

Of course, it might be possible and suggestive to point to the need for and priority of such an account. Providing it, while avoiding the classic failures of the materialist and counter-Enlightenment traps, is another story. But the considerations offered above at least begin to suggest some of the dangers in considering the field of medical ethics as a kind of subdiscipline, dominated by problems of judgment in hard cases, once some basic commitment to a deontological or consequentialist or religious principle frames the discussion. Inevitably in all such cases, some sort of a decisive and usually silent commitment to one or another narrative of modernity and theory of society itself will also come into play. Some notion of the normative status of the modern family, the real authority and duties of parents, the status of religion, the ethical dimensions or relative importance of exchange relations, the nature of institutions in modern societies, the function of law in modern states, even the notion of modern nation-states would all be relevant to such a narrative. The fact that we cannot properly understand one crucial element of medical ethics, the legitimate authority of a physician, without implying such an account, and the fact that it appears so sweeping and hard to manage do not mean that an implied reliance on such notions of modernity and modern societies is any less pervasive or foundational.

With respect to physicians' authority, such a project would have to involve some re-examination of the (putatively misleading) ways in which modern assumptions about any fair or just or good exercise of authority have come to dominate our discussion of these issues. On the one hand, the autonomy ideal itself, which enjoins us to work toward some full, free,

---

[14] See also Engelhardt 1991.

fair exchange between reflective, adult reasoners, who in effect bargain fairly with each other over some real transfer of goods, is itself so thin, so much an expression of what is often simply presumed to be an absence of any common ethical culture, that it is an easy target for skeptics and inspires all the predictable counters. It is in reaction to such an idealized and mostly unreal assumption that critics of the liberal tradition and those suspicious of the role of markets and power in social relations make the contrary assumption: that everyone's position in any social dealing is already some sort of reflection of some power relation, that everyone is always a witting or unwitting partisan of such ongoing struggles and never a detached, critical, or autonomous agent. The wholly negative or dangerously utopian and revolutionary implications of such an attack are well known.

A central move among those who have argued that this situation and the dead ends that lead from it could be avoided is the claim that we should discard the presupposition that only individual, voluntary associations generate ethical obligations or norms of all sorts (and so the counterassumption that all contemporary social relations, in the very large respects in which they are not "really" chosen or autonomously chosen, are "really" involuntary and oppressive, no matter how they seem). The question (and I recognize that nothing has here been established about the prospects for answering such a question), then, would be whether there would be some sorts of involvements in institutions, some ongoing participation in some sort of public life that is not voluntary (as in individually "chosen," consensual) but not thereby involuntary (as in unfree, not what would have been willed in a wholly undistorted context). This would mean that it might be possible to discuss what a physician, all things considered, ought to do, where that notion is not tied strictly to what he promised to do, what any reasonable consumer would expect he would have pledged to do, and so forth. It is not, after all, counterintuitive to appeal to such considerations in determining what a statesman, parent, or teacher "should do." (There are the briefest of hints about what such social ties among physicians and their colleagues, profession, and patients would look like in chapter 4 of William May's discussion of "covenants" in medical practice.) [15]

As already noted, I don't believe much detail will be forthcoming in such accounts without a fuller account of the distinct characteristics of modern, now even late modern societies and the sorts of norms consistent

---

[15] May 1983.

with such societies. (My account here is only a prolegomena to such an account and is meant to argue against the insulation of medical ethics as a subfield and the predominance of casuistical, dilemma case, and libertarian issues in it.)

Again, the motivation behind examining institutional roles and role-based norms stems directly from a recognition of the character of late modern ethical life, as fragmented and tension-filled as it is. In the exercise of their professional capacities, a physician simply cannot act exclusively as a paid agent of the patient (although she certainly is at least that); and in accounting for what, as a doctor, she ought to do, she cannot rely wholly on scientifically sanctioned therapies (although she must at least do that). Moreover, it will not be of much help to insist that, in response to the patient's suspension of judgment, she must act conscientiously, or in terms the doctor would herself approve, were she the patient. The patient is not a physician and not that particular person, her physician. It is clear that in acting conscientiously, the physician acts in recognition of the norms of the profession itself, and that these (1) always reflect much more than technical competence and (2) are themselves unintelligible apart from a general theory of modern civil societies. These norms, that is, reflect a common view of our stake in some social whole.

We certainly tend not to believe there are such norms in late modern societies and think that suggestions about such roles lead us toward a nostalgia for a "my station, my duties" approach to normative issues or a vague and so dangerous communitarianism. And yet participants in such societies constantly evince an interest in issues such as reputation, pride, and professional respect and act in ways that cannot be accounted for by attention to consensual exchange relations or the maximization of expected utility. Medical practice and the problem of medical authority, I have suggested, are cases in point.

I make no claim here about the prospects for such a reconsideration of these sorts of norms. I want only to claim that the basic ethical issue in medical practice should be seen to be the issue of authority and that the conventional understanding of the sources of such authority and the familiar criticisms of such authority do not do justice to the problems faced by anyone wishing to understand what, to invoke a famous phrase, Hegel called modern "ethical life."

# PART IV

# EXPRESSION

# 12

## "The Force of Felt Necessity"

### *Literature, Ethical Knowledge, and Law*

### I

By now, the "law and literature" topic has come to include a wide array of issues. One might consider the literary treatment of law and lawyers *in* literature, mostly in novels and plays, and one might thereby learn something about the socio-historical status of the legal profession and the everyday understanding of how the law works (or does not) from studying such works. (Dickens's novel *Bleak House* is probably the most obvious example.)[1] Literature itself raises a number of problems *for* the law, and so the law's regulation of literature might form a natural subdiscipline. (Intellectual property law and copyright issues would be clear instances.) One might study the literary *style* of judicial opinions, with an eye toward understanding the rhetoric of famously persuasive decisions or toward understanding the distinctive style that sets apart a certain legal school of thought, perhaps more clearly than do legal principles.

But there are two issues of greatest philosophical interest. Most people would concede that the law itself must be interpreted in order to be effectively applied, and this has seemed to many to open the door to a broad set of controversial issues concerned with theories of interpretation. According to some in the "Law and Literature" movement, written statutes and constitutions are texts and like texts are often ambiguous and vague and subject to multiple possible readings, perhaps, so goes the suggestion, like literary texts. Now we commonly understand the distinction between literary objects and, say, scientific prose or journalism to

[1] I rely here on the layout of issues presented in Posner 1998.

be the fact that there is always an implied reality/appearance distinction in literature. One misunderstands a literary work when one understands only the facts of the plot or the literal meaning of poetic images and does not appreciate that those details force on us the question of meaning, significance, intention, and judgment. These issues are not on the surface; they are hidden, in effect, in a metaphorical sense, invisible, and must be *sought*. In literary appreciation, some of this seeking obviously involves reliance on historical scholarship, knowledge of literary conventions (poetic diction, say), and experience with literary analysis. But some of it, at a deeper level, is of a piece with the attempt at understanding and assessing of other human beings and decisive events, such as love, betrayal, and death.[2] Literary texts are initially unclear or vague not because they are poorly written but because the understanding of literary meaning (and therewith of human meaning) is a distinct kind of very difficult achievement. (Or, if the text's meaning *is* obvious, on the surface, then we have an example of very bad, didactic literature, perhaps not even literature but propaganda.) Various literary theories tell us how such meaning is possible, what is distinctive about it, and how to find such meaning (or why it cannot be found), and one might assume that when constitutional principles or precedents are applied to new cases, a similar sort of *literary* interpretation must go on and that literary theories or even very general theories of meaning or Being, might therefore be relevant to the study and practice of law. (Hermeneutics, semiotics, structuralism, discourse theory, and deconstruction might then be of relevance in treating the law "as a text, like anything else" – and sometimes these theorists really do mean "like '*anything*' else." As is well known, this inflation of the scope of textuality is often accompanied by a deep skepticism that an authoritative meaning can ever be defended or is possible only in a biased way.)[3]

---

[2] I try to show what such a claim might amount to in Pippin 2000c.

[3] Posner 1998, 226–54, has offered a number of criticisms of the application of such "postmodern" theories of interpretation (or, to use Sontag's old phrase, theories "against interpretation"), many of which I agree with. But I find his own views on legal interpretation puzzling. He notes that the contexts and purposes of interpretation are different in legal and literary cases, that the legislator intends to issue commands, while the poet intends to create a work of beauty (whether or not anyone can see "through" it to that or other intentions). But the main reason Posner gives for at least attempting to do all we can to discern legislative intent or what the legislator would do were he confronted by novel situations is basically that that's all we've got to go on, that judges need guidance and need to avoid arbitrariness, and such a standard is the only realistically available one (see 231). This is like saying that since human life needs guidance, and since we are not

Second, there is the question of judicial *judgment*, and, secondarily, how it might be taught in law schools. Most judicial judgments are a lot like what Kant called "determinative" judgments, the application of a principle or rule, to a specific case. (In some instances, a case or a series of similar cases might be so novel or distinctive that the task of judgment is to find and formulate a new legal principle to cover such cases, closely consistent with analogous principles, but still novel. This would be an example of what Kant calls "reflective judgment.") In both cases, though, as Kant famously and influentially pointed out, while we might have a kind of literal, technical understanding of a rule (we can at least formulate semantically equivalent versions), we do not really *understand* a rule unless we understand how to apply it in a wide variety of cases. But there cannot be another *rule* for such application problems, since we would also understand that application rule only if we knew how to apply *it*, and that would set off a regress. Rather, Kant claimed, the correct application of a rule is more like "wit," or a kind of practical wisdom. (Pascal called it an *esprit de finesse* and contrasted it with the *esprit geometrique*, and of course Aristotle originated the discussion of the unique status of practical, especially "equitable" judgments.) Kant called it the "power of judgment" (*Urteilskraft*), and the term has an appropriate judicial ring. We expect judges to be able to decide with sagacity ("with good judgment") and with a great sensitivity to a wide variety of possible aspects and dimensions of a case and an imagination rich enough to imagine what "it must have been like to be X" or "what Y must have intended" as well as to foresee the implications of decisions in practice. All this, even while we concede, following Kant, that we cannot expect someone who does this well to provide an explicit account of *how* he or she does it well or to be able to give us a rule or method for doing so. We tend to think "experience" is the key component here, but we also know that there is no reason why someone of poor judgment cannot have many years of such "experience," merely demonstrating constantly that he or she cannot learn anything from experience and that

very good at figuring out philosophically how to guide a life (see Posner's comments in this chapter on Dworkin's philosophical reconstruction theory), we are stuck with the revealed word of God, which is at least a rule book of sorts. That is a reason of sorts, but it is not a very good one. In the legal context, it does not answer the question of whether such an approach gives us the best legal system in the normative sense of "best." We just resign ourselves to the only possible one. Not to mention that psychological interpretation of intentions or thought experiments about then and now are not likely to provide answers any more determinate than those provided by Dworkin or Fish. (I note that Posner also claims that consideration of pragmatic consequences must supplement an original intent theory.)

he or she repeats the same obtuse literal-mindedness and moralism (or sentimentalism and condescending pity) over and over again. Faced with this problem, one might propose great literature as a way of "educating," "refining," "opening up" judicial sensibility. The idea would be just the opposite of drawing "lessons" from literature that could then be applied in cases but proceeds on the assumption that a sensitivity to the complexity of the moral particulars of a case requires the education of the imagination, even the emotions in a way that cannot rely on lessons and principles. Lessons and principles are not the ways the imagination or a perceptual and emotional sensibility *can* be educated. Shakespeare might be of more use in improving such sensitivity (and so a judgmental, discriminating power) than legal textbooks, even ones with lots of rich examples.

Since I have used the Kantian formulation of the problem, I should hasten to point out that this judgment/moral knowledge problem is *not* the issue that would have interested say, Kant or Schiller, to cite the two philosophers from the German Idealist period who expressed the greatest hope for the relevance of beauty, and in Schiller's case art, for the moral life. In Kant's case, while he thought some cultivation of taste was possible and while he thought that that was a morally significant fact, he did not pursue the matter very far. The capacity for a disinterested pleasure, one not desire-driven, and the purposiveness evinced by beauty in nature were both morally reaffirming and reassuring in some sense, and literature was assigned some role in moral education, but that was a pretty simplistic, didactic role, and beauty's being a symbol of the morally good was not allowed to obscure in any way the absolute self-sufficiency of morality. And for Schiller, just as with Kant, the basic problem in living rightly is not a matter of moral knowledge or judgmental excellence. It appears that for both of them, we always could determine what we ought to do. The problem was *moral motivation* and the ideal of a harmony between moral law and sensibility; how we could come to do what reason demanded of us, without such an exercise of freedom being in reality a form of self-enslavement and permanent alienation. As Schiller famously said in the *Letters*,

If Truth [in this case, moral truth] is to gain victory in the struggle with Force [in this case, natural necessity], she must first become herself a force, and find some impulse to champion her in the realm of phenomena; for impulses are the only motive forces in the realm of phenomena. (48)

Moral weakness, on the one hand, and a kind of legalistic, formalistic "barbarism," on the other, are the central problems to be addressed, and art plays a "mediating" role, once the problem is set up that way. Hegel will drastically transform this landscape (returning us to a more Aristotelian, less Christian picture of the basic situation); we will thereby be returned to the problem of judgment and the potential relevance of literature, and I want to discuss some broad aspects of Hegel's view (without reference to Hegel's controversial texts). But we need first to understand the additional difficulties faced by an account of *legal* judgment.

II

The two issues on the list above have been much in the news in the last twenty-five years or so.[4] I am skeptical of the relevance of postmodern theories of meaning to understanding legal texts, mostly because I am skeptical about those theories themselves. But I do not address that issue here, and at any rate the problem of judgment independently suggests a number of distinct, interesting literary and philosophical issues.

However, this last "judgmental dimension" quickly becomes extremely complicated (and even more resistant to a formal or method-based approach) when one considers the extraordinary range of desirable goals we expect judicial decisions to accomplish, all at the same time, and how specific they are to the judicial context, perhaps nontransferable, too disanalogous to what goes on in literary appreciation. For example, we of course always want the decision to be (and to appear to be) just, to conform to a general, clear standard of rectitude. We want the decision to be consistent with results of analogous cases so that the application of the law does not seem to be lurching first in one direction, then in another, with no overall coherence (*stare decisis*), even if a judge so lurches in the name of justice. In many cases, we take for granted that the question of what a statute or constitutional principle means has got to have *some* connection with the original intention of the legislators or founders. To ignore completely such a consideration suggests an ad hoc legislating, not judging, and this creates the suspicion that judges are asserting power for the sake of their individual political philosophy or even interests, not acting the role of judges. Moreover, we do not consider the social results of the decision irrelevant; we do not want the decision to result in an increase of suffering. Indeed, we want the result, when considered as the standard for like cases and applied consistently as such, to benefit the

---

4 This is the case if one accepts Posner's dating, that "law and literature" as a field of organized study first got going with the publication of White (1973).

citizens affected by the ruling. Further, while consistency is important, we do not want to purchase it at the expense of flexibility in the face of social and historical change. We also want to make sure the judgment ends up punishing the wicked. A decision that, however consistent with precedent and legally just, does not end up doing so is thought to be flawed. Judges themselves might want a result to reflect a whole, coherent political philosophy. We want to make sure the costs of the decision are borne by those who can afford to pay, not those who cannot, and so on. And finally, we must satisfy what has been called a "meta-imperative":[5] We must ensure that all these desiderata must be given (or must appear to be given) some due in a decision. We cannot seem to be purchasing consistency with precedent at the cost of justice, or justice at the cost of coherence with precedent, or justice at the cost of great social pain, or minimizing social pain at the cost of proper punishment, and so forth.

The ability to fulfill these legal desiderata does not necessarily involve anything connected with what might be involved in becoming good and better readers. But the whole complex of judgmental goals rests ultimately on a "proper appreciation" of an individual case or cases and on a sensitivity to analogy. Such capacities, for all the special problems of legal judgment, still seem to involve a discriminatory capacity that is connected in some way with the powers of imagination and perception, a sensitivity to the "lived out" implications of choices (a sensitivity to the "logic" of life itself or to what has been called the "life world") and a capacity to link up principles and cases, universals and particulars that all do seem related to something like a literary or a broadly aesthetic sensitivity. And the same is true with regard to the question of what, in each case, actually counts as fulfilling each imperative. For example, we do not want judges who are so impressed and bewildered by the extraordinary uniqueness and distinctness of individual situations that none of the cases seems really to fit, to be properly subsumable under *any* principle, any more than we want a judge who sees every case so abstractly that each is *nothing but* an instance of some relevant rule, so quickly subsumable because so formally treated, that the law seems applied mechanically, hard-heartedly, lifelessly.

And, correspondingly, literary cases provide the best example of what Hegel called the "concrete universal," such that "proper appreciation" of such instances manifests the kind of excellence in judging that we are

---

[5] Menand 2001, 339, in his account of Oliver Wendell Holmes. Menand also presents a clear summary of the desiderata just discussed and of how Holmes tried to figure out how to satisfy them.

looking for. That is, reading about Emma Bovary is not something like reading journalism or a case history of a particular provincial doctor's wife who ruined herself financially and committed suicide, any more than it is reading about one of many such instances of a type, say, an instance of a Freudian law of development, of alienation among the bourgeoisie, or of a moral law about the evil of adultery, and so forth. In the former case, we want to say that there is something at stake, something of some generality, in the fate of Madame Bovary that is not a matter just of her personal fate, as is suggested everywhere by the many references to the Revolution, to the importance of the pharmacist, Homais, for understanding the new sort of society being formed after the Revolution, and to the romantic aspirations of Emma. On the other hand, the great vividness of Emma as an individual, with a claim on our attention as an individual, is lost in any hasty generalizing, not to mention that the great literary achievement of *Madame Bovary* – Flaubert's creation of an individual who seems alive, real – would also thereby be neglected.

At any rate, these are some of the considerations that led Oliver Wendell Holmes to declare, famously, "The life of the law has not been logic; it has been experience," to define experience as "the felt necessities of the time," and to assert that being able to recognize such necessities required "insight, tact, and specific knowledge." Now Holmes himself thought that such "balancing act" judgments would involve an experience-based sensitivity to likely *outcomes*, to "probabilities" (he said that the "man of the future" would be "the man of statistics and the master of economics"), and so a judgmental style oriented to consequences and predictions was the right way to flesh out his famous "reasonable man" standard, and his positivistic theory of legal decision making placed a heavy emphasis on predicting what other and future judges would say. And there are, of course, other obvious solutions to the excellence in judgment problem, but all such approaches will have to begin with the particulars, with the right (rich enough, nontendentious) description of the particulars and some sort of feel for which principles apply and in what way.[6]

As noted already, one might think that the requirements of discriminatory finesse in such balancing-act judgments could be improved by

---

[6] One might have an even more pragmatic, utilitarian approach to these issues (such as the law and economics school), pull back to a strictly formal theory, or adopt a historicist and sociological third-person point of view and see any result as merely and inescapably the reflection of the powers that be in some time and in some society, and so forth.

a literary training, by learning to see the complexity and interrelation of issues. We might be helped to understand the way the implications of judgments would acquire a distinct "lived" meaning in the lives of those affected by relying on what literary masterpieces can help us to see. It might then be that literature is one of our best means of access to the complexities of the "felt necessities of our time." Even if we end up concluding that such felt necessities were multiple and not consistent, understanding *that* with the proper appreciation might create an appropriate sort of humility, qualifying an otherwise dangerous illusion of certainty and righteousness. What such reliance on literature might mean, whether it is reasonable to expect it to have such an effect, and what implications it might have for lawyers are the issues I address in the next section.

## III

The basic question, then, is how to describe what it is judges must in some sense *know* in applying rules to cases and in balancing legal desiderata, if that knowledge cannot be formalized or formulated as a methodology, and whether some notion of literary knowledge is of help here. This takes us immediately into a contested area of contemporary ethical theory. It introduces not just the question of the relation between philosophical theories and literature, but the status of ethical theory itself. (Nussbaum has divided up the camps into the "alliance" partisans, who see both ethical theory and literary imagination as ineliminable and complementary, and the "adversarial" writers, such as Cora Diamond, or perhaps Bernard Williams, who are skeptical of the possibility of ethical theory at all.) If we take the problem of moral knowledge and moral discrimination as the central component of any account of excellence in judging, this would be a debate about the relative usefulness, harm, benefit, and so on of a greater or exclusive reliance on analytical argument, or literary exemplification in any attempt to improve such a capacity.

I do not think we need to go too far into that dispute, since we want first an understanding of just what literature might contribute to moral knowledge in the first place, not whether it does so better or exclusively or in an alliance with philosophy and argument. (I hope that it is clear that I mean moral knowledge very broadly here, so that it includes what one ought to do, what is appropriate to say, what makes someone a good friend, or what shows that a legal decision exhibits good judgment.) We should be careful, though, right away, in stating the claim for the relevance of literature to judgment and should immediately distinguish two claims. The first is the claim (1) that there is an important component of literary appreciation, of satisfying the norm "being a good reader," that is analogous to and can help to illuminate what excellence in judging in general consists in, and so can illuminate what counts as satisfying the norm "being a good (or wise) judge." The heart of *that* claim is the relation between universality and particularity in the practice of judging and understanding the conditions (social, psychological, historical) under which the realization of some putative ideal would be more or less likely. We might also go so far as to claim that one could not *be* a good judge if one did not simply *have* just those qualities that make one a good reader or even that it is in becoming a better reader that one, perforce, becomes a better judge in general; that that is just what it would be to become a better discriminator of particulars and applier of principle. The *other* very different claim (very often confused with the first) is sometimes thought to be an implication of the first: (2) that one of the best ways *to become* a better judge is *by* reading literature; that literature might sensitize us in the proper way, improve our discriminatory powers and sensitivity to morally salient features of situations, and so on. That this is not a direct implication of the first claim, and so must be defended separately, is obvious when we note that it is not at all clear (and very likely untrue) that one even becomes a better reader in the sense that we are interested in simply (or only) *by* reading, by reading more, by reading certain types of literature, or even by having certain conversations about literature. This is as implausible (or at least as radically incomplete) as the claim that one becomes better morally by doing better moral philosophy, or moral philosophy at all. Such staples of the defense of high culture may be good ways to convince state legislators in democratic societies (and especially in extremely pragmatic, utilitarian societies) to hire philosophy and literature professors, but there is very little evidence that it is true. The idea of literary sensitivity training, besides being somewhat sentimental and potentially simplistic, does not properly state the relevance of literature and literary understanding to the problem of judgment.

## IV

To see the problem better, consider two recent, prominent examples (by, respectively, a philosopher and a literary critic) who move from (1) to (2) without providing the argument that I claim is necessary. In her book *Poetic Justice* and in many articles, Martha Nussbaum has been defending what she calls a "literary/Aristotelian conception of practical judgment"[7] and so the relevance of literature to the development of the "special excellence of practical reasoning."[8] (She also invokes Adam Smith's notion of the ideal or judicious spectator.) At one point, she argues, with respect to Dickens's novel *Hard Times*,

> We are in effect being constituted by the novel as judges of a certain sort. As judges we may dispute with one another about what is right and proper; but in so far as the characters matter to us, and we are active on their behalf, we do not feel that the dispute is about nothing at all, that we are merely playing around.[9]

This suggests a problem right away, as soon as we suggest any relevance outside the world of the novel, as Nussbaum quickly does. Whatever we come to appreciate about a character's limitations or moral flaws, however we are made by the novelist to see aspects of issues that we would not have seen in ordinary life, we just thereby face *another* problem of judgment: that is, the problem of trying to appreciate properly what may be analogous or similar cases in life (or not), for which our broadened perceptual powers would now be relevant. We also face the problem of why, under which conditions, one would even care in the first place to seek out that relevance. Literature cannot be a means to improve *this* capacity, because that is the capacity (and the caring) by virtue of which literature could be relevant in the first place, and there is no clear reason to think that reading itself contributes anything to appreciating the broadened relevance or importance of the issues we confront in novels. (My objection, in other words, is not to the moral or legal relevance of *literature*, in sense no. 1 above, but to claims for the moral relevance of *reading*.) No one, in other words, could be said to be "reading well" many of the novels of J. M. Coetzee if she did not appreciate the way the novels exhibit and in their own way demonstrate how spiritually deforming and dehumanizing the exercise of oppressive, illegitimate power is for the oppressor as well as the oppressed, how horribly poisoned the oppressor's own life becomes by that exercise. Indeed, there are very few "demonstrations" of this point anywhere, in philosophy or literature, as compelling as Coetzee's. Yet it is not hard to imagine an American reader of *Waiting for the Barbarians* who sees clearly and is deeply moved by such a demonstration and yet who just does not see that in his treatment of his wife or his family or his employees he is re-enacting precisely what he

---

[7] Nussbaum 1995, 82.
[8] Ibid., 86.
[9] Ibid., 83.

had "appreciated" in the novel. In the long run, of course, it is unlikely that someone could respond in such a way to a novel and be *so* blind in his own life, but in the long run, I want to suggest that a good deal more is going on than can be explained by attention to literary appreciation.[10]

Even more difficult issues emerge when Nussbaum tries to specify the sort of moral sensitivity that literature (presumably, qua literature) promotes. Again, when writing about *Hard Times*, she says:

> In this way our thought will *naturally turn* in the direction of making the lot of the worst off more similar to the lot of the rich and powerful: since we might be, or become, either of these two people, we want to raise the floor [my emphasis].[11]

I see no reason to believe that so "learning the facts," as she says, will just *thereby be* "acquiring a motivation to alter them." There is a suggestion of the Rawlsean Original Position argument, but that would be subject to all the standard objections. Why assume that we, as readers, would not rather gamble that we will end up better off, and admire, even envy, the wealthy? Rather than be so motivated, would it not be more "natural" to feel grateful that we are not as bad off as Louisa and Blackpool, perhaps to pity them, and move on? Perhaps not, but there are many ways of responding to their suffering consistent with having appreciated the contingency and undeservedness of their lot, and it is certainly not obvious that a "turning" to egalitarian action will ensue "naturally."

There is even less reason to believe that the modern realist novel "promotes habits of mind that lead towards social equality in that they contribute to the dismantling of the stereotypes that support group hatred."[12] Is there any reason to believe that there is this "connection between literary spectatorship and a concern for equality"? In some general sense, it might be true that prejudice rests on stereotypes and is at a certain

---

[10] Or consider the lead character in Coetzee's novel, *Disgrace*, David Lurie. David is (or was) a professor of romantic literature and believes himself to be aware of the soul-deadening mediocrity of modern societies, unencumbered by bourgeois illusions, and defiantly antihypocritical. Some of his attitude is fueled by his belief that he has learned from his mentors – Wordsworth, Byron, Blake – about the authenticity of erotic desire, the "god within" in his nature that David thinks he is courageously refusing to tame. Such literary sensibilities, however, involve little more than self-serving self-deceit, so profound and deep that even the rape of his daughter does not seem to awaken him to the complexities and dangers of eros (and his own, especially). He learns finally a good deal more, even about moral integrity (more than he ever did from literature) by tending sick dogs at a nearby clinic. This makes David's final deed for the dogs at once transformative and genuinely ennobling and pathetic.

[11] Nussbaum 1995, 91.

[12] Ibid., 92.

distance from the reality of particular lives and that gripping literary accounts of such individuals might begin to make one uneasy about one's prejudices, but if the novel is not very good (like Dickens's dreadful *Hard Times*, and like other novels out to make such a point), it is just as likely that "the individual" presented will instantiate just another Christian cliché, the good-hearted worker uncorrupted by power and money, or that the villains will be stereotypes and one's moral reaction will amount to an all-too-easy rejection of the villain (Who could take Grandgrind seriously as a character? He's right out of the Disney kitsch factory), or that one's reaction itself will be stereotypical, will amount to a self-satisfied feeling that one has rejected Grandgrind and has a good heart, that one's sympathies are all in the right place.

This is all going quite wrong, I think, and stops well short of appreciating the sort of unease, anxiety, disquiet, and excitement we feel with great literature. For one thing, we usually end up far more confused than armed with egalitarian weapons in our encounters with great work. The very simplicity of the categorizations used by Nussbaum to discuss *Hard Times* reminds us of the novels where such oppositions would be quite clumsy. *Madame Bovary*, again; *Anna Karenina*; Julien Sorel in the *Red and the Black*; Hardy's novels. Think only of Charlus in Proust's novel. Charlus is a study in "inversion," as the Narrator calls it, but his treatment is far more complex than the "see what a *real* person Maurice is" plot in Forster's (also dreadful) novel about the subject. Charlus is vain, cruel, a snob, hypocritical, unreliable, grotesquely egotistical, but all of that seems somehow compensated for or offset in some way by the furious intensity and passion with which he leads his life. He is also, in other words, intensely interesting; endlessly complex and himself an aesthete with genuine taste, someone who cares most of all (knowledgeably) about beauty (and would of course be horrified at any form of egalitarianism). One would be a bad reader indeed to respond to Charlus in moral terms alone. Something about one's misunderstanding the place of moral judgments in a life, some error of judgment, would be exhibited were one's reaction merely to wag one's finger at the Baron.

## V

That great Schillerian theme – the moral significance of beauty and art – appears more and more irresistible in contemporary commentators and is no doubt some aspect of the "law and literature" movement itself, an attempt to acquaint oneself again with the value and indispensability of humanistic learning after decades of attack. That yearning is manifest not only in a clear, recent aesthetic return to the beautiful as aesthetic standard[13] but in claims for the moral and political significance of the aesthetic dimension. This much larger theme of beauty is treated as morally and politically important in a much discussed recent book by the Harvard critic Elaine Scary, called *On Beauty and Being Just.* Scary is out to offer a defense of beauty against the "taboo"[14] that pronounces a love of the beautiful as a form of reification or an exhibition to be an elitist, inegalitarian sensibility, against the way "the vocabulary of beauty has been driven underground in the humanities for the last two decades."[15] But she does not offer this apologia in the language of aesthetic autonomy, or *l'art pour l'art.* Like Nussbaum, she defends the moral significance of an attention to beauty and champions the transformative, politically positive effects of aesthetic experience. Some of these defenses are not news (such as her Kantian claims about the non-self-interested quality of aesthetic delight – Scary calls the phenomenon "radical decentering"),[16] although they are all stated with a sweeping, almost oracular confidence that makes the nineteenth-century German claims for *Bildung* look pale by comparison. For example: "The willingness continually to revise one's own location in order to place oneself in the path of beauty *is the basic impulse* underlying education" (my emphasis).[17] And: "By perpetuating beauty, institutions of education help incite the will toward continual creation" (presumably, a good thing).[18] Beauty is "life saving . . . it makes life more vivid, animated, living, worth living," and, as in Plato's famous account, the desire for the beautiful is "bound up with" the desire for truth, and this by acquainting us with a kind of "conviction" and certainty such that "ever afterward one is willing to labor, struggle, wrestle with the world to locate enduring sources of conviction – to locate what is true."[19]

The most extreme of her claims concerns the relation between beauty and equality, but it should first be noted that these sorts of claims could be taken seriously only if they were accompanied by some attention to

[13] Cf. one of the most unusual of such attempts, Hickey 1993.
[14] Scary 1999, 117.
[15] Ibid., 52.
[16] Ibid., 111.
[17] Ibid., 7.
[18] Ibid., 8.
[19] Ibid., 31.

the historical fate of the beautiful in modern art and literature. The appreciation of the beautiful was traditionally understood as primarily a sensible and emotional regarding, and such a capacity has been understood as "taste." Sometime after the first third of the nineteenth century, aesthetic value came to be understood in a way less and less tied to the experience of harmony or even pleasure; the "painful" effects of the sublime were more in evidence; modernist art came to be more and more occupied with itself, eventually more ironic; and the capacity for appreciation became much more a matter of "criticism" than taste. The growing disenchantment with, disinterest in, even suspicion of the beautiful as a value is not a "mistake" made by humanities departments in the last two decades, a mistake that can be "corrected" by an essay that reminds us of all the good things associated with beauty. This was a profound transformation in our self-understanding that Hegel, virtually alone, foresaw and tried to account for, as in his famous claim that fine art, with respect to the "highest needs of the spirit," had become for us a "thing of the past," and with such claims as:

The *philosophy* of art is therefore a greater need in our day than it was in days when art itself yielded full satisfaction. Art invites us to intellectual consideration, and that, not for the purpose of creating art again, but for knowing philosophically what art is. (A, 11)[20]

And I note that this historical dimension is largely missing from Nussbaum, too, who wanders from Sophocles to Ralph Ellison and Henry James as if they were all contemporaries of Dickens. Some classics have perennial themes and as art works have stood the test of time. But that does not mean that the role or the possible role of such works in the moral life of communities is pretty much the same or can be easily transferred from one epoch to another.[21] (It is much more likely that "classics" are classics because they can play multiple, different roles in different places and times.) The importance of understanding "*what happened* to

---

[20] And in his remarks about "the self-transcendence of art but within its own sphere and in the form of art itself" (A, 80).

[21] We of course like to believe that critical and legal self-criticism is always available to us, but we might recall that the U.S. Supreme Court supported the grotesquely unconstitutional Japanese internment laws and several repressive security measures enacted during the McCarthy era for many years before they were finally nullified – not to mention the Court's recent, disgraceful partisanship.

the beautiful" before we can begin a campaign of aesthetic-moral rearmament is clear from the results of ignoring it.[22]

But it is Scary's treatment of the *political* dimension of beauty that reminds us again of the difficulty of understanding the relation between the aesthetic and the normative domains. Like Nussbaum, she concludes that a good reader or good appreciator very likely would have to be "good" in a more full-blooded sense, especially good in the modern, political sense: an egalitarian, an appreciator of particularity and the equal importance of different individuals. Here are some of her remarkable claims. Beauty "intensifies the pressure we feel to repair existing injuries."[23] She exploits the twin resonances in "fairness" and "symmetry" as both aesthetic balance and political equality to suggest that beautiful things "give rise to the notion of distribution, to a life-saving reciprocity, to fairness... in the sense of 'a symmetry of everyone's relation to one another.'"[24] And she concludes that "folded into the aesthetic surfaces of the world is a pressure toward social equality."[25]

As with Nussbaum's claim, I see little reason to expect that aesthetic sensitivity will "give rise to" any such notion and see plenty of reasons to think otherwise. Consider first something Scary does not: the classical and quite plausible claims about the deep *tension* between the claims of beauty and the demands of justice. The Diotima passage in Plato's *Symposium* suggests one problem, and the *Republic* another. The desire for the beautiful turns out to be completed by the eternal *possession* of the beautiful. It need not be a possession that also excludes. (Philosophical possession of truth, for example, is not like this, and is beautiful. Sharing such knowledge does not thereby mean that one has less of it.) But, as Henry James, among others, suggested, there is one sort of important, very typical attachment to the beautiful that is expressed by "collecting,"

---

[22] For another thing, with respect to Scary's thesis, to state the obvious, Kant was overwhelmingly successful in arguing that the significance of the beautiful was "subjective." The capacity to have the experience told us something about ourselves, not about palm trees or symmetry. The experience had its uniquely occasioning (formal) objects, inspired a "sense" of the purposiveness of nature, and consisted in an unusual sort of normative claim on others, but the experience's deepest significance resided in its relation to our moral destiny as free persons. Kant could have accepted the claims that Scary makes about the beautiful thing and the subject "welcoming" each other (Scary 1999, 90) only if interpreted in this idealist way.

[23] Scary 1999, 57.

[24] Ibid., 95.

[25] Ibid., 110.

a nice way of saying "exclusively owning." This is partly so that one may see the objects whenever one likes, but this itself is technically impossible without regulating who else may see it, and it is partly a desire whose negative side is jealousy. Delight in the beautiful has always in some sense inspired a need to guard and protect and keep for one's own. This may all be pathological, of course, or not typical, or Plato might be wrong to think it an important worry, but the issues of possession, exclusion, and jealousy seem so close to this topic (eros for the beautiful) that some deeper tension with the desire for justice seems a reasonable concern.

Second, there is the kind of tension evinced so famously by *The Republic*, where, for the sake of justice, beauty (poetic beauty at least) must be in some sense excluded. (The first "political" attack on beauty is in the name of justice.) This partly has to do with the doctrine of the passions in that work and the relation between the intellect and the passions, but there is also some suggestion that justice always requires some sort of application of a measure or criterion *at odds with* the attachment to particularity, to a beauty that cannot be commonly shared and appreciated or that expresses a particular, concrete attachment that has nothing in common with the public or the city. The Platonic view seems to be that beauty is experienced and comes to be loved privately, inevitably, and closes off rather than opens up the passions and needs we share, the proper domain of justice. (This is not to mention the Platonic suspicion that beauty can easily contribute to deception and illusion, can intoxicate us with the love of appearances in a way that forecloses, hardly leads to, a concern with truth.)

And this raises questions about Scary's case for the link between aesthetic symmetry (and other properties, such as balance, harmony, or proportion) and *equality*. Originally, justice (*dike*) simply denotes that things are in their right place, that all is fitting, mete, or, most famously, as she herself notes, *kalos*. This can certainly mean that there are inequalities expressed and perhaps embraced by a regime, but the regime is still just if the order and form is "as it should be," for the good of all, and so on, not necessarily only if the regime embodies some large commitment to moral (or some other sort?) of equality. There is even, we all have experienced, something scary and ugly in symmetrical and orderly attempts at public displays and affirmations of "beautiful equality," from May Day parades to Mao jackets. A common or equal measure for all seems antithetical to a concern with the beautiful. Isn't the most intuitive beginning thought on this subject that beauty *among persons* is "unjustly" or unequally distributed and so at some odds with egalitarian sensibilities, that beauty can thereby inspire hatred and especially envy as well as love, that the capacity to appreciate beauty is also unequally distributed, and that the enjoyment of beauty requires a leisure and education very likely not possible (or not possible soon) for the many but only for a few?[26] Beauty and our love of the beautiful is, in a word, dangerous, something not noted in Scary's anodyne formulations.

## VI

By denying that there is any clear link between being a good reader or a good appreciator of beauty and having any practical reason to do anything, certainly any reasons to "equalize," I do not mean to align myself with either aesthetic purists or with those Humeans and Kantians who seek to separate sensible and intellectual perception from motivating reasons, and want instead to cast my lot in with those such as McDowell, Wiggins, and Nussbaum who defend a neo-Aristotelian picture of ethical knowledge, and so the inseparability of the perception of an action as base and that being the reason not to do it. But where Nussbaum had spoken of the way literature inspires a "natural turn" toward attempts to equalize position and status, we should, I am arguing, substitute the neo-Aristotelian, Hegelian notion of a "second nature" in that claim and admit that what we are inspired to do is much less clear and more historically sensitive. That will help us to appreciate that what a work of literature evokes or does not evoke in a reader is a complex function of an ongoing historical form of life (that second or cultivated nature), an interrelated set of a community's practices, and that initiation into such practices is not a matter of learning rules or principles, *or* of being *directed* one way or another *by* a work of literature. Such initiation is, famously, a matter of habit and a slow, extremely complicated process of socialization, out of which (and only out of which) good reading and good judgment arise and flourish. Literature and art certainly play an important role in such education, in *Bildung*, but "always already in that world," if one might borrow a Heideggerianism. Both the reader and the book are embedded in a kind of life at a time and the practice of reading or reading well, appreciating, must always be understood as an expression of that life.

This is not to deny that such forms of life become self-conscious and self-critical, to be committed to relativism, or to deny that work from other times and places is accessible to us or that oppressive forms of life

---

[26] Cf. also the remarks about Clarissa, Lovelace, and beauty in Coetzee 2001, 23–33.

can be undermined by the simple act of reading. The point is, rather, that were a work of art to have such a capacity in such a culture, it would be as much because of the requirements of that culture at that time as the qualities of the work and that we cannot expect such a work to have that effect "by itself." If lawyers and judges should read Shakespeare and Proust, such reading must be (must have been) folded into the fabric of a life, continuously and early on, not picked up as means to improve perception. Down that latter road lies moralism, sentimentality, "reverse" stereotyping, and a historical blindness that "thins out" a work to its most obvious and obviously relevant dimensions. Said another way, works of art primarily help us understand who we are and what we have become, and only thereby and in those terms what we can or ought to be. The exercise of practical judgment has to rely first of all on the "felt necessities of the time" for bearings, and the cultivation of excellence in judging and reading is much more a matter of development, changes, in those felt necessities over time, usually over a long time. Literature can help us to understand the normative assumptions, the "felt necessities," behind the law and its practice at a time, but there is little that reading or appreciating can do on their own about such necessities.

# 13

## What Was Abstract Art? (From the Point of View of Hegel)

### I

The emergence of abstract art, first in the early part of the twentieth century with Kandinsky, Malevich, and Mondrian, and then in the much more celebrated case of America in the 1950s (Rothko, Pollock, et al.) remains puzzling.[*] Such a great shift in aesthetic standards and taste is not only unprecedented in its radicality. The fact that nonfigurative art, without identifiable content in any traditional sense, was produced, appreciated, eagerly bought, and even, finally, triumphantly hung in the lobbies of banks and insurance companies provokes understandable questions about both social and cultural history, as well as about the history of art. The endlessly disputed category of modernism itself and its eventual fate seems at issue.

Whatever else is going on in abstraction as a movement in painting, it is uncontroversial that an accelerating and intensifying self-consciousness about what it is to paint, about how painting or visual meaning is possible, came to be at issue, leading ultimately to the transformation of painting itself into the object of painting (all issues already in play since impressionism) are at issue. Given that heightened conceptual dimension, one might

[*] I am much indebted to Thomas Pavel for his comments on an earlier draft of this chapter, to Thomas, Eric Santner, and Terry Pinkard for many fruitful conversations about Hegel's *Lectures* during a seminar in the spring of 2001, to Stephen Houlgate and Michael Fried for helpful comments and criticisms, and to the audience at a conference on abstract art held at the University of Chicago in October 2001, where an earlier version of this chapter was first presented. I have been pressed about several of the major issues by Martin Donougho, and I am grateful for his remarks.

turn for some perspective on such developments to that theorist for whom "the historical development of self-consciousness" amounts to the grand narrative of history itself. Even if for many, Hegel is, together with Locke, *the* bourgeois philosopher (the philosopher of the *arrière-garde*), he is also the art theorist for whom the link between modernity and an intensifying self-consciousness, both within art production and, philosophically, about art itself, is the most important. And the fairly natural idea of abstraction as a kind of logical culmination of modernist self-consciousness itself, that way of accounting for the phenomenon, is the kind of idea that we owe to Hegel. More broadly, the very existence of abstract art seems to represent some kind of deliberate departure from the entire tradition of image-based art, and so involves some sort of implicit claim that the conditions of the very intelligibility of what Hegel calls the "highest" philosophical issues have changed, such that traditional, image-based art is no longer as important a vehicle of meaning for us now, given how we have come to understand ourselves, have come to understand understanding. And Hegel was the only prominent modern philosopher who in some way gave voice to that departure, who argued – at the time, outrageously – that traditional art had become "a thing of the past" and that it no longer served "the highest needs of human spirit" (that is, it still served many extremely important human needs, was hardly "over" or finished, but had declined in importance, could not represent "the highest" or most important self-understanding).

Of course, all these ideas – that a form of art could in some sense be required historically by some sort of conceptual dissonance in a prior form, that a historical form of self-understanding could be called progressive, an advance over an earlier stage, that various activities "of spirit," art, politics, and religion could be accounted for as linked efforts in a common project (the achievement of self-knowledge and therewith the "realization of freedom"), and so forth – are now likely to seem naïve, vestigial, of mere historical interest. But the justifiability of that reaction depends a great deal, as in all such cases, on how such Hegelian claims are understood. For example, it is no part at all of any of the standard interpretations of Hegel's theory that, by closing this particular door on the philosophical significance of traditional art, he could be understood to have thereby opened a door to, to have begun to conceptualize the necessity of, non-image-based art. And given when Hegel died, it is obviously no part of his own self-understanding. But there is nevertheless a basis in his philosophical history of art for theorizing these later modern developments. Or so I want to argue.

## II

Consider the most obvious relevance: the general trajectory of Hegel's account. The history of art for Hegel represents a kind of gradual dematerialization or developing spiritualization of all forms of self-understanding. Put in the terms of our topic, the basic narrative direction in Hegel's history of art is toward what could be called something like greater "abstraction" in the means of representation – "from" architecture and sculpture "toward" painting, music, and finally poetry. "Abstraction" is not the word he would use (he would insist on greater "concreteness" in such a progression), but his stress on less reliance on "representation" and on greater reflexivity is consistent with the colloquial sense of that term. (The putative inadequacy of "representational" notions of intelligibility is, of course, tied to very large themes in Hegel's account of the famous "subject-object" relation. In general, he wants to deny that such intelligibility requires that subjects be both cut off from and connected with the objects of understanding by some mediating medium, by means of which we are directed to some intentional object, a general picture of the mind-world relation that also generates unsolvable skeptical problems. On the Hegelian account of modernism, the question becomes something like what, say, painting looks like, how it presents a notion of intelligibility, without reliance on such a representational model.) So, within the narrative of developing self-consciousness presented by Hegel, not only would it not be surprising to hear that at some point in its history, art might come more and more to be about "abstract" or conceptual objects, such as "paintingness," but we might also hope to find some explanation of why the development of art might have brought us to this point. There will be much that remains surprising, especially the dialectical claim that with such a topic the "world-historical" capacities of art – its role in satisfying "the highest need of human spirit" – itself would be exhausted, would no longer be adequate to its own object, but the cluster of topics raised by the question of the meaning of abstraction naturally invites an extension of Hegel's narrative.[1]

---

[1] This is *not* at all the same thing as saying that the development of Western art tends toward ever greater "formalism," in the sense of a preoccupation with "pure" form, understood as "without the content." So, again, "abstraction" can be a misleading word. But in aesthetic theory as well as ethical theory Hegel claims to have been able to show how there can be "concrete universals," a *kind* of independence from particularity that is not the adoption of a "mere one among infinitely many" stance. An analogy: when we say that abstract painting is "formal," we ought to mean that it has only itself, or painterly possibilities as its own content (possibilities within the norm of painting, once we have come to

Sketching this trajectory already indicates what would be the philosophical significance of this development for Hegel: that human beings require less and less sensible, representative imagery in order to understand themselves (with respect to "the highest issue" – for Hegel, their being free subjects), that such a natural embodiment is less and less (on its own, considered just in itself) an adequate expression of such a genuinely free life, especially since the essential component of such a free life is an adequate self-understanding.

It is within this narrative that we hear the final, famous Hegelian verdict that artistic expression in Western modernity, tied as it ever was to a sensible and "representative" medium, could no longer bear a major burden of the work in the human struggle toward self-understanding, was no longer as world-historically important as it once was, was no longer as necessary as it once was to the realization of freedom. (Hegel's claim about becoming for us "a thing of the past" is thus not about the end of art, however much he is associated with that phrase, but the end of a

---

understand that that norm is "self-legislated"), in the same way that for Hegel the content of speculative philosophy is nothing but the history of philosophy itself. Or Proust's novel is about novel writing and so has its own form *as* its content. But the novel is not "*empty*" of content. Or when people say that Henry James novels are "too stylized," are "formal" experimentations, they often do not appreciate that such a stylization represents an independence from a fixed perspective on content that has itself a profound moral meaning, *that* content ("independence from a fixed perspective on content"; see Pippin 2000c). Given the work of Arthur Danto, this is an important point to stress. Hegel's claim about the *end of art mattering in the way it always had* is not a claim about the "end of art" in Danto's sense (the end of the purchase *of the category of art*, of the art/nonart distinction.) Art remains distinguishable as art (that issue is never Hegel's concern, and a great number of issues are confused by Danto's invoking Hegel in the name of such an issue); art remains an *aesthetic* object (Danto's own reasons for distinguishing art and the aesthetic are too involved to go into here; they may be good reasons, but they have little to do with Hegel (see Danto 1981)); its mode of embodiment in sensuous material is not abandoned (as if on the way to "conceptual art"); and what is overcome in later modernity is the normative *authority* of nature, not nature itself. Modern art finally becomes philosophical in Hegel's sense, but it does not become philosophy. (Cf. by contrast Danto 1986, on "art having finally become vaporized in a dazzle of pure thought about itself, and remaining as it were, solely the object of its own theoretical consciousness" (111).) This sort of reading of Hegel (the "end of history," "victory over matter," etc.) is not an uncommon one. See Michelson 1982, esp. 8. (Mondrian's "art of pure relations" *does* approach Hegelian ideas in an interesting way, if we forget about Theosophy, 10.) On the more explicitly Hegelian elements (teleology, the concrete universal, dialectic) in De Stijl in general, and van Doesburg and especially Mondrian in particular, see Cheetham 1991, 52–8, and on their appearance in Kandinsky, 79–83. The theosophical elements again distort the deeper relevance of Hegel's theory of art since they lead Cheetham to attribute to Hegel notions of "essentialism," "purity," freedom as identification with the absolute," and so forth that miss the deeper elements connected with Hegel's theory of normativity.

*way* of art's mattering, something he thinks he can show by presenting a kind of history and logic and phenomenology of anything "mattering" to human beings, within which art plays a distinct and changing role.[2] (Said another way, the prior question for Hegel is always the human need for art.)[3] Again, the claim is not that there will not be art or that it will not matter at all but that art can no longer play the social role it did in Greece and Rome, in medieval and Renaissance Christianity, or in romantic aspirations for the role of art in liberation and *Bildung*. Each of these historical *worlds* has come to a kind of end, and, the claim is, there is no equivalently powerful role in bourgeois modernity. (In a way, what could be more obvious?) Accordingly, if Hegel's account is roughly correct, art must either accept such a (comparatively) diminished, subsidiary role (whatever that would mean) or somehow take account of its new status by assuming some new stance, perhaps "about" its own altered status, perhaps by being about, exclusively and purely, its formal properties and potentials, perhaps by being about opticality as such, perhaps about purely painterly experiments as the final assertion of the complete autonomy of art, or perhaps by still announcing some form of divine

---

[2] More specifically, it is "with respect to its [art's] highest vocation [*nach der Seite ihrer höchsten Bestimmung*]" that it does not matter as it once did (A, 11). Second-place on a list with *that* criterion would still rank awfully high. References refer to Knox's translation, but where there might be some confusion, I have added the problematic German phrase.

    It would take an independent, book-length study to work out the nature of Hegel's "phenomenological" narrative, but these two elements – the problem of mattering, significance, and importance and the claim that politics, religion, art, and philosophy should all be understood as always aspects of and manifestations of a continuing project of self-knowledge itself understood as the key element in the progressive realization of freedom – should be contrasted with Danto's narrative in Danto 1986, "The End of Art," 81–115. Danto's narrative is internal to art history itself. He sees it as about a problem of "optical fidelity" (90), or the "cultural imperative to replace inference with direct perception" (91), and so ends up with "resolutions" of that problem in photography and film; hence a crisis in what art can now be. Danto's narrative thus ends up paradigmatically with Duchamp, or an un-Hegelian "indeterminate negation" of art's distinctness. More of Hegel's own theory is highlighted, I am suggesting, if we see abstraction *in* painting (and not abstraction as an early move *away from* painting as aesthetic enterprise) as an exemplification of the trajectory of his theory. How to extend that trajectory beyond the New York art world of the 1950s is another question, briefly discussed below. See also Danto 1986, "Art, Evolution, and the Consciousness of History" (187–210), where again the concerns of an "optics of fidelity" are grafted onto Hegel's account and made to provoke a crisis that is not relevant to Hegel's concerns. Danto here seems quite influenced by Alois Riegel and some of the analogous ideas of Hans Belting about art "before art." See Danto 1997, "Three Decades after the End of Art" and the beginning of "Modernism and the Critique of Pure Art: The Historical Vision of Clement Greenberg," 61ff.

[3] See Houlgate 2000, 61–82. (I disagree below in note 10 with Houlgate's version of what Hegel would have disagreed with in Greenberg's famous account of abstraction.)

revelation after the death of God, but a revelation without content and indifferent to audience (as perhaps in the work of Rothko).[4] It could then matter in all these different ways that there be art, a way not like its prior roles and one more consistent with the situation of European modernity, but a way not imagined by the historical Hegel, even though some such altered stance might be said to have been anticipated in his theory.

## III

It is certainly true that Hegel seems to have had some presentiment of the great changes that were to come in post-Romantic art, to have appreciated the significance of those changes, and to have realized that they amounted to much more than a change in artistic fashion. Contemporary artists, Hegel says, "after the necessary particular stages of the romantic art-form have been traversed," have liberated themselves from fixed or required subject matter, from any nonaesthetically prescribed determinate content:

Bondage to a particular subject-matter and a mode of portrayal suitable for this material alone, are for artists today something past, and art therefore has become a free instrument which the artist can wield in proportion to his subjective skill in relation to any material of whatever kind. The artist thus stands above consecrated forms and configurations and moves freely on his own account (*frei für sich*), independent of the subject-matter and mode of conception in which the holy and eternal was previously made visible to human apprehension.... From the very beginning, before he embarks on production, his great and free soul must know and possess its own ground, must be sure of itself and confident in itself. (A, 605–6)[5]

---

[4] I refer here to the set of issues raised by the well-known letter of Gershom Scholem to Walter Benjamin, quoted and glossed in a very interesting way in Santner 2001, 38. The relevance of the Hegelian position here is complicated. As he had made clear in GW, for Hegel, "the religion of modern times is 'God is dead.'" There is no "Jenseits," no Beyond or transhuman transcendence. But humankind's *self*-divinization can seem to be just as much a successful glorification as it can be something merely left standing when all else is gone. If there is "only" human law, posited in time, binding us as such only if we submit to it, then the revelation is as much an intimation of Pascal's eternal silences as it is the discovery of an autonomous human being standing in the place that was to be occupied by a genuine, exogenous revelation.

[5] In one respect, all Hegel might be saying here is that the production and appreciation of art in the modern era has become something important in itself, and not because of some religious or civic function. What else he might mean, especially about art's self-reliance, is what is at issue in any interpretation of Hegel's aesthetic theory.

Admittedly, again, the historical Hegel would never have imagined the extent of the "freedom" claimed by modernists and would no doubt have been horrified by abstract art. He was a pretty conservative fellow. But the principle articulated in this quotation, as well as the link to freedom as the decisive issue, is what is important for our purposes. And Hegel seemed to have foreseen the shift in the modernist understanding of artistic experience, away from the sensuous and beautiful and toward the conceptual and reflexive:

> The *philosophy* of art is therefore a greater need in our day than it was in days when art itself yielded full satisfaction. Art invites us to intellectual consideration [*denkenden Betrachtung*], and that, not for the purpose of creating art again, but for knowing philosophically what art is. (A, 11)

Art (like the modern social world itself) had thus "become philosophical," invited as much a philosophical as a purely aesthetic response, and so, for that reason, could be said now to be superceded in world-historical terms by philosophy itself, by the very philosophy it itself calls for.

This is certainly a distinctive, bold candidate among other more familiar explanations. It competes with what can loosely be called the Marxist claim about the dissolving coherence of late bourgeois culture reflected in the self-images expressed in such art or the neo-Marxist claim about the active "negation" of that culture by an art produced so that it could not be assimilated, consumed, or even understood within it. (A link between modernism in the arts and resistance to the cultural logic of capitalism – not just expressive of it and its failure to make sense – is also characteristic of the sophisticated new account by T. J. Clark.)[6] It competes as well with more so-called essentialist or reductionist accounts, such as Greenberg's: how painting, threatened with absorption by the mass culture and entertainment industries, retreated (or advanced, depending on your point of view) to the "essence" of painting as such, flatness and the composition of flat surface, an insistence on art's purity and autonomy as a way of resisting such absorption or colonization by other, especially narrative, art forms. And there is Michael Fried's compelling emphasis on the attempt by modernists to continue to make *great* art, art that did not at all reject or refuse

---

[6] Clark 1999. A standard classification of such philosophic narratives: There is the Kant-Greenberg (and some people assume Michael Fried) line (the last depends on how one interprets philosophically the categories of "theatricality" and "absorption"), the Hegel-Marx-Clark line, and the Nietzschean line, visible in very different ways in Adorno, Benjamin, and Heidegger, where the whole possibility of sense making breaks down, initiating a different, perhaps more archaic role for art.

its tradition and aspired to be an art that could stand together with the great art of the past. Such art had to be produced under such radically different historical conditions as to make this most unlikely, especially conditions of intense, expanding, and deepening self-consciousness about the painting itself both as artificial object beheld and as directing the beholder to the painting's intentional object. Given such self-consciousness, painters had to respond by creating a different sort of painterly presence and by solving in ever more complicated ways what Fried has called the problem of the painting's "theatricality." Hegel's account of our growing awareness of the limitations of a traditionally representationalist notion of intelligibility (for the expression of "the highest things") and the consequences of this development for the status of visual art in our culture (its way of mattering) is a bold entrant in such a sweepstakes. The core of that case is Hegel's argument for the explanatory priority of the notion of spirit, *Geist*, a collective subjectivity, and its development, that such notions amount to a more comprehensive and fundamental *explicans* in accounting for conceptual, political, and aesthetic change than appeals to "capitalism," "negation," the "essence" of painting, and so forth. This, in turn, obviously commits him to showing just how such an appeal to spirit's self-alienation, externalization, and eventual reconciliation does in fact account for fundamental shifts in aesthetic values, especially in what is for Hegel its end game, its "culmination" as art itself.

There are, of course, hundreds of elements in such claims that specialists and philosophers will want to attack. There are no grander grand narratives than Hegelian ones, and his have been put to such strange and implausible uses that one might be advised to stay well clear of any claim about abstraction (understood as a turn to reflexive self-understanding as its own object) as the culmination or completion or exhaustion of the Western art tradition.[7] But there must be *something* of some generality and scope that we can say about the historical experience of the

---

[7] One should also note that in most respects, Hegel's lectures on fine art do not present an "aesthetic theory" in the sense that came to be established in British, French, and German thought in the eighteenth century. He deals only in a glancing way with one of the three canonical questions in that aesthetics:

(1) What is the *ontological* status of the art work or of aesthetic properties? How are such objects to be distinguished from craft works, natural objects, and how are properties such as beautiful, sublime, or ugly to be distinguished? (Or, What is beauty, a question Hegel rarely takes up as such, merely pronouncing that it is the appearance, the shining, of the idea (*das sinnliche Scheinen der Idee*).)

(2) What is distinctive about aesthetic *experience*? How is it different from simple pleasure in sights, tastes, and so on, or simple perception, for that matter? (What do we know or understand when we understand that something is beautiful?)

inadequacy of traditional representational art, just then and just there (i.e., at the forefront of European modernization), and whatever there is to say, it is unlikely we will get a handle on it without understanding the relation between this momentous, epochal shift in art history and the history of modernity itself, as well as corresponding changes in religious, institutional, and socio-political life.[8]

So *why* then did traditional, representational art come to be experienced as inadequate, a kind of historical relic rather than a living presence? To understand Hegel's (or "the Hegelian") answer to this question, we also face right away the difficult question of gaining any adequate access to the twelve hundred pages of lecture notes organized by his student Hotho in what we now know as the standard edition of Hegel's lectures.[9] But we can start reconstructing a Hegelian reaction to abstractionism by noting several peculiarities of Hegel's aesthetic theory. I note four such distinct peculiarities because, I try to show below, they are the most important in understanding a comprehensive Hegelian view (or possible view) on the issue of abstractionism.

## IV

The first and most peculiar is how Hegel ties art ubiquitously, in all cases, to *the divine*. In a way that greatly complicates his use of the term, Hegel

(3) And what can be said about the possibility of distinguishing expressions of aesthetic preferences ("I like this") from *aesthetic claims* ("This is beautiful")? Do aesthetic judgments have any normative authority, and if so on what basis?

There is some Hegelian discussion of the first issue, in connection with the relation among art, religion, and philosophy. This is already not a traditional categorization issue, and Hegel does not deal with the standard issues. Rather, Hegel's project might be said to offer an account of what Dieter Henrich has variously called the "resonance" of art in human life and a "diagnosis of the state of art in our time." See Henrich 2001. Henrich's account is one of the very few to have appreciated, and with great subtlety, the possibility of a link between Hegel's philosophy of art and modernism (although I doubt very much that he would agree with the approach to Hegel presented here). Clark's, in a very different way, is another.

[8] This again distinguishes Hegel's attempt from Danto's, whose account does not attempt the links with nonaesthetic phenomena that Hegel's does and remains linked to the representational problem of fidelity, without a "Hegelian" account of the significance of art that goes beyond such a technical problem. On the other hand, Danto understands the problem of "what art can be" after the crisis reached in that progression to conclude in the result that art "can be *anything.*" Nothing could be more un-Hegelian than this last notion of "freedom."

[9] The lectures certainly do have a kind of Protestant, anti-Catholic, Reformation tone, as if the point were something like the growth of such a Reformation spirit of inwardness and anti-idolatry in visual art ("to the Lutherans truth is not a manufactured object," PH, 416; W, vol. 12, 496). And see A, 103.

does not confine that issue solely to explicitly religious art of the classical Greek, Roman, medieval, Renaissance, and early modern periods. All art, no matter the subject matter, from still life to portrait to landscape to historical scenes, is understood as an attempt "to portray the divine." This ought right away to alert us that this sweeping reference is, to say the least, nonstandard and will require considerable interpretation. Art is called "one way of bringing to our minds and expressing the Divine, the deepest interests of mankind, and the most comprehensive truths of spirit [*Geist*]" (A, 7). This set of appositives appears to gloss the divine *as* "the deepest interests of mankind and the most comprehensive truths of spirit" rather than vice-versa, and this quite radical humanism (or divinization of the human) is prominent elsewhere in the lectures, too. The divine is often treated as if its relevant synonyms were *das Wahre* and *das Wahrhaftige*, the true and the "real truth," and art is regularly treated as the attempt by spirit to externalize its self-understanding in a sensible form, and thereby to appropriate such externality as its own, to be at home therein, and to express more successfully such a self-understanding. (And all of *that* is called an expression of the divinity in man. As Hegel is wont to put it, this is the truth that the Christian religion tries to express in its "representation" of a father-god externalized in his son.) Art, in other words, is treated as a vehicle for the self-education of human being about itself, ultimately about what it means to be a free, self-determining being, and when Hegel calls *that* dimension of aesthetic meaning "divine," he seems to be rather flattering the seriousness and finality of the enterprise (its independence from sensual need, utilitarian interest, and so forth; its "absolute" importance) than in any sense worrying about the God of revealed religion. Another way to put Hegel's quite heretical view would be to say that for Hegel artistic activity is not about representing divinity but about *expressing* divinity and even *becoming* divine. "God," he says, "is more honored by what spirit makes than by the productions and formations of nature," and this because "there is something divine in man, but it is active in him in a form appropriate to the being of God in a totally different and higher manner than it is in nature" (A, 30).[10] (This is all the basis of Hegel's fantastic, extravagant claim that in effect *religion* is an inadequate vehicle of the divine.[11])

[10] Cf. Schiller's remark in (1965), 63: "Beyond question Man carries the potentiality for divinity within himself; the path to divinity, if we may call a path what never reaches its goal, is open to him in his senses."

[11] Religion is always said to be a mere "representation." Contrast here Stephen Houlgate's interpretation in (1997), 1–19. Houlgate argues that because art has "lost" its link with

## V

Likewise, second, Hegel is one of the very few philosophers or writers or artists of this period – I would guess the only one – for whom *the beauty of nature was of no significance whatsoever*. Nature's status as an *ens creatum*, as a reflection of God, or natural beauty as an indication of purposiveness, are of no importance to him, and he expresses this while evincing no Gnostic antipathy to nature itself as fallen or evil. Nature is simply "spiritless," *geistlos*, or without meaning, even boring. (Hegel goes so far as to claim that a landscape painting is the proper object of human attention and speculative contemplation, not a natural landscape itself (A, 29), or, in a near-Kafkaesque claim, that a portrait of a person can be more like the individual than the actual individual himself (A, 866–7).)[12] When a natural object or event is portrayed aesthetically, it acquires a distinct sort of meaning, what it is within and for a human community, that it would not have had just as such an object itself. (Hegel is, after all, an idealist of sorts, and we return to this reflexivity or doubled meaning of art objects below.) The object becomes suffused for the first time with a human meaning.[13] In a memorable passage, Hegel notes that it is as if an artistic treatment transforms every visible surface into an eye, the visible seat of the soul's meaning, such that in looking at such painted surfaces – looking at, he says, "the thousand-eyed Argos" – we search for what we search for in looking into another human's eye: meaning. It is crucial to note that Hegel describes looking at art objects this way, as

---

the "divine," it can no longer serve our highest interests and needs, which, presumably, on his view are still religious. Cf. Houlgate's remarks on p. 9, when he claims both that Hegel approved of Protestant art because it "freed art from dominance by religion" and so allowed it to become "*fully* secular" (my emphasis) *and* that such art allowed us to see "secular forms of activity" as "*not* simply falling outside the religious, monastic life but as 'holy' in themselves" (my emphasis). He wants to say both these things because, in his view, Hegel treats modern secular activities, such as labor, marriage, the family, and citizenship, as forms of religiosity truer than the monastic virtues of poverty, chastity, and obedience. Both these claims seem to me right, but not yet to make clear the limitations of art for Hegel within this new post-Reformation sense of religiosity. I am indebted to Houlgate for correspondence about this issue.

[12]  Hegel is discussing Titian's portraits.

[13]  Hegel's expression is that art creates a reality that is itself "ensouled [*für sich beseelt*]" (A, 834). Another way to put Hegel's point would be to note his appreciation of some dimension of what would be called the "disenchantment" of the world (the term used by Weber, borrowed from Schiller), but that such a realization does not consign us to a banal fate. An appreciation of the "divinity" of human freedom does not re-enchant the world; it elevates us above the need for enchantment, an elevation that can have a painterly presence all its own. Cf. Clark 1999, 34.

if each one had eyes (which, whatever it means, does not mean we are looking *through* the image to a source or original; a human soul is not literally visible inside the eye). Nor are we looking at art objects the way subjects look at objects. That would be like looking at *persons* that way and suggests a different sort of link between art and morality than what Kant wanted to suggest[14] (A, 153). And this is all also part of Hegel's case that painting is the first "romantic art" (in his hierarchy of art), and therewith first on the way to an adequate expression of human freedom. This is so because, for example, in a painting the object "does not remain an actual spatial natural existent, but becomes a reflection [*Widerschein*] of spirit." The "real" is thus said to be "canceled" and transformed into something "in the domain of spirit for the apprehension by spirit" (which natural objects are not) (A, 805).[15]

This touches on an important point that *is* part of the traditional Hegel reading: that Hegel played a very large role in shifting aesthetic appreciation from one founded on taste, beauty, and pleasure to one concerned with criticism, meaning, and a kind of self-education. But the point here about the importance of Hegel's indifference to nature and beauty introduces a more radical one.[16] In fact, fine art, and especially its history, Hegel claims, should be understood as a *liberation from nature*, not a rejection of its (or our) inherent inadequacy but the achievement of a mode of self-understanding and self-determination no longer set, or limited by nature as such, as well as a humanizing transformation of the natural into a human world. (Art is said to enable a "free subject" to "strip the external world of its inflexible foreignness and to enjoy in the shape of things only an external realization of himself" (A, 31).)[17] Hegel starts out from a premise in which art is treated cognitively, as a way of becoming

---

[14] Kant's traded on the notion of "disinterestedness."

[15] See also A, 809, on natural and artificial light. There are several other issues in Hegel that are relevant here but that would require a separate discussion. Especially important are Hegel's claims in what is published as the second volume of the lectures, where he defends a hierarchical system of the arts themselves and where the "place" of painting, especially with respect to literature, is an important theme, relevant here as well.

[16] It should be noted that these remarks about nature are heretical in another sense, too: from the viewpoint of traditional Hegel interpretation. This has it that Hegel held a position somewhat like Plotinus' (or at least Schelling's), in which the sensible, natural world was an emanation of and so linked to God, or the One. Nature was supposed to be the externalization of God, finally fully self-conscious or "interiorized" in absolute spirit, in philosophy. These passages make that interpretation implausible. More specifically and more clearly put by Hegel: "[T]he connection between the beautiful and ourselves is that we catch sight of our own essence in the beautiful" (V, 57).

[17] These are the kinds of passages that prompt the kind of characterization of the Narcissistic Hegel, he of the great devouring Maw of Subjectivity, familiar to readers of Adorno.

more self-conscious about aspects of intelligibility, meaning, and the activity of meaning making itself, and so is said to be *the sensible shining or appearing of the Idea*, where "the Idea" is that comprehensive, sought-after self-conscious understanding of "rendering intelligible." And it is *this* function that is treated as partaking of a kind of divinity. ("The universal need for art, that is, to say, is man's rational need to lift the inner and outer world into his spiritual consciousness as an object in which he recognizes again his own self" (A, 31).) From there he proceeds to a conclusion that runs so counter to contemporaries such as Kant, Schiller, and Schelling: that art "liberates man . . . *from the power of sensuousness*" and "lifts [man] with its gentle hands [*mit milden Händen*] out of and above imprisonment in nature" (A, 49).

In what we now characterize as the romantic dimension of post-Kantianism, most visible in Schiller, the significance of beauty and art, its mattering as it does, was an expression and experience of an original harmony between our corporeality or natural fate and our agency, spontaneity, and freedom, a harmony partially lost in the assertion of modern autonomy or self-rule but that could be recovered in the "play" of the imagination's spontaneity "at work" in, not on, the sensuous immediacy of perception and delight. Hegel's formulation indicates that if there is to be such a reconciliation, it must be achieved rather than recovered, and that part of that process will be an active negation in some way of the "power" of sensuousness and "imprisonment" in nature (not, it should be stressed, of "nature" as such). Nature will be not lost or rendered a mere object in this process (which is, after all, a "gentle" process) but transformed, remade into a "second nature."[18] A standard example of such a transformation is Hegel's account of the habits of mind and unreflective practices of "ethical life" (*Sittlichkeit*) and another might be, I am suggesting, the achievement of those habits of mind, sorts of lived embodiment, for which modernism in the arts becomes timely, appropriate.

Admittedly, this is a difficult position to understand. Hegel neither is appealing to some subjective act of "investing" the natural world with an imposed, human/divine meaning, nor is he ascribing to aesthetic experience a religious function, as if a revelation of divine or even "in itself" purposiveness in the natural world. And the putative inadequacies of representational meaning and of natural embodiment in art are not

---

Again, it all depends on what one takes the claim to mean. See remarks on this issue in Pippin 1997c.

[18] Like many of the terms of art necessary to state Hegel's position, "second nature" is another that deserves a book-length treatment. Cf. chapter 9 in this volume.

introduced in order to suggest a rejection of all representation or to introduce some possible transcendence of natural embodiment. As noted before, the "inadequacy" issue concerns only the issue of "the highest" matters of human importance, and Hegelian transcendence (or *Aufhebung*) is always also a preservation and recollecting, even if with an altered sense of such "matterings." Without a fuller account than is possible here of such a "highest" self-understanding and the place and status of nature in such an accomplishment, not to mention his final take on the mind-world issue, his position on the "limitations" of traditional fine art cannot be adequately understood, but we shall have to make do here with such a provisional account.

Likewise in Hegel's account this development is not a result of a growing realization of the inadequacy of the iconic relation to a transcendent God, as Alain Besançon has recently claimed.[19] What Hegel describes is a much more practical struggle with the natural world, such that the achievement of various forms of real independence from natural determination is reflected in the self-images manifested in art. There is, in other words, no negative theology in Hegel's strange humanistic theology. His progressivism is everywhere decisive; we have *broken* free of a fundamental dependence on such sensible images not so much because of *their* inadequacy as because of *our* having made ourselves independent of them, and art must be understood as part and parcel of that work. Again, none of this means that we become or realize we always were supernatural beings or that we can now ignore our corporeality. We remain finite, constrained in all the obvious ways by natural limitations. But the experience of, the very meaning of, such naturality is now to be regarded as a human achievement, in the way that the natural desire to reproduce has become inseparable from romantic values and the norms of familial and social existence – or inseparable from egoistic or hedonistic or any other such value. (The unavailability of mere nature, as such, within experience, is the point at issue.) As Hegel puts it in a famous passage:

No matter how excellent we find the statues of Greek gods, no matter how we see God the Father, Christ and Mary so estimably and perfectly portrayed: it is of no help; we bend our knee[20] no longer [before these images]. (A, 103)

---

[19] Besançon 2000, 219–20.

[20] Cf. "Modernism turns on the impossibility of transcendence." Clark 1999, 22. As indicated above, what is "left" without such transcendence is the issue, and for Hegel, and for Hegel's modernism, what is left is neither mere materiality as such (resistant to sense, to the work of painting) nor a mere object to be transformed and humanized by the

## VI

Third, Hegel is well known as the philosophical founder of the historical study of art, the most important proponent of the idea that art works must be understood as "of their time," where such a time could itself be understood comprehensively as an integrated whole, a point of view or *Weltanschauung*. And this premise contributes as well, in quite an unusual and unexpected way, to the thesis that art cannot matter for us now as it used to, that representational art has become, with respect to the highest things, a "thing of the past." We can begin to see how this works by noting that Hegel, although associated with the philosophical romanticism of the late eighteenth and early nineteenth century in Germany, veers off that course pretty radically on this historical issue. He sees "what his age requires," what is a "need of spirit," in quite a different way, and that will be quite important for the "fate of art" issue.

By contrast, Kant, for example, fits the romantic pattern much better and provides a useful foil for appreciating this point. Kant had denigrated the importance of fine art because the experience of fine art involved not a wholly "free" but what Kant called a "dependent" beauty, and so inevitably, he claimed, was too much a matter of concepts and conceptualizing. An art product was always of a kind, produced with a certain, recognizable intention, within a school, after a style, and so on. And this hindered (though it did not absolutely prevent) the "free play" of the faculties that Kant thought essential to aesthetic pleasure. Art works tend to be instances of kinds, and recognizing and cataloguing instances was not what the experience of the beautiful was about. Aesthetic experience involved precisely a kind of inconceivability, together, nonetheless, with some intimation of harmony and meaning, all of which the rule-governed production of fine art made very difficult. This was all connected in Kant to much larger issues, especially his attempt to distinguish the separate contributions of sensibility and the understanding, contra the Leibnizian school. And because Kant insisted on the limited role of the understanding in aesthetic intelligibility, he was somewhat unwittingly preparing the way for a much stronger emphasis on artistic autonomy and even on the aesthetic as a *superior* mode of intelligibility.[21]

---

"labor of the concept." What that all amounts to is a large independent issue. For an indication of Clark's view, see the analysis of David's *Death of Marat*, esp. 48.

[21] All of this Hegel would dispute, but without, I think, a reversion to classicism. The fact that *art* belongs to the domain of the self-articulation of reason tell us something about Hegel's notion of reason and hardly makes a point about his regressive classicism.

The historical Kant clearly intended by such an argument (especially in his insisting on beauty's dependence on some extrahuman source of significance, on the "supersensible") to accentuate the theological and moral importance of natural beauty. However, Kant's legacy for the art world was to accentuate the greater importance of genius and the sublime in fine art, the former because the unprecedented, inimitable creation of the genius allowed a kind of novelty or delightful surprise that Kant thought essential to aesthetic experience, and the latter because the defeat of our imagination by the magnitude, dynamism, or, in later romantic versions, the horror of the sublime also allowed a kind of intelligibility and experience not rule-bound or intellectualizable.[22] One might hypothesize that such a notion corresponded to a new modern need, for a kind of divine significance without any determinate transcendent realm, without the metaphysics that Kant's first *Critique* removed from the philosophical agenda, a place marked out from and higher than the utilitarian calculation and mass politics already on the horizon or from the "iron cage" beginning to descend on European societies.

The contrast with Hegel could not be sharper, more antiromantic. Hegel regarded the experience of the sublime as historically regressive, an indication of a much less well developed understanding of "the divine," in all the manifold, elusive senses discussed above. Vague intimations of an indeterminate, horrifying power were, by virtue of their very indeterminacy, already an indication of a much less self-conscious and even less free stage of being in the world. Products of genius also traded, for Hegel, on a kind of indeterminacy and elusiveness that he thought amounted to mere *Schwärmerei*, or romantic clap-trap, which were only vestigial in the modern age.

Of course at this point one might wonder, if Hegel is right that such suspicion of indeterminacy, mystery, ineffability, the awe-inspiring, and so forth does comprise our starting position with respect to the "spirit of the times," what then *could* be said for the contemporary role of art, the way it might matter (as high art, not as mere decoration or monuments from the past)? Without further ado, it might seem that Hegel almost treats the domain of art itself as atavistic, as if a bit like reading bird entrails or

---

[22] The Kantian sublime should also be distinguished from modern, religious views of the sublime, as in nature's void or infinity in Calvin and Pascal, and that will make clear the heretical character of Kant's position. Rather than provoke a humbling awe, the experience of the sublime is a *two*-step process in Kant and finally confirms a sense of man's absolute supremacy over all of nature by virtue of his moral vocation and its independence from any natural condition or power.

astrology. As we have seen, the question at issue for Hegel is not the end of art making and appreciating but something like a shift in its status and social role. But we can now see that this modern displacement occurs for him for an unusual reason. Put simply, one of the main reasons for Hegel's view that image or content-based art seems to matter less and less derives from his comprehensive view of the nature of the modern world. It is, he repeats frequently, a *prosaic,* unheroic world, not much of a subject for the divinizing or at least idealizing transformations of aesthetic portrayal at all. (The "Idea" *need* not "sensibly shine" any longer because it can be grasped conceptually; norms get their grip on us without primary reliance on the sensual. But, said the other way around, it *cannot*; the sensible appearances of modern ethical life themselves are not fit vehicles for such "shining" because they and our very sensual lives have themselves been rationalized, transformed into practices, habits, and institutions with some sort of rational transparency to themselves.)[23] *The modern social world itself may be rational, in other words, but it is, to say it all at once, just thereby not very beautiful, and its "meaning" is not very mysterious.* It has its own kind of domestic and rather small-screen beauty, we can say – hence all that Hegelian praise for Dutch celebrations of the bourgeoisie – but the "sacredness" of orderly city streets, piano playing, milk pouring, needlework, and fine clothing, does not, given that Hegel's aesthetics is so content-driven,[24] satisfy very lofty aesthetic ambitions. ("Spirit only occupies itself with objects so long as there is something secret [*Geheimes*], not revealed [*nicht Offenbares*], in them ... [but now] everything is revealed and nothing obscure" (A, 604–5).)

This introduces a complicated topic in Hegel studies, especially with regard to his political theory, because such a position represents quite a change from Hegel's younger days and his Hölderlin-intoxicated hopes for a beautiful Christian community of love. He appears to have become quite impressed with the altered situation of modern individuals, with, let us say, the "dispersed" character of subjectivity in modern societies, all reflecting an acknowledgment of the spiritual effects of ever more

[23] I am of course aware that, glancing back at European history in the twentieth century, expressing such Hegelian views without irony or qualification can seem a little naïve. But, as in so many cases, we need a comprehensive view of what Hegel means by insisting on the "rationality" of modern ethical life, and I do not believe that such an interpretation is yet available among the prominent competitors, descendants of the nineteenth-century left-right Hegel wars. For what I hope is a start, see Pippin 1997d.

[24] "Works of art are all the more excellent in expressing true beauty, the deeper is the inner truth of their content and thought" (A, 74).

divided labor first apparent in Rousseau. In such a world, no one simply could be heroically responsible for much of anything (and so could not be beautiful in action), and the legal and administrative tasks, the daily life, of modern society are indeed, in his favorite word, prosaic (not beautiful). We have already discussed the aesthetic consequences of a disenchanted nature. And it is a striking oddity in Hegel's project that the full realization of art *as art* should occur quite early in his story about art, that he should insist that Greek art, the art of the Greek polis, *qua art* is "better" art, but that modern romantic art is simply better, a greater human accomplishment. But however complicated the issue and Hegel's reasons for this alteration, such an antisentimental, realist modernism (Hegel does not even credit what would be Baudelaire's aesthetics of the beauty of modern speed and instability), together with Hegel's Protestant secularization of the divine and with his view that art evinces the self-image of an age, are all clearly playing a role in Hegel's restraint with regard to the social and spiritual role of traditional art. This represents a kind of wager on Hegel's part that the satisfactions of modern (or bourgeois) romantic, familial, economic, and political life were, in a sense, *enough*, that we could do without beautiful depictions of ourselves and our lives or even sublime warnings about its potential emptiness, and so could do without the living role for fine art imagined later. I think that it is fairly clear by now that, to say the least, this was a bad bet, as the whole phenomenon of aesthetic politics (especially in fascism) demonstrates, but that is surely another and a longer story.

## VII

The last or fourth peculiarity in Hegel's treatment of art is the most important and the most difficult to discuss economically. It involves the basic reason why Hegel opposed the grandiose hopes of many of his contemporaries for a renewal of monumental, culturally important, transformative art, and claimed instead that in a certain (world-historical) respect, art (or what we would now regard as premodernist art) had become for us a thing of the past. That reason has much more to do with a new understanding of the mind-world and self-other relations, and at the heart of this new understanding is an altered picture of sensibility, perceptual meaning, and "lived" sociality, or a new sense of what it is to be a materially embodied being for whom experience can mean what it does. Hegel's full case about the status of art within a modern society ultimately relies on a case for a great alteration in the way things basically make sense to us, and a large component of that "basically" involves an altered relation to our own sensibility, something most clearly at play in visual art and its historical transformations.

After all, up to this point one might still characterize Hegel's position as some sort of return to classicism, especially with his definition of beauty as the sensible appearing of an intelligible, essentially non-sensible ideal. Since Hegel understands art cognitively, as a way of apprehending the truth (he rarely mentions aesthetic pleasure as such), and understands that way as a sensible "shining" or appearing, the inference that Hegel was some kind of neo-classicist would not be unreasonable. But Kant's revolution in philosophy, which Hegel, despite criticisms, enthusiastically accepted,[25] essentially destroyed the classical picture of the sensible-intelligible relation. Sensibility could not now be understood as an unclear representation of the world that reason could work to clarify or could represent better, nor could it be understood as a vivid, "lively" impression, guiding the abstracting and generalizing intellect. In Kant's famous phrase (the one most relevant for the altered situation within which, according to Hegel, art must make sense now), the senses do not err, not "because they always judge rightly, but because *they do not judge at all*" (A293; B350).[26] The content of sensibility was, after Kant, to be understood as the material object of the understanding's synthesizing, active work, and the entire intelligible domain (any "possible experience") was now understood as a result of the activity of the understanding, the product of its work. Sensory data became representative as a result of this work by the understanding, and considered apart from such enforming, conceptualizing activity, it counted as mere stuff, preintelligible materiality. This all also meant that not *all* aspects of our knowledge claims could be said to be guided by the world, from without. The ultimate authority or legitimacy of our knowledge claims had also to be in some respect *self*-authorizing, required as a condition of there being any sensible evidence.[27] In another of Kant's memorable phrases: Reason does not beg from nature; it commands (A653, B681) – a

---

[25] Another endlessly contested issue. See Pippin 1989 for the argument defending a reading of Hegel through Kantian lenses.

[26] Immanuel Kant, *Critique of Pure Reason*, trans. Norman Kemp Smith (New York: St. Martin's, 1965).

[27] The central problem in that endeavor is the one that Kant created for aesthetics and that after him, with the rejection of his formalism, became the core modern problem: genuine lawfulness but without a determinate law and without a possible appeal to a determinate law. And therewith another preview of the modernist spirit. See no. 39 of Kant's *Critique of Judgment* and Ferry 1993, 15 and 96. The principle that Hegel will settle

phrase that already sounds the deepest theme of what would become modernism in the arts, that is, the theme of freedom.[28] (Indeed, Kant had himself so spiritualized religion, risking blasphemy by insisting on discussing it "within the limits of reason alone" and making it merely a moral postulate or practical faith, that any sort of "representation" of the divine had already become, thanks to Kant, not inadequate, but simply irrelevant.)

Hegel's narrative of an expanding critical self-consciousness thus fits the modernist refusal to take for granted what a painting or art was, what writing or being an artist was. Such notions were now treated as norms not fixed by nature or human nature but actively (and in Hegel historically) "legislated" and subject to criticism. And with such questions raised this way, it would be no surprise that art making and novel writing would themselves become the subjects of art; Proust and James, de Kooning and Pollock being only the most obvious examples.

With this in mind, then, the official Hegelian claim goes like this. The basic principle of modern philosophy (i.e., post-Kantianism), modern politics (liberal, republican politics, after a fashion), and modern religion (Protestant post-Reformation religion) has become what Hegel calls "subjectivity" or "reflection," ultimately a version of critical and rational self-consciousness about the way we actively render the world intelligible, or legislate normative constraints on claims and conduct.[29] Normative

---

on in his account of this possibility is basically similar to that introduced by Kant in the third *Critique*: "An der Stelle jedes anderen denken" (no. 40).

[28] When the "ideal," after Kant, could no longer be identified with a distinct intelligible world (but was instead a goal of ideal and complete intelligibility, the postulation of the "unconditioned"), the status of the sensible also changed dramatically. For the modern Anglophone tradition, it meant the problem of formulating a coherent empiricism, one consistent with mathematical physics, with self-knowledge, memory, and personal identity, one that could deal with the problem of skepticism, and so on. On the other hand, one prominent feature of what is called the "Continental" tradition, viewed in this light, is a much heightened attention to the significance of aesthetic sensibility, the significance of the fact that a merely empirical apprehension of an art work is inappropriate. Cf. the first four chapters of Ferry 1993, and Jay Bernstein's interesting 1992 discussion. (The much discussed "subjectivization" of the aesthetic realm is thus not a relocation of aesthetic meaning "from" objective perfectionism, classical rules and formulae, and so forth inward, not an interiorization of what had been "out there." Self-reliance, self-certitude, and constructivism are not in isolation the modernist problems (for Hegel) but a making, the products of which fully embody the freedom of the maker, reflect that freedom adequately.)

[29] Cf. Clement Greenberg: "I identify Modernism with the intensification, almost the exacerbation, of this self-critical tendency that began with the philosopher Kant" (1993, "Modernist Painting," 85). For a different account that makes the same beginning, see

claims to knowledge, rectitude, spiritual life, or even *to be making art* or that *that was good* are now made with the self-consciousness that the authority of such claims can always be challenged and defeated (or such claims could simply "die out," lose historical authority) and must be in some way defensible to and for subjects if they are to be defensible at all. The pre-Hegelian situation is one in which we acted on the basis of such norms but could not fully understand their autonomous status and so proposed social and philosophical justifications to each other that could not be reconciled and always betrayed an element of "positivity" or mere contingency or power. (One of the most important things Hegel says about this situation, the one most relevant to his use of religious terminology, is that the basic state of human dissatisfaction or alienation is a *self*-alienation, not one from a transcendent God or even from the truth. Spirit, human being itself, is said *to be* a "wound" that it inflicts on itself, but that it can heal itself (A, 98).) Art is to be understood as an aspect of the age's reflection on itself (that healing), a way for the spirit of such an age not just to be lived out, but itself aesthetically thematized.

To put the point in another way: An enduring, continuous human life is not an event or occurrence, a happening, like others. Lives do not just happen; they must be actively led, steered, guided, which we now, for the

---

Pippin 1999a. Greenberg treats modernism as beginning with a kind of Kantian inspiration not to take painting itself (as color on a flat surface) for granted anymore but to explore *what it is* to put color on a flat, limited (framed) surface. It doesn't seem to me possible to understand *the significance* of that without understanding the significance of the ideal of critical autonomy, and that move always seems to appear to Greenberg "impure," an attempt at the tyrannization of painting by something that is not painting, such as philosophy or social theory (very un-Hegelian dichotomies). Cf. the difficulty in his position in Greenberg 1993, "The Case for Abstract Art," 80, where such a move to abstraction is treated as an antidote against hyper-self-interested, materialistic, anticontemplative mass society (this is what the art *means*) even while he insists it functions as an example of something that "does *not* have to mean" (my emphasis). From Hegel's point of view, this is not a debater's point but an indication of how deeply Kantian Greenberg's program remains. What results from this unclarity in Greenberg is his occasional odd homage to empiricism, scientism, and scientific experimentation in abstract painting. See the extraordinary claims about the "results" of what appears to be modernist "research" in ibid., "After Abstract Expressionism," 131. The point where Greenberg and Hegel join forces is in their opposition to sentimentality in criticism, or to the "aesthetics of sentiment" generally, and a commitment to the conceptual intelligibility of modernist art. This does not necessarily commit either of them to one side of dualism, as Ferry has claimed. Ferry's view seems to be that if you are not with Bouhours and Debos, you must be attempting to circle back to Boileau. Cf. Ferry 1993, chap. 4. See also Danto's remarks about the brushstroke, as against Greenberg's "flatness," in Danto 1997, 74–77.

first time, fully appreciate. As in the Stoic tradition that influenced the
German through its influence on Kant, had it, living a human life is not
the natural realization of an essence, the great problem being to find a
way to "allow" it to grow and flourish in the conditions "naturally" right
for it. Rather, it is fundamentally a self-relation, a self-directing agency;
at the very minimum a life must be *actively* preserved and protected. A
subject must not only "take up the reins" of a life in order to do this but
must do so continuously and with an eye toward the unity and integration
without which lives cannot be coherently led. Moreover, leading a life in
this way is reflexive because it always involves actively taking a point of
view or stand on some relevant event, person, or state in the world, *and*
this in an always challengeable and revisable way. In the (Kierkegaardian)
language developed by Heidegger and Sartre to make this point, one *is* a
subject (does not flee such an unavoidable self-responsible stance in bad
faith or inauthenticity) only by not presuming simply *to be* a subject or *to
be* an anything, even while one is not some free-floating mere possibility,
not nothing at all.

All of this was necessary to state what is for Hegel the essential limitation of traditional art, and it is not a religious limitation: *Representational
art cannot adequately express the full subjectivity of experience, the wholly self-
legislating, self-authorizing status of the norms that constitute such subjectivity, or,
thus, cannot adequately express who we (now) are.* Only philosophy can "heal"
such a self-inflicted wound and allow the self-determining character of experience its adequate expression. ("Only philosophy," that is, on Hegel's
official account. I am trying to suggest that there is no reason a form
of art, like abstraction, could not make such a point in a nondiscursive
way.)[30] After such a "healing," of course, fine art will certainly continue

[30] A remark in the spirit of such a reading of Hegelian modernism is T. J. Clark's on a
photograph of Picasso's paintings at Sorgues: "Painting at Sorgues, says the photograph,
stands on the threshold of a new order and chaos; and not just painting, by the looks of
it, but picturing in general; and not just picturing, but maybe perceiving; and not just
perceiving but maybe being-in-the-world, or at least having-the-world-be-visible; maybe
the world itself" (174). Although Clark thinks that such hopes for modernism are forlorn,
he is quite right, I think, to quote at this point an apposite passage from Hegel on the
world historical individual. (My differences with Clark concern a number of points of
emphasis, especially the range and depth and usefulness of appeals to categories such
as "capitalism" and "socialism" and his melancholic treatment of a putative "failure" in a
social reconciliation between autonomy and embeddedness in a community, reflected in
the "failure" of modernism. See Clark 1999, esp. chap. 4, on "Cubism and Collectivity";
chap. 6, on Pollock as "unhappy consciousness"; and, inter alia, 1–13 and 259. Although
he insists that he is praising abstract expression, Clark's reliance on these social categories
also leads him to characterize the painting movement as "vulgar," or "the style of a certain

to be produced (indeed, Hegel says that he hopes art will always "rise higher and come to perfection" (A, 103)).[31] But what is now possible in post-Kantian speculative philosophy makes the limited and only partially realized subjectivity or self-legislation embodied in works of representational art (art tied directly to "objecthood," to borrow Fried's phrase)[32] clearer by comparison, and art becomes "a thing of the past."[33] It is the historical realization of subjectivity in the modern world (especially the greater realization of freedom in philosophical and political life) that makes representational art (or all art up to and including Romantic art) matter less for us than it once did and had to.[34] In an obviously deeply contestable claim: What has come to matter most to us has less and less to do with a visual or even corporeal intelligibility based on what we might now call "pre-Kantian" assumptions about representation and intelligibility,

petty bourgeoisie's aspiration to aristocracy, to a totalizing cultural power" (389). But despite such disagreements, the spirit of the narrative in *Farewell to an Idea* certainly qualifies it as the most ambitiously "Hegelian" treatment of modern art, known to me anyway.)

[31] At the close of the lectures, Hegel appears to give fine art a new, different, and quite important function: "Art itself is the most beautiful side of that history [the unfolding of truth in world history – RP] and is the best compensation for hard work in the world and the bitter labor for knowledge" (A, 1236–7). Note, too, that Hegel claims that the supercession of art by philosophy also provides "an inducement for taking up the essence of art too in a profounder way" (A, 21).

[32] Fried 1998, 148–72. I agree with what I take to be Fried's attitude: There was no failure of modernism, no exhaustion by the end of abstract expressionism. Rather, there was (and still is) a failure to appreciate and integrate the self-understanding reflected in such art (the same kind of failure to appreciate modernism, or the same kind of straw-men attacks, in what we call postmodernism). The aftermath – minimalism, "literalism," op and pop art, postmodernism – can be understood better as evasions and repressions than as alternatives.

[33] Again, this is a thing of the past only with respect to what Hegel called the "realization of the Absolute." Hegel's position does not entail the dispensability of art, especially when viewed from other perspectives, such as rhetoric and education. In fact, Hegel treats both art and religion itself as forms of "representation" that, while inadequate philosophically, are nevertheless indispensable elements of modern life, however imperfect when viewed from the Olympian heights of "the Absolute."

[34] There is a tension here in Hegel's position, relevant again to Danto's. Prior to the Hegelian stage of modernity, the intuitive expression of "the truth" that art alone made possible was counted as a necessary element in the becoming-self-conscious of such a truth, while after that stage, art was merely to express sensibly a truth attained properly by philosophy. But this would mean that in such a philosophical stage, art would no longer be functioning *as art*. As art, it is an aspect of a sensible reflection of truth *unavailable in any other way*. See the discussion by Henrich 1979, 107–33. See especially Henrich's note on p. 114 about Hegel's 1828 aesthetics lectures. (This essay is a catastrophically bad translation of a powerful, original article by Henrich that compellingly defends the relevance of the Hegelian analysis for modern art, even given the problem just noted.)

all because what unavoidably must matter now is the realization of a kind of freedom: autonomy.

## VIII

There are lots of questions here worth asking, especially since it seems much more intuitive to say that, if the underlying theme of modern art is the achievement of freedom, traditional visual art could just give us one indispensable perspective on the lived meaning of freedom, and philosophy, perhaps a modernist philosophy, discursively, *another*. Hegel's disjunction and claim to hierarchy seem extreme. But it is at least clear that this line of thought in Hegel has very little to do with many of the conventional qualifications on the status of art, almost all of them religious in tone: such things as the Platonic worry about art as illusion or the Christian worry about art as idolatry. And Hegel's historicist stance excludes any nonhistorical answer at all to the question of "the" status of the sensible image or "the" nature of art.[35]

That is, Hegel's view of the limitations of aesthetic intelligibility should not be understood as a reflection of what Hegel would call a philosophy of finitude, in the way that religious concerns about the adequacy of the sensible image for representing the divine would express. Such iconoclastic worries amount to a claim about limitations, boundaries, and so forth, because of either our inadequacy or the awesome majesty of the represented object, or both, which Hegel, unlike every other post-Kantian modern philosopher except Nietzsche, explicitly rejects. (That is why the "finitude" framework fits Kant so well. It fits Heidegger's denigration of the "ontic" spectacularly well, but that is another story altogether.) Hegel never tires of distinguishing himself from such a stance. This means that he thinks fine art *is* doing what the "finitists" say it cannot: Represent "the divine" (just that it does so partly or incompletely, and under the assumption of Hegel's own heretical notion of the divine). The contrast to such iconoclasm is not mysticism, negative theology, the ineffable, or

---

[35] Hegel's position is not easy to get out on the table for a hearing, not least because post-Nietzschean and post-Heideggerian European philosophy have been so hostile to and so suspicious of the notion of "subjects leading their lives reflexively." Subjects have become epiphenomena of social forces, texts, discourses, language, gender, the unconscious, Being, the ethnos, and so forth. Hegel's attempt to enlist art in the project of the actualization of self-conscious subjectivity is viewed under the shadow of that suspicion, and so his even wilder claim that Romantic art finally revealed the limitations of art as such in such a project is now not taken very seriously.

some sort of authenticity. According to Hegel, it is "the philosophy of infinity," a discursive account of the whole human world, and therewith the realization of God. By this, Hegel does not mean a philosophy of the limitless void or the like but an understanding of the "absolute" status of human autonomy, a life understood and lived out – very much in a corporeal, affective, sexual, laboring world – as a collective, rational self-determination, not one determined by nature and fate.

Admittedly, this all amounts to no more than a prolegomena to a full Hegelian case for modernism in general and for abstraction (a conceptual function for art) in particular. Why traditional art might have become a thing of the past, a reminder of a different sense-making practice still partially invoked but no longer endowed with authoritative priority, why on Hegel's view that is the right way to put it, and so forth, are all one set of issues. What might be reconstructed in any detail in a Hegelian position about future art is quite another thing, and the variety of artistic moments in any account of the trajectory of modernism is obviously overwhelming.[36] But there are some elements of such a bridge between Hegel's narrative and later modernism that, by now I hope, stand out. The most important issue is that discussed in the last section above about the historical conditions of sense making, intentional content, practical authority, and so forth. These issues are much like those already obvious much earlier, in post-Impressionism, say, especially in Cezanne, as the constituent elements of painterly meaning begin to "come apart" or perhaps come to seem more and more to be a result of having been actively put together (held together in order to belong together), and where all that becomes thematized as such. (Seurat's points and Cubism's lines and planes could serve the same function.) The relationship among shape, plane, and a sense of weight, actual components in the density of objects, and so their very objecthood, can be now thematized as such. It becomes historically possible, in the extended post-Kantian aftermath that Hegel's narrative relies on, for a sensible take on such individual and independent components *to make sense* as a painting, a material "image," a new way of capturing the mind-world relation (a spontaneity-in-receptivity), because and only because a lot of other aspects of political, religious, and philosophical life have come to make sense, to succeed in invoking

---

[36] Danto's astonishing list is instructive: "Fauvism, the Cubisms, Futurism, Vorticism, Synchronism, Abstractionism, Surrealism, Dada, Expressionism, Abstract Expressionism, Pop, Op, Minimalism, Post-Minimalism, Conceptualism, Photorealism, Abstract Realism, Neo-expressionism" (1986, "The End of Art," 108).

a norm, in analogous, interconnected new ways, too. There is a new historical whole within which these new sorts of "painterly claims" can make sense. That is the heart of the Hegelian prolegomena.[37]

Correspondingly, we can then begin to see that painterly and indeed sensible representations cannot be understood on some mimetic model of seeing through the image (or sensation) to the object itself and that without the work of (historically variable) meaning making in perception, the constituents of meaning are shapes, borders, dots, frames, and so forth, *potentialities*, not just as such, but understood conceptually, as moments of sensible meaning that painting can be *about*, thus being about both itself and the possibility of sensible meaning itself. Said another way, the bearer of visual meaning can no longer be taken to be the sensible image just as such or even the idea, the mental state as such. The bearer of meaning is the concept of painting as such (it is "*abstract*" in this sense), itself a collectively constituted norm (like all norms, after Hegel) and "realized" as such in modernism. "Abstraction" in this Hegelian sense does not mean abstraction of "everything that was not intrinsic to art as such"[38] but abstraction from dependence on sensual immediacy, and so a kind of enactment of the modernist take on normativity since Kant: *self*legislation.[39] (There is an obvious danger here, the temptation of irony, the suspicion that "structures of depiction" are "purely contingent, nothing but devices."[40] Overcoming such temptations is an important element of Hegel's treatment of Diderot's *Rameau's Nephew* and Schlegel's

---

[37] I am assuming that it is obvious that none of these claims depends on demonstrating any actual historical influence of Kant on modernist painters. The "realization" of philosophy in the historical, social world is a complex, contentious topic, but there is no reason to set out by limiting such realization to instances of painters reading the *Critique of Pure Reason*. And perhaps it would be better to call this an introduction to a prolegomena. We would still need a defense of a number of controversial notions to make the Hegelian account more philosophically defensible: the notions of *distinct historical epochs*, a distinctly *philosophical diagnosis* of an epoch, of the *causality of fate* or of *philosophical fate*, and the sense of *historical rationality* invoked, the claim that there is a way of considering a major cultural change as a *rational outcome* in some way of a prior form of life.

[38] Belting 2001, 295.

[39] Again, a very long story. For an abstract formulation, see Pippin 2003a.

[40] Clark 1999, 221. One more remark about Clark. The difference between his take on modernism and mine involves a different tone in the invocation of Hegel. Hegel's defense of the modernity of art (Romanticism, in his view, even if of diminished importance with regard to the highest things; modernism, even abstraction, in the view I am attributing to the immortal Hegel) is indeed a defense of the ultimacy of "bourgeois modernity." But, as with everything else, that depends on what that involves. Hegel's soberness about what it involves can be bracing, but it is not, to invoke an old term from Marcuse, "one-dimensional." On the contrary. Cf. Pippin 1999a, chap. 7, "Unending Modernity."

doctrines in the *Phenomenology of Spirit* and goes to the issues raised earlier as "second nature.")

As indicated above, the elusive motto for all this, the broad implications of which Hegel understood better than Kant, is Kant's dense redefinition of any possible object: "that in the concept of which the manifold of a given intuition is united" (B137). This would provide the context for seeing abstraction as self-conscious, conceptual, not, as with Greenberg, reductionist and materialist. Paintings by Pollock and Rothko are not presentations of paint drips and color fields and flat canvas. They thematize and so render self-conscious components of sensible meaning that we traditionally would not see and understand as such, would treat as given. Said another way, they present the materiality of such components in their conceptual significance; such materiality is mentioned, cited, or quoted, as well as used, as well as occupying space on a stretched canvas. And this can make sense because the "result" character of even sensible apprehension, a generalized idealism evident even in the likes of Nietzsche and Proust, has come to be part of the intellectual habits of mind of modern self-understanding, even if unattended to as such. Such is for Hegel the new way nonrepresentational art might matter.[41]

---

[41] Does this mean that *all* future art should look *something* like New York 1950s Abstract Expressionism? I don't think so. Hegel is basically making use of the very idea of modernity in art to argue that there cannot be a genuinely historical way of (ever) "overcoming" the self-consciousness of normativity as both self-legislated and subject to the demand for reasons, ultimately genuinely sharable reasons. That has nothing to do with time stopping or art ending, either as an activity or a category, and the meaning of any such claim about the achievement of such a self-consciousness about freedom always has to be historically inflected. So I agree with Danto that Hegel's great contribution was to insist on the historicity of all art criticism, and so that there ought to be a "Hegelian" account of postabstract art. But Danto's is not it, in my view, and this is also because of the "indeterminate negation" problem raised earlier. If all of this (the Hegelian account as I see it) is on the right track, then we will need an account of Literalism, Minimalism, Pop, art trouvé, and so on. But we also still need to hold open as a possibility in such an account the categories of mannerism, phoniness, posturing, commercialism, show biz, and so forth. (To some extent this is Danto's view, too (1986, xiv). The prospects for art without a history do not seem good, if "anything goes" means or has only so far meant "immense and bombastic, puerile and portentous, shallow and brash.") Likewise in Hegel, not everything that happens historically is world historical. In Hegel's view, history can take a holiday for a few centuries, spin its wheels in insignificant repetition and a kind of pathological self-satisfaction. To give up this distinction (between art and phony art) is simply to pander to the art market. Moreover, the owl of Minerva takes flight only at dusk, when a form of life is dying. It is not often enough appreciated that Hegel thus must believe that he is writing at a time when the modern bourgeois world was, in fact, beginning to die, if not in the indeterminate, "failure of meaning" sense

Modernism after Hegel would then look something like what Hegel prophesied after Romantic art: "the self-transcendence of art but *within its own sphere and in the form of art itself*" (A, 80, my emphasis).[42] One could say that for both Hegel and a major strand of modernism (the strand that culminates in abstractionism), the decisive modern event was the end of the authority of nature as such, in itself, as a norm, a hard-fought practical achievement, together with the insight that this did not, could not mean what the traditionalists always feared: mere "normlessness." What, instead, a kind of self-authored normativity or human freedom might *be* is a terribly difficult question to answer. But perhaps, over the last hundred years, and especially in the experiments of abstraction, we now have some sense of what it *looks like* (thus both confirming and undermining Hegel's claim about the way art could now matter).[43]

---

that interests Clark. What that might mean is something that we ought to be able to see in some way in the art and literature of the twentieth century.

[42] As far as I can determine, Danto's account, which cites Hegel so often, does not attempt an interpretation of this passage.

[43] This last remark pulls hard at only one thread intertwined with many others in Hegel's assessment of the state of art at the end of Romanticism. On specific aesthetic issues – his evaluation of the greater importance of color over drawing and linear perspective, his apparent commitment to the paramount importance of human beings and objects that reflect human moods, and his apparent linking of aesthetic with ethical ideals (with regard to Christian love, for example) – would all need further treatment before this suggestion of a Hegelian sympathy for abstraction could be defended. But Stephen Houlgate, in the two articles noted above, already seems to me to go too far in excluding the abstractionists from the Hegelian aesthetic realm, the realm of inwardness and "objectless" freedom. The question is not really about abstraction but about which historical forms allow what Hegel, in his comments on late Romantic art, described as the attempt to preserve something "substantial" in art (A, 602; an impetus that already sounds "Friedian"). And that issue cannot be assessed in modernism without attention to the rather heterodox view of freedom that Hegel defends as the modern "substantiality." This whole situation is, again, made somewhat more difficult by the influence of Greenberg's criticism, which treats the autonomy of art so purely, so "surrenders" (to use Greenberg's telling word) to the flatness and materiality of painterly expression that he makes it hard to answer the obvious Hegelian question: What does it mean (why does it matter) that such self-authorizing painterly norms (flatness and frame) came to lay claim on the aesthetic imagination so exclusively?

# 14

## On "Becoming Who One Is" (and Failing)

### *Proust's Problematic Selves*

### I

Oscar Wilde once noted that for antiquity and for long afterward, the great imperative in human life was to "Know thyself."* This was the path to wisdom given by the oracle at Delphi and was often cited by Socrates as his greatest task in life. It did not imply in antiquity what it might to us; it had much less the sense of "avoid self-deceit," "be true to yourself," or "know your limits." It had much more the sense of "avoid ignorance about what it is to be a human being and what happiness for such a creature consists in." However, said Wilde, for us moderns, the major life task had become something different. It is now: "*Become* who you are." This imperative has also been of central concern in a strand of modern European and American philosophy (sometimes called a "romantic" strand) that stretches from Rousseau to Hegel, Emerson, Thoreau, Nietzsche (with whom the phrase itself is now probably most associated), Heidegger, and Sartre.[1] A kind of anxiety that in our official or public roles we are not really or authentically "who we are," that we are not what we are taken to be by others, now seems familiar to us as a characteristic problem in modern Western life.[2]

---

* I am much indebted to John Coetzee, Nikolas Kompridis, Glenn Most, and Thomas Pavel for comments on an earlier draft of this chapter, and to Jonathan Lear, James Chandler, Joshua Landy, Lanier Anderson, and Candace Vogler for conversations about its content.

[1] There is a thoughtful comparison of Nietzsche and Proust in Nehamas 1985, 167–70. I shall be stressing here much more the ineliminable social dimension to any "self-fashioning." See also my discussion in Pippin 1999a, 99–113.

[2] Cf., though, Pindar's Second *Pythian Ode* (2.72), where one is encouraged to "[b]ecome such as you are, having learned what that is" (1997, 239). Pindar, as the context reveals,

However familiar, the imperative and the issue also seem to be quite paradoxical. Why would you need "to become who you are"? Who else could you be? And even if that could be worked out, the idea of a contrast between the two maxims is paradoxical for other reasons. How can the imperatives be separated and contrasted? Doesn't one have to know who one is, before one can struggle to become who one is, struggle to resist the temptation to be false to oneself?

To answer the first concern we have to appreciate that the subject in question – the "you" that you are to become, at least in the explorations undertaken in the modern novel or confessional poetry – has little directly to do with the familiar philosophical questions about the minimum conditions of self-identification, personal identity, and so forth. At issue is not the Humean worry about the possibility of an awareness of an enduring, stable self but something like acknowledgment of (and faithfulness to) one's "practical identity," what is sometimes referred to as one's character (*what* one is "being true to" when one is "being true to oneself"). Or, as it is sometimes put, the problem is not of individuation but of individualization; the problem of the self's unity is not so much the formal problem of possible continuity over time but the substantive problem of self-knowledge, ego ideals, grounding commitments, all understood as an ethical as much as an epistemological problem.[3] What most seems at stake is what is meant when, *in extremis*, someone might say: "I couldn't live with myself if I did that" or, more commonly, "I don't know why I did that; I don't recognize myself in that deed." And, said the other way around, many people, after all, have self-images that they count as solid self-knowledge but that are better described as self-indulgent fantasies or delusions. They especially might be said to need to become in reality the person they take themselves to be (because they are not or are not yet). Put in a much more general way and anticipating my conclusion: Being the subject of one's life, a subject who can lead a life rather than merely suffer what happens, who can recognize her own agency, the exercise of her subjectivity, in the deeds she produces, also means *being able to fail to be one*. That already indicates that being such a subject cannot be something

*is* talking about a kind of integrity, being true to yourself no matter what the "cunning slanderers" say. But there is no sense that *who* one is might just consist in a constant, experimental "becoming," one that never ends in a realization. Proust's vision is much more like this latter, ever suspended, unresolved becoming, I want to show. (I am grateful to Glenn Most for discussions about the topic.)

3 Contra, to some extent, the approach suggested in Landy 2001b.

one just substantially "is" over time and so can report.[4] As we see below several times, a "practically relevant self-knowledge" is the question at issue, and such first-personal knowledge cannot be understood on models of introspecting an inner essence, on the model of *being S* or *not being S*, but it is more like the expression of a commitment, usually a provisional commitment, which one can sustain or fail to sustain, and so is something one can always *only* "be becoming" (or failing to become).[5]

Accordingly, the answer given by philosophers such as Nietzsche and novelists such as Proust to the second concern (the apparent priority of self-knowledge over self-becoming) is to deny such priority, and so to suggest a deeper paradox. They want to say something like: Any settled piece of self-knowledge or presumed fixed commitment or ego ideal is, because of considerations like those just advanced, *always*, necessarily, provisional, in constant suspense, always subject to pervasive doubt.[6] The reality of such a self-image, what turns out to confirm it, is not fidelity to an inner essence but is ultimately a matter of action, what we actually do, a matter of engagement in the world, as well as, in a way, a kind of negotiation with others about what, exactly, it *was* that one did. (So, to determine

[4] I am going to take up and follow the psychological language with which Proust treats problems such as this, but the general ontological puzzle that this introduces (being a subject by not really "being," being identical with, anything at all) can be understood as a framework for understanding the condition of literary and aesthetic modernism. (In this context one need only replace the "becoming who one is" language with a "Marcel writing himself into existence" formulation to see the relevance of the provisionality and "ungroundedness" in the former to the textuality problems of the latter.) This means a great self-consciousness about what it is to "be an artist," say, without the question ever being such as to allow an "answer." I discuss this general issue a bit more below.

[5] Cf. Leo Bersani's apposite remark: "For Marcel, personality – his own and that of others – is by definition what has not yet happened or has not yet been revealed; it is in essence a secret" (1965, 77). One might also put the point by stressing the nonpropositional character of the content of self-knowledge. One must always " *make* true" what one claims to know about oneself, rather than " *find* such true propositions." A contrast between "reports" and "avowals" in first-person knowledge is discussed in Richard Moran's valuable 2001 book, although he retains a sense of first-person authority that, I think, emerges quite "scathed" in Proust's treatment, even though it does not disappear. I have also benefited a great deal from David Finkelstein's fine 2003 book.

[6] See the very typical "hesitation" style in this simple "report" on the Balbec elevator boy and his reluctance to enter conversation:

But he vouchsafed no answer, whether from astonishment at my words, preoccupation with his work, regard for etiquette, hardness of hearing, respect for holy ground, fear of danger, slowness of understanding, or the manager's orders.

All references will be to the C. K. Scott Moncrieff and Terence Kilmartin translation (Proust 1982). References will be cited in the text and refer to the volume and page number of this edition (I, 715–16).

that something is true about myself is much more like resolve than discovery.)[7] As such, our actual practical identity is always also the subject of contested interpretations and appropriations by others (another mark of its provisionality). And there is very often a kind of struggle to hold fast to such an image or to alter it properly in the face of finding out that one "was not whom one took oneself to be." The idea is that it is only *in* trying to become who one (provisionally) thinks one is that one can begin to find out who one really is (what one would really do), even though that putatively discovered result is only a provisional pledge of sorts to act in certain ways in the future. That is, this finding out does not discover a stable essential self thereby simply "revealed" in action. We get, at best, another temporary resting place that further demands on us could and very likely will dislodge. In this context, the question of whether there can ever be any end to this provisionality, reformulation, and re-engagement is obviously a pressing one.

So is another necessary struggle: for some perspective from which the unity of such deeds and manifestations can be made out. We need to achieve some such coherent connections among deeds – to be able to understand why someone who did *that* would do *this* – or we will not be able to recover the deeds as *ours*, to recognize ourselves in them. Some will seem strange, alien episodes, absent such connectability; more like things that happen to us rather than things we do. (And again, all such claims to unity by any individual, even to himself, are *claims*, are also subject to dispute and denial by others, especially when we act on such a self-understanding and affect what they would otherwise be able to do.)

This is the problem of recovering "lost time," attempting to retrieve what really happened as one's own or to recover who one "really" was. It is the attempt to avoid being trapped in some wish-fulfilling fantasy or in yet another, merely successive provisional point of view. And it is the attempt to avoid being subject to the interpretive will of another. This issue is, of course, the chief subject of Proust's great novel, at issue in questions such as Marcel (or Swann) becoming "a writer," what it is to be truly "in love," why social prestige and snobbery (or radical social dependence) are so

---

7 The following is a typical passage indicating Proust's sense of this issue, from *The Fugitive* (Marcel is hesitating after he has told his mother he will not leave Venice with her):

I was well aware that in reality it was the resolution not to go that I was making by remaining here without stirring, but to say to myself: "I'm not going," which in that direct form was impossible, became possible in this indirect form: "I'm going to listen to one more phrase of 'O sole mio.'" (III, 669)

important, and why there is such an insistent repetition of the theme of "theatrical" selves, selves that seem to exist only as "displayed" and only in the perceptions of others – actresses, prostitutes, closeted homosexuals, and socially successful (Swann) or socially ambitious (Bloch) Jews.

Moreover, the suggestion of such maxims as "become who you are" is that this possibility of a gap between self-image and reality must be *overcome*, that exercising your agency is always an active becoming, a struggle against some barrier, some temptation to conformism or forgetfulness or bad faith or inauthenticity (or some unavoidable contestation with others about what it is that one did, over whom one is revealed to be, or about whom one gets to be). This gap can either be some sort of real barrier to becoming who you are (such as a political barrier or some social convention), where that struggle is based on already achieved (if still provisional) self-knowledge, or it could be required because of a gap between self-image and self-knowledge. Self-knowledge, on this view, should be understood as a product of long experience, profound struggle, and negotiations with others, never a moment of epiphanic insight. It is a retrospective of what we learn in some struggle (with and often against others) to become whom we believe we are.

I want to focus some attention on this theme ("become who you are") in Proust's novel, *Remembrance of Things Past*, by isolating four different facets of the novel where this problem is engaged and extensively treated, where the logic of such a provisional and developmental sense of self is thematized and explored. The four facets concern: (1) The extremely complicated narrative strategy of the novel. (Complicated formally, anyway. As has been pointed out, the plot of this massive work is very simple: Marcel becomes a writer.)[8] Here the surface of the novel, with the young Marcel apparently finally "becoming" the actual author, Proust, is particularly deceptive and elusive. (2) Becoming a self-in-society. The suggestion above was that the basic struggle "to become who one is" is a *social* struggle and involves a complicated negotiation of dependence and social independence that Proust explores with great subtlety. (3) Selfhood and love. Here the possibility of failing (at times, it seems *necessarily* failing) to become who one is is most evident. One never seems to know who the (provisional, possible) beloved is, and one constantly finds that one is not who one assumed one was or is frequently surprised at how different one is "in relation to A" when compared with "in relation to B." And (iv) Marcel's self-identity as an artist and the role of artistic idealization,

[8] Cf. Genette 1980.

fantasy, self-fashioning, and creation in, paradoxically, knowing the truth, especially the truth about oneself. More generally then, the novel invites us to entertain, as a premise for what it will work through, Marcel's unusual anxiety that he will fail to find, or will always have lost, his "self," whom he is to become, and this "in time" (that there might be no successful narrative point of view), in love (the beloved remains unknown, his desires never stabilize), in rejection from society, and in failing to become a writer. What is it to be worried about such a matter?

## II

In the novel, a narrator, near the end of his life, now mostly isolated from society, alone, often ill, attempts to remember and reconstruct narratively the story of his boyhood and early adulthood. (At two and only two very isolated moments in the novel, this object of memory, the narrator's younger self, is called "Marcel.") For the most part, he is nameless and speaks in the first person, as the narrator seems to assume the persona of, seems to enact or re-enact the voice of this younger person, expressing things as this young Marcel would, as well as apparently sometimes stepping outside him to comment on what was really happening to the younger Marcel, as if this were accessible not to that character then but to his older self. To complicate matters, the novel is also often interrupted by what appear to be long, independent philosophical reflections on love, jealousy, time, art, memory, and human psychology. It is often unclear whether these reflections capture the young Marcel's thinking at the time, reflect the narrator's considered view, or are philosophical insertions by the real Proust, the absent author of the narrator's reflections. Many readers have stumbled over this issue, taking it as simply unproblematic that the reflective passages are bits of "Proustian philosophy" meant to illuminate the narrative passages. But the presence and meaning of those passages are quite problematic indeed, something to be thought about, not a given, and it is more likely that Vincent Descombes has it right when he suggests in his recent book that the situation is rather the other way around: that the narrative helps us to contextualize and understand the reflections and especially the limitations of the quite specific point of view that they express. A "philosophical reading" can occur only after this is appreciated.[9] Put much more simply, we have to be as constantly aware as

---

[9] Descombes 1992, 6. See also his very useful formula summarizing his approach: "The thoughts reported *in the narrative* do not coincide with the thoughts communicated *by the*

Marcel that nothing is what it seems. Society matrons are ex-prostitutes, manly aristocrats are homosexual masochists, one's beloved is a lesbian, and the book we are reading does everything possible to convince us it is a memoir; a reportage of inner states, a psychological work. But it is not. There is no historically real Marcel, no real narrator. And characters report their inner states, even to themselves, in ways that turn out to be fundamentally untrustworthy, prompting a constant search for truth, and this more "in" (always contestable) social action than in "deeper" psychological insight.[10]

There is a passage from Proust's letters, quoted by Descombes, that sums up this problem:

No, if I had no intellectual beliefs, if I were trying simply to remember and to create through memory a useless depiction of days gone by, I would not, ill as I am, take the trouble to write. But this evolution of a mind – I have chosen not to analyze it in an abstract way, but rather to recreate it, to bring it to life. And so I am forced to depict errors, but without feeling bound to say that I hold them to be errors. So much the worse for me if the reader believes I hold them to be the truth. The second volume will encourage this misunderstanding. I hope the last volume will clear it up.[11]

And the novel itself warns us, even if that warning appears hard to remember for most readers: "A book in which there are theories is like an article which still has its price tag on it" (III, 916).

So, in testimony to the relevance of our problem (how one becomes who one is), the novel directs us to three main personae, and the relation among them is not clear. (And I should emphasize that I mean three *main* narrative "I's." Marcel Muller has argued for seven narrative

---

*narrative*" (30, my emphasis). See also 272. Descombes's book is invaluable, but I disagree with his interpretation of Proust's modernism in chap. 8, esp. 138–9 ("For remembrance systematically eliminates public events as a source of exaltation or despair. The Dreyfus affair is a mere topic of conversation" (138)). My claim is that Proust (the "philosophical novelist," as that notion is brilliantly deployed by Descombes, or the "implied author," as Wayne Booth would deploy that term) has understood something essential about the relation between public and private, social and individual, not somehow dismissed the former, and so has avoided the simplified dichotomies presupposed in such questions as about the "sources" of inspiration. Also extremely helpful on this theme is Bersani 1965.

[10] There are signs throughout the novel that Proust is well aware of this problem. One of the clearest occurs in *The Guermantes Way*, when Marcel realizes that "Elstir the painter" is much "more daring" than "Elstir the theorist"; that in general, there need be no tight connection between the two (II, 436).

[11] Quoted by Descombes 1992, 4–5. See also Landy 2001b, 109.

voices sharing the first-person pronoun; Joshua Landy, five.)[12] There is
the younger Marcel, the object of the narration, as well as the imitated
subject of thoughts and reflections in the novel; the older narrator, whom
the younger is becoming – as if becoming who he is – and the absent au-
thorial narrator, Proust himself. These characters are three, but as just
noted we tend to collapse them into one and want that one to be the
real Proust.[13] This theme is expressed by the earliest object of Marcel's
writing, the three church spires at Martinville, which look like three from
one angle, but from another and farther away, meld visually into one
spire. (The more distant our perspective on the book, the less close our
reading, the more likely we are to submit to an optical illusion, to mistake
all three for one, for Proust himself?)[14]

And the specific problem in the novel is quite relevant to our theme:
The young Marcel considers himself, from very early on, a writer; that
is his self-understanding; and he is very much trying to become who he
believes he is, trying to become a writer. And this is indeed portrayed as
a struggle, and the struggle concerns the right relation to his audience,
among many other things. (Again the deceptively simple "plot": Marcel
wonders what it is to be a writer, is eager to imitate models, enters and
succeeds in high society, where people become ever more (or less) socially
prominent. Dinner parties are held. Beach resorts are visited. People grow
old. Some die. Marcel becomes disillusioned about society, but finally
does become a writer (while offstage, frustratingly enough, and during a
long temporal gap in the narration), and, if we accept the conventional
point of view, the book we are reading is the product of that decision.)[15]

---

[12] Muller 1965; Landy 2001b, 124. (Landy has a fine book, *Proust, Philosophy and Fiction*,
forthcoming from Oxford University Press, in which many of these narrative and chrono-
logical details are clearly sorted out; some, as far as I know, for the first time.)

[13] Indeed, the temptation to read the novel as a roman à clef, and such curiosity about
"who" the "real" author is, is a bit like the obsessive need to know if Albertine is a lesbian,
if Odette was with Forcheville, and so forth.

[14] This expands on a brief suggestion in Shattuck 2000, 32. I should stress that there most
definitely *is* also a sense in which the three *are* one. So many readers automatically assume
this, though (that what Marcel thinks, what the narrator says in his philosophizing,
and what Proust believes are the same thing) that while the three-in-one, one-in-three
structure of the novel is the complete picture, the difficulty of simply identifying all
the thoughts in the book with Proust's should be especially stressed. The view from far
off cannot be wholly deceptive, since the narrator himself uses the "distance" metaphor
when he claims that he can see only from "far off," though with a telescope. I am indebted
to conversations with Jim Chandler on this point.

[15] Landy has established in his forthcoming book that this is not so, *even from the novel's*
(narrator's) own point of view.

For a very long time, though, Marcel is a writer who does not write or writes very little as he struggles to understand how a writer lives, how one responds to and tries to understand the people around him "as a writer would" and struggles to find out whether he can ever become in reality, however much he actually writes, "a real writer."[16] The issue that he is most puzzled about – what does it mean *in this society* to become a writer? – is already prominent in the narrative or more formal structure of the novel, which is often built on "surprising revelations."

That is, Marcel, in this quest to know who he is, to know whether he is a writer, finds that his beliefs about that issue and many others (especially about what he should do, given those beliefs), almost inevitably fail to correspond with how he actually does react to events and are out of sync with the way in which what he does is understood by others. He is sure he is not in love with someone and is then devastated by some slight or neglect or indifference; he is sure the attainment of some goal is crucial to his happiness, yet finds himself indifferent in acquiring it. (An important example: Marcel is frustrated by his father's opposition to his becoming a writer, but when, influenced by M. Legrandin, his father drops his opposition, Marcel immediately finds the prospect dubious.) We are thus shown that reports of self-knowledge are very likely not reports of mere inner facts, gained by some special access the subject alone has (as if one could discover whether one had a writerly essence or not). The relation between such beliefs and their expression in actions is much tighter than this; the latter turns out to be crucial to the truth of any such former claim, and such truths often turn out different from how a provisional, prior expectation would have it. Introspection is thus singularly unreliable, as in this extraordinary passage:

Now, since the self is constantly thinking numerous things, since it is nothing more than the thoughts of these things, when by chance, instead of having them as the objects of its attention, it suddenly turns its thoughts upon itself, it finds only an empty apparatus, something unfamiliar, to which, in order to give it some reality – it adds the memory of a face seen in a mirror.[17]

---

[16] During this "apprentice" time Marcel pays very close attention to three ideal or model artists – the novelist Bergotte, the painter Elstir, and the composer Vinteuil – trying to understand what makes them artists and how they are both formed by and help to form their milieu. (They appear to be arranged in some order of importance in the novel, and one of the most important passages is in the last volume: It presents a reflection on a septet by Vinteuil and its implications for the self. I discuss it in section V below.)

[17] This is from a passage not included in the French edition used by Moncrieff; quoted by Bersani 1965, 106–7.

As Sartre would later put it, these reports of self-knowledge reflect provisional promises or pledges at a certain time (in effect, promises to oneself and others) to act in certain ways, which one may fail to keep for all the sorts of reasons people fail to keep pledges.[18] To summarize several of these points at once: The fact that Proust's narrator is *also a character in the novel we are reading* is not merely the exploration of an unusual point-of-view technique; it manifests the paradox and tensions of *any* self-reflection, and so the necessary link between such reflection and action; it *manifests* these tensions more than perhaps any other book, or so I am trying to claim.[19]

And often these reflective failures are not matters of simple weakness or moral failure; they can be results of the simple pressures of time. One has to make such pledges at some moment, before one can even begin to know how to understand the implications of the commitment, something one learns only "as time unfolds," given some principle of narrative connectedness. For this reason, "the bluff" – pretending, when some situation calls for action, that one knows what one is about, knows what should happen, and so on – is an important, unavoidable, and often hilarious social mechanism throughout *Remembrance*[20] and thereby also a valuable way to learn about oneself in a fairly standard (not absolutely unique, first-personal) way.[21] And for similar reasons the novel itself embodies, constantly exhibits, a narrative and point-of-view uncertainty and complexity consistent with the often confusing temporal and social instabilities exhibited in its details. While much in the novel conspires to have us believe that the vain, social-climbing young Marcel grows into a wise, reflective narrator Marcel who writes the books we have just read and that

[18] This despite the fact that Sartre almost willfully refuses to notice those passages in Proust so similar to the views of *Being and Nothingness* and treats him as if wholly wedded to an introspective account of self-knowledge. Bersani 1965 is very good on this issue (106).

[19] I agree with Bersani that the absence of omniscient narrators in novelists such as Proust or Henry James not merely is a matter of technical experimentation but evinces a historical and social crisis manifest in literary modernism and one ultimately most threatening to that bourgeois consolation that had been so often evoked as a refuge from the secular harshness and uncertainties of the bourgeois world: romantic love. See the discussion in Pippin 2000c.

[20] There is a fine description of the bluff and its dialectical twists in III, 360–1.

[21] There are philosophical controversies aplenty here. As stated, this "Proustian" theory is quite incomplete. It especially leaves unclarified our strong intuition that there nevertheless *is* something distinctive and unique about the first-person perspective on "who I am," distinctive, that is, from one's knowledge of other persons and objects. The novel is, in effect, "disputing" that. But for the purposes of this chapter, those refinements are not yet relevant.

*that* narrator is "really" Proust himself, the novel does nothing to establish that there is or even can be any point of view "outside" the narrative flux and instability described, that Marcel's quasi-religious discovery of "real time past" in the last novel is anything other than *yet another* moment in a temporal story that has led Marcel in hope to, and then in disappointment away from, other idealizations: Swann, Berma, the Guermantes, his grandmother, art itself, Albertine, *time regained,* and so forth.[22] There is no reason to take *Marcel's* "death bed" conversion away from the radical temporal instability we have just seen as any more authoritative than these other putative moments of redemption.[23] If Marcel is to become who he is, it will not be in any such moment of stalled or stopped time. We have just read the account that shows why it cannot be.

Put one final way, the problem I have called Marcel's "becoming who he is" amounts to his becoming a determinate agent, someone who leads his life, both carries the past into the future in a certain way and does so, acts, in the light of some conception of the subject he is struggling to become. But this is mostly manifested by a kind of *via negativa,* the often palpable sense in the novel of the great and almost intolerable burden of the demands of such agency and the sweet pleasures to be gained by avoiding such a burden. We are introduced to this theme in a famous archetypal scene, Marcel's intense pain at being separated from his mother, that great rip in the fabric of presubjective, harmonious being that can never be avoided or ever healed. But the figure for this problem actually begins earlier in the first novel, in its first, most famous line: "For a long time, I used to go to bed early." We are thus subtly introduced to the odd desire, not just for the nighttime kiss, but also for "earlier sleep," a desire for some release from the burdens of "waking" agency that introduces the recurring images of passivity and its many pleasures: being pursued, being a beloved, and even the later themes of masochism and betrayal, being made an object. It is enough to note here the importance and potential, perhaps very deep irony of this theme in Marcel's (that

[22] I note that this claim, which I return to at the end of this chapter, does not undermine Marcel's experience of the way past time can be "held" in objects, sounds, sights, and food, like a genie in a bottle, to be released in an involuntary rush when the right key happens to be found. At issue is what Marcel makes of this, needs to make of it, especially the way he tosses around the notions of "truth" and "reality."

[23] This introduces an extremely large issue that has dominated much European philosophy since Heidegger. Cf. Gadamer's remarks in *Truth and Method*: "Reconstructing the original circumstances, like all restoration, is a futile undertaking in view of the historicity of our being. What is reconstructed, a life brought back from the past, is not the original." (1999, 167).

is, not "Proust's") enormous faith in "involuntary memories," supposedly the key to the novel's success.[24] This would be to make a point, by way of attention to irony, that Benjamin makes in a different way: that Marcel's near sanctification of involuntary memory figures a failure, a kind of breakdown, in modern temporal experience. For Benjamin that failure consists in a gap opening wide between individual and collective, inherited memory, or tradition, an inability to place oneself in such a collective memory that means it is wholly "a matter of chance whether an individual forms an image of himself, whether he can take hold of his experience."[25]

III

A great part of such a struggle to become who one is, an agent, obviously concerns our proper relation to people around us, concerns our social self. A self-image, for example, that is not at all reflected or accepted in practice by others or, especially, that is contradicted by the way one is treated or regarded would have to count as some sort of failure to become who one is. An obvious example: the reputedly large number of our contemporaries who think of themselves as poets, novelists, writers, or artists but whose work (the objectification of such a self-understanding) is universally rejected. (At a certain level of rejection, being such a bad writer, for example, has to count as not being a writer at all.) And the case is even more obvious in those who profess such self-knowledge but who have not yet even begun to write, who know somehow that in their inner being, a great writer lurks, waiting only for the time and leisure to escape. A self-image never realized in social space, never expressed in public action, has to count as more a fantasy than a piece of self-knowledge, even though when expressed in such action, the public deed cannot be said to be exclusively owned by the subject, to have the meaning that the subject insists on. It is "up for grabs" in a certain sense. One's self-image becomes a social fact through action, and its meaning can then

---

[24] In fact, reliance on such memories is what we might call ideological, something Marcel needs badly to believe rather than what is in itself believable. As Adorno pointed out, no past memory is ever safe, neatly stored away; it can be "revoked in its very substance by later experience. He who has loved and who betrays love does harm not only to the image of the past, but to the past itself" (MM, §106, 166). Cf. also Leo Bersani's remark: "And the act of memory seems to involve such a liberal re-creation of the past, rather than a mere fidelity to past impressions, that some of the theoretical positions that inspired the narrator's work are made obsolete by the work itself" (1965, 18).

[25] Benjamin 1977, 158. I think the irony goes even deeper.

no longer be tied to the intention or will of the agent alone. This is, of course, exactly why many people forever postpone such action, never write that book, send off that manuscript, finish that dissertation.[26]

And yet, on the other hand, there are clearly people whose self-image, whose practical identity, has been formed so extensively by the expectations and demands and reactions of others that, while their own self-image does circulate successfully in society, their view of themselves is indeed very well mirrored in how they are regarded and treated; it has to be said that they have become the person whom "*they*" want one to be, that one does not have one's own identity, has not become who one is. As noted above, this type of slavish conformism has to count as just as much a failure to become who one is as the action of the fantasy-indulging narcissist we just discussed.

We are also often shown another implication of this theme: that the "you" who you can become is not entirely "up to you." For one thing, our self-identity is very much linked to some commitment to values, and we do not think of ourselves as committing to values arbitrarily or of values themselves as just expressions of our preferences. *They* make some claim *on* us. When we say that we know ourselves very well, we often mean to imply that we know something such as where we would draw some line beyond which we would never cross, that our sense of self is essentially a sense of values we cannot give up in the face of demands by others. (Having a practical identity – husband, father, professor, American – always involves something like commitment to a norm, something that I must initiate in response to such a claim and actively sustain over time. I do not regard myself as having the option of just abandoning such a commitment.)

For another, the realization of such value must make some sense within the historical, social world in which we live. We can adopt the values of chivalry and try to become a knight in the modern world, but we won't be able to become a real knight; we'll end up a comic character, a Quixote.[27] (The growing absurdity of Charlus's aristocratic pretensions is connected with this theme. His decline into sadomasochistic farce is not at all simply a matter of psychological deterioration but is both an effect of

---

[26] Cf. the formulation by Bersani: "Our knowledge of the outer world is, then, dramatic rather than conceptual; unable to describe it, we nevertheless spend our lives meeting it" (1965, 134). I discuss this issue at considerably more length in Pippin forthcoming a.

[27] As is often pointed out, a great deal of the nineteenth-century realist novel obviously involves such a "lack of fit" between idealistic expectation and the emerging social reality of bourgeois Europe.

and a manifestation of "social deterioration," from the Guermantes to the middle-class Verdurins.[28] This is a new world in which his fantasy of feudal power is sustainable only if he can experience himself as creating his new submissive, dependent role, and so in sadomasochism. And Swann's inability to write his Vermeer book is not mere "writer's block." It has everything to do with Swann's sense of audience or lack of audience.)

Finally, such social treatments of the "real self" question (and the narrative fractures and ambiguities they entail) are also presented within a specific socio-*historical* context by Proust. Geographically, the vast novel is divided for the most part into three regions: Combray, the country village where Marcel's parents have their vacation home; Paris, where Marcel's father is a doctor and where they have their principal residence (eventually sharing a building with the famous Duc de Guermantes's family); and Balbec, a seaside resort, both a kind of transition place for the young Marcel and a social scene where rigid class distinctions do not apply as much as in ancient Combray but which is not yet as unstable as modern Paris. (He first visits Balbec with his beloved grandmother, and so it remains a piece of his boyhood, but it is also where he meets the fabulous Guermantes, especially the dashing whirlwind of a character, Robert de Saint-Loup, and the most complex, colorful, and sad character in the book, the great Baron de Charlus.)

But these geographical regions also sound a historical resonance. Combray is an almost prehistorical social world; at least premodern and largely feudal. There is little historical time present. Life there is as repetitious as nature's own cycles, and it has a rigid and largely unchanging social hierarchy. It is important that the character most associated with this world, the maid Françoise, is the rock of ages in the book, outside modern, historical time, supremely self-confident, unchanging, full of the opinions and superstitions her ancestors would have expressed. She has no need to "become who she is"; the question itself would no more arise for her than it would for Eumaios in the *Odyssey*.[29] But the world of Paris, and to a growing extent the intermediary world of Balbec, is a world where the experience of vast, rapid social change is omnipresent, disorienting,

---

[28] Or it is a manifestation of the even more deflating revelation that there was essentially never any difference between these social cliques.

[29] Descombes 1992, 166, notes that because no real events happen in Combray (anomalies that might seem like novelties, such as the social success of Swann or Legrandin, are successfully filtered out), this "world" is not a novelistic world, as is the world of Paris. Throughout his book, Descombes makes an interesting case, using Proust for a historical theory of the novel, similar in ambition to Girard's.

and, when properly appreciated, simply will not allow the intelligent and aware characters a "Françoise-like" solution. (Even a character such as the Duchesse de Guermantes prefers not to observe rigid social hierarchies based strictly on family and fancies herself a social adventuress, thus raising the question that the Parisians must now face: What is it to "make" a society in these altered social conventions? How does one play the great and unbelievably complex "game" of invitations and refusals?)

The evidence for such change is often slipped in quietly in the narrative details but begins to accumulate as the events in the novel head for two decisive historical and social crises: the Dreyfus affair and World War One. These details include enormous technological change: the arrival of electric lighting in the home, the telegraph and railway, Marcel's first telephone call, and, above all, the arrival of the automobile. (In a famous passage in *Cities of the Plain*, Marcel actually weeps when he first sees an airplane (II, 1062).) These are all shown to contribute to a great "compressing" of social life, as if various communities grow more and more compacted together, making more and more impossible the isolation of little villages, such as Combray, and so exposing everyone more and more to more social pressures than before, resulting in greater conformism and anxiety about authenticity.[30] It is all presented as if these devices, by drawing people closer together, in ever more rapid physical and communicative contact with each other, rather than increase communicative closeness and daily intimacy, mostly increase the sense of being regarded, of being monitored ever more constantly and effectively by others, as if, in effect, there are fewer and fewer places to "hide," fewer reasons to avoid contact, fewer real opportunities for solitude and the development of a socially independent self.[31]

[30] Some aspects of technology also are shown to distort, narrow, or at least drastically affect aspects of social understanding, as when Marcel speaks to his grandmother on the telephone, hears her isolated voice, the voice of a frail old woman, not his grandmother. And when he rushes to see her, he now cannot avoid seeing her in this way, a "mad old woman, drowsing over her book, overburdened with years, flushed and coarse . . . a stranger whom he has never seen." Cf. Beckett 1931, 15.

[31] Cf. Adorno's remarks in no. 20, *Minima moralia*, "Die Entfremdung erweist sich an den Menschen gerade daran, dass die Distanzen fortfallen" (MM, 45). ("Alienation is manifested precisely in the elimination of the distance between people.") Thomas Pavel has pointed out to me that people lived on top of each other and complained about it well before such technologies. But I mean to suggest here that the rapidity and efficiency of communication and travel introduces a qualitative change into this longstanding problem, a level and a kind of odd, paradoxical (because also anonymous) intimacy and regard that alters the nature of social experience. The line between "inside" and "outside" is harder to maintain and what one can regard as one's own point

Finally, another consequence of the socio-historical Proustian world is even more important but harder to summarize without a separate chapter (or book). A simple term for it would be the untrustworthiness of direct or immediate experience, something that seems linked to the inadequacy of the historically specific evaluative and descriptive terms available to Marcel. We all know that the official Proustian doctrine is supposed to be that immediate experience is experienced too quickly, caught in too great a jumble of associations and affective responses, to be fully intelligible. Experiences "according to Proust" supposedly reveal their true meaning in a *mémoire involuntaire*, when they supposedly can jolt their way through the surveillance of quotidian consciousness and appear as, it would seem, the thing in itself, an experienced moment in its original meaning and importance. But we sometimes neglect to note that such "experiences of not clearly or reliably experiencing" in the historical present are not treated as epistemological theses but as a record of such flux and uncertainty in a certain historical world. Françoise's world, the largely premodern world of Combray, we can easily infer, suffers no such confusions or uncertainties, since within it the patterns of repetition and reidentification familiarize the familiar and screen out what does not fit. Marcel, however, in a world where the unprecedented is common, a world always overdetermined in meaning, cannot even directly experience the greatest life event in the novel, his grandmother's death. He must later, at Balbec, re-experience what he paradoxically did not originally experience. This is yet another image of the inevitably reflective and thereby unstable characterization of experience in the novel, a feature that I would argue is historically indexed, tied to the sort of world where sexual identities can seem to change instantaneously, information circulates rapidly and often without context, and moral hierarchies crumble and are rebuilt unpredictably. (It is also in, and probably *only in*, such a world that such extreme claims about the power of involuntary memory can seem to make sense. That is, we need again to be attentive as well to *Marcel's need* for such a touchstone – something independent of any supposed Proustian theory – before we can properly evaluate what Marcel thinks he experiences in the novel's final volume.)[32]

---

of view, developed by oneself, is harder to have some faith in. Marcel himself complains about how the automobile, by bringing villages "closer," is also homogenizing them.

[32] See Walter Benjamin's discussion on involuntary memory, experience, and Proust in "On Some Motifs in Baudelaire," in 1977, esp. 162–3.

## IV

In the novel's many love affairs, the issue of being or becoming a lover or beloved is raised in both a temporal and more directly psychological framework. The temporal problem in human relations is pronounced and stressed very frequently, almost ad nauseam. A typical passage:

> Every person is destroyed when we cease to see him; after which his next appearance is a new creation, different from that which immediately preceded it, if not from them all. . . . Remembering a strong and searching glance, a bold manner, it is inevitably, next time, by an almost languid profile, a sort of dreamy gentleness, overlooked by us in our previous impression, that at the next encounter we shall be astonished, that is to say almost uniquely struck. (I, 979)

Because of this phenomenon of instability, the very attainment of desire is treated as temporally complex and problematic. For when we achieve what we thought we desired, we often find that we are "no longer the person who desired that," that we formed the desire at a time and under conditions specific to that period, not any longer to this new one.[33] (And I stress again the terrible complication: All we know is that this is what the *narrator* believes about such matters, perhaps for his own defensive, still obsessional motives. As always, we as readers have to try to figure out just who is speaking, as the speaker or rememberer is also trying to figure out who he is or was. These opinions are part of that process and so part of ours.)

Moreover, Proust treats imagination and fantasy as essential to desire, especially necessary to intense, powerful desires such as romantic love, which are formed and sustained largely under the influence of fantastic idealizations of the beloved or lover. (In the language used here, one forms various aspects of one's self- and other image under the inevitable sway of these erotic illusions.) Without such fantasies, love could become too much like that dreary contract between consenting partners for the reciprocal use for pleasure of each other's bodies that Kant so infamously defined as the basis of any ethical marital relation. Yet such fantasies – so essential to a person's self-identity – also cannot withstand the great pressure of having finally to acknowledge the humdrum reality behind such illusions, and so the identities of lover and beloved are in constant suspense.

---

[33] To be able to be satisfied now with what we desired "then" is as "illogical," Beckett notes in his book about Proust, as "to expect one's hunger to be dissipated by the spectacle of Uncle eating his dinner" (1931, 3).

For this and many other reasons (such as the unreliability of experience sketched above), the central plot event in the novel is disappointment after disappointment after disappointment. The great actress,
Berma, whom Marcel yearned to see with every fiber of his body, turns out
(at first, anyway) to be a prosaic disappointment. The imagined ancient
church at Balbec is in reality prosaically stuck among some shops in a dull
village. The great, mysterious Swann is a pathetic dilettante, captured in
a love affair with a woman whom he does not even like, tortured by constant jealousy. The mysterious world of the Faubourg St. Germain, the
Guermantes's world, turns out to be a collection of petty, venal, essentially worthless people. In fact, society itself, the very necessary condition
under which one forms a sense of who one is and should become, looks to
be little more than a tissue of lies, evasions, delusions, vain pretensions, a
hall of mirrors for social posturing, with each figure trying hard to imitate
those regarded as the originals, the setters of fashion, who are themselves
trying to imitate those who are trying to imitate them. (There is even a
Groucho Marx element to this disappointment: Marcel's constant sense
that the objects of his desire must be so valuable and rare and difficult to
achieve that if he, poor Marcel, has attained them, they must be worthless in reality, thus confirming Groucho's law that he would not want to
be a member of any club that would have him as a member.)

In this doomed economy of love, the beloved wants the lover, but that
means wanting the lover to want her, and so she wants to become what
the lover wants to love. "Success" in such an enterprise is then obviously
double-edged, since she is always left wondering whether the lover really
loves *her*, the "real her," and what will happen when he "finds out" who she
really is, behind all the mystery, makeup, fine clothes, tailored persona,
and so forth. And as she is assessing what the lover wants, she is also
assessing the lover's self-presentation to the beloved, which is of course
*his* attempt to be whom he thinks she wants a lover, or him, to be.

And we see over and over again that the enemy of love's intensity is the
grinding, soul-deadening familiarization of habit and the everyday. (Cf.:
"stupefying habit, which during the whole course of our life conceals
from us almost the whole universe, and in the dead of night, without
changing the label, substitutes for the most dangerous or intoxicating
poisons of life something anodyne that procures no delight" (III, 554).)[34]

---

[34] "Habit then is the generic term for the countless treaties concluded between the
countless subjects that constitute the individual and their countless correlative objects"
(ibid., 8).

Proust suggests that it is almost as if we had a motive to *find* constant occasions for jealousy, to *want* to consider the beloved as eluding us, absent (thereby defeating habit, even if in a Pyrrhic victory). Marcel wants to convince himself that he does not really know Albertine and so must constantly experience a great anxious unsettled doubt about her life apart from his. This, though, however painful, means that their love has not been completely settled, has not become a matter of habit. The difficulty of becoming who one is, in other words, is something one easily and unavoidably and sometimes eagerly projects onto others, too; one realizes that the beloved may not really be the person that the lover, or even she herself, takes herself to be or that she may suddenly, given some chance encounter with another, not just reveal herself to be in fact other than she appeared, but might become someone else. (Marcel's Law seems to be: Anxiety and jealousy make the heart grow fonder.)

Now Marcel appears to react to this with an almost insane possessiveness, tries to keep Albertine a prisoner. But this, too, is treated with great irony by Proust. We see pretty quickly that Marcel is as much, if not much more, the captive of Albertine as vice versa, and the situation itself is already paradoxical. (The jailer must be constantly on guard lest his prisoner escape; they are in effect chained to each other, the jailer as much a prisoner.)[35]

Finally, this whole set of considerations – escaping from habit, avoiding the dullness of familiarity, and so forth – is another reason why, in a novel that is so much about remembering, forgetting is so important. Moments of past time must be lost, however painful that is, so that they can escape the control of habit and habitual associations and then be (apparently) recaptured in moments of sudden, unplanned, involuntary memory. Said another way, the picture Marcel presents suggests that our real life, wherein we can come to understand ourselves, understand what it is to become who one is, is so wholly false, routinized, saturated with habit, familiarity (and the contempt it breeds), as well as, paradoxically, so subject to radical temporal flux, that it can be really *lived* only "too late," afterward, in (mostly involuntary) recollection and a kind of intense re-experiencing. (We can become who we are only when, in a way, we cease

---

[35] There are many other examples of this issue in society. For example, there is the story of Oriane, who in order to demonstrate or even create her independence, makes a show of not attending the party of Mme. de Saint-Euverte and pretends to have a sudden desire to see the fjords of Norway. The suggestion is that she is no more free of social pressures than if she had accepted (II, 495; see also Descombes 1992, 282). There is a fine discussion of this problem in Earle forthcoming.

to be, at least cease to be so "in control.") In his famous, sad phrase: The "true paradises are the *paradises we have lost*" (III, 903). (If they are lost, forgotten, they at least have a chance of escaping habit and can reappear with some freshness and vivacity as "true" paradises. This is a mirror of the earlier point – that the only successful (sustainable) love is unrequited love.) The suggestion is that while we like to think of ourselves as living our life forward, as if a life were in the control of a subject, enacting a clear self-identity, in fact that direction would not make much sense unless we were able to live it constantly "backward," too, making sense later of what could not make sense at the time. This is already the beginning of a claim for what amounts to the priority of art to life itself in the novel, for a radical aestheticism as the solution of sorts to the "become who you are" imperative.[36] Since *lives* are such backward-looking narrated *novels*, the best narrator is the wisest judge, the most successful at life; he is perhaps most of all "who he is." Or at least he is the most self-conscious. And this is also an answer of sorts to the obvious question raised by the book's title. *Why* must lost time be searched for? Because that is where your life lies hidden, Marcel seems to say. Contrary to the conventional wisdom – "Don't live in the past" – Marcel often suggests that one can truly *live* only in the past, at least live in a way that can make some sense, can be rescued from habit, the rush of time, the confusing swirl of immediate impressions, and the difficulties arising from one being a character in the novel one is narrating – all if such lost time can be "found."[37]

In the treatment of love in high society, what would otherwise seem to be a rather bizarre intense, frequent emphasis on male and female homosexuals (what Proust calls "inversion") and prostitutes is more intelligible as linked to the social dimensions of this identity theme. This is so

---

[36] At one point, Marcel can confuse relations of original and image to such an extent that he can describe the moonlight as "copying the art of Hubert Robert" (I, 124).

[37] This central theme in the novel – unrequited love – deserves a book-length treatment. It could easily be invoked as a figure of sorts for the condition of modernity itself. Even the resolutely prosaic Kant must resort to it to describe our condition, fated to ask questions we cannot answer, in love philosophically with an unattainable goal: that the subject's relation to metaphysics is like that of an unrequited lover (*Kritik der reinen Vernunft*, A850/B878). It's a prominent image in Nietzsche. He notes that "our passion," "the drive to knowledge,"

has become too strong for us to be able to want happiness without knowledge or [to be able to want the happiness] of a strong, firmly rooted delusion; even to imagine such a state of things is painful to us! Restless discovering and divining has such an attraction for us, and has grown as indispensable to us as is to the lover his unrequited love, which he would at no price relinquish for a state of indifference – perhaps, indeed, we too are unrequited lovers. (1982, 428)

because such characters allow Proust to raise frequently the question of the "theatrical self" (existing only in the beliefs and perceptions of others) or the importance of role playing, acting, and so the nature of the difference between the public self (in conventional terms, often false, hypocritical, as with homosexuals who present a straight face to the world, one full of hostility for gays, or prostitutes such as Odette Swann, who have become society matrons and try hard to stay well to the right of any social issue of the day, as in the Dreyfus affair.) Indeed, this concatenation of themes – homosexuals, prostitutes, actors, Jews – seems designed to raise the question of the relation between "inner" and "outer" self and the link with the nonsocial/social dialectic noted earlier. For secularized Jews, it was the problem of what it was to "be" Jewish (or to deny being Jewish) in those heated times. For some women, it was a question at least as old as Mary Magdalene: How does one *become* a thoroughly "ex-"prostitute after one has been one? And the acting theme (and so the difference between pretense and reality) is everywhere, as one might expect in a work where Proust is in effect "acting the part of himself" all the way through.

This theatricality, then, also carries us back full circle to the romantic theme, and so to the question of how to distinguish between regarding a persona as a finely crafted work of art, something that does express one's self or the artist's truth but that takes account of what can be socially understood and circulated (and so avoids the simplistic solution – just be who you are honestly and forget about what the world thinks), and, on the other hand, as being inauthentic and deluded, a victim of a self-serving conformism. (A typical anxiety of Marcel's: "[O]ur social personality is the creation of the thoughts of other people" (I, 20).)

## V

Now, if one tried to sum all this up too quickly, one would end up with a vast novel of horrible disillusionment. "Becoming who one is" would simply look impossible in such a society with no sense of what is worth wanting and why it would be worth wanting, trapped inside an endless cycle of snobbery, fashion, and hypocrisy, without genuine worth, unsettled every second by the radically temporal, mutable nature of the human subject. Or such a goal seems possible only in a pure, rarified aesthetic domain, bought at the price of a great distance from life-as-it-is-lived, at the price, to use such a frequent modern image, of an isolating illness, making real contact with others impossible, but just thereby allowing separation and insight, a living death or *nunc stans*, outside time but thereby outside life. (At one point in the last volume, the narrator remarks that people think he has looked at them under a microscope, but it was really a telescope, far away enough for distance, but with the power to magnify from that distance (III, 1098).)[38] We seem left with a human world with no possibility of adult, romantic love; one where love is possible (if it is) only within the family.

And there is almost a religious dimension to such an attitude. It is in one sense true that Proust seems to show us only the vanity and corruption "of the world," in some Augustinian way (or the reduplication in the modern world of the diseases of court culture, an old, tried and true theme in French literature), and to propose salvation only in another realm, isolated, nonsocial (or proposed for a thoroughly idealized society), a religion of art.[39] But *real* society is also what makes possible Marcel's education, his *Bildung*, his meeting Bergotte, Elstir, and Swann (all of which is made possible by his grandmother's social position and her social and aesthetic taste); there are genuine friendships (Bergotte's beautiful ministrations to the grandmother when she is dying; the early friendship with Saint-Loup); and there is the telling and rich spectacle of Charlus's disintegration and what it teaches Marcel. So there are various things about the "human mystery" that appear to require not just a social existence but a complex form of social sensibility, refined over time, and that turns out to be indispensable for Marcel's vocation. How to state properly this relation of dependence (the novel is, after all, about the social world, and not in a moral, or condemnatory way) and social independence (there must be some break – the sanatoria stays and his later isolation – for Marcel to gain the perspective he needs to write) remains the riddle that must be solved.

That is, the novel seems to suggest a kind of "capacity" view of one's practical identity and unity, and the capacity in question is an ability to negotiate properly the relation of dependence and independence with one's fellow agents, what to accept of how others take up and interpret

---

[38] As Walter Benjamin has pointed out, the significance of Proust's snobs extends far beyond French society. They are avatars of that deadly modern type, the consumer, who wants to be flattered for his discriminating taste but whose taste amounts to nothing more than liking what will get him flattered, taking refuge in brand names and high-end merchandise, much as the snob does in supposedly high-end people. A whole society looms where no one is or even wants any more to be "who one is" – another Nietzschean nightmare. See Benjamin 1974.

[39] I am grateful to Thomas Pavel for noting the relevance of this Augustinian theme in French literature and its continuing relevance to Proust.

and react to one's deeds, what to reject. Swann seems at first to negotiate the aristocratic social world with some proper measure of independence and integrity, in what appears to the young Marcel, anyway, to be an ideal way. Bloch's pretended integrity is as false as, ultimately, Charlus's. There seems to be an endless dance of domination and submission in all the love affairs. But the social world in which all this occurs and its great temporal and psychological instability seem to leave no place for such a settled balanced capacity, no space even for it to develop properly.

But such a pessimistic reading would be much too hasty. For one thing, neither our narrator nor the younger Marcel can be granted complete authority in what they pronounce about these issues. Marcel is shown to be vain, deceptive, weak-willed, neurotic, hysterical, and untrustworthy, and he spouts a lot of half-baked philosophy about idealism, solipsism, egoism, the impossibility of love, the prevalence of vanity, and so forth, views that have no independent weight in the book and are opinions that themselves undergo considerable, manifest change over time. Accordingly, as in all great novels, we have to pay attention to what is shown much more than what is said if we are to come to any conclusions about the possibility of becoming who one is.

And we are shown a great deal. We are shown how the possibility of "becoming who you are" and all that comes with that – sustaining a commitment to a value, living in a social world without living under the suffocating, conformist weight of that world, living a coherent, relatively unified life (being able to narrate one's life, to live backward as well as forward, and so forth) – should all also be understood as some sort of function of the kind of society one lives in as well as a result of a refined capacity one might develop. (Generalizing from such a society to the "in itself" or essential problem would be dangerous.) As the novel shows, a practical identity, our sense of our own individuality, is the coherent real-ization in deeds of such a self-consciousness and so such a capacity, a kind of (relatively fragile, easily lost) achievement, not a simple discovery, and in all such achievements one needs help from others, and the right kind of help. Social dependence need not itself mean a loss or qualification on independence and so a restriction of the achievement of individuality; it all depends on the sort of dependence.

And the most salient feature of the society of aristocrats that becomes Marcel's world is that they have nothing to do with, are part of no social project larger than preserving privilege and the system that enhances them; they are desperately dependent on each other, and so some aspect of this theme in the novel must appear in a distorted way. They are, as

Ortega y Gasset said, like plants: rooted in their natural spots, moving only to turn to catch the rays of the sun of flattery and esteem, without which they would surely wilt and die, and so they have no help to offer in any common project. They have no project. Or they are more like strutting, well-dressed animals in a zoo than human beings.[40] They have no historical time because they have no future, have no way of stretching the past on along into the future, the modern world. They only have one way of making sense of their past, "narrating backward," as we said earlier: lineage and genealogy. (By contrast, the peasants of Combray are privileged with the burden of necessity; they must work and their lives are purposive and ordered by means of the structure of this work.) There is a description of Swann that is telling in this regard:

> The fact was that Swann had reached an age whose philosophy – encouraged, in his case, by the current philosophy of the day, as well as by that of the circle in which he had spent much of his life, the group that surrounded the Princess des Laumes, where it was agreed that intelligence was in direct relation to the degree of skepticism and nothing was considered real and incontestable except the individual tastes of each person – is no longer that of youth, but a positive, almost medical philosophy, the philosophy of men, who, instead of exteriorizing the objects of their aspirations, endeavor to extract from the accumulation of the years already spent a fixed residue of habits and passions which they can regard as characteristic and permanent, and with which they will deliberately arrange, before anything else, that the kind of existence they choose to adopt shall not prove inharmonious. (I, 304–5)

For a good part of the novel, until a large temporal break at the end (Marcel's illness requires two very long stays at sanatoria), Marcel struggles (and fails) to become who he is in *this* sort of world, modeled on that world, struggles to become what would be an artist for this audience, at such a time. He clearly at first regards their leisure and education and worldliness as the key to their freedom from necessity and so their capacity for an undistorted view of the higher things. If there is any group, he seems to reason, where a free appreciation of the best aspects of human life can be had, especially an appreciation of beauty and nobility, this must be it. That is all, we are shown (especially in the case of Charlus, whose pretense of near god-like independence is finally revealed as in reality a craven masochism, as he enacts this cult of dependence in sexual-pathological terms), and it leads to a hopeless counterfantasy about art. At first, it is only once free of *such a community* (one that regards art as an

---

[40] See Bersani on "Le royaume de néant" (1965, 166–77).

escape into some realm of purity and eternity, away from life) that he can write, he can be for himself a writer.[41] Not being able to become who he is is not the difficulty it is because of some intrinsic limitation, some inherent tragedy in human life, dooming us to perpetual alienation, and it is not due to some inherent falseness of the modern world. It has everything to do with Marcel's historical world.

What he comes to appreciate, I would suggest, is that artists have no secure place in this society because this society, both the remnants of the feudal, *ancien régime* and the new "fast" society of consumption, rapid technological change, great social instability, and a new power of fluid capital, is about nothing, stands for nothing, devours its artists as entertainment or fetishizes them as sacred priests, disguising in Mme. Verdurin's paroxysms of aesthetic delight its own vapidity. Bergotte, Elstir, and Vinteuil are in the novel served by, their aims are realized by, and their social reality is largely determined by acolytes such as Mme. Verdurin, Berma, Rachel, Swann, Charlus, and Morel. The relations among patrons, artist, and audience have always been complex, but there is not much hope for the artist as such when he is bounded on either side by such unrelenting phoniness and self-servingness or, in cases such as Swann's, such cynicism and boredom.

Marcel's reaction to this realization is complex. Such a "negotiating capacity" still has to be *directed* in some way, in one direction rather than another, under some assumption or other about who one is, who one takes oneself to be, however provisionally. And this still raises the question of the conditions for the success of such a goal. He *does*, after all, become who he is in spite of all this, he becomes a writer, and the conditions for his success are presented in a complex or double-edged way, not just as an escape from a concern with society (a flight that would suggest the naïveté of a claim for complete societal independence, a "beautiful soul"). In the simplest terms, he can become a writer when he *gives up* the search for something like the "writerly essence" inside him, ceases looking inward at all, and begins the *act* of writing, an action that is inevitably also an exposure to the social world. And this is all of a piece with what we have seen before: Marcel's breaking free of understanding the first-person perspective as introspective and observational, such that he comes to see that attitude as more projection than reportage, projections, or pledges that

---

[41] It should perhaps be stressed that this is the opposite of many standard readings of Proustian "Platonism," the final aesthetic *defeat* of time. Beckett is often on a better course.

must be sustained and backed up. His hesitancy in the writing case is a product of the somewhat ludicrous elevation of art's importance that he inherits through his grandmother and his grandmother's relation to art, is, as Shattuck has pointed out so well, a kind of *idolatry*, an absurd project of investing in art virtually every dimension of human value and of thinking of that activity and its creators in essentialist, Platonic ("antitemporal") terms. This is, after all, a woman who gives a small boy a George Sand novel, so risqué or adult that his mother must censor so much in reading to Marcel that nothing makes any sense. (The fact that the novel, *François le Champi*, is almost about incest, about a foundling who marries a woman who is "like a mother to him," is a topic best left for another discussion.) Likewise, there is something hysterical and defensive about the "aristocratic" (and late nineteenth-century) relation to art, as if in compensation for the sterility, the nongenerative character of their lives (another link to the homosexuality theme), and both influences set up Marcel's hopelessly Platonic aspirations for art, as a way of rescuing truth from time or communing with eternal essences and revealing them all to everyone.[42]

The central transformation that makes possible not only Marcel's success in becoming who he is but a Proustian way of thinking about such an issue in an age where such identities, practices, and types are always in suspense and contestable and cannot be secured by anything, any value or reality that transcends the wholly temporal human world, is that his time so long away from society has broken the hold of such "Platonic" illusions.[43] He comes to understand that his world's not being redeemable in this sense *is* his subject, and an infinitely variable one it is, too, making some sense now of the modern anxieties of love and jealousy, the prevalence of vanity, his constant disappointment with society. It was, in other words, by failing to become "what a writer is," to realize his inner "writerly essence" – as if that role must be some transcendentally important or even a definite, substantial role – that Marcel realizes that such a becoming is important

[42]  There are several hilarious send-ups of the members of the Verdurin salon on this score and of the "High Art" religion of Charlus and his crowd. See *The Captive*, vol. III, 250ff. Moreover, the narrator has set out these examples with some design in view. Elstir, the painter, is sometimes described as "stopping" time by painting moments of it; Vinteuil as composing a purely temporal art, leading to the suggestion that Bergotte and the novel form represents some possible synthesis.

[43]  In Beckett's apt phrase, "from the victory over Time he passes to the victory of Time, from the negation of Death to its affirmation" (1931, 51). See also 61ff. for Beckett's discussion of Proust's "romanticism."

by *not* being secured by the transcendent, *by* being wholly temporal and finite, always and everywhere in suspense, and yet nonetheless capable of some illumination. (Marcel thus accepts the idea that his own book "will never be completed.") This realization is expressed a number of ways:

> How much more worth living did it appear to me now, now that I seemed to see that this life that we live in half-darkness can be illumined, this life that at every moment we distort can be restored to its true, pristine shape, that a life, in short can be realized within the confines of a book. (III, 1088)

And when talking about the readers of his book and pointing us away from the notion of the book's "content":

> For it seemed to me that they would not be "my" readers but the readers of their own selves, my book being a sort of magnifying glass like those which the optician at Combray used to offer his customers – it would be my book, but with its help I would furnish them with the means of reading what lay inside of themselves. (III, 1089)

At another point, the emphasis on the instability and temporariness of any such putative inner "self" we might become is not invoked as a reason to despair:

> For I realized that dying was not something new, but on the contrary, since my childhood, I had died many times. . . . These successive deaths, so feared by the self which they were destined to annihilate, so painless, so unimportant once they were accomplished and the self that feared them was no longer there to feel them, had taught me by now that it would be the merest folly to be frightened of death. (III, 1094–5)[44]

And Marcel goes on here to contemplate with the same equanimity the death of his book itself ("Eternal duration is promised no more to men's works than to men" (III, 1101)).

But how can the "illumination" of these successive deaths and even successive selves, this acknowledgment of contingent temporality as sweeping as that very soon thereafter embraced so famously by Heidegger, serve as some sort of answer to the question of "how one becomes who one is"?

---

[44] This is the theme that begins very early, as in this passage from *Swann's Way*:

> And so it was from the Guermantes way that I learned to distinguish between these states which reign alternately within me, during certain periods, going so far as to divide each day between them, the one returning to dispossess the other with the regularity of a fever; contiguous, and yet so foreign to one another, so devoid of means of communication, that I can no longer understand, or even picture to myself, in one state what I have desired or dreaded or accomplished in another. (I, 200)

It seems to be saying, when all is said and done, that you will be several (contested, provisional) "selves" in your life and that most of these will not care very much about the past others and the ones to come, and the best thing to be said about all that is that at least you will be well prepared for your actual death.

Proust's treatment here is quite deliberately indirect, and his response to this question involves an even further shift away from thinking of one's self-identity as a kind of content revealed in a redemptive moment. This is to be expected, of course. The emphasis we have seen on breathtaking temporal transformations (that of Marcel's friend Saint-Loup being, for Marcel, one of the most painful, since it involves the death of a friend; the "death" of his love for Albertine is another), the effects of habit on daily perception and understanding, and the overdetermination of possible meaning in the words and gestures of other people are all just as relevant to self-understanding as the understanding of anything in society. If Marcel has become who he is, and this somehow continuous with and a product of the experience of his own past, it is unlikely that we will be able to understand that by appeal to a substantial or underlying self, now discovered, or even by appeal to successor substantial selves, each one linked to the future and past by some sort of self-regard.

If the details of the novel suggest that becoming an individual is a kind of achievement, one that involves an implicit, not formalizable or thematizable capacity to negotiate the social world in a way true to the inevitable dependencies and relative independence required, is there a right or better way to embody this, and a wrong or worse way? If one never becomes who one is but is always, inevitably becoming and revising a practical identity in exercising this capacity, if one is always in a kind of suspense about who one will turn out, yet again provisionally, to be, what is the *proper* acknowledgment of this state of affairs?

Even the right formulation of the question suggests an important, required acknowledgment. It reveals that it is a matter of some significant Proustean irony that "Proustianism" or "Proustian idealism" is supposed to consist in a solipsism beyond the merely methodological or even epistemological; that it reaches metaphysical dimensions. Yet the questions that dominate the interior monologue of the narrator and Marcel – What do I really believe? What do I really want? – are revealed never to be asking, cannot be asking, "Do I *have* such a determinate belief? Do I *have* such a determinate desire?" Marcel constantly *surprises himself* by what he *turns out* to desire, and so in some sense learns (or at least we learn) that the content of the desires ascribable to him is manifest only in deeds, demurrals, social interactions, and actual struggles, "out there." And even "there," where it is manifest, it is not ever wholly or fully manifest. What is manifest is a subject of contestation, possible retraction; provisional yet again. That is why the book is a novel, not a lyric poem, and the "unfinished" character of this provisionality tells us something of why it is not a work of philosophy. (The logic of the claim Proust is implicitly making is important to stress. It is not that Marcel is simply self-deceived (although he often is), not that his true practical identity, the true commitments have already been made and lie somewhere hidden. Again: He becomes who he is only when he acts in some way, and even then what he intended to do and what he did are both subjects for much uncertain retrospective contestation.)

A different "answer" of sorts is suggested by a long passage about a musical concert in *The Captive*. What we are presented with is a different way of thinking about who one is, one that, oddly, undermines any way of thinking of such an achievement as a possible intentional goal that can finally be reached and that shifts our attention from center to periphery in the "search for self." The concert occurs in one of the funniest and yet pathos-filled party scenes, the one organized by Charlus for his lover, the violinist Morel, at the home of Mme. de Verdurin. The party is a social catastrophe, as Charlus's posh friends treat the Verdurins like the butler and maid and titter openly about their social pretensions, thus ruining forever Charlus's relations with the Verdurins and so his relation with Morel. But at this party, Marcel hears a new piece of music, a "septet"[45] by Vinteuil, a composer who, along with an earlier piano sonata, has figured intermittently and importantly in the novel since *Swann's Way*. The sonata serves as a figure for the Swann-Odette story and perhaps as well for what that story could have meant to us "then," all to be contrasted with the now much more complex "septet," figuring as it does the culmination of our experience of love in the novel. (It is important, too, that the septet was written by Vinteuil in a kind of code or shorthand and required translation, especially since Marcel has already referred to the writer's task as translation. Whatever the meaning of Vintueil's notes, the record of temporal movement, they will require as much interpretive or

---

[45] This is the standard translation of "septuor," but it is a bit misleading. I quote Joshua Landy's note on the subject, from his forthcoming *Proust, Philosophy and Fiction*: "In Proust, the term 'septuor' does not appear to mean a piece for seven players – a septet – but rather a piece whose primary theme has seven notes. Thus Vinteuil's masterwork can be a 'septuor,' even though it is a 'pièce pour dix instruments,' because it is 'a song on seven notes'" (note 93, from the Introduction).

decoding work as is demanded of the reader of *Remembrance*.) Marcel's reflections on the differences between that earlier, "prettier" piece and this more complex, almost discordant, but much more "profound" work provide a context for an indirect reflection on his own history and his relation to art and identity. (It can even be read as an indirect manifesto for modernism in the arts, the aesthetic analogue to the social suspension of the self's stability.) The earlier works of Vinteuil are called "timid essays, exquisite but very slight, besides the triumphant and consummate masterpiece now being revealed to me" (III, 253). This seems to be a reference to his own little pieces, his small essay for *Figaro*. He continues to use the language of youth and innocence to describe that sonata ("lily-white," III, 256), and the language of a dawning maturity to describe the septet, but he also begins to realize that the two pieces are profoundly linked, and his reflections on how they are linked seem like reflections on the question Marcel has always asked himself, "Who am I?" While the earlier sonata is "so calm and shy, almost detached and somehow philosophical," and the later septet "so restless, urgent, imploring," they, Marcel realizes,

were nevertheless the same prayer, bursting forth like different inner sunrises, and merely refracted through the different mediums of other thoughts, or artistic researches carried on through the years in which he had sought to create something new. (III, 257)

Although the works are so different, Marcel realizes that they teach him that "in spite of the conclusions to which science seemed to point, *the individual did exist*" (ibid., my emphasis) and that that individual exists as a kind of "*accent*" throughout so much temporal change. (It is thus important that the image is musical, where such an accent is not exactly an inflection *on* content. Since there is no independent content in music, it, the accent, *is* the "content," the music, and by its existence serves as "a proof of the irreducibly individual existence of the soul" (III, 258).) All artists are thus like travelers from an unknown land that they have forgotten, but which stamp their talk and manner nonetheless, to which fatherland they remain all our lives "unconsciously attuned," able thus to express "who they are" only as an "ineffable something" more than the substantial content of their roles and practices and ideals.[46]

As noted before, I have adopted the largely psychological language invoked by Marcel to describe this notion of transformation. But Proust's

---

[46] Cf. a similar image in Nietzsche's *The Gay Science*: "One thing is needful – To 'give style' to one's character" (1974, §290), and see the discussion in Nehamas 1985, 170–99.

novel is not only or not even primarily a *Bildungsroman*. These figurative references to art and artists are not casual and already intimate a view of modernism in the arts that underlies "what has happened" to Marcel and to the condition of art. For Marcel, despite his own memorializing, nostalgic hope for the pure return of the past, has in effect implicitly had to give up the notion of some sort of internal teleology in his life, and therewith the notion of having *arrived* somewhere, either at the essence of (finally autonomous, formally self-reflexive) art or at the dissolution of the art/nonart distinction, the inauguration of art as mere play. To use more contemporary language, writing, as manifested in the theme of the text, is not pure text, nor an endless constitutive writing about writing, nor the overcoming of writing through pure insight, rescued from time. All such resolutions are moments of rather grand "arrival," and it is understandably what part of Marcel still devoutly wants, as he faces the end of his own time, his death. What it is to have given up the notion of *arrival* but yet still to *be* somewhere and someone is what is being hinted at with such notions as tone and accent.[47]

We as readers have thus also come to the strange "place and time" to which Marcel has come; we understand who he is, but not by knowing anything substantial directly about him; we have not "arrived" at "the end," in any eschatological sense of finality. We and Marcel are simply close to his end, his and the characters' death. We know what we do know by having become "attuned," after three thousand pages and months and months of reading, to this "accent," the musical image for his *distinct* capacity, his "attunement." And this result has a number of implications. It suggests that "one's true self" is not a thing one can pursue directly, that it is much more something like "the bloom of health in a youth." Trying to find "it" almost ensures that it will be artificial. (And many of the other grand themes have this quality: You cannot really seek love or

---

[47] This all also means that the romantic idea of "creating" yourself, writing yourself into existence, and so forth must be invoked very carefully in this context. Such a question always raises the issue of what it would be to create successfully in this way or not, what it would be to fail. As the novel in effect "teaches," such a normative dimension requires that we consider the role of others in any such self-constitution and the much more difficult problem of self-location in time. The "finality" of the realization that Marcel seems to undergo at the end thus has two dimensions: the alleged or hoped-for finality of the retrieved "essence" of lost time, truly what it was to have been so and so or to have experienced such and such, and the temporal finality, nonrepeatability, the absence of much possible future re-experiencing in a different context, at a different time, simply for Marcel and these subjects. They are facing death, in other words, a much different sort of finality. And, as Heidegger would put it, death is not an arrival, and is final only in the latter sense.

certainly cannot seek to be "in love"; you cannot achieve social prestige by trying to achieve such prestige. Even Mme. de Verdurin has to fake her aesthetic swoons of appreciation. You cannot write by imitating the essence of writing. In all such cases, including this practical identity, these are things that one cannot achieve alone; they reflect quite a complicated social and temporal dependence.)

This would mean, too, that any expression of putative self-knowledge is always something provisional and hypothetical, a matter of dispositions with uncertain realizations and commitments of uncertain strengths. (This position again bears comparison with Sartre's early position in *The Transcendence of the Ego*, with his claim that one's "self" is so linked to action and possible action that it can be said to be "out there," as much "in the world" as anything else.)[48] More important, lest this sound like the familiar kind of aestheticism ascribed to Proust, accents also exist *in being heard* in contrastive contexts and interpreted for what they show about origin; they have their own social dimension as well and, in the same sense noted throughout, can never "settle" anything. Our own difficulty in settling on what we really believe, are committed to, is thus as much a problem as the reader's difficulty in identifying "which" Marcel is speaking, from which stage of development, in which relation to the absent Proust. And that is paradigmatic for the problem itself in the novel. (To know anything about anyone is not to have propositional knowledge about an object but to be able to inhabit, to become the point of view of such a person; more simply, to be able to imagine what they would do. In a deeply paradoxical way, Proust is suggesting, this is just as true of self-knowledge. It is the task of "becoming who one is.") Indeed, finally, our narrator goes very far to make his point, so far as to say that it is *only* in art (or in the aesthetic dimensions of our own lives) that this "ineffable something . . . which we call individuals" can be known:

A pair of wings, a different respiratory system, which enabled us to travel through space, would in no way help us, for if we visited Mars or Venus while keeping the same senses, they would clothe everything that we saw in the same aspect as the things of Earth. The only true voyage of discovery, the only really rejuvenating experience, would be not to visit strange lands, but to possess other eyes, to see the universe through the eyes of another, of a hundred others, to see the hundred universes that each of them sees, that each of them is; and this we can do with an Elstir, with a Vinteuil; with men like these we really do fly from star to star. (III, 260)

---

[48] Sartre 1989.

# Bibliography

## Abbreviations

### *Adorno*

DE: *Dialectic of Enlightenment* (Max Horkheimer, co-author), trans. John Cumming. New York: Seabury, 1972.

EF: "Der Essay als Form." In *Gesammelte Schriften* (GS), Bd. 11. Frankfurt a.M.: 1997. English translation: "The Essay as Form." In *Notes to Literature*, vol. 1, trans. S. Nicholsen, ed. R. Tiedemann. New York: Columbia University Press, 1992, pp. 3–23.

MM: *Minima moralia.* GS, Bd. 4. English translation: *Minima moralia*, trans. E. Jephcott. London: Verso, 1974.

ND: *Negative Dialektik.* GS, Bd. 6. English translation: *Negative Dialectics*, trans. E. Ashton. New York: Continuum, 1973.

PT: *Philosophische Terminologie*, Bd. 1. Frankfurt a.M.: 1973.

### *Arendt*

EJ: *Eichmann in Jerusalem: A Report on the Banality of Evil*, rev. ed. New York: Viking, 1964.

OT: *The Origins of Totalitarianism.* New York: Harcourt Brace Jovanovich, 1973.

PRD: "Personal Responsibility under Dictatorship." *The Listener* 72 (August 6, 1964).

R: "A Reply." *Review of Politics* 15 (January 1953).

### *Fichte*

F: *Foundations of Transcendental Philosophy (Wissenschaftslehre nova methodo (1796/99))*, trans. and ed. Daniel Breazeale. Ithaca: Cornell University Press, 1992.

GA: *Gesamtausgabe der Bayerischen Akademie der Wissenschaften,* ed. Reinhard Lauth and Hans Jacob. Stuttgart: Frommann-Holboog, 1965.
WL: *Wissenschaftslehre nach den Vorlesungen von Hr.Pr. Fichte.* In GA, Bd. IV.


## Frank

KH: *Kaltes Herz, unendliche Fahrt, neue Mythologie: Motiv-Untersuchungen zur Pathogenese der Moderne.* Frankfurt a.M.: Suhrkamp, 1989.
SVL: "The Subject v. Language: Mental Familiarity and Epistemic Self-Ascription," trans. Lawrence K. Schmidt and Barry Allen. *Common Knowledge* (October 1995): 30–50.
TC: "Two Centuries of Philosophical Critique of Reason." In Freundlieb and Hudson 1993, 72–93.
WIN: *Was ist Neostrukturalismus?* Frankfurt a.M.: Suhrkamp, 1983. English translation: *What Is Neostructuralism?* trans. Sabine Wilke and Richard Gray. Minneapolis: University of Minnesota Press, 1989.


## Gadamer

HD: *Hegel's Dialectic: Five Hermeneutical Studies,* trans. P. Christopher Smith. New Haven: Yale University Press, 1976.
PG: *The Philosophy of Hans-Georg Gadamer,* ed. Lewis Edwin Hahn. Chicago and LaSalle: Open Court, 1997.
SHR: "The Scope of Hermeneutical Reflection." In *Philosophical Hermeneutics,* trans. and ed. David E. Linge. Berkeley and Los Angeles: University of California Press, 1976, pp. 18–43.
TM: *Truth and Method,* 2nd ed., trans. and rev. Joel Weinsheimer and Donald G. Marshall. New York: Crossroad, 1989.
WM: *Wahrheit und Methode,* 3rd ed. Tübingen: Mohr, 1972.


## Hegel

A: *Aesthetics: Lectures on Fine Arts,* 2 vols., trans. T. M. Knox. Oxford: Clarendon, 1975.
BK: *Belief and Knowledge,* trans. W. Cerf and H. Harris. Albany: SUNY Press, 1977.
D: *Differenz des Fichte'schen und Schelling'schen Systems der Philosophie.* In GWe, Bd. IV. English translation: *The Difference between Fichte's and Schelling's System of Philosophy,* trans. H. Harris and W. Cerf. Albany: SUNY Press, 1977.
EL: *Hegel's Logic, Being Part One of the Encyclopedia of the Philosophical Sciences (1830),* trans. William Wallace. Oxford: Clarendon, 1982.
EnL: *Enzyklopädie der philosophischen Wissenschaften, Ertser Teil, Die Wissenschaft der Logik.* In W, Bd. 8.
GW: *Glauben und Wissen.* In GWe, Bd. IV.
GWe: *Gesammelte Werke,* ed. Rheinisch-Westfaelischen Akademie der Wissenschaften. Hamburg: Felix Meiner, 1968– .
PH: *The Philosophy of History,* trans. J. Sibree. New York: Dover, 1956.

PhG: *Die Phänomenologie des Geistes*, Bd. II: *Hauptwerke in sechs Bänden.* Hamburg: Felix Meiner Verlag, 1999.

PhR: *Elements of the Philosophy of Right*, ed. A. Wood, trans. H. B. Nisbet. Cambridge: Cambridge University Press, 1991.

PhS: *The Phenomenology of Spirit*, trans. A. V. Miller. Oxford: Oxford University Press, 1998.

PR: *Grundlinien der Philosophie des Rechts.* In W, vol. 7.

SL: *Hegel's Science of Logic*, trans. A. V. Miller. London: George Allen & Unwin, 1969.

SS: *Hegel's Philosophy of Subjective Spirit*, trans. and ed. M. Petry. Dordrecht: Riedel, 1978.

V: *Vorlesung über Ästhetik (Berlin, 1820–1)*, ed. Helmut Schneider. Frankfurt a.M.: Peter Lang, 1995.

W: *Werke.* Frankfurt a.M.: Suhrkamp, 1996.

WL: *Wissenschaft der Logik.* Bds. I and II. Hamburg: Felix Meiner, 1969.


*Heidegger*

BT: *Being and Time*, trans. John Macquarrie and Edward Robinson. New York: Harper and Row, 1962.

GA: *Gesamtausgabe.* Frankfurt a.M.: Klostermann, 1975– .

IM: *Introduction to Metaphysics*, trans. Gregory Fried and Richard Polt. New Haven: Yale University Press, 2000.

N: *Nietzsche*, 2 vols. Pfullingen: Neske, 1961.

PS: *Plato's Sophist*, trans. Richard Rojcewicz and André Schuwer. Bloomington: Indiana University Press, 1997.

SZ: *Sein und Zeit.* Tübingen: Niemeyer, 1972.


*Kant*

AA: *Gesammelte Schriften.* Berlin: Preussische Akademie der Wissenschaften: 1910– .

A/B: *Kritik der reinen Vernunft.* In W, vols. 3 and 4. English translation: *Critique of Pure Reason*, trans. and ed. P. Guyer and A. Wood. Cambridge: Cambridge University Press, 1998.

GL: *Grundlegung zur Metaphysik der Sitten.* In AA, vol. 4, pp. 385–463. English translation: *Grounding of the Metaphysics of Morals*, trans. and ed. M. Gregor. Cambridge: Cambridge University Press, 1998.

I: *Idee zu einer Allgemeinen Geschichte in Weltbürgerlicher Absicht.* In AA, vol. 8, pp. 15–31. English translation: "Idea for a Universal History with a Cosmopolitan Intent." In *Perpetual Peace and Other Essays*, trans. T. Humphrey. Indianapolis: Hackett, 1983, pp. 29–40.

KU: *Kritik der Urteilskraft.* In W, vol. 10.

P: *Prolegomena zu einer jeden künftigen Metaphysik.* In AA, vol. 4, pp. 251–83. English translation: *Prolegomena to Any Future Metaphysics*, ed. L. W. Beck. Indianapolis: Bobbs-Merrill, 1950.

PC: *Philosophical Correspondence 1759–99*, ed. A. Zweig. Chicago: University of Chicago Press, 1967.

R: *Religion innerhalb der Grenzen der bloßen Vernunft.* In AA, vol. 6, pp. 1–202. English translation: *Religion within the Boundaries of Mere Reason,* trans. and ed. A. Wood and G. di Giovanni. Cambridge: Cambridge University Press, 1998.

W: *Werkausgabe,* ed. W. Weischedel. Frankfurt a.M.: 1968.

*McDowell*

C: "Comments on Hans-Peter Krüger's Paper." In *Philosophical Explanations* 2 (May 1998).

HWV: "Having the World in View: Sellars, Kant, and Intentionality." *Journal of Philosophy* 95, no. 9 (September 1998): 451–70.

LFI: "Lecture II: The Logical Form of an Intuition." *Journal of Philosophy* 95, no. 9 (September 1998): 451–70.

MW: *Mind and World.* Cambridge, Mass.: Harvard University Press, 1996.

P: *Perception. Philosophical Issues,* vol. 7, ed. Enrique Villanueva. Ridgeview: Atascadero, 1996.

PTE: "Projection and Truth in Ethics." In *Mind, Value, and Reality,* Cambridge, Mass.: Harvard University Press, 1998, pp. 151–66.

R: "Reply to Commentators." In *Philosophy and Phenomenological Research* 63, no. 2 (June 1998): 403–31.

RM: "Responses." In Smith 2002, 269–305.

TSN: "Two Sorts of Naturalism." In *Mind, Value, and Reality.* Cambridge, Mass.: Harvard University Press, 1998, pp. 167–97.

*Strauss*

CCM: "Correspondence Concerning Modernity," trans. Susanne Klein and George Tucker. *Independent Journal of Philosophy* 4 (1983): 105–19.

NRH: *Natural Right and History.* Chicago: University of Chicago Press, 1968.

OT: *On Tyranny,* ed. Victor Gourevitch and Michael S. Roth. New York: Free Press, 1991.

PAW: *Persecution and the Art of Writing.* Chicago: University of Chicago Press, 1980.

PL: *The Argument and the Action of Plato's Laws.* Chicago: University of Chicago Press, 1975.

PPH: "Political Philosophy and History." In WIPP, 56–77.

RCP: *The Rebirth of Classical Political Rationalism: An Introduction to the Thought of Leo Strauss,* ed. Thomas L. Pangle. Chicago: University of Chicago Press, 1989.

SCR: *Spinoza's Critique of Religion,* trans. E. M. Sinclair. Chicago: University of Chicago Press, 1997.

WIPP: *What Is Political Philosophy?* Chicago: University of Chicago Press, 1988.

Sources

Ameriks, K. 2003. "On Being Neither Post- nor Anti-Kantian: A Reply to Breazeale and Larmore Concerning *The Fate of Autonomy.*" *Inquiry* 46, no. 2: 272–92.

———. 2000a. *The Cambridge Companion to German Idealism.* Cambridge: Cambridge University Press.

2000b. "Introduction: Interpreting German Idealism." In Ameriks 2000a, 1–17.

2000c. *Kant and the Fate of Autonomy: Problems in the Appropriation of the Critical Philosophy*. Cambridge: Cambridge University Press.

2000d. *Kant's Theory of Mind: An Analysis of the Paralogisms of Pure Reason*, 2nd ed. Oxford: Oxford University Press.

2001a. "Pure Reason of Itself Alone Suffices to Determine the Will." In *Immanuel Kant: Kritik der praktischen Vernunft*, ed. O. Höffe. Berlin: Akademie Verlag, pp. 99–114.

2001b. "Zu Kants Argumentation am Anfang des Dritten Abschnitts der Grundlegung." In *Systematische Ethik mit Kant*, ed. Hans-Ulrich Baumgarten and Carsten Held. Freiburg: Alber, pp. 24–54.

Anderson-Gold, S. 1991. "God and Community: An Inquiry into the Religious Implications of the Highest Good." In *Kant's Philosophy of Religion Reconsidered*, ed. P. Rossi and M. Wreen. Bloomington: Indiana University Press, pp. 113–31.

Baum, M. 2000. "The Beginnings of Schelling's Philosophy of Nature." In Sedgwick 2000b, 199–215.

Beck, L. W. 1969. *Early German Philosophy: Kant and His Predecessors*. Cambridge: Belknap.

Beckett, S. 1931. *Proust*. New York: Grove.

Beier, C. 1977. *Zum Verhältnis von Gesellschaftstheorie und Erkenntnistheorie. Untersuchung zum Totalitätsbegriff in der kritischen Theorie Adornos*. Frankfurt a.M.: Suhrkamp.

Beiser, F. 1993. *The Fate of Reason: German Philosophy from Kant to Fichte*. Cambridge: Harvard University Press.

2002. *German Idealism: The Struggle against Subjectivism. 1781–1801*. Cambridge: Harvard University Press.

Belting, H. 1987. *The End of the History of Art?*, trans. Christopher S. Wood. Chicago: University of Chicago Press, 1987.

2001. "The Dream of Absolute Art." In *The Invisible Masterpiece*, trans. Helen Atkins. Chicago: University of Chicago Press, pp. 294–314.

Benjamin, W. 1974. "Zum Bilde Proust." In *Gesammelte Schriften*, Bd. II, 3, ed. R. Tiedemann and H. Schweppenhäuser. Frankfurt a.M: Suhrkamp, pp. 310–24.

1977. *Illuminations*. New York: Schocken.

Bennett, J. 1966. *Kant's Analytic*. Cambridge: Cambridge University Press.

Bernstein, J. 1992. *The Fate of Art: Aesthetic Alienation from Kant to Derrida*. University Park: Penn State University Press.

2001. *Adorno: Disenchantment and Ethics*. Cambridge: Cambridge University Press.

Bersani, L. 1965. *Marcel Proust: The Fictions of Life and Art*. New York: Oxford University Press.

Besançon, A. 2000. *The Forbidden Image: An Intellectual History of Iconoclasm*, trans. Jane Marie Todd. Chicago: University of Chicago Press.

Bird, G. 1996. "McDowell's Kant: Mind and World." *Philosophy* 71, no. 276: 219–43.

Bowie, A. 1990. *Aesthetics and Subjectivity from Kant to Nietzsche.* Manchester: Manchester University Press.

1996. "John McDowell's *Mind and World,* and Early Romantic Epistemology." *Revue Internationale de Philosophie* 3: 515–54.

1997. *From Romanticism to Critical Theory: The Philosophy of German Literary Theory.* New York: Routledge.

Brandom, R. 1994. *Making It Explicit: Reasoning, Representing and Discursive Commitment.* Cambridge: Harvard University Press.

1996. "Perception and Rational Constraint: McDowell's *Mind and World.*" In *Perception: Philosophical Issues,* vol. 7, ed. E. Villanueva. Ridgeview: Atascadero, pp. 241–60.

1998. "Perception and Rational Constraint." In *Philosophy and Phenomenological Research* 58, no. 2: 369–74.

2002. "Holism and Idealism in Hegel's *Phenomenology.*" In *Tales of the Mighty Dead: Historical Essays in the Metaphysics of Intentionality.* Cambridge: Harvard University Press, pp. 178–209.

Braun, C. 1983. *Kritische Theorie versus Kritizismus. Zur Kant-Kritik Theodor W. Adornos.* Berlin: de Gruyter.

Brody, H. 1992. *The Healer's Power.* New Haven: Yale University Press.

Bubner, R. 1983. "Adorno's Negative Dialektik." In Friedberg and Habermas 1983, 35–40.

Buchanan, A., and D. Brock. 1989. *Deciding for Others: The Ethics of Surrogate Decision Making.* Cambridge: Cambridge University Press.

Buck-Morss, S. 1977. *The Origin of Negative Dialectics: Theodor W. Adorno, Walter Benjamin and the Frankfurt Institute.* Hassocks, U.K.: Harvester.

Canovan, M. 2000. "Arendt's Theory of Totalitarianism: A Reassessment." In *The Cambridge Companion to Hannah Arendt,* ed. Dana Villa. New York: Cambridge University Press, pp. 25–43.

Carey, J. 2002. *The Intellectuals and the Masses: Pride and Prejudice among the Literary Intelligentsia, 1880–1939.* Chicago: Academy.

Carmen, T. 2003. *Heidegger's Analytic: Interpretation, Discourse and Authenticity in Being and Time.* Cambridge: Cambridge University Press.

Carnap, R. 1959. "The Elimination of Metaphysics through Logical Analysis of Language." In *Logical Positivism,* ed. A. J. Ayer. New York: Free Press, pp. 60–81.

Cassirer, E. 1951. *The Philosophy of the Enlightenment.* Princeton: Princeton University Press.

Cavell, S. 1979. *The Claim of Reason.* Oxford: Oxford University Press.

1969. *Must We Mean What We Say?* New York: Scribner.

Cheetham, M. 1991. *The Rhetoric of Purity: Essentialist Theory and the Advent of Abstract Painting.* Cambridge: Cambridge University Press.

Clark, T. 1999. *Farewell to an Idea: Episodes from a History of Modernism.* New Haven: Yale University Press.

Coetzee, J. 2000. *Disgrace.* New York: Penguin.

2001. "Samuel Richardson, *Clarissa.*" In *Stranger Shores.* New York: Viking, pp. 23–33.

Corcoran, Paul. E. 1977. "The Bourgeois and Other Villains." *Journal of the History of Ideas* 38, no. 3 (July–September): 477–85.

Crowell, S. 1991. "Lask, Heidegger, and the Homelessness of Logic." *Journal of the British Society for Phenomenology* 23, no. 3: 222–39.

Dahlstrom, D. 1991. "Heidegger's Kantian Turn: Notes to His Commentary of the *Kritik der reinen Vernunft.*" *Review of Metaphysics* 45: 329–61.

2001. *Heidegger's Concept of Truth.* Cambridge: Cambridge University Press.

Danto, A. 1981. *The Transfiguration of the Commonplace.* Cambridge: Harvard University Press.

1986. *The Philosophical Disenfranchisement of Art.* New York: Columbia University Press.

1997. *After the End of Art: Contemporary Art and the Pale of History.* Princeton: Princeton University Press.

Descombes, V. 1992. *Proust: Philosophy of the Novel,* trans. C. Macksey. Stanford: Stanford University Press.

Dottori, R. 1984. *Die Reflexion der Wahrheit: Zwischen Hegels absoluter Dialektik und der Philosophie der Endlichkeit von M. Heidegger und H. G. Gadamer.* Heidelberg: Carl Winter.

Dreyfuss, H. 1992. *Being-in-the-World: A Commentary on Heidegger's* Being and Time, Division One. Cambridge: MIT Press.

Earle, B. Forthcoming. "Proust and the Object of Literature."

Ehrenreich, B., and J. Ehrenreich. 1971. *The American Health Empire: Power, Profits and Politics.* New York: Vintage.

Elias, N. 1996. *The Germans: Power Struggles and the Development of Habitus in the Nineteenth and Twentieth Centuries,* ed. Michael Schroeder, trans. Eric Dunning and Stephen Mennell. New York: Columbia University Press.

Engelhardt, H. 1991. *Bioethics and Secular Humanism: The Search for a Common Morality.* Philadelphia: Trinity Press International.

Faden, R., and T. Beauchamp. 1986. *A History and Theory of Informed Consent.* Oxford: Oxford University Press.

Ferry, L. 1993. *Homo Aestheticus: The Invention of Taste in the Democratic Age,* trans. R. de Loaiza. Chicago: University of Chicago Press.

Finkelstein, D. 2003. *Expression and the Inner.* Cambridge: Harvard University Press.

Flathman, R. 1980. *The Practice of Political Authority.* Chicago: University of Chicago Press.

Føllesdall, D. 1979. "Husserl and Heidegger on the Role of Actions in the Constitution of the World." In *Essays in Honor of Jaakko Hintikka,* ed. E. Saarinen, R. Hilpinen, I. Niiniluoto, and M. P. Hintikka. Dordrecht: Riedel.

Förster, E. 2000. *Kant's Final Synthesis: An Essay on the Opus Postummum.* Cambridge: Harvard University Press, 2000.

Foucault, M. 1975. *The Birth of the Clinic. An Archaeology of Medical Perception,* trans. A. M. Sheridan Smith. New York: Vintage.

1995. *Discipline and Punish,* trans. A. Sheridan. New York: Vintage.

Frank, M. 1997. *Unendliche Annäherung: Die Anfänge der philosophischen Frühromantik.* Frankfurt a.M.: Suhrkamp.

Franks, P. 2000. "All or Nothing: Systematicity and Nihilism in Jacobi, Reinhold, and Maimon." In Ameriks 2000b, 95–116.

Frege, G. 1960. *Translations from the Philosophical Writings of Gottlob Frege*, ed. Peter Geach and Max Black. Oxford: Blackwell.

1979. *Posthumous Writings*, ed. H. Hermes, F. Kambartel, and F. Kaulbach, with the assistance of G. Gabriel and W. Rödding; trans. P. Long and R. White, with the assistance of R. Hargreaves. Vol. 1. Chicago: University of Chicago Press.

Freundlieb, D., and W. Hudson, eds. 1993. *Reason and Its Other*. Oxford: Berg.

Fried, G. 2000. *Heidegger's Polemos: From Being to Politics*. New Haven: Yale University Press.

Fried, M. 1998. "Art and Objecthood." In *Art and Objecthood: Essays and Reviews*. Chicago: University of Chicago Press, pp. 148–72.

Friedberg, L. von, and J. Habermas, ed. 1983. *Adorno-Konferenz, 1983*. Frankfurt a.M.: Suhrkamp.

Friedman, M. 2000. *A Parting of the Ways: Carnap, Cassirer, and Heidegger*. Chicago and LaSalle: Open Court.

2002. "Exorcising the Philosophical Tradition." In Smith 2002, 25–57.

Fuchs, V. 1974. *Who Shall Live? Health, Economics and Social Choice*. New York: Basic Books.

Furet, F. 1999. *The Passing of an Illusion*, trans. Deborah Furet. Chicago: University of Chicago Press.

Genette, G. 1980. *Narrative Discourse: An Essay in Method*, trans. Jane E. Lewin. Ithaca: Cornell University Press.

Goldman, A. 1980. *The Moral Foundations of Professional Ethics*. Totowa, N.J.: Rowman & Littlefield.

Greenberg, C. 1993. *The Collected Essays and Criticism: Modernism with a Vengeance, 1957–1969*, ed. John O'Brian. Chicago: University of Chicago Press, 1993.

Grier, M. 2001. *Kant's Doctrine of Transcendental Illusion*. Cambridge: Cambridge University Press.

Guzzoni, U. 1981. *Identität oder Nicht: Zur kritischen Theorie der Ontologie*. Freiburg: Alber.

Habermas, J. 1971. *Hermeneutik und Ideologiekritik*. Frankfurt a.M.: Suhrkamp.

1987. *The Philosophical Discourse of Modernity*, trans. Frederick Lawrence. Cambridge, Mass.: MIT Press.

Hamilton, R. 1982. *Who Voted for Hitler?* Princeton: Princeton University Press.

Haugeland, J. 1992. "Dasein's Disclosedness." In *Heidegger: A Critical Reader*, ed. H. Dreyfuss and H. Hall. Oxford: Blackwell, pp. 27–44.

2000. "Truth and Finitude: Heidegger's Transcendental Existentialism." In *Heidegger, Authenticity and Modernity, Essays in Honor of Hubert Dreyfuss*, vol. 1, ed. Mark Wrathall and Jeff Malpas. Cambridge, Mass.: MIT Press, pp. 43–78.

Henrich, D. 1966. "Kunst und Kunst Philosophie der Gegenwart." In *Poetik und Hermeneutik* 2: 11–33 and 524–31.

1979. "Art and Philosophy of Art Today: Reflections with Reference to Hegel." In *New Perspectives in German Literary Criticism*, ed. R. Amacher and

V. Lange, trans. D. Wilson et al. Princeton: Princeton University Press, pp. 107–33.

1982. *Selbstverhältnisse.* Stuttgart: Klett-Cotta.

1991. "Der Weg des spekulativen Idealismus." In *Konstellationen: Probleme und Debatten am Ursprung der idealistischen Philosophie (1789–1795).* Stuttgart: Klett-Cotta.

1994a. "The Concept of Moral Insight and Kant's Doctrine of the Fact of Reason," trans. Manfred Kuehn. In *The Unity of Reason.* Cambridge: Harvard University Press, pp. 55–88.

1994b. "Ethics of Autonomy," trans. Louis Hunt. In *The Unity of Reason.* Cambridge: Harvard University Press, pp. 89–122.

1997. *The Course of Remembrance and Other Essays on Hölderlin,* ed. E. Förster. Stanford: Stanford University Press.

2001. *Versuch über Kunst und Leben.* Munich: Karl Hanser Verlag.

Herf, J. 1984. *Reactionary Modernism.* Cambridge: Cambridge University Press.

Hickey, D. 1993. *The Invisible Dragon: Four Essays on Beauty.* Los Angeles: Art Issues.

Hollis, M. 1998. *Trust within Reason.* Cambridge: Cambridge University Press.

Honneth, A. 1979. "Communication and Reconciliation: Habermas's Critique of Adorno." *Telos,* no. 39: 45–61.

1991. *The Critique of Power: Reflective Stages in a Critical Theory of Society,* trans. Kenneth Naynes. Cambridge, Mass.: MIT Press.

2000. *Suffering from Indeterminacy: An Attempt at a Reactivation of Hegel's Philosophy of Right.* Introduction by Beatte Rössler, trans. Jack Ben-Levi. Assen: Van Gorcum.

2002. "Between Hermeneutics and Hegelianism: John McDowell and the Challenge of Moral Realism." In *Reading McDowell: On Mind and World,* ed. Nicholas H. Smith. New York: Routledge, pp. 246–65.

Horstmann, R. 1991. *Die Grenzen der Vernunft: Eine Untersuchung zu Zielen und Motiven des Deutschen Idealismus.* Frankfurt a.M.: Anton Hain.

Houlgate, S. 1997. "Hegel and the 'End' of Art." In *Owl of Minerva* 29, no. 1: 1–19.

2000. "Hegel and the Art of Painting." In *Hegel and Aesthetics,* ed. W. Maker. Albany: SUNY Press, pp. 61–82.

Illich, I. 1976. *Medical Nemesis: The Expropriation of Health.* New York: Pantheon.

Jacobi, F. H. 1968. *David Hume über den Glauben, oder Idealismus und Realismus. Über den transzendentalen Idealismus.* In *Werke,* Bd. 2, ed. Friedrich Köppen. Darmstadt: Wissenschaftliche Buchgesellschaft.

Kateb, G. 1983. *Hannah Arendt: Politics, Conscience, Evil.* Totowa, N.J.: Rowman & Allanheld.

Kisiel, T. 1995. *The Genesis of Heidegger's* Being and Time. Berkeley: University of California Press.

Korsgaard, C. 1993. "The Reasons We Can Share: An Attack on the Distinction between Agent-Relative and Agent-Neutral Reasons." In *Altruism,* ed. E. F. Paul, F. D. Miller, and J. Paul. Cambridge: Cambridge University Press, pp. 24–51.

1996a. *Creating the Kingdom of Ends.* Cambridge: Cambridge University Press.

1996b. *The Sources of Normativity.* Cambridge: Cambridge University Press.

Kuehn, M. 1987. *Scottish Common Sense in Germany, 1768–1800: A Contribution to the History of Critical Philosophy.* Kingston and Montreal: McGill-Queen's University Press.

Landy, J. 2001a. "Les Moi en Moi: The Proustian Self in Philosophical Perspective." *New Literary History* 32, no. 1: 91–132.

2001b. "The Texture of Proust's Novel." In *The Cambridge Companion to Proust,* ed. Richard Bales. Cambridge: Cambridge University Press, pp. 117–34.

Forthcoming. *Proust, Philosophy and Fiction.* Oxford: Oxford University Press.

Lear, J. 1998. "Transcendental Anthropology." In *Open-Minded: Working Out the Logic of the Soul.* Cambridge, Mass.: Harvard University Press, pp. 247–81.

Locke, J. 1967. *An Essay Concerning Human Understanding,* ed. A. S. Pringle-Pattison. Oxford: Clarendon.

Lukes, S. 1978. "Power and Authority." In *A History of Sociological Analysis,* ed. R. Nisbet and T. Bottomore. New York: Basic, pp. 633–76.

MacIntyre, A. 1981. *After Virtue.* Notre Dame: University of Notre Dame Press.

Maimon, S. 1965. *Versuch über die Transzendentalen Philosophie.* In *Werke,* Bd. II, ed. V. Verra. Hildesheim: G. Olms.

May, W. 1983. *The Physician's Covenant: Images of the Healer in Medical Ethics.* Philadelphia: Westminster.

Mayer, A. 1975. "The Lower Middle Class as Historical Problem." *Journal of Modern History* 47, no. 3 (September): 409–36.

Meier, H. 1996. *Die Denkbewegung von Leo Strauss.* Stuttgart: Metzler.

Menand, L. 2001. *The Metaphysical Club: A Story of Ideas in America.* New York: Farrar, Straus and Giroux.

Michelson, A. 1982. "De Stijl, Its Other Face: Abstraction and Cacaphony, or What Was the Matter with Hegel?" *October* 22: 3–26.

Moran, R. 2001. *Authority and Estrangement: An Essay on Self-Knowledge.* Princeton: Princeton University Press.

Muller, M. 1965. *Les voix narratives dans À la recherche du temps perdu.* Geneva: Dorz.

Nehamas, A. 1985. *Nietzsche: Life as Literature.* Cambridge, Mass.: Harvard University Press.

Neiman, S. 2002. *Evil in Modern Thought.* Princeton: Princeton University Press.

Nietzsche, F. 1969. *On the Genealogy of Morals,* trans. Walter Kaufmann. New York: Vintage.

1974. *The Gay Science,* trans. W. Kaufmann. New York: Vintage.

1982. *Daybreak,* trans. R. J. Hollingdale. Cambridge: Cambridge University Press.

1988. *Morgenröte.* In *Kritische Studienausgabe,* Bd. 3, ed. G. Colli and M. Montinari. Berlin: de Gruyter, 1988.

Nussbaum, M. 1995. *Poetic Justice: The Literary Imagination and Public Life.* Boston: Beacon.

Paton, H. J. 1951. *Kant's Metaphysics of Experience: A Commentary on the First Half of the* Kritik der reinen Vernunft. London: George Allen & Unwin.

Pellegrino, E., and D. Thomasma. 1993. *The Virtues in Medical Practice.* Oxford: Oxford University Press.

Pernoud, R. 1960. *Histoire de la bourgeoisie en France.* Paris: Éditions du Seuil.

Pindar 1997. *Olympian Odes, Pythian Odes,* ed. and trans. W. Race. Cambridge, Mass.: Harvard University Press.

Pinkard, T. 2002. *German Philosophy, 1760–1860: The Legacy of Idealism.* Cambridge: Cambridge University Press.

Pippin, R. 1979a. "Negation and Not-Being in Wittgenstein's *Tractatus* and Plato's *Sophist.*" *Kant-Studien* 70, no. 2: 179–96.

1979b. "The Rose and the Owl: Some Remarks on the Theory-Practice Problem in Hegel." *Independent Journal of Philosophy* 3: 7–16.

1982. *Kant's Theory of Form: An Essay on the Critique of Pure Reason.* New Haven: Yale University Press.

1989. *Hegel's Idealism: The Satisfactions of Self-Consciousness.* Cambridge: Cambridge University Press.

1993. "'You Can't Get There from Here': Transition Problems in Hegel's *Phenomenology of Spirit.*" In *The Cambridge Companion to Hegel,* ed. Fred Beiser. Cambridge: Cambridge University Press.

1997a. "Avoiding German Idealism: Kant, Hegel, and the Reflective Judgment Problem." In Pippin 1997e, 129–53.

1997b. "Hegel, Freedom, The Will: *The Philosophy of Right,* #1–33." In *Hegel: Grundlinien der Philosophie des Rechts,* ed. L. Siep. Berlin: Akademie Verlag, pp. 31–53.

1997c. "Hegel, Modernity, and Habermas." In Pippin 1997e, 157–84.

1997d. "Hegel's Ethical Rationalism." In Pippin 1997e, 417–50.

1997e. *Idealism as Modernism: Hegelian Variations.* Cambridge: Cambridge University Press.

1997f. "Kant on the Spontaneity of Mind." In Pippin 1997e, 29–55.

1997g. "The Modern World of Leo Strauss." In Pippin 1997e, 209–32.

1997h. "On Being Anti-Cartesian: Hegel, Heidegger, Subjectivity and Sociality." In Pippin 1997e, 375–94.

1999a. *Modernism as a Philosophical Problem: On the Dissatisfactions of European High Culture,* 2nd ed. Oxford: Blackwell.

1999b. "Naturalness and Mindedness: Hegel's Compatibilism." *European Journal of Philosophy* 7, no. 2: 194–212.

2000a. "Fichte's Alleged One-Sided, Subjective, Psychological Idealism." In *The Reception of Kant's Critical Philosophy: Fichte, Schelling and Hegel,* ed. S. Sedgwick. Cambridge: Cambridge University Press, pp. 147–70.

2000b. "Hegel's Practical Philosophy: the Realization of Freedom." In Ameriks 2000b, 180–99.

2000c. *Henry James and Modern Moral Life.* Cambridge: Cambridge University Press.

2000d. "Kant's Theory of Value: On Allen Wood's *Kant's Ethical Thought.*" *Inquiry* 43 (Summer): 239–65.

2000e. "What Is the Question for Which Hegel's 'Theory of Recognition' Is the Answer?" *European Journal of Philosophy* 8, no. 2: 155–72.

2001a. "A Mandatory Reading of Kant's Ethics? Critical Study of Paul Guyer's *Kant on Freedom, Law and Happiness.*" *Philosophical Quarterly* 51, no. 204 (July): 386–93.

2001b. "Rigorism and 'the New Kant.'" In *Kant und die Berliner Aufklärung: Akten des IX. Internationalen Kant-Kongresses*, ed. V. Gerhardt, Rolf-Peter Horstmann, and Ralph Schumaker. New York: de Gruyter, Bd. 1, pp. 313–26.

2003a. "Die Begriffslogik als die Logik der Freiheit." In *Der Begriff als die Wahrheit: Zum Anspruch der Hegelschen Logik*, ed. Anton Koch, Alexander Overauer, and Konrad Utz. Paderborn/Munich: Ferdinand Schöningh, pp. 223–37.

2003b. "Über Selbstgesetzgebung." *Deutsche Zeitschrift für Philosophie* 6: 905–26.

2004. "Recognition and Reconciliation in Hegel's Phenomenology." In *Internationales Jahrbuch des Deutschen Idealismus/International Yearbook of German Idealism*, vol. 2, pp. 249–67.

Forthcoming a. *Hegel's Practical Philosophy: Rational Agency as Ethical Life*.

Forthcoming b. "Mine and Thine? The Kantian State." In the *Cambridge Companion to Kant*, 2nd ed., ed. Paul Guyer.

Forthcoming c. "On Giving Oneself the Law." To appear in a volume edited by Richard Velkley, Catholic University Press.

Forthcoming d. "The Kantian Aftermath: Reaction and Revolution in German Philosophy." In *Cambridge History of Nineteenth Century Philosophy*, ed. A. Wood.

Pirenne, H. 1939. *Les villes et les institutions urbaines*. Paris: Librairie Félix Alcan.

Posner, R. 1998. *Law and Literature*, 2nd ed. Cambridge, Mass.: Harvard University Press.

Prauss, G. 1971. *Erscheinung bei Kant. Ein Problem der Kritik der reinen Vernunft.* Berlin: de Gruyter.

Proust, M. 1982. *Remembrance of Things Past*, trans. C. Moncrieff and T. Kilmartin. 3 vols. New York: Vintage.

Redding, P. 1996. *Hegel's Hermeneutics.* Ithaca, N.Y.: Cornell University Press.

Rorty, R. 1970. "Strawson's Objectivity Argument." *Review of Metaphysics* 24: 207–44.

1971. "Verificationism and Transcendental Arguments." *Nous* 5: 3–14.

1979. *Philosophy and the Mirror of Nature*. Princeton: Princeton University Press.

1991. "Solidarity or Objectivity?" In *Objectivity, Relativism, and Truth*. Cambridge: Cambridge University Press, pp. 21–34.

1998. "The Very Idea of Human Answerability to the World: John McDowell's Version of Empiricism." In *Truth and Progress, Philosophical Papers*, vol. 3, pp. 138–52.

Rosen, S. 1973. "The Absence of Structure." *Kant-Studien* 64, no. 2: 246–61.

1980. *The Limits of Analysis*. New York: Basic.

1987. *Hermeneutics as Politics*. Oxford: Oxford University Press.

1993. *The Question of Being: A Reversal of Heidegger*. New Haven: Yale University Press.

1999. "Philosophy and Ordinary Experience." In *Metaphysics in Ordinary Language*. New Haven: Yale University Press, pp. 218–39.

Santner, E. 2001. *On the Psychotheology of Everyday Life: Reflections on Freud and Rosenzweig*. Chicago: University of Chicago Press.

Sartre, J.-P. 1989. *The Transcendence of the Ego: An Existential Theory of Consciousness*, trans. F. Williams and R. Kirkpatrick. New York: Hill and Wang, 1989.

Scary, E. 1999. *On Beauty and Being Just.* Princeton: Princeton University Press.

Schiller, F. 1965. *On the Aesthetic Education of Man*, trans. R. Snell. New York: Fredrick Unger.

Schlegel, F. 1962. *Philosophische Vorlesungen (1800–07)*, Erster Teil, Bd. XII, *Kritische Friedrich-Schlegel-Ausgabe*, ed. J.-J. Anstett. München-Paderborn-Wien: Verlag Ferdinand Schönigh.

Schnädelbach, H. 1983. "Dialektik als Vernunftkritik. Zur Konstruktion des Rationalen bei Adorno." In Friedberg and Habermas 1983, 66–93.

Schneewind, J. 1998. *The Invention of Autonomy.* Cambridge: Cambridge University Press.

Schulze, G. E. 1969. *Aenesidemus, oder über die Fundamente der von Herrn Prof. Reinhold in Jena gelieferten Elementarphilosophie.* Aetas Kantiana series. Brussels: Culture et Civilization.

Searle, J. 1992. *The Rediscovery of the Mind.* Cambridge, Mass.: MIT Press.

Sedgwick, S. 1997. "McDowell's Hegelianism." *European Journal of Philosophy* 5, no. 1 (April): 21–38.

2000a. "Hegel, McDowell, and Recent Defenses of Kant." *Journal for the British Society of Phenomenology* 31, no. 3: 229–47.

2000b. *The Reception of Kant's Critical Philosophy: Fichte, Schelling and Hegel.* Cambridge: Cambridge University Press.

Sellars, W. 1963. "Philosophy and the Scientific Image of Man." In *Science, Perception and Reality.* London: Routledge, pp. 1–40.

1968. *Science and Metaphysics.* New York: Humanities Press.

1969. "Metaphysics and the Concept of a Person." In *The Logical Way of Doing Things*, ed. Karel Lambert. New Haven: Yale University Press, pp. 248–52.

Sennett, R. 1980. *Authority.* New York: Knopf.

Shattuck, R. 2000. *Proust's Way: A Field Guide to In Search of Lost Time.* New York: Norton.

Shell, S. Forthcoming. "Natural Right and the Historical Approach."

Smith, Nicholas, ed. 2002. *Reading McDowell: On Mind and World.* New York: Routledge.

Starr, P. 1982. *The Social Transformation of American Medicine.* New York: Basic.

Stern, R. 1999. "Going beyond the Kantian Philosophy: On McDowell's Hegelian Critique of Kant." *European Journal of Philosophy* 7, no. 2 (August): 247–69.

Strawson, P. F. 1966. *The Bounds of Sense.* London: Methuen.

Stroud, B. 1969. "Transcendental Arguments." In *The First Critique*, ed. T. Penelhum and J. MacIntosh. Belmont, Calif.: Wadsworth, pp. 54–69.

Taylor, C. 1975. *Hegel.* Cambridge: Cambridge University Press.

Theunissen, M. 1983. "Negativität bei Adorno." In Friedberg and Habermas 1983, 41–65.

Thyen, A. 1989. *Negative Dialektik und Erfahrung: Zur Rationalität des Nichtidentischen bei Adorno.* Frankfurt a.M.: Suhrkamp.

Truffaut, F. 1985. *Hitchcock.* New York: Simon and Schuster.

Tugendhat, E. 1967. *Der Wahrheitsbegriff bei Husserl und Heidegger.* Berlin: de Gruyter.

1986. *Self-Consciousness and Self-Determination*, trans. P. Stern. Cambridge, Mass.: MIT Press.

Velkley, R. Forthcoming. "Natural Right and History as a Response to the Challenge of Martin Heidegger."

Weber, Max. 1968. *Economy and Society*, ed. G. Roth and C. Wittich. New York: Bedminster.

Wellmer, A. 1985. "Adorno, Anwalt des Nicht-Identischen: Eine Einführung." In *Zur Dialektik von Moderne und Postmoderne: Vernunftkritik nach Adorno.* Frankfurt a.M.: Suhrkamp, 141–63.

White, J. 1973. *The Legal Imagination.* Boston: Little, Brown.

Wiggins, D. 1987. "A Sensible Subjectivism?" In *Needs, Values, Truth.* Oxford: Basil Blackwell, pp. 185–214.

Wildavsky, A. 1977. "Doing Better and Feeling Worse: The Political Pathology of Health Policy." *Daedalus* 106: 105–24.

Williams, B. 2002. *Truth and Truthfulness.* Princeton: Princeton University Press.

Williams, M. 1996. "Exorcism and Enchantment." *Philosophical Quarterly* 46, no. 182: 99–109.

Wolff, R. P. 1963. *Kant's Theory of Mental Activity.* Cambridge, Mass.: Harvard University Press.

Wood, A. 1999. *Kant's Ethical Thought.* Cambridge: Cambridge University Press.

Zaner, R. 1988. *Ethics and the Clinical Encounter.* Englewood Cliffs, N.J.: Prentice Hall.

# Name Index

Adorno, T., 20, 23, 77, 98–120 passim, 147n, 149, 249, 285n, 290n, 318n; *Dialectic of Enlightenment*, 102n, 116; *Minima moralia*, 98, 321n; *Negative Dialectics*, 98–120, 147. *See also specific subject entries*
Aenesidemus. *See* Schulze, G.
Aeschylus, 84
Allen, W., 237
Althusser, L., 172
Ameriks, K., 29n, 45n
Anderson, L., 307n
Antigone, 73, 220
Arendt, H., 146–67 passim; *Eichmann in Jerusalem*, 147; *The Origins of Totalitarianism*, 147–67 passim. *See also specific subject entries*
Aristotle, 80, 130, 199, 202, 215, 219n, 223, 225, 263; *Poetics*, 123n
Austin, J. L., 133

Barthes, R., 172
Bartleby (in Melville's 'Bartleby the Scrivener'), 73
Baudelaire, C., 296
Beattie, J., 28
Beauchamp, T., 246n
Beck, L. W., 28n
Beckett, S., 107, 323n, 331n, 332n
Beier, C., 113n
Beiser, E., 31n, 38n
Belting, H., 283n
Benjamin, W., 284n, 285n, 318, 322n, 328n

Bennett, J., 46n
Bernstein, J., 99n, 106n
Bersani, L., 309n, 313n, 315n, 316n, 318n, 319n
Besançon, A., 292
Bichat, M. F. X., 250
Bird, G., 187n
Blumenberg, H., 57–58, 170
Boileau, N., 299n
Booth, W., 313n
Bouhours, D., 299n
Bouveresse, J., 168n
Bovary, Emma (in Flaubert's *Madame Bovary*), 267
Bowie, A., 39n
Brandom, R., 18n, 19, 48, 61n, 183n, 195, 208
Braun, C., 113n
Brody, H., 247
Bubner, R., 108n, 220n
Buck-Morss, S., 23n
Burke, E., 128

Calvin, J., 294n
Canovan, M., 151n
Capra, F., 237
Carmen, T., 62n
Carnap, R., 58, 72
Cassirer, E., 63
Cavell, S., 18n, 20–21, 133, 142n
Céline, F., *Bagatelles pour un massacre*, 163
Cézanne, P., 303
Chandler, J., 307n, 314n

# Subject Index